C000049409

THE GROWNUP'S GUIDE®

LIVING WITH KIDS IN MANHATTAN

Also by Diane Chernoff-Rosen

THE GROWNUP'S GUIDE® VISITING NEW YORK CITY WITH KIDS
with Lisa Levinson

THE GROWNUP'S GUIDE®

LIVING WITH KIDS IN MANHATTAN

Revised, Updated & Expanded Edition

Diane Chernoff-Rosen

GROWNUP'S GUIDE® PUBLISHING LLC

To the reader:

The information in this book was accurate at the time of publication. However, due to the dynamic nature of small businesses and the Internet, business names, addresses, phone numbers and web addresses may change in the future.

The author and publisher apologize for any errors and, if notified, will adjust them for future editions of this book. If we have not included your favorite resource or you want to make us aware of additional information to be included in subsequent editions, you can contact the publisher at info@grownupsguide.com.

As of February 1, 2003, all calls within New York City will be made by dialing 1 plus the three-digit area code plus the seven-digit phone number. Unless otherwise indicated, all phone numbers listed in this book are in area code 212.

Copyright © 2003 by Diane Rosen

All rights reserved. No part of this book may be reproduced or transmitted in any form or by any means without permission in writing from the publisher.

Published by Grownup's Guide Publishing LLC, New York, New York.
Find us online at www.grownupsguide.com

Library of Congress Control Number 200319507

ISBN 0-9663392-3-1

Book and cover design by Elizabeth Woll

Manufactured in the United States of America

10 9 8 7 6 5 4 3 2 1

To my three favorite New Yorkers,
Amanda, Oliver and Matthew.

Table of Contents

Acknowledgments

A huge thank you to the many parents, friends, administrators, business owners and others who shared information and insights with us. A special thanks to Lisa Levinson, who co-authored the first edition of this book for her continued support, thoughtful advice, creative energy and perspective and for being an all-around excellent friend, colleague and amazing person. Also, thanks to our copy editor Karen Lane and researcher Alison Hagge for all their hard work. Last, but never least, thanks to my family for their patience and support.

Chapter 1

City Life

Manhattan is an incredible place to raise children. City life is not without its challenges, but once you learn to navigate your way through what this city has to offer to its youngest population and their parents, you begin to see just how manageable, if not terrific, family life in Manhattan can be.

The first edition of this book was originally conceived when we, as Manhattan parents, found ourselves spending our "free" time researching the things we needed to know, such as selecting a pediatrician, locating parenting classes, hiring a babysitter, applying to nursery schools and then ongoing schools, finding activities for our children, locating children's stores and just generally getting around town. Using a variety of sources—word of mouth, giveaway publications, bulletin boards, general city guides and the telephone book—every inquiry seemed to require an extraordinary amount of our most precious and scarce resource, time. So, like the instruction manual you wish your child was born with, we longed for a comprehensive guide to living with kids in Manhattan that would take care of the basics. The result was the 1998 edition of *The Grownup's Guide to Living with Kids in Manhattan.*

In the years since the publication of the first edition of *The Grownup's Guide to Living with Kids in Manhattan,* many things have changed in New York. We elected a new mayor, the dot.com bubble expanded and then burst, the Dow climbed way above and then fell way below the 10,000 mark, businesses opened and closed, fortunes were made and lost, people moved in and moved out, trends spiked and fizzled, using the Internet and e-mail became commonplace and on September 11, 2001, our city suffered the worst attack on American soil in the history of our nation, an experience from which New Yorkers continue to valiantly recover.

During the same period, however, the job of parenting has, for the most part, remained much the same. Babies were born, bottles and pacifiers were introduced and given up, toddlers had tantrums, use of the potty was mastered, pre-schoolers learned to ask "why?", children played too many video games, watched too much television and crept into bed with parents in the middle of the night, homework was checked, clothes and accessories were bought and grown out of (or rejected!), adolescents sulked, siblings argued and made up, childcare arrangements got made and unmade, schools were chosen, after-school schedules were juggled, pediatricians were visited, apartments were renovated, family vacations were taken, parents fretted, children explored and grew and fun was had. In short, all kinds of issues were addressed and problems solved.

As the landscape of the city evolved, it seemed time to revisit the material contained in the first edition and bring it up to date. And so, for you, the harried parents of New York, this updated and revised edition of *The Grownup's Guide to Living with Kids in Manhattan* compiles even more of the information you need in a single volume geared toward making our job as parents in Manhattan not only somewhat easier but perhaps significantly more enjoyable.

This is a guide for parents of children ages 0 through 14. It is not a resource guide for pregnancy and postpartum issues. Once you have your bundle of joy, or if your bundle of joy is becoming a bundle, we will show you how to get the best out of this wonderful city. Regrettably, this book will take you only through the early teen years. Once we have helped you successfully get your children that far, we wish you good luck, because from our own experience, that is what you will need plenty of, no matter where you raise your kids.

It is not our intention to serve solely as a telephone book, so if another source already exists that covers a specific subject, you will be directed to it. This is our way of making sure you are equipped for a given project without having to make this book a sequel to *War and Peace*. Note that all telephone numbers are 212 area code unless otherwise indicated.

Please note that we do not recommend specific individuals, businesses or services (medical practitioners, tutors, schools, agencies, classes, services, etc.). Because Manhattan is full of so many qualified people doing so many different jobs, it would be virtually impossible to check each one's credentials and capabilities or anticipate your goals and expectations in retaining someone's services or purchasing particular products. Our goal is to tell you how to find people, services and organizations and, where appropriate, how to determine whether they are properly credentialed or right for the situation you are seeking to address.

Our hope is that this resource will enable you to draw on the best, most current and thorough information when making decisions. On that note, enjoy.

The Ten Principles of Living with Kids in Manhattan

Whether you are a New York City veteran or a recent arrival, once you become responsible for rearing a child here, you quickly learn that city life with a child in tow is a far cry from your pre-child existence. You will discover many wonderful places and things about New York City about which you were previously unaware and find businesses, services and people you never knew existed. However, at the same time that you are delighting in all this city has to offer to its parents and children, you will also unfortunately learn that the Big Apple is not always child friendly to its core and that living here with children can be hard work.

So how do you organize your life with children in this city to maximize the pleasure and minimize the pain? We have identified ten principles of living with kids in Manhattan that have helped us through many a tough moment. These rules of thumb were distilled from the experiences of many seasoned Manhattanites and are presented with the intention of making your life a little less complicated. Our ten principles are hardly the only coping strategies you will develop or rely on, but we hope that they provide a good starting point. At the very least, they can help you avoid some of the pitfalls and pratfalls of city life.

▶ **1 Know what works for you.** Life in Manhattan can often feel like a test of your wits, and parents and others caring for children are hardly excused from the exam. In an attempt to be the best parents, aunts, uncles, and so forth we can be, we may seek advice from friends, colleagues, family, parent educators and parenting books. Often, we are more willing to follow the advice of others, who may or may not know us or our children, than to follow our own instincts. In any event, we frequently find ourselves trying to sort out what is the right way, the best way or even just some clue as to how to do something.

OK, so despite what the experts may say about letting your children sleep with you, your family of four somehow finds itself sleeping in the same bed somewhere around 4 a.m. As in all family matters, within the boundaries of basic health and safety, there are no right or wrong ways to parent here or anywhere else. Hence the first principle, **know what works for you**. What works for you may be different from what works for your friend or even all of your friends, but you know better than anyone else what you and your children can handle.

If you do not establish your own personal parenting limits, you will find that it is you, and not your child, who is having the temper tantrum in the middle of the supermarket. Take it from those who have been there, it is not a pretty place to be. Even when you must endure the disapproving looks and rolled-up eyes of others, feeling secure that you are doing what works best for your family will help you get through many a trying moment.

▶ **2 Plan Ahead.** So, knowing what works for you, you have determined that you can handle only three hours in the park. You are equipped with a portable potty or a mental map of the area coffee shops, stores or hotels with public rest rooms. You have mastered the art of diversion as you pass every candy store, toy store, fast-food stop and ice cream vendor, but you forgot to factor in that it is rush hour and the crosstown bus to Central Park is jammed. The kids are getting antsy and you can tell that they need this outing to get off the ground. You stand at the bus stop, barely holding it together, hoping in vain for a taxi when it starts to rain. This brings us to the second principle, **plan ahead**.

Planning can make all the difference. This does not mean that you have to schedule the spontaneity out of your life, but it does mean that it is worth spending some time anticipating the logistics of your activities and the limitations of your children. The basics: when and where to eat and rest and how to deal with boredom. Children inevitably get hungry, thirsty and tired at inopportune times. Depending on where you will be, consider packing snacks (or knowing where to procure one on short notice) or bringing the folding stroller. Many outings can be saved with a surprise treat or rest stop.

Dealing with a fidgety, bored child may be more of a challenge. It is always advisable to have something in your bag for your child to play with: crayons, books, lanyard, a Walkman, handheld electronic games or anything else that is self-contained. Many problems can be avoided altogether by being realistic in your planning. Can a two-year-old really sit through a long movie? Will your three-year-old appreciate a guided tour of the Whitney Biennial? Can your five-year-old sit through a four-course dinner? Can your seven-year-old amuse himself or herself while you get your passport renewed? Whenever possible, schedule your adult activities solo, but if you must bring your child, bring some entertainment with you.

Remember that children have a short attention span, lose interest in adult outings and do not graciously accept things like traffic, long lines, being closed out of a movie, bad weather, waiting for food in a restaurant or a change in plans. So whenever you can, think ahead, anticipate timing, and be aware of what causes your children to experience meltdown. With the right diversions, even a trip to the Department of Motor Vehicles can actually be fun . . . well, at least not a total disaster.

► **3 Never take more than you want to carry.** Having observed the second principle, you have meticulously planned ahead. When it began to rain, you ducked into a coffee shop, got everyone a bagel, waited out rush hour and got a taxi. Invoking Plan B, you head to the Metropolitan Museum. You, your two children, the stroller, toys, baseball bat, juice boxes, snacks, hats and sunglasses arrive at the Met. You know better than to schlep up all those lovely steps, so you enter at the street level. The problem is that you are carrying all that stuff. It is one thing to dump it in a pile at the park and quite another to drag it around a museum. You are in luck because you can check your things at the Met, but it does bring us to the third principle, **never take more than you can carry**.

Being prepared is a noble thing, but it is possible to be too prepared. In Manhattan, we walk a lot and when we are not walking, we are taking cabs or buses or riding in a hole in the ground to our destinations. You cannot count on your children to haul any of their gear for too long, and overloaded strollers tend to tip over as soon as your child leaps out. Worse yet, if you do not have a stroller, you will rapidly begin to resemble and feel like a pack mule. What to do? Be realistic about what you need for where you are going, pack accordingly, and stick to your guns when the kids drag out more paraphernalia for you to carry.

► **4 Make sure that you and anyone caring for your children are equipped to handle an emergency.** Despite the odds, you have a great outing. You return home and leave your children with the caregiver, so that you can get that important assignment to FedEx before your cover as a freelancer is blown or just so you can have some grownup time for yourself. You are barely out the door when your nine-year-old jumps off the couch and hits his or her head. While your caregiver is phoning the pediatrician, your three-year-old comes into the room with an empty bottle of cough medicine that he or she seems to have just swallowed.

Now what? Fortunately for you, this would never be a problem. The three-year-old could not swallow the cough medicine because your home was properly childproofed and even if he or she had, the poison control number (and every other emergency number) is clearly posted. You have also sent your caregiver to an emergency care course and instructed her on emergency procedures.

Hence the fourth principle, **make sure that you and anyone caring for your children are equipped to handle an emergency**. This principle is not unique to New York parents, but it is especially important here. What is unusual about our city is the diversity of individuals with whom we share this city and in whose care we often leave our children. For that reason, you can never assume that what makes sense to you in an emergency will make sense to someone else. It is crucial to instruct caregivers as to how you want them to handle an emergency and give them the tools to do so, such as a list of people to call (and in what order), emergency money (for cab fare), instructions on how to handle themselves in an emergency room and, whenever possible, training in specific emergency procedures (such as CPR).

▶ **5 Safety First.** Most New York City kids are very savvy, very early. By age six, most children are well versed on social issues such as homelessness and union strikes. It is, however, important to arm our children with the strategies needed to keep themselves safe. And though your child does not need to learn CPR, he or she does need to know age-appropriate safety basics, and parents need to invoke the fifth principle, **safety first**.

While there are many specific things you can do to ensure your child's safety, most issues require a cautious, informed approach and a judgment call. For example, once you have checked a prospective babysitter's references, you must still rely on your instincts when deciding to hire. When sending your five-year-old to a new friend's house after school for the first time, you and your child might feel more comfortable if you or your babysitter tag along.

However, by a certain age, you will discover that it is not possible to be with your child at every turn to make those judgment calls and safety assessments. This is why we cannot emphasize enough to all parents, and Manhattan parents in particular, that the seeds you plant early on to help your children to develop judgment and a sense of confidence combined with caution will ultimately allow them to become responsible for themselves and their own safety.

▶ **6 Choose your battles.** Living in Manhattan is a fast-paced business. City children are exposed to a lot from a very young age and become quite adept little negotiators and maneuverers very early on. New York parents tend to be extremely busy, heavily scheduled and frequently stressed out. As we orchestrate our complicated lives and those of our children, it is easy to become overwhelmed with the minutiae of family life, and the smallest of matters can easily take on seemingly gargantuan significance.

As you escort your children through the various stages of their development, they will cleverly and creatively challenge your patience and authority every step of the way. At each juncture, as you try to do the right thing and keep your children safe while teaching good values, you can begin to feel like the military police as you find yourself in a constant state of battle with your progeny and hear yourself saying no more often than not.

In New York, where very busy families face a constant stream of apparently endless choices and possibilities, the ability to focus on what matters most, not to sweat the small stuff and to **choose your battles** seems unusually appropriate and ranks as our sixth principle.

Using this technique to deal with the myriad complaints and grievances of your kids is more than just a peace-keeping strategy. It forces us to slow down and deliberately decide what really matters to us and, whenever appropriate, to give the kids an opportunity to chart their own courses. While it may feel that to give in is to relinquish control, in fact you are giving your children the chance to experience a modicum of self-determination as well as to observe the grownups in their lives compromise.

▶ **7 See the bigger picture.** As we navigate our families through Manhattan's extraordinary number and variety of activities, schools, organizations and institutions, it is likely that the day will come when something you or your child desired or counted on will fall through. Perhaps your child does not get accepted to the preschool or ongoing school of your choice, gets cut from the soccer travel team, is not asked to dance in the *Nutcracker*, does not qualify for the chess nationals, does not make the middle school baseball team or does not make the Metropolitan Opera children's chorus.

As grownups, we understand that life is not always fair and that there are disappointments and even tragedies to deal with in life. Yet somehow, when disappointment or loss touches our children, we often cannot bear the unfairness or unhappiness and feel somehow compelled to get out there and make it right, or at least better. Many parenting gurus note that learning to deal with disappointment is a healthy skill, and parents do children a huge disservice when we try to correct all the (real or perceived) wrongs suffered by our children rather than letting, or helping, them learn to process, cope with and even find inspiration following disappointment, frustration or loss.

To that end, perhaps as parents we can remind ourselves and teach our children to **see the bigger picture** and to understand that one cannot always be the best, brightest, prettiest, most clever, most talented, most popular or the winner of every competition. Rather, lessons can be learned from failures, what seemed like the end of the world will feel less so as circumstances and preferences change over time, future opportunities will arise, and chances are created to go back and work hard for something that matters. In the face of a setback, allowing for the possibility best summed up by the old adage that 'when one door closes another one opens' can be a gift for the whole family.

▶ **8 Relax.** Parenting in Manhattan can sometimes feel like an extreme, competitive sport. An afternoon in the park with a group of aggressive parents can leave you feeling as if you missed the good parent boat. Somehow, the other parents seem to have the inside track on everything. While you are just barely getting through the day, their children seem to have been accepted into the most exclusive programs (that you did not even know existed); speak several languages; are musical prodigies and accomplished performers in all of the arts; can read and write and calculate cube roots before they enter preschool and so on, and so on, and so on.

As you retire to a bench on the far side of the playground to lick your wounds and contemplate where you went wrong, we urge you not to fall victim to predator parents and instead to follow the eighth principle and step back, take a deep breath and **relax**. In the pressure cooker that is New York, some parents feel the need to appear more knowledgeable, better informed and ahead of the curve on everything related to their children. Often, what you are seeing is a big show with very little substance.

The truth is that even if a child is unusually precocious, did gain admittance to an exclusive program or the parents do have access to special information, that does not mean that that child has a lock on future success or that his or her advantage creates a disadvantage for your child. More important, another child's achievement or access does not in any way diminish your child's happiness, potential or opportunities. Keeping your perspective and reminding yourself that it is possible to create our own opportunities, even under less than perfect conditions, is the best defense against Manhattan's special breed of über parents.

▶ **9 Too much of a good thing can be too much.** Remember how big your elementary school seemed when you were six years old? Well, imagine how big this city must feel at times even to a 12-year-old. Day in and day out, there is nonstop noise, visual stimulation and the routine of the day to get through. In addition, there are so many options available to fill our children's free time that it is often hard to avoid the temptation to overschedule them. By the age of seven, most city kids will have sampled an incredible number of extracurricular activities, from gymnastics to violin, and some will be deeply engaged in a particular discipline, such as dance, music, chess, or sports, to name only a few. And so, our ninth principle: **too much of a good thing can be too much.**

Whatever you or your child may choose to participate in, we urge you to keep in mind how very important it is to carve out time each day or, at the very least, each week, for your child to reflect and quietly contemplate, without a play date, television or a video game. And even if you believe that your child is destined to be the next Einstein or Martha Graham, remember that a personal balance comes only when there is a genuine desire on the part of the child to make a commitment to an activity or endeavor. With your guidance and sensibility, it is easy to let your children direct you as you help them to discover their own paths.

▶ **10 Attitude is everything.** As you approach the job of parenting in Manhattan, or anywhere really, it is essential to remember the final principle, **attitude is everything.** Do not be dismayed when even the best laid plans run awry. Keeping your cool as Murphy's Law wreaks havoc on your day will certainly help you enjoy life's surprises, even if you are the one left picking up the pieces.

Biting into the Big Apple

As big and impersonal as this city can seem at times, there is a piece of the Big Apple carved out especially for kids, and it is delicious. Manhattan has never lacked the ability to dazzle the eyes of a child, but the place we call home is more than a candied apple. There is no denying that having made the choice to live here with your family, organizing your life in Manhattan with children requires much thought, patience, planning and a sense of humor, if not of the absurd.

To our minds, the price we pay to live in this great metropolis is well worth the value we, and our children, receive from the experience. We hope that our ten principles and the information you find in this book will help you and your family enjoy your New York community and eliminate some of the aggravation that comes with parenting and living in one of the biggest and most exciting cities in the world.

Chapter 2

Hometown New York

The Big Apple shines for those who call it home. Somehow, despite all that the residents of the city must endure, there is a great sense of satisfaction in being part of a place that is so notoriously dynamic. The familiar refrain "If you can make it here, you can make it anywhere" is a driving force behind many a hard-working New Yorker.

The fast-paced city life to which we have become so accustomed affects how New Yorkers connect to our surroundings. Although Manhattan is packed with people and bustling with activity, there is not the automatic sense of community most often associated, rightly or wrongly, with the suburbs. Time is compressed, and acquaintances outnumber friendships built over time and from mutual support. The idea of the whole of New York as a "community" is, for many, an oxymoron. Yet there are many healthy, if diverse, communities thriving in Manhattan, waiting to be discovered.

▶ **Bringing up baby Manhattan style.** When you first become a parent, a strange metamorphosis begins to take place. Certainly in the first few months, new parents start to see the world with an altered perspective. For some, the air quality they endured for a decade becomes intolerable with the introduction of baby into their lives. For others, the long hours at work, which seemed so normal before, suddenly feel unhealthy.

For almost all new parents, the nesting instinct begins to extend beyond their apartment walls. Most parents quickly realize that without the support of friends, family, other parents and even community organizations, parenting would not only be lonely, but could drive a sane person totally mad. For as much as parenting is an individual experience, it is also very much a collective endeavor. As a result, parents begin looking for a community beyond the dry cleaner, video rental shop and greengrocer. So, while New York has virtually everything to offer, some things cannot be ordered up by phone. Community is one of them.

Each of us must find or develop our own sense of community through our interests and affiliations and, as our families grow, through those of our children. However you create a sense of community for your family and however many disparate communities in which you find yourself participating (even in the course of a single day), you will discover over time that you are indeed a full-fledged community member.

Many parents who have decided to raise their families in New York City find themselves at a loss as to how to make the city their hometown. Surprisingly, each of Manhattan's neighborhoods has more of a sense of community than you might imagine. It is however, more or less up to the individual to seek it out. Depending on what stage your family is in, there are different ways to become involved. In this chapter, we will provide you with some suggestions and resources to draw upon to make New York your hometown. The rest is up to you. Remember, the more you put in, the more you get out.

▶ **You have a friend.** The best thing about setting out to become part of a community when you have kids is that you immediately

eliminate the first major obstacle to making a connection—finding something in common. You have your children. You will be amazed at the number of people in your building, the park, children's classes, parenting groups, the pediatrician's office and even the gym that you will meet and become friendly with when you have small children. Especially for first-time parents, infant and parenting classes are great for developing friendships and feeling connected, not to mention having people with whom to compare notes on feeding, sleeping and car seats.

Relationships are sometimes forged in the most unlikely situations. When you ask couples how they met, you will hear many funny stories. There are couples who met at Fairway, in the Hamptons, at the gym or while working on the floor of the stock exchange. The same sort of thing occurs among families. Fathers meet at weekend Park Bench classes, nannies meet in the park and introduce the moms, mothers find each other at the Children's Museum.

You will be amazed at the number of people... that you will meet and become friendly with when you have small children.

Sometimes you connect with other parents simply because you are on the same circuit. You take your child to a Little Orchestra Society concert and sit next to a family with a child around the same age. Next you see them at the Museum of Natural History annual family party and maybe on several other occasions over the next few months. Before you know it, you are looking for each other at events and making play dates. If the kids hit it off, you may end up with a friend for life.

Once your children enter school, your family will automatically become part of the school community of families. Fear not, the PTA is alive and well and always recruiting. Becoming active in the school is a wonderful way to make friends, achieve a sense of belonging and be informed about what goes on at the place where your child spends a huge amount of time. There is the added benefit of sending a message to your child that you care about what goes on at his or her school and are willing to invest your time being a part of it. Parents have many ways to get involved, from volunteering in the classroom to working on fund-raising and parent–faculty committees. Most school administrators recognize that many families have two working parents and make an effort to hold meetings, schedule events and organize volunteer efforts to accommodate working moms and dads.

The Parents League of New York is an all-around excellent resource for families and provides a valuable network for the community. Founded in 1913, the Parents League is a not-for-profit organization of parents and independent schools that offers current information on education, entertainment and enrichment opportunities. The Parents League maintains resource files for activities, babysitters/mother's helpers, family travel information, parenting help and support and tutors. The Parents League distributes the *New York Independent Schools Directory* and publishes the *Parents League Guide to New York and Calendar, Parents League Review, Summer in New York City, The Toddler Book* and "The Parents League News." During the course of the year, the Parents League sponsors several workshops and panel discussions on such topics as child safety, homework, independence, learning styles and sibling relationships. You can become a member of the Parents League for a well-worth-it $85 per year (or $225 for three years) by calling 737-7385 or visiting www.parentsleague.org.

When the time comes to begin your search for nursery and ongoing schools (much more about this in Chapter 8!), the Parents League and its two indispensable publications, *The Independent Schools Directory* and *The Toddler Book*, can be of enormous assistance. Well-informed parent volunteers can help you navigate your way through the admissions process in New York independent schools and provide information on summer programs for all ages. Advisory services are available to members free of charge. The Parents League also sponsors annual lectures on the application process and Independent School Day.

Beyond classes and schools, there are numerous religious institutions and community centers affiliated with churches and synagogues that work very hard to create a community for members. Although membership in a congregation may not have been very important before becoming parents, once there are children in the picture, religious and cultural traditions, religious school and attending services at a place of worship may become more appealing. Many families experience a sort of religious rebirth when thinking about the moral and ethical education of the children and become reconnected to their faith. Since there are so many and such diverse opportunities in Manhattan, if you are looking for a congregation to join, or if you feel that the congregation with which you are affiliated does not meet your needs, there are many alternatives available.

Manhattan is home to several Y's, a list of which can be found at the end of this chapter. The various Y's offer many types of family programs, classes for all ages, sports facilities and fitness centers, lectures and performances, and some even operate their own preschools and day camps. Your local Y can provide a place to meet other families and become involved in your neighborhood. A recent addition to the Manhattan landscape is the full-service JCC in Manhattan, which also offers many programs and classes as well as a fitness facility at its new building on the Upper West Side (334 Amsterdam Avenue, 646 505-4444, www.jccmanhattan.org).

For true grass-roots community participation, you can become involved in your local Community Board. There are 12 Community Boards in Manhattan, each of which comprises up to 50 unsalaried members. A full-time salaried District Manager and other staff run each district office. The Board members are appointed by the Manhattan Borough President in consultation with the Council members, who represent any part of the district under the jurisdiction of that Community Board. Any person who resides or operates a business in, or has a professional or other significant interest in, the community is eligible for appointment to the relevant Community Board.

Community Boards meet once a month to address items of concern to the community. Board meetings are open to the public. Special hearings are conducted as needed on particular issues such as the city budget and local land use. Boards also process block party and street fair permits, coordinate neighborhood cleanup programs, publicize special events and in some districts organize merchant and tenant associations. To learn more about Community Boards, you can contact the office of the Manhattan Borough President at 669-8300, www.cvfieldsmbp.org.

Local publications are an invaluable resource for city and neighborhood happenings and essentially serve as our community bulletin board. The *New York Times* has a "For Kids" column in its weekend section, and *New York Magazine* and *Time Out New York* have listings of cultural activities for children. In addition, there are a number of family-oriented publications distributed for free throughout the city at supermarkets, retail establishments, libraries, schools and pediatricians' offices that list numerous activities in the city and metropolitan area for and about children. And if you want to let your fingers do the walking at your computer, there are many websites devoted to family life. The resource list at the end of this chapter provides the names of local publications to look for and websites to explore.

The resource list at the end of this chapter provides the names of local publications to look for and websites to explore.

Neighborhood houses, many of which began as "settlement houses" in the late 19th century, can be another avenue for becoming involved in your community. Today's neighborhood houses develop programs to meet the changing needs of their constituents. They mobilize neighborhoods to address complex social issues and provide services for local residents, such as early childhood education and Head Start programs, day care for children and seniors, after-school programs, teen centers, language classes, job training, tutoring, recreation centers, counseling services and classes in art, music and drama.

The United Neighborhood Houses of New York, Inc. (967-0322, www.unhny.org) is the umbrella organization for the 37 neighborhood houses in New York City, 20 of which are in Manhattan (and listed at the end of this chapter). It is certainly worth finding out whether your local neighborhood house offers any classes, programs or projects of interest to you and whether it provides opportunities for volunteering or getting involved with issues relevant to the community.

▶ **Sharing your piece of the Apple.** Community is more than just meeting people and participating in programs. An often overlooked aspect of being a member of a community is the notion of giving something back to the other members. This feature is for many people a complicated part of connecting to the communities in which we function. With our spare time so tightly scheduled and limited by the reality of attending to the needs of our own families, most of us just do not have the time to give to ourselves, let alone to someone we do not know.

On the other hand, we experience a wonderful spirit of community when we donate even the least bit of time or expertise to an organization that exists solely to assist other people, to promote an important cause or to enhance the cultural life of our city. While it is easy to feel you are doing your part by writing a check to this or that charity, getting out there yourself and helping to affect the life of even one person in your community can be personally gratifying.

Which charity or institution you give your time to or how much time you can donate is less important than the fact that you are making the effort. A little bit of your time or talent can mean a lot to most people, and that is really what community is all about. Keep in mind, too, that children learn by example, and your volunteering is a wonderful way to teach them how people work together to make the world a better place.

There are many organizations to become involved with if you want to volunteer your time or talent. The best way to start is by focusing on an issue of interest to you and volunteering with an organization involved in that issue. If you do not know where to begin, you can contact the Mayor's Voluntary Action Center at 788-7550 or www.nyc.gov/volunteer, the Volunteer Referral Center at 889-4805 or www.volrefcen.org, New York Cares at 228-5000 or www.nycares.org, Volunteer Match at www.volunteermatch.org or Givingwell at www.givingwell.org. Opportunities for children to volunteer can be found at Kids for Community at 759-1462 or www.kidsforcommunity.org.

▶ **Next stop Bedford Falls.** After a somewhat rocky transition into parenthood, it has been our experience that as we grew into our roles as parents, our feeling of belonging to a community grew exponentially. As we take the time to get to know the community that surrounds us and to see the people around us as neighbors and fellow parents all trying to do the best for our children, New York

City continues to inspire and charm us. And if all of us, regardless of ethnicity, finances and religion, treat others as we would like to be treated ourselves, our daily travels might prove more fulfilling.

This city is a special place to raise our children. There is no right way to do the job or ready-made community to simply join, but New York is diverse and full of options. We hope that you, too, are able to discover the hometown within the Big Apple.

RESOURCES

Parents League of New York, Inc. (open only during the school year)
115 East 82nd Street, New York, NY 10028
737-7385, www.parentsleague.org

Community Boards

Community Board Services Coordinator
788-7426

Office of the Manhattan Borough President
1 Centre Street, 19th floor
New York, NY 10007
669-8300
www.cvfieldsmbp.org

Board No. 1
49-51 Chambers Street, Room 715
New York, NY 10007
442-5050
www.cb1.org

Board No. 2
3 Washington Square Village, Apt. 1A
New York, NY 10012
979-2272

Board No. 3
59 East 4th Street
New York, NY 10003
533-5300
www.home.earthlink.net/~cb3nycm

Board No. 4
330 West 42nd Street, 26th floor
New York, NY 10036
736-4536/7
www.manhattancb4.org

Board No. 5
450 Seventh Avenue, Suite 2109
New York, NY 10123
465-0907

Board No. 6
866 United Nations Plaza, Room 308
New York, NY 10017
319-3750
www.neighborhoodlink.com/manhattan/cb6m

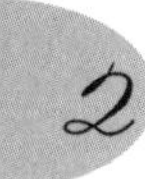

Board No. 7
250 West 87th Street, 2nd floor
New York, NY 10024
362-4008
www.cb7.org

Board No. 8
505 Park Avenue, Suite 620
New York, NY 10022
758-4340
www.decny.com/cb8

Board No. 9
565 West 125th Street
New York, NY 10027
864-6200
www.neighborhoodlink.com/manhattan/com9

Board No. 10
215 West 125th Street, 3rd floor
New York, NY 10027
749-3105

Board No. 11
55 East 115th Street
New York, NY 10029
831-8929/30
www.cb11n.org

Board No. 12
711 West 168th Street, ground floor
New York, NY 10032
568-8500

Jewish Community Center

JCC in Manhattan
334 Amsterdam Avenue, New York, NY 10023
646 505-4444, www.jccmanhattan.org

Neighborhood Houses

United Neighborhood Houses of New York, Inc. (UNH)
70 West 36th Street, 5th floor, New York, NY 10018
967-0322m www.unhny.org

UNH Member Houses in Manhattan (provide services and provide volunteer opportunities)

Boys and Girls Harbor, Inc.
1 East 104th Street
New York, NY 10029
427-2244
www.boysandgirlsharbor.net

Chinese-American Planning Council, Inc.
150 Elizabeth Street
New York, NY 10012
941-0925
www.unhny.org

Educational Alliance
197 East Broadway
New York, NY 10002
780-2300
www.edalliance.org

Goddard Riverside Community Center
593 Columbus Avenue
New York, NY 10024
873-6600
www.goddard.org

Grand Street Settlement
80 Pitt Street
New York, NY 10002
674-1740
www.grandstreet.org

Greenwich House, Inc.
27 Barrow Street
New York, NY 10014
242-4140
www.unhny.org

Grosvenor Neighborhood House, Inc.
176 West 105th Street
New York, NY 10025
749-8500
www.unhny.org

Hamilton-Madison House, Inc.
50 Madison Street
New York, NY 10038
349-3724
www.hmh100.com

Hartley House
413 West 46th Street
New York, NY 10036
246-9885
www.unhny.org

Henry Street Settlement
265 Henry Street
New York, NY 10002
766-9200
www.henrystreet.org/site/PageServer

Hudson Guild
441 West 26th Street
New York, NY 10001
760-9800
www.unhny.org

Lenox Hill Neighborhood House, Inc.
331 East 70th Street
New York, NY 10021
744-5022
www.lenoxhill.org

Lincoln Square Neighborhood Center, Inc.
250 West 65th Street
New York, NY 10023
874-0860
www.unhny.org

RENA-COA Multi-Service Center, Inc.
1920 Amsterdam Avenue
New York, NY 10032
368-3295
www.unhny.org

SCAN/LaGuardia Memorial House
207 East 27th Street
New York, NY 10016
683-2522
www.unhny.org

St. Matthew's and St. Timothy's Neighborhood Center
26 West 84th Street
New York, NY 10024
362-6750
www.unhny.org

Stanley M. Isaacs Neighborhood Center, Inc.
415 East 93rd Street
New York, NY 10128
360-7620
www.isaacscenter.org

Third Street Music School Settlement
235 East 11th Street
New York, NY 10003
777-3240
www.unhny.org

Union Settlement Association
237 East 104th Street
New York, NY 10029
828-6000
www.unionsettlement.org

University Settlement Society of New York, Inc.
184 Eldridge Street
New York, NY 10002
674-9120
www.universitysettlement.org

Publications

The Baby Guide. 914 381-7474, www.parenthood.com. Biannual. Free. Available at pediatricians' offices, schools, libraries and stores.

Big Apple Parent. 889-6400, www.parentsknow.com. Monthly. Free. Widely distributed throughout the city. Produces an annual Parents' Source Book. Subscriptions available.

Expectant and New Parent Guide. 787-3789, www.expectantandnewparentguide.com. Four issues per year (fall, winter, spring, summer). Free. Available at obstetricians' offices, childbirth class facilities, maternity stores, juvenile stores, Lamaze instructors, midwives, parent educators, corporations and professional firms.

Family Entertainment Guide. 787-3789, www.buzzguide.com and www.familybuzzguide.com. Five issues per year (seasonal plus holiday). Free. Available at schools, libraries and family facilities.

New York Family. 914 381-7474, www.parenthood.com. Monthly. Free. Available at pediatricians' offices, schools, libraries and stores. Subscriptions available. Produces an annual family resource guide called *Can't Live Without It.*

New York Magazine. www.metronewyork.com. Weekly magazine.

New York Times. www.nytimes.com. Daily newspaper.

PARENTGUIDE. 213-8840, www.parentguidenews.com. Monthly. Free. Available at pediatricians' offices, schools, libraries and stores. Produces several annual resource guides. Subscriptions available.

Time Out New York. www.timeoutny.com. Weekly magazine.

Volunteering

Some of the following organizations provide opportunities for children to participate in community service programs and some offer hands-on volunteering possibilities.

American Red Cross in Greater New York
150 Amsterdam Avenue
New York, NY 10023
787-1000
www.nyredcross.org
www.redcross.volunteermatch.org

Citizens' Committee for Children
105 East 22nd Street
New York, NY 10010
673-1800
www.kfny.org

Citizens Committee for New York City
305 Seventh Avenue, 15th floor
New York, NY 10001
989-0909
www.citizensnyc.org

City Harvest
575 Eighth Avenue, 4th floor
New York, NY 10018
917 351-8700
www.cityharvest.org

Citymeals-On-Wheels
355 Lexington Avenue
New York, NY 10017
687-1234
www.citymeals.org

Federation of Protestant Welfare Agencies
281 Park Avenue South
New York, NY 10010
777-4800
www.fpwa.org/getinvolved

Food for Survival—the Foodbank of New York City
Hunts Point Cooperative Market
355 Food Center Drive
Bronx, NY 10474
www.foodbanknyc.org

Givingwell.org
c/o Logicworks Inc.
11 Beach Street, 3rd floor
New York, NY 10013
625-5371
www.givingwell.org

Jewish Community Center in Manhattan
Volunteer Bank
334 Amsterdam Avenue
New York, NY 10023
646-505-4455
www.jccmanhattan.org/jccworks.asp

Kids for Community
206 East 63rd Street, 5th floor
New York, NY 10021
759-1462
www.kidsforcommunity.org

Mayor's Voluntary Action Center
49-51 Chambers Street, Suite 1231
New York, NY 10007
788-7550
www.nyc.gov/volunteer

New York Cares
116 East 16th Street
New York, NY 10003
228-5000
www.nycares.org

New York Catholic Center
1011 First Avenue
New York, NY 10022
371-1000
www.ny-archdiocese.org/charities/center.cfm

Project Sunshine
25 West 45th Street
New York, NY 10036
354-8035
www.projectsunshine.org

Salvation Army of Greater New York
120 West 14th Street
New York, NY 10011
337-7200
www.salvationarmy-newyork.org

UJA-Federation of New York
130 East 59th Street
New York, NY 10022
980-1000
www.ujafedny.org/Get_Involved/Volunteering

United Way
2 Park Avenue
New York, NY 10016
251-2500
www.unitedwaynyc.org (see Volunteers in Action database)

Volunteer Match
www.volunteermatch.org

Volunteer Referral Center
161 Madison Avenue, 5th floor
New York, NY 10016
889-4805
www.volrefcen.org

Websites

www.familycares.org

www.nick.com (click on Big Help)

www.shine365.com

For additional ideas on volunteering, some of which are appropriate to do with your children, and a source of both national and New York City organizations, see *How to Save the Children*, Amy Hatkoff and Karen Kelly Klopp (Simon & Schuster/Fireside, 1992); *Volunteering in New York City*, Richard Mintzer (Walker & Company, 1996); and *The Kids Guide to Social Action*, Barbara Lewis et al. (Free Spirit Publishing, 1998).

Y's

Chinatown YMCA
100 Hester Street
New York, NY 10002
219-8393
www.ymcanyc.org/chinatown

14th Street Y
Sol Goldman YM-YWHA of the Educational Alliance
344 East 14th Street
New York, NY 10003
780-0800
www.edalliance.org

Harlem YMCA–Jackie Robinson Youth Center
180–181 West 135th Street
New York, NY 10030
281-4100
283-8543
www.ymcanyc.org/harlem

McBurney YMCA
125 West 14th Street
New York, NY 10011
741-9210
www.ymcanyc.org/mcburney

McBurney YMCA Chelsea Center
122 West 17th Street
New York, NY 10011
741-8715
www.ymcanyc.org/mcburney

92nd Street Y
1395 Lexington Avenue
New York, NY 10128
996-1100
www.92ndsty.org

Vanderbilt YMCA
224 East 47th Street
New York, NY 10017
756-9600
www.ymcanyc.org/vanderbilt

The West Side YMCA
5 West 63rd Street
New York, NY 10023
875-4112
www.ymcanyc.org/westside

The YWCA of the City of New York
610 Lexington Avenue
New York, NY 10022
755-4500
www.ywcanyc.org

Chapter 3

NAVIGATING THE CITY

Navigating the city's streets can, on occasion, seem as challenging as driving the Amalfi Coast at night with a blindfold. In such a big city it is difficult not to feel lost at times. For anyone who has lived in Manhattan for any length of time, getting around town is second nature and not something about which to spend much time pondering. When living in Manhattan with kids, however, the number of trips we make around town seems to multiply, as does the amount of baggage we cart. In this chapter, you will find information about getting around town with your children, which we hope will make for smoother sailing as you navigate the island we call home.

Getting Around Town

Physically getting around New York requires an understanding of traffic flow, a great memory for which streets are under construction and a basic knowledge of the city's ever-changing landscape. Helpful extras, depending on your mode of transportation, might include plenty of quarters or tokens, a MetroCard, small bills for taxi fare, a wallet-size street map and a good pair of walking shoes.

Getting from Point A to Point B does not have to be a test of your endurance, thanks to the number of transportation options. There are subways, buses, taxis, car services or the family car. For the adventurous, bikes, Rollerblades and scooters are available, although the number of individuals you can transport may be severely compromised. Last but not least, there is the most reliable mode: your own two feet. Depending on the time of day you are traveling and how important it is that you be on time, if you are going fewer than ten blocks and your children are good walkers or still in the stroller, it is generally faster to walk. No matter which mode of transportation you choose, if you are toting a tot or shuffling a school-age kid around the city, it is advisable to take the path of least resistance.

▶ **Yellow Medallion Taxis.** New York City is known for many things: bagels, Central Park, hotdog vendors, the Empire State Building and of course those world-famous yellow cabs. Taxis now come in as many shapes and sizes as their drivers do, but a genuine New York City yellow cab will always have a medallion on the hood of the vehicle. The driver's name, license number and the medallion number must be displayed in the taxi and are usually located to the right of the meter on the dashboard or on the partition separating the front and back seats. The medallion number must also be displayed on the exterior of both rear doors, the roof light, the hood and the license plates.

Yellow medallion taxis are hailed on the street by pedestrians (there are also several taxi stands, which are listed at the end of this chapter). Taxi fares are regulated and set by the Taxi and Limousine Commission (TLC). Rates are posted on the doors of the taxi, and meters are required to be calibrated accordingly. There are special fares for trips to airports and rules governing the fares that may be charged for trips outside of the five boroughs, which are posted in the back seat of the taxi. Tipping is customary. The standard tip is 15–20 percent of the fare. Drivers are not required to change bills over $20. It is wise to travel with small bills, as drivers often do not have change for a $20 bill, even though they are supposed to.

A yellow cab with its rooftop light illuminated (indicating that it is for hire) that stops to pick you up must take you to any destination within the five boroughs, although a driver is permitted to refuse to take you outside New York City. A driver who asks you where you are going and declines to take you anywhere within city limits on hearing your destination is in violation of the regulations governing the operation of yellow cabs.

The TLC has promulgated specific rules governing service, including the Taxi Riders Bill of Rights. The Taxi Riders Bill of Rights, which must be posted in the back seat of each medallion cab, states that as a taxi rider, you have the right to: direct the destination and route used; be taken to any destination in the five boroughs; a courteous, English-speaking driver who knows the streets in Manhattan and the way to major destinations in other boroughs; a driver who knows and obeys all traffic laws; air conditioning on demand; a radio-free (silent) trip; smoke and incense-free air; a clean passenger seat area and trunk and a driver who uses the horn only when necessary to warn of danger. Refuse to tip if these basics are not complied with. State law provides that a driver may not operate a hand-held cell phone while driving.

The TLC recommends that passengers abide by their suggested Basic Rules of Common Courtesy. Passengers are encouraged not to ask the taxicab driver to violate traffic laws (for example, asking the driver to make a U-turn or exceed the speed limit) and to inform the driver of all stops and destinations at the start of the trip. The TLC asks that all fares be paid before the passenger exits the taxicab. It is illegal for a passenger to remove any stickers or take the passenger information maps from the interior of the cab.

◪ **The rules of the road.** Taxi drivers get a bad rap in part because, from the viewpoint of the passenger, the whole taxi riding experience can be a rather arbitrary one. Some drivers ask you your route preferences, help you with your packages, know their way around town and are polite, while others seem to go out of their way to make your trip as unpleasant as possible. The problem is that no one really seems to know what the rules of the road are, and when the rules are known, they are inconsistently applied. As a result, passengers and drivers alike are not really clear as to what services are required to be provided, a situation that is further complicated by cultural diversity among drivers and passengers and the occasional less-than-perfect manners of some individuals.

According to the TLC, taxi drivers are supposed to follow certain basic operating parameters. Knowledge of these guidelines affords you the opportunity to tip generously when service is above average, not to tip when you are dissatisfied and to file a complaint against the driver if you are treated inappropriately. And if you want your children to say please and thank you, remember to show them your good manners too. The rules applying to cabdrivers can be found at www.nyc.gov/html/tlc/pdf/drivrules.pdf.

◉ *How many kids can fit in a cab?* You are with another parent, and between the two of you there are four children. You hail a cab but when the driver pulls over and sees how many passengers you have in your group, he wants nothing to do with the whole lot of you. Was the driver being rude or does he have the right to refuse the fare? TLC regulations state that a driver is not allowed to have more than four passengers in a four passenger cab or more than five passengers in a five passenger cab (who has ever seen one of these!!!!) except that an additional passenger must be accepted if such passenger is under the age of seven and is held on the lap of an adult. However, according to the TLC, a cab driver is required to take only up to three adults (in the back seat) unless the driver determines it is safe to, and he chooses to, allow a fourth passenger to sit in the front seat. There is no formula to calculate how many children fit in a cab. For instance, two children do not necessarily equal one adult. So, if you are traveling by cab and your group includes two adults and two kids you are probably fine. If your gang is more than four, well, hope for an agreeable driver and tip accordingly.

◉ *Does the safety belt law apply to taxis?* Among the joys of taxi riding, when you can find a taxi, is that you can slip in and out of the back seat without having to be responsible for the car. For many, it is a pleasure not to have to deal with the dreaded car seat. For most of us, for whom is it second nature in our own cars to buckle ourselves and children into our seats, in a taxi the whole idea of buckling up is often as well received as a pothole. The law requires that there be three back seat belts in working order and available for passengers to use, but strangely, the law does not require that you use them (although the TLC recommends that all passengers be strapped in by a safety belt). Even though you are not in violation of the law if you are not wearing your seat belt, if you are injured in an accident, your not having worn a seat belt may affect your insurance claim or a claim against the driver. Ask your pediatrician for a recommendation on how to transport your small child.

◉ *How much is too much to ask of a cab driver?* You went a little too far on your walk with your baby and it starts to rain. You attempt to hail a cab. After several minutes and the loss of the now-drenched paper shopping bag you were toting, you stand holding its contents and finally your luck changes. A cab comes to your rescue—or so you think. You open the door, manage to put your belongings on the seat and start stripping down the stroller. Holding the baby with one arm, you get the stroller to collapse and as you go to put the stroller in the front seat you hear the trunk pop open. You place the stroller in the trunk, get in the cab, shut the door and out of total frustration and exhaustion hardly get the address said before the driver says, "I can't hear ya." Most parents would agree that this situation should be grounds for having one's taxi license revoked, but is that the case? As annoying and counterintuitive as it may seem, a taxi driver is *not required* to assist a passenger or to allow the front seat to be used for cargo such as a stroller even though the regulations provide that upon request, the driver must help load or unload the passenger's luggage or possessions in or from the *trunk*. So, do not be outraged if a driver does not help you fold your stroller and get you settled in the back seat. When you are in a situation where you are provided with only the most basic service and when clearly you could have benefited from some assistance, you may want to consider returning the favor and pay the driver only the basic fare.

◩ **To file a complaint.** Do not hesitate to file a complaint against the driver with the TLC if: the driver was not driving safely; the driver did not know basic thoroughfares; the driver could not communicate in English; the physical condition of the taxi was poor or the driver was discourteous.

To file a complaint, you can either call the TLC Consumer Hotline at NYC-TAXI (692-8294); write to the TLC at 40 Rector Street, 5th floor, New York, NY 10006; or file your complaint on-line at www.nyc.gov/html/tlc/html/tlccompl.html. You will need this necessary information to file a complaint: the medallion number; the driver's name and license number; the date, time and pickup and destination points of the ride; and your mailing address and daytime phone. All complaints are confidential. Always remember to ask for a meter receipt when in a taxi, because it contains the medallion number of the vehicle and the time of the ride.

▶ **Mass Transit.** With one of the largest public transportation systems in the nation, the Metropolitan Transportation Authority (MTA) operates New York City's subways, public buses and railroads and the local bridges and tunnels, moving 2.3 billion commuters via subway, bus or rail and more than 300 million vehicles per year.

The bus and subway systems are so vast that if you are not already familiar with them, the thought of getting acquainted while you are trying to travel with your children may seem overwhelming. Fear not, mass transit does not take much savvy to master and there are advantages to using it. To begin with, taking the bus or subway can create an instant activity for your children, because for most, especially young kids, it is an adventure. If you travel by subway, you do not have to deal with traffic or gridlock and can reach your destination quickly.

Using mass transit can save you a bundle because children under 44-inches tall travel free. There is no official limit to the number of children who can travel for free with a single adult. Note that when boarding a bus, you can use the bar that separates the bus driver's area from the passenger side as a rough height guide, since it is approximately 44 inches from the floor of the bus.

There are a few things to keep in mind when using mass transit to better ensure that you make it to your destination safely. Strollers

must be folded to board a bus or subway. On a bus, make sure the child is seated correctly in the seat. If you must stand, hold your child's hand in case of sudden stops and starts. The Department of Buses offers "The Insiders Guide," a free brochure that answers many of the questions you may have about the bus system. To obtain a copy of "The Insiders Guide," call the Bus Customer Relations Center Monday through Friday between 7 a.m. and 5 p.m. at 718 927-7499.

When traveling by subway, ride the escalators to and from the subway platform with care. Strollers should be folded and children should hold a grownup's hand, not the handrail. Stand away from the sides, because clothing can get caught as can shoes, shoelaces, sneakers, boots or sandals if you fail to step off. Never allow a child to run or sit on the steps or handrail of the escalator. The safest way to travel with your baby on the subway is to hold your child and fold the stroller before you enter the subway. If you do not fold the stroller while riding the subway, make sure to do the following: strap your child into the stroller, never place the stroller between closing subway doors, be aware of the gap between the platform edge and the train, engage the stroller brake while the train is in motion, keep the stroller away from the platform edge, and board the subway at the center of the train, in plain sight of the conductor.

Current fare for bus and subway is $1.50 (going up to $2.00 in mid-2003), payable in coins or by MetroCard. You can buy a MetroCard from any subway station, the St. George Ferry Terminal in Staten Island or at over 3,200 neighborhood newsstands, delis, groceries, banks, pharmacies, check cashiers and other stores. You can also buy a MetroCard online at www.mta.nyc.ny.us/metrocard/subcool/index.html. When you use the MetroCard, the fare will be automatically deducted and your remaining balance indicated. If you do not have enough money on your MetroCard to cover the fare, you cannot pay the additional amount needed with change. You can add money to your card at subway stations and at the St. George Ferry Terminal. The MetroCard cannot be replaced if lost or stolen. A MetroCard can be used until the expiration on the back of the card, after which you can transfer any remaining money to a new card at any subway station or the St. George Ferry Terminal.

You can buy MetroCards in denominations from $3 to $80 or unlimited ride MetroCards (1-, 7- or 30-day cards). For more information about MetroCard, free transfers and student fares, visit www.mta.nyc.ny.us/metrocard or call customer service at METROCARD (638-7622) within New York City or 800 METROCARD (800 638-7622) outside New York City between 9 a.m. and 11 p.m. Monday through Friday or between 9 a.m. and 5 p.m. on weekends and holidays. Reduced-fare benefits are available for senior citizens and customers with eligible disabilities, who can also obtain an application for a personalized photo-identification MetroCard by calling 718-243-4999 between 9 a.m. and 5 p.m. Monday through Friday.

For route and schedule information, you can get maps of the transit system from token booths, bus drivers and at approximately 4,000 other locations around the city, including libraries and museums, or by calling 718 330-1234.

If you are traveling by subway, it is important to be street smart. As a general rule, it is best to travel the subways during the day and avoid deserted stations or travel in the evenings. While waiting for a train, stand where there are other people and do not stand close to the platform edge. Do not let children wander away from you and always have them within your view. It is best not to open purses or bags in the subway station and always hold your purse or other bags close to your body. Expensive or flashy jewelry is best left at home when you know you will be riding the subways. If you see an unsavory character or feel ill at ease or threatened in any way, seek help or leave the station.

As a general rule, it is best to travel the subways during the day and avoid deserted stations or travel in the evenings.

▶ **Car Services.** While it may seem frivolous to transport your children by hired car, having an account with a car service can be a great convenience. Although car services can be expensive—they are not subject to the yellow taxi rate schedule and each company sets its own rates—there are many reasons why parents have come to rely on them. For example, if requested, the car will wait for you while you pick up or drop off a child in bad weather. You can make reservations for a car to drop off and pick up you or your children at prearranged times, which can be enormously helpful when you need to get to and from hard-to-reach places during busy traffic times. Car services can be of great use when you have a very sick child, when the additional service makes an otherwise traumatic visit to the doctor easier to maneuver. It is also possible to hire a car service at an hourly rate if you need to be transported among a variety of destinations on a particular day (which can end up costing less and being far more convenient than taking a series of cabs). In addition, car service drivers typically help you with your stroller and help load and unload your packages. In times of stress or just simply to make your busy life easier, a car service can be quite a parent's helper.

Car services and other for-hire vehicles differ from yellow medallion taxis, because they are not supposed to pick up passengers hailing from the street. The law requires that car service companies, vehicles and drivers be licensed by the TLC.

In order to obtain a license: company owners must not have a criminal record in New York State, the company must have a legitimate place of business, the owners and location of the business must be on record with the TLC, the vehicle must be insured for the specialized job of carrying passengers for hire (other cars may not be covered or may have no insurance at all), vehicles must be inspected three times a year for safety defects, drivers must pass a physical that checks for conditions that could cause problems behind the wheel and, finally, all drivers must pass a New York State criminal record check.

All licensed car services should have cars displaying a diamond-shaped decal in the windshield. If you do not see the decal, do not get in. The cars bearing "Livery" plates are registered outside of the five boroughs and can drop passengers off in Manhattan but are not supposed to pick up fares within New York City. There are other cars for hire bearing "TLC" license plates (such as limousines), which are not supposed to pick up passengers in the street and are subject to regulations of their own. It is often hard to determine if a for-hire car looks legitimate or not. Certainly there are plenty of "gypsy" (i.e., unlicensed by the TLC) cabs driving the streets, but for your own safety, it is recommended by TLC officials that you only take yellow taxis and prearranged licensed cars.

Names of car services can be found in the telephone book. When you call a car service company, make sure to confirm that the service is licensed. Unfortunately, there is no governmental office to contact to get a list of licensed car services. Discuss rates, reservations procedures, how to open an account, whether they use vouchers, billing periods, identification procedures (are you given a car number in advance?), waiting time and multiple stop policies and last-minute requests. If someone other than a family member is authorized to request service, advise the car service in advance. You may have to try a few car services before you know which service is the most reliable and has the friendliest drivers, a fleet of vehicles in good condition and the most reasonable prices.

All complaints against drivers and services can be filed with the TLC in the same manner as complaints are filed against yellow cab drivers.

If you have your own car and want an alternative to a car service, you may want to consider hiring a professional driver who will operate your car for an hourly fee. Most services charge between $15 and $20 per hour and require a three-to-four-hour minimum. This service can be a lifesaver when you have multiple errands to do or will be carting children back and forth among a variety of destinations on a particular day. Several services are listed at the end of this chapter.

▶ **The family car.** One of the many things suburban and urban parents have in common is the problem of transporting kids to school, activities and play dates. As your children's social circle expands and their activities and school friends begin to be further from home, family cars start to hit the weekday streets. As long as you avoid midtown during business hours (where parking is hard to find), there can be many benefits to driving in Manhattan. Believe it or not, parking in a parking lot can often be cheaper than a round-trip taxi fare. If you are willing to park in the street, driving can be a downright bargain. In your own car, you can use age-appropriate safety seats, transport a lot of children with all of their gear, avoid getting stuck without transportation at inopportune times and yes, you can even carpool.

Some tips for city drivers: pay attention to parking signs or be prepared to pay a small fortune to the city in tickets; keep a roll of quarters hidden in your car or you will be forever begging people on the street for change; and when feasible, patronize the many stores and businesses that offer parking credits. By all means, if you do find yourself in the car often, make sure to stock it with creature comforts from home. From our suburban friends we have learned that there is nothing like a few favorite snacks, books or toys (self-contained with no little pieces to fall between the seats) to keep kids busy when stuck in traffic. Additionally, if you take along a change of clothing for your child, an unexpected downpour or spill will not require you to retreat home. Keep a small garbage bag and wipes (or that modern miracle, hand sanitizer) in the car for easy clean up.

◩ **Traffic strategy.** Traffic is endemic to New York City, and its constant presence provides a good reason to leave the car behind. You will rarely find yourself alone on the road. You can count on hitting traffic during rush hour, but there are other traffic obstacles to be on the lookout for, including parades (usually on weekends, but not always), street fairs, visits to the city by the president or other dignitaries, construction and roadwork. You can tune in to WINS 1010 AM, www.1010wins.com or CBS-AM 880 AM, www.newsradio88.com for frequent traffic reports and updates (or visit the websites before you head out), which can help you avoid traffic jams if you are in a position to change your route. If you cannot change your route, at least you will have an explanation for the wait. Another major time-saver for drivers living in the tri-state (New York, New Jersey and Connecticut) area is the E-Z Pass, a local electronic toll-collecting system. For information call 800 333-TOLL (800 333-8655) or visit www.e-zpassny.com.

◩ **Parking.** The magnitude of the problem of what to do with your car as you work through your day should not be underestimated. You have only two choices. You can either park on the street or park in a garage facility. Neither option is ideal. While parking on the street is cheap (free at unmetered spaces and typically 25 cents for 15 minutes at metered spaces), it is often difficult to find a space that is near where you want to be. While garages are somewhat plentiful, they are expensive and, depending on the time of day you show up, do not always have space available. That said, if you have the time and patience or are prepared to shell out for a garage, you will be able to park.

◉ *Garages.* While there are many garages all over Manhattan, it is inevitable that whenever you need one, there is not one to be found. With all the wonderful contraptions that many cars come equipped with these days, a parking lot locator would be our preference for standard city car equipment. The closest thing to such a tool is the *Parking Guide to New York City* produced by the Department of City Planning, Transportation Division (see the resources at the end of this chapter for more information). The *Guide* provides maps of off-street parking facilities located south of 72nd Street in Manhattan.

For additional parking information, you can visit the Department of City Planning website, www.nyc.gov/html/dcp/html/dcptd/index.html, which offers maps showing the location of over 2,400 licensed parking facilities in the five boroughs. Without the *Guide*, above 72nd Street or without a visit to the Internet, the only way to find a private parking garage is by cruising the streets. The city does operate three Municipal Parking Lots in Manhattan, which are listed at the end of this chapter.

One of the great New York mysteries is understanding how private parking lots calculate their rates. Daily parking rates vary greatly, not only among garages but among neighborhoods, without rhyme or reason. Even more mystifying is that although there is a detailed rate schedule posted by law at every facility, when you go to get your car, the amount you are charged seems to bear no relationship to the rate schedule, and somehow, whatever is up on the board seems not to apply to you. To add insult to injury, an 18.25 percent tax (outside of Manhattan, 10.25 percent) will be added to your bill. If you are parking for the day in midtown Manhattan, expect to pay upwards of $25 for the privilege; prices will be lower outside midtown.

If you are parking a large sports utility vehicle (SUV) or a high-end luxury or sports car (think Rolls Royce or Ferrari), expect to pay a parking surcharge. In fact, the larger SUVs, including the Lincoln Navigator, the Ford Expedition and Toyota Land Cruiser to name a few, are not welcome at many garages.

Be sure to inspect your car before leaving a parking lot or garage. If you find that your car has been damaged, request a claim form and, when possible, get a police report. If the matter is not resolved to your satisfaction with the garage owner, you can file a complaint with the Department of Consumer Affairs. Most garages post signage indicating that the management is not responsible for valuables left in the car, and so whenever possible, do not leave anything valuable in the car. If you have separate keys for the engine and the trunk of the car, you can store items in the trunk and take that key with you when you leave the garage.

If you keep a car in Manhattan and rent a monthly parking space in a garage, be sure to apply for your Manhattan Parking Tax Exemption. Manhattan residents qualify for an exemption from the 8% New York City Surtax levied on Manhattan parking services if such Manhattan resident rents a long-term parking space, has a car registered to the resident's Manhattan address and the car is used exclusively for personal use. Applications for the exemption can be downloaded at www.nyc.gov/html/dof/html or obtained from the New York City Department of Finance Parking Tax Exemption Unit, 25 Elm Place, 3rd floor, Brooklyn, NY 11201, 718 935-6080 or obtained via Tax Fax at 718 935-6114. Be sure to ask your garage if you are entitled to any parking discounts at any other garages operated by the same owner.

◉ *Street parking.* Parking on the street is always an option, but you may find it difficult to find a space when and where you need one. If you do park on the street, be sure to read the street signs, since all city streets are officially tow-away zones. If you are concerned about your car being stolen or broken into, it is best to park in busy, well-lit areas.

Some New York parking basics:

- Alternate-side-of-the-street parking requires that at designated times during the day or week, parking is permitted on only one side of the street to allow for street cleaning. On certain holidays this rule is suspended. You can call the Department of Transportation's 24-hour hotline at 212/718 CALL DOT (225-5368) for more information.

- A "No Stopping" sign means you are not permitted to wait or stop in that space to pick-up or drop-off people or packages.
- A "No Standing" sign means you can stop to pick-up or drop-off passengers, but you cannot wait or leave the car to stop to pick-up or drop-off packages.
- A "No Parking" sign means that you cannot wait or leave the car, but you can stop to pick-up or drop-off packages or people.
- Double-parking of passenger cars is illegal.
- You may not park within 15 feet of either side of a fire hydrant.
- Pursuant to New York's Vehicle and Traffic Law 1959, all of the city is a tow-away zone. This means that if your car is parked illegally or does not have a current registration or inspection sticker displayed on the windshield, it can be towed.
- Parking tickets begin at around $55 dollars. This is a big source of income for the city, so read the parking signs.

It's the law. Remember, seat belts save lives, and in New York City, as in the rest of New York State, you are required to wear a seat belt in your vehicle. Children ages four and under are required to be in age- and size-appropriate car seats. All front-seat passengers and passengers under the age of 16 must be buckled in. It is illegal to turn right at a red light in Manhattan, and never, never "block the box" (get stuck not being able to move completely through an intersection before the light turns red). Blocking the box will cost you money and may result in penalty points on your license. Under state law, the driver of a vehicle may not operate a hand-held cell phone while driving (except in an emergency).

▶ **A word about bicycles.** Like their suburban neighbors, city children do learn to ride bicycles, and family urban biking outings are becoming more commonplace. While it is absolutely not recommended that you send your children out on the busy streets on their bikes unaccompanied by an adult, it is possible that the spirit may move you to embark on a two-wheeled adventure with your kids. If you must, your best bet is to confine your riding to the large parks, such as Central Park or Prospect Park, and always to stay on the populated roads. It is not a good idea to explore deserted paths.

If you ride in the street, familiarize yourself with the bicycle traffic laws: ride in the direction of traffic (not against traffic), obey all traffic laws, come to a complete stop at stop signs and red lights, use a bike path or lane if one is available and use hand signals to indicate turns. Bicyclists must ride on the street, not on the sidewalk. The exception is riders under 13 riding a bicycle with wheels smaller than 26 inches, who may ride on the sidewalk. Children must be carried in a properly affixed child carrier, and a child under the age of one is not permitted to be carried on a bicycle. Cyclists under the age of 14 must wear a safety helmet.

The streets of New York are certainly not paved in gold, so there are many things to watch out for, including potholes, traffic, aggressive drivers, bicycles, emergency vehicles and pedestrians who sometimes dare you to hit them. It can get ugly, so take it easy and do not feel compelled to beat out the taxi drivers.

Getting Out of Town

Although the city offers endless sources of entertainment and activities for families, city dwellers often long for a break from the hustle and bustle of urban life. Whether you are looking for a daytime adventure, are visiting suburban friends or family or just want to explore beyond the five boroughs, there are many options for transporting your crew out of town.

▶ **By Train.** If you are planning a long or short excursion, consider the train. Kids love the adventure of it, there are generally few hassles involved with train travel and the price may be just the ticket.

If you are traveling within the metropolitan area, the train is a great way to travel out of the city for a day trip or other excursion. There are four local commuter rail systems serving New York City: Metro-

North, with more than 100 stations in New York and Connecticut; the Long Island Railroad (LIRR); New Jersey (NJ) Transit (consisting of the Hoboken and Newark Divisions and the Atlantic City Rail Line); and PATH, the Port Authority Trans-Hudson Corporation.

Amtrak, which operates trains throughout the United States, provides the rail service into New York from points both inside and outside of the metropolitan area. Compared to the European rail system, Amtrak is not as reliable or as extensive a system, but for going from city to city, particularly along the East Coast, it is generally fast, reasonably priced and convenient, and Amtrak offers many special packages and promotions.

There are two major train stations in Manhattan. Grand Central Terminal (aka Grand Central Station), perhaps the most famous station in the country, is located on 42nd Street and Park Avenue in Manhattan. Metro-North operates out of Grand Central. Pennsylvania Railroad Station, aka Penn Station, is located on Seventh and Eighth Avenues between 31st and 32nd Streets, directly underneath Madison Square Garden. Penn Station is home to Amtrak, the LIRR and NJ Transit trains.

◪ **General information.** On most train lines, children under the age of 12 travel at either a discount or for free. Depending on the train line, the price of a child's ticket may be contingent on the time of travel. It is wise to be aware of fare restrictions and policies so that you can plan to travel at the most advantageous time. Note that in general, purchasing a ticket on the train rather than at the station will add to the cost of an adult fare and, on certain train lines, perhaps to the cost of the child's ticket as well. We have included information about discounted children's fares, but be aware that policies are subject to change, and it has been known for the railways to provide inconsistent information about their policies!!

Strollers are allowed on all trains and are not necessarily required to be folded. They cannot, however, interfere with the conductor's ability to move easily through a train car. Therefore, if you are not able to park your stroller out of the way, you will probably be asked to fold it. Make sure that while your child is in a stroller, he or she is properly secured during travel. It is recommended that when traveling with a child in a stroller, you do so during off-peak hours when space is more available.

Bathrooms are available on all trains with the exception of the PATH trains. Since the facilities are far from hygienic—and definitely not spacious—it is always a good idea to "try" before you get on the train.

There are two weekday commuter rail "rush hours" that impact travelers. Each commuter railway will define its own rush hour in terms of "peak" times, meaning the time when the rail service is most used by commuters. Generally speaking, it is safe to assume that the morning rush ranges from about 5:30 a.m. to 9 a.m. and the afternoon rush ranges from about 4:30 p.m. to 6 p.m.

Although there are more trains running at peak (rush hour) times than during "off-peak" times, during peak times, commuter trains will be crowded and it will be hard to get taxis at the train station (especially in bad weather). Unless you need to arrive or leave the city during rush hour, try to avoid rush hour when you travel with children. Refer to train schedules for on- and off-peak time periods.

If you use the commuter rails, take along a schedule for the train line you will be riding (also called a "branch schedule"), so that if your plans change, you'll have the information you need to select an alternative departure time. Remember to check the dates for which the schedule is effective, as schedules tend to change a few times a year, typically around the change of seasons.

◩ **Amtrak.** While traveling by air is often perceived as being the fastest way to get from place to place, it can be far from the truth once you factor in getting to and from the airport and dealing with airport issues such as check-in and retrieving your luggage. For instance, if you are traveling to Baltimore, Washington, D.C., New Jersey, Pennsylvania, upstate New York, Boston or New England, consider taking Amtrak. Its express trains, such as the Metroliner and Acela (a high-speed train that runs between Boston and Washington, D.C.), deposit you in the heart of Manhattan at Penn Station and provide a reasonable alternative to flying or driving. Children under two travel for free. One adult can take up to two children between the ages of 2 and 15 for half the adult fare. Amtrak often runs specials that make it even less expensive to travel by rail. To explore all that Amtrak has to offer, including schedule and fare information, call 800 USA-RAIL (800 872-7245) or visit www.amtrak.com.

◪ **Metro-North.** The Harlem Line, the Hudson Line and the New Haven Line carry thousands of people each day from as far north as Wassaic into Grand Central Terminal and back home again. Traveling with kids under the age of 12 is a relative bargain on any one of these lines. One adult can travel with up to four children between the ages of 5 and 11 for only 50 cents per child. Children under five are free. The catch is that you may not depart from the station before the conclusion of the morning rush hour. Rush hour is usually considered over after 10 a.m., although this may vary for certain stations. This fare restriction does not apply to evening peak hours or weekend schedules. If you must travel during the morning rush hour, children between the ages of 5 and 11 will be charged half the adult fare. Children 12 and over pay the adult fare. For schedule and fare information outside the city call 800 METRO-INFO (800 638-7646), or call 532-4900 from within New York or visit www.mnr.org.

◪ **LIRR.** The Long Island Rail Road maintains nine lines and over 130 stations serving Nassau and Suffolk Counties as well as Queens, Brooklyn and Manhattan. Trains originate from Penn Station in the heart of Manhattan and travel up to 120 miles from Manhattan to Montauk at the eastern tip of Long Island. Children under five travel for free on the LIRR regardless of the time of day. During peak hours, children between the ages of 5 and 11 pay half the adult fare; off-peak, the fare is only 50 cents per child. Up to five children can travel with a paying adult and receive the discounted off-peak fare. There are surcharges for tickets purchased on trains when station ticket offices are open. For specific fare and schedule information call 718 217-LIRR (718 217-5477) in New York City, 516 822-LIRR (516 822-5477) in Nassau County and 631 231-LIRR (631 231-5477) in Suffolk County. Information can also be obtained on-line by visiting www.mta.nyc.ny.us. Visit the website or call 718 558-7498 for information about special excursions.

◩ **NJ Transit.** NJ Transit has 614 trains servicing more than 380,000 passengers daily. It provides access via three train divisions—the Hoboken Division, Newark Division and Atlantic City Rail Line—to points in New Jersey, New York and Philadelphia. The lines and branches include the Atlantic City Line, the North Jersey Coast Line, the Northeast Corridor, the Pascack Line, the Main/Bergen Lines, the Boonton Line, the Raritan Valley Line and the Morris & Essex Lines (which include the Morristown Line and the Montclair and Gladstone Branches). Trains leave out of and arrive at one of three stations: Penn Station, Hoboken and Newark's Penn Station. For specific fare and schedule information call 973 762-5100 outside of New Jersey and toll free in New Jersey at 800 772-2222. The official website of the NJ Transit can be found at www.njtransit.com. There is an "unofficial" site at www.nj.com/njtransit.

Up to three children under four years of age ride free with an adult passenger paying a full fare. Children from 5 to 11 years of age pay half the adult fare, provided that they are traveling with an adult passenger paying a full fare. The fare for children is the same off- or on-peak

◩ **PATH.** The PATH system links New Jersey urban communities and suburban commuter railroads to Manhattan. Over 1,000 trains run daily, operating 24 hours a day, as frequently as every four to six minutes during rush hour. The PATH fare is a flat rate of $1.50 for a ticket, regardless of the distance being traveled. Children under five ride for free. Trains leave from Newark, Jersey City and Hoboken and arrive in lower Manhattan, making stops along the route on Sixth Avenue. In Manhattan, you can catch a PATH train at various locations along Sixth Avenue between Christopher Street and 33rd Street. The World Trade Center and Exchange Place stations are expected to re-open in 2004. Schedules can be obtained at the stations, on-line at www.panynj.gov/path or by calling 800 234-PATH (800 234-7284).

The Newark station is New Jersey's Penn Station and should not be confused with New York's Penn Station located in the heart of Manhattan.

By Ferry. Believe it or not, getting to and from the city by ferry is not only possible but is also how thousands of people get to work every day. You can travel by ferry between Manhattan and Staten Island, Brooklyn, Queens and New Jersey. There are also seasonal schedules for ferries between Manhattan and Yankee Stadium and Shea Stadium.

By Bus. If you are traveling within the metropolitan or tri-state (New York, New Jersey and Connecticut) area, a number of local bus companies offer service. See the resources at the end of this chapter.

Bus service between the city boroughs is extensive and offered by seven different franchised private companies with over 91 routes. The bus lines and the areas they service are listed in the resource section of this chapter.

RESOURCES

Bus Service

Port Authority Bus Terminal
Eighth Avenue at 40th–42nd Streets
Information 564-8484
www.ny.com/transportation/port_authority.html

George Washington Bridge Station
178th–179th Streets between Fort Washington and Wadsworth Avenues
Information 800 221-9903

Connecticut

Connecticut Transit (New Haven) 203 624-0151, www.cttransit.com

Connecticut Transit (Stamford) 203 327-7433, www.cttransit.com

Greenwich Shuttle 800 982-8420, www.norwalktransit.com

Inter-Borough Bus Service

General information 212 or 718 CALL-DOT (225-5368)

Liberty Lines Express 718 652-8400, www.libertylines.com, service to the Bronx

New York Bus Service 718 994-5500, www.nybus.com, service to the Bronx

Command Bus Company 718 277-8100, www.commandbus.com, service to Brooklyn

Green Bus Lines 718 995-4700, www.greenbus.com, service to Queens

Jamaica Buses 718 526-0800, www.jamaicabus.com, service to Queens

Queens Surface 718 445-3100, www.qsbus.com, service to Queens

Triboro Coach 718 335-1000, www.triborocoach.com, service to Queens

Long Island

Long Island Bus 516 542-0100, www.mta.nyc.ny.us/libus

National and Regional Bus Lines

Adirondack Trailways 800 858-8555, www.trailways.com (see member companies)

Bonanza Bus Lines 800 556-3815, www.bonanzabus.com

Greyhound Lines 800 231-2222, www.greyhound.com

Olympia Trails 212 964-6233, www.olympiabus.com

Peter Pan Trailways 800 343-9999, www.peterpanbus.com

Shortline 800 631-8405, www.shortlinebus.com

New Jersey

New Jersey Transit Information Center 800 772-2222 (within New Jersey), 973 762-5100 (outside New Jersey), www.njtransit.com

New York

Dutchess County 845 485-4690, www.dutchessny.gov

Putnam County 845 878-RIDE (914 878-7433), www.putnamcountyny.com/part/part.html

Rockland County 845 364-3333, www.co.rockland.ny.us

Westchester County 914 813-7777, www.beelinebus.com

Driver Services

Chauffeurs Unlimited, 787-2800

City Valet, 752-0022

Executive Club Chauffeurs, 499-7424

Metropolitan Chauffeurs, 604-0444

Driving Resources

American Automobile Association
Emergency Road Service 800 AAA-HELP (800 222-4357)
www.aaa.com
www.aaany.com (Automobile Club of New York, Inc.)
Executive offices 516 746-7730
Bronx, Brooklyn, Queens 718 224-2222
Long Island 516 746-7141
Manhattan 757-2000
Rockland County and Westchester 914 948-4600

E-Z Pass 800 333-TOLL (8655), www.e-zpassny.com

New York City Department of Transportation
www.nyc.gov/html/dot/home.html
24-hour hotline 212/718 CALL DOT (225-5368)
24-hour Towed Vehicle Information and Borough Tow Pound 971-0770/1/2/3 (Manhattan tows only). You will need $185 in cash to retrieve your car.
Parking Violations Helpline 718 422-7800 (800 813-9183 out of state)
www.nyc.gov/finance to find a towed car.

Parking Pal (motorists' rights organization) 800 41 PARK PAL (727-5725), www.parkingpal.com

Ferries

Liberty Landing Marina 201 985-8000, www.libertylandingmarina.com, service to Liberty State Park, NJ

New York Fast Ferry 732 291-2210 or 800 NYF NYFF (693-6933), www.nyff.com, service to New Jersey and Shea Stadium

NY Waterway (formerly Port Imperial Ferry) 800 53 FERRY (800 533-3779), www.nywaterway.com, service to New Jersey, Brooklyn, Queens and Yankee and Shea Stadiums

Seastreak (formerly Express Navigation) 800 BOAT RIDE (800 262-8743), www.seastreak.com, service to New Jersey and Yankee and Shea Stadiums

Staten Island Ferry Information 718 815-BOAT (718 815-2628)

Department of Transportation General Information 212/718 CALLDOT (225-5368), www.nyc.gov/html/dot/html/get_around/ferry/statfery.html www.siferry.com

Garages

Municipal parking facilities

Municipal parking facilities are generally open 24 hours a day, seven days a week. Metered parking only. Meters take either quarters (20–30 minutes per 25 cents) or NYC Parking Cards.

www.nyc.gov/html/dot/html/get_around/park/prkintro.html

NYC Parking Cards (pre-paid parking meter cards available in values of $10, $20 and $50) can be used at most municipal parking lots and can be purchased by calling 718 786-7042 or downloading an application from www.nyc.gov/html/dot/html/get_around/park/municard.html.

Broome and Ludlow Municipal Parking Field, Broome Street, between Ludlow and Essex Streets (4-hour limit)

Delancey and Essex Municipal Parking Garage, 107 Essex Street, just North of Delancey Street

Leonard Street Municipal Parking Field, Leonard Street, between Lafayette and Centre Streets (2-hour limit)

NYC Parking Cards can also be used at special on-street meters at the following locations:
Second Avenue from 30th to 33rd Streets
30th Street between First and Second Avenues
43rd to 59th Streets between Fifth Avenue and Broadway
72nd Street
8th Street (NYU area)
Battery Park
Orchard Street

Private parking facilities

For a copy of The Parking Guide, visit
www.nyc.gov/html/dca/html/parkguide.html

For information on licensed parking facilities, visit
www.nyc.gov/html/dcp/html/dcptd/index.html

Mass Transit

MTA New York City Transit
www.mta.nyc.ny.us
Travel Information Center 718 330-1234
Travel information for non–English-speaking people 718 330-4847
Department of Buses "Insider's Guide" 718 927-7499
Travel information for people with disabilities 718 596-8585
Hearing impaired 718 596-8273
Lost Property Office 712-4500
Elevator/Escalator Hotline 800 734-6772

MetroCard
www.mta.nyc.ny.us/metrocard
638-7622 (within New York City)
800 METROCARD (800 638-7622) (outside New York City)
M–F, 9 a.m.–11 p.m. and Saturday, Sunday and holidays, 9 a.m. to 5 p.m.
Reduced fare information 718 243-4999
Purchase MetroCard online
www.mta.ny.us/metrocard/subcool/index.html

Port Authority of New York & New Jersey
www.panynj.gov
435-7000

www.straphangers.com (subway directions)

Parking Tax Exemption

New York City Department of Finance Parking Tax Exemption Unit
25 Elm Place, 3rd floor, Brooklyn, NY 11201
718 935-6080
www.nyc.gov/html/dof
Tax Fax 718 935-6114
Taxpayer Assistance Hotline 718 935-9500, M–F, 9 a.m.– 4:30 p.m.
City Tax Dial (recorded tax information) 718 935-6736

Taxi Service

Taxi and Limousine Commission
40 Rector Street, 5th floor, New York, NY 10006
676-1000
24-Hour Consumer Hotline NYC-TAXI (692-8294)
www.nyc.gov/html/tlc/
To file a complaint on-line: www.nyc.gov/html/tlc/html/tlccompl.html

Dispatcher-Operated Taxi Stands

Citicorp Center, Lexington Avenue between East 53rd and East 54th Streets

Grand Central Terminal, Vanderbilt Avenue and East 42nd Street

Penn Station
Seventh Avenue and West 32nd Street
Eighth Avenue and West 33rd Street

Peter Minuit Plaza at Staten Island Ferry Terminal

Port Authority Bus Terminal
Eighth Avenue between West 40th and West 41st Streets
Eighth Avenue between West 41st and West 42nd Streets

Other Taxi Stands

Taxi stands are located at major transit hubs, hotels, office and retail centers and hospitals in Manhattan. At these stands, drivers are permitted to wait to pick up passengers. Taxi-stand signs are affixed to guide rails and lampposts on the sidewalk.

Train Service

Grand Central Terminal, Park Avenue at 42nd Street,
www.grandcentralterminal.com

Pennsylvania Station, Seventh and Eighth Avenues at 32nd Street,
http://www.amtrak.com/stations/nyp.html

Amtrak Information, 800 USA-RAIL (800 872-7245), www.amtrak.com

Long Island Rail Road
- www.mta.nyc.ny.us
- 718 217-LIRR (718 217-5477) (inside New York City)
- 516 822-LIRR (516 822-5477) (in Nassau County)
- 631 231-LIRR (631 231-5477) (in Suffolk County)
- Special packages and promotions 718 558-7498
- Lost and Found 643-5228 M–F, 7:20 a.m. to 7:20 p.m.
- Police 718 558-3300/3301

Metro-North Information
- www.mnr.org
- 532-4900 (inside New York City)
- 800 METRO-INFO (800 638-7646) (outside New York City)
- Police 878-1001
- Lost and Found 340-2555

NJ Transit
- Official website www.njtransit.com
- Unofficial website www.nj.com/njtransit
- 800 772-2222 (inside New Jersey)
- 973 762-5100 (outside New Jersey)

PATH, 800 234-PATH (800 234-7284), www.panynj.gov/path

Chapter 4

Doctor, Doctor

Manhattan probably has the highest concentration of health-care practitioners in the nation, if not the world. Whether you are seeking a pediatrician, family physician, specialist, therapist or homeopath, there are myriad professionals from whom to choose. Finding your way to the right person for the needs of your child and family takes some work on your part, but investing the effort and energy in times of relative calm can save you aggravation and anxiety—and precious time—in times of illness or emergency.

New Yorkers tend to have very strong views about which doctors are "good." Because Manhattan is indeed the home of many world-renowned medical centers and famous physicians, it is easy to fall into the trap of seeking a celebrity doctor or a hot practice. Notwithstanding the lure of using a popular doctor or a medical star, the most fundamental issue in organizing health care for your family is finding competent practitioners who will pay attention to you, whose judgment you trust and with whom you can communicate about issues large and small.

In this chapter, we will guide you through the process of finding pediatric professionals, dentists and specialists. At the end of this chapter, you will find a list of resources to assist you in getting the best care for your children.

About Pediatricians

For every neurotic New Yorker who has a Filofax filled with the names of specialists for all types of ailments and consults with a doctor for every sneeze, there is another New Yorker who has not seen a doctor since his or her last school-mandated physical. Whether you love to go to the doctor or go only under duress, once you become a parent, you will need a primary-care physician for your child. Your infant will need regularly scheduled visits for immunizations, checking growth and physical condition and assessing development. In addition, there will be your fair share of visits for respiratory infections, rashes, stomach viruses and other things you could not have even imagined before you were a parent. As your child gets older, you will need a doctor to complete required forms for preschool, school, camp and other programs regulated by the health department.

▶ **Pediatrician vs. Family Physician.** Before beginning your search for a doctor, you need to decide whether you want a pediatrician or a family physician. A pediatrician is a doctor who has completed specialized training in pediatrics and sees only children. A pediatrician has particular expertise in dealing with children and childhood illnesses and is able to recognize and treat conditions ranging from the mildest to the most severe. By virtue of his or her practice, the pediatrician has a broad range of experience, will likely be well informed on the latest information in the specialty and have seen more unusual childhood diseases or behaviors, thereby broadening his or her diagnostic skills.

The family physician, a descendant of the general practitioner, on the other hand, does not limit his or her practice to children, but rather sees patients of all ages. Since family physicians tend to treat the entire family, they may be better able to spot emotional problems arising from family dynamics, be more aware of family conditions (such as allergies) and treat contagious illnesses that run through the family. Essentially, you must decide whether you prefer a specialist who treats only your children or more of a generalist who can be the primary physician for your whole family.

▶ **What type of practice?** Once you have decided what type of doctor you want, the next thing to think about is the type of practice you prefer. In Manhattan, the most common types of pediatric practices are individual (solo) or group. Solo practitioners maintain their own practices without partners. The advantage of the solo practice is that your child will always be seen by the same doctor, who will come to know you and your family very well. Individual practitioners must arrange coverage for times when they are unavailable. Most doctors tend to create coverage networks with colleagues affiliated with the same hospital, so that in the event hospitalization is required, your child will be admitted to the hospital where your doctor has privileges.

While most solo practitioners make every attempt to be available to their patients at all times, it is not always possible to do so. Therefore, the disadvantage of using a doctor with an individual practice is that there will be times when you must deal with a covering doctor who does not know you or your child and has no access to your child's records. Some parents have found that covering doctors may be less inclined to see a child in the office during off hours and, if possible, prefer either to treat over the telephone, arrange to meet a very sick child in an emergency room or try to arrange for the patient's own doctor to see the child.

There tend to be two types of group practices. In the pure group practice, your child is a patient of the group rather than an individual doctor. While you may choose to see a particular group member for well visits, typically your child will see whoever is available for a sick visit. In the other type of group practice, several doctors will share office space (and probably certain office personnel), but each doctor will maintain a separate practice. In this type of practice, the doctors will have a schedule of off-hour coverage among group members during which the patients of any group members will be seen.

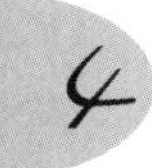

The benefits of using either type of group practice are that a covering doctor will have access to your child's records, group practices tend to have extended office hours (evenings and weekends) so that you can take your child to a familiar office for an off-hour sick visit, and many groups have doctors with specialties, which can be helpful for additional on-site consultations. Over time, most parents and children become familiar with all of the doctors in a group practice.

There are also what are known as faculty practices, which operate in conjunction with, and are salaried by, a hospital. These tend to be more common at teaching hospitals and for specialty practices and are often located on or near hospital premises. Faculty practices tend to operate like group practices with a number of affiliated members.

▶ **Special Credentials.** The American Board of Pediatrics (www.abp.org), a national organization, certifies general pediatricians and pediatric specialists (including specialists in adolescent medicine) who complete an approved residency program and pass a written exam that the Board administers (this exam is in addition to the credentialing exam required by the New York State Board of Regents). Certification signifies that the doctor has achieved a certain level of competency and recognition in the profession. Certification used to be for life, but pediatricians certified after 1988 must be recertified every seven years. It is not necessary to be board certified to practice pediatrics in New York.

You may hear the term "board eligible" to refer to doctors who have complied with all certification requirements but have not sat for the certification exam. The Board no longer uses this term, and if you inquire as to a doctor's board status, you will only be told whether or not he or she is certified. You can visit the American Board of Pediatrics website at www.abp.org or call 919 929-0461 to find out if a pediatrician is board certified or for a referral to a local certified pediatrician.

Board-certified pediatricians may also be members or fellows of the American Academy of Pediatrics (www.aap.org). The Academy's website allows you to search by name to determine whether a physician is board certified (which is a requirement of membership) and to get referrals to member doctors. The Academy also produces materials on many subjects pertaining to the health and care of children, which can be obtained by accessing its affiliated website at www.medem.com.

The American Board of Family Practice (www.abfp.org), also a national organization, certifies family practitioners who complete an approved residency program and pass a written exam that the Board administers (this exam is in addition to the credentialing exam required by the New York State Board of Regents). Board-certified family physicians must be recertified every seven years. It is not necessary to be board certified to be a family physician in New York. You can find out whether a family physician is board certified by visiting the website at www.abfp.org and choosing "Diplomate Verification" or by calling the American Board of Family Practice at 859 269-5626 (note that you must have the physician's social security number to confirm certification). You can also search the website for local members.

The American Academy of Family Physicians (www.aafp.org) is an organization of family physicians/doctors who have completed a three-year residency in family practice at an approved institution. Academy members must complete 150 hours of continuing education every three years. For a list of family physicians in New York City, visit the affiliated website at www.familydoctor.org. The Academy can also provide you with information on anything from specific ailments to improving your relationship with your doctor.

▶ **Hospital Affiliation.** Affiliation with a New York City hospital is not automatic and must be applied for by a doctor. Each hospital has its own criteria for granting hospital privileges—the right to admit and treat patients at the facility—to a physician. While all hospitals require that the doctor be licensed by the state, many require that he or she be board certified and/or be recommended by peers (or have professional references). In return for being granted privileges, most hospitals require the doctor to give something back to the hospital. In teaching hospitals, it may be a teaching requirement. In other hospitals, it may be some other type of service, such as seeing clinic patients. Because of the service obligation, as a practical matter, most doctors tend to have only one affiliation. While it is possible to practice without a hospital affiliation, the downside to using an unaffiliated doctor is that if your child needs to be hospitalized, your primary doctor can neither admit nor personally treat your child at the hospital.

▶ **Insurance.** Finally, before considering individual doctors, families must determine the specifics of their insurance coverage. Insurance coverage may permit an unlimited choice of doctors, provide lists of network doctors or limit choices to doctors at a specific facility. Each family must decide whether it will stay within insurance limits or use doctors for which all or a portion of the fees will not be reimbursed. The good news is that there are so many terrific doctors in Manhattan that whatever your insurance coverage may be, you will in all likelihood be able to find a doctor who meets your needs.

▶ **Finding Dr. Right.** You may want to focus your search for a doctor on certain criteria such as the age or gender of the doctor, hospital affiliation, location of office, style of practice (formal or informal, group or individual), or you may prefer to meet a variety of doctors to see what suits you best. It is customary to interview one or more doctors before selecting one or bringing your child in for a visit. In fact, most expectant parents interview and select a pediatrician or family practitioner before their baby is born so that their own doctor can see the baby in the hospital following the birth.

To generate a list of prospective pediatricians or family-practice physicians, your first step is to seek referrals from people whose opinion you value. Excellent sources include your own physician, obstetrician or other medical specialists, friends, family and other parents. You can also get referrals from the American Board of Pediatrics or the American Board of Family Physicians. Most hospitals maintain physician referral services, but be aware that in some cases participants may pay the hospital to be included on such lists and in others the list may be an alphabetical list of physicians whose are "referred" in alphabetical order. Your health insurer will probably provide a list of doctors covered in its network.

Once you have a list, schedule consultations with the doctors. Some doctors do not charge for interviews. However, it is becoming more common for doctors to charge for interviews due to the great number of families seeking consultations, which can take up a great deal of the doctor's time. You can expect the fee for a consultation to range from $50 to $125. Frequently, doctors who charge for the interview will apply the amount paid for the consultation against the first visit with the child. It is best to clarify the cost issue at the time you schedule the appointment.

▶ **The interview.** Your initial contact with a doctor's office provides your introduction to the practice. Were you treated courteously when making your appointment and upon arrival in the office? Was it easy or difficult to get an appointment (how full is the doctor's schedule)? Are the staff friendly and helpful? Look around the office. It should be neat, clean, have books and toys for children of all ages and be generally child friendly. Is the office cheerful? Are the toys clean and in good repair? Is there a place to play while waiting? How long are patients kept waiting before seeing the doctor? Is equipment modern and up to date? What diagnostic equipment is kept in the office (e.g., for vision and hearing tests)? Are examining rooms pleasant for the children? Is the office formal (lab coats and nurses' uniforms) or more casual?

A question many parents ask is whether sick and well children are separated. While many suburban pediatricians have sick and well waiting areas, in Manhattan, where real estate is very dear, it is not often that you find a physician's office large enough to accommodate separate waiting areas. Also, segregated waiting areas may be difficult for parents to honor when bringing more than one child to the doctor's office. In most offices, very sick or contagious children are sent immediately to an examining room rather than remaining in the reception area. It is worth observing while you are waiting to see the doctor and asking the doctor how this is handled.

Before your meeting with a doctor, you may want to jot down your questions or the issues you want to discuss. Some ideas:

- Inquire about the doctor's training and professional experience, specialties, credentials, certifications, professional memberships, continuing education and hospital affiliations.
- Ask how the practice runs. What are the scheduled office hours? How is off-hour coverage handled (e.g., will the doctor meet you in the office over the weekend)? How can you reach your doctor in an emergency: beeper, service, voice mail? Is the doctor willing to communicate by e-mail? Who will treat your child when your doctor is not available? If your child is admitted to the hospital, would your doctor be able to treat him or her? Discuss the doctor's rates for routine checkups, sick visits and consultations. If it is a group practice, can you choose which doctor you want to see for well or sick visits?
- Discuss office procedures. How are phone calls handled during office hours? Does the doctor have scheduled phone hours for non-emergency inquiries? Does the doctor use nurses or physician's assistants to answer certain questions and if so, under what circumstances are you put through to the doctor? Who performs various procedures such as taking blood, administering injections, conducting hearing and vision tests? What is the doctor called by the children? Are there giveaways for children, such as stickers?
- Find out about the doctor's interest in behavioral, psychological and development issues. Does the doctor run or participate in parent support groups or educational seminars? For example, some offices sponsor groups for new parents. If groups are sponsored, who runs them and does the doctor participate? How involved does the doctor get in referrals for non-medical issues such as speech therapy, psychiatric and psychological treatment, occupational therapy, and work with learning specialists? Some doctors take an active interest and role in helping parents of children with special issues while others prefer to refer to specialists and limit their role in non-medical treatments.
- Be sure to discuss any other issues that are of special concern to you or relevant to your situation. For example, you may want to know the doctor's views on breastfeeding, nutrition, use of bottles, toileting, when to begin classes for the child, sleep problems or reaching developmental milestones. If you are interested in nontraditional medicine, ask whether the doctor will support you in seeking alternative treatments. How does the doctor feel about prescribing medications?

4

▶ **The doctor–parent relationship.** According to Manhattan pediatrician Dr. Barry Stein, the most important feature of a sound doctor–parent relationship is trust. You will be relying on this person's judgment to tell you when your child is well and for diagnosis, treatment and guidance when your child is ill. You need to be able to communicate with your pediatrician or family practitioner and feel free to raise whatever questions and issues may be on your mind. If you feel intimidated and cannot fully express your concerns or if you feel that the doctor does not listen to you or is regularly unavailable, then you are not with the right doctor.

Providing good health care, however, is not the sole province of the doctor. Parents are an integral part of a team. It is unrealistic to expect your pediatrician or family practitioner to assess your child's total health and developmental profile from a 30-minute examination. You must alert the doctor to all matters—physical, psychological and environmental—that you think may impact your child's health. For example, stresses in the family (of which a child may be only subliminally aware) may contribute to such things as sleep disturbances, tantrums, withdrawal or eating problems.

It is also important to point out any changes in behavior or habits that you notice or differences between your child and his or her peers that you observe and about which you are concerned. To this end, the input of caregivers, teachers, parents or other family members can be quite relevant in assessing whether the behavior at issue is within normal ranges or requires further investigation.

Dr. Stein recommends that in advance of a visit to the doctor, parents should prepare a written list of questions, concerns and issues they would like to discuss. It may make sense to make a separate appointment with the doctor, without the child present, to talk about issues in greater depth or with respect to which it would not be appropriate to have the child in the room. The more information you provide to the doctor, the better prepared he or she is to assess your child's situation in the proper context and recommend a course of action.

Last, but certainly not least, your child must like the doctor too.

Last, but certainly not least, your child must like the doctor too. Your child will inevitably have a relationship with his or her doctor, particularly as the child approaches adolescence. While all children will experience fear or anxiety about visits to the doctor at some time (or even every time!), how the doctor handles such situations is paramount. You will want a doctor who is kind, gentle and empathetic, relates well to children and attempts to assuage your child's fears rather than fuel them. You will also want a doctor who actually likes and listens to children, engages them and makes them feel comfortable. As Dr. Stein reminds us, a child can usually tell you whether the doctor is a good one.

▶ **Specialists.** There will likely be occasions when your child will need to pay a visit to a specialist of some type. The first source for referrals is your pediatrician or family practitioner, who can both direct you to the type of specialist you need and give you names. If you want more than one opinion, you should not hesitate to ask for more than one name. Your doctor should be able to recommend specialists from several hospitals.

You can do research on your own to find specialists. As with finding any medical professional, good sources include your own physicians, friends who have faced similar medical problems and other parents. Your insurance company may be able to provide you with names of specialists who are in the network. In some situations, school psychologists may be helpful in providing lists of specialists, particularly in the area of speech and learning problems. You can contact the professional organization of the specialty you need for a list of practitioners. If you are not sure how to find the relevant professional organization, the American Medical Association can help direct you to relevant Boards, Academies and other organizations, as can the American Board of Medical Specialties (see resource list at the end of this chapter). You can network via organizations set up to deal with particular problems or diseases, parent support groups or the Internet. For resources relating to specific medical, mental health and learning issues, see the resources listed at the end of Chapter 13.

During times when you do need to work with a specialist, the relationship you have built with your pediatrician or family practitioner can be most valuable. The doctor can help you to understand

The American Dental Association (ADA) can provide consumers with information on particular dental problems and procedures. You can contact the ADA at 312 440-2500 or www.ada.org. The ADA produces written materials on many topics of interest to parents, and it will send them to you on request. This material—as well as dentist referrals—can be found on the website at www.ada.org. The New York State Dental Association also has a "Dentist Search" feature on its website at www.nysdental.org.

As is the case with finding a physician, you will probably have many questions you want to ask the pediatric dentist about his or her credentials and training, office procedures for handling off-hours emergencies, who performs what procedures, how and what type of anesthesia is administered, how the dentist handles a frightened child, fees and office procedures and policies.

Although parents tend not to interview pediatric dentists before selecting one, it is possible to do so. In any event, when you visit the office, either with or without your child in tow, you would want to see an office that is child friendly, cheerful and clean. It should have modern equipment and a variety of activities for children to get busy with in the waiting room. If your child has special needs, be aware that most pediatric dentists receive special training to treat mentally and physically challenged children, so be sure to ask whether the practice can meet your child's needs.

▶**Your relationship with the pediatric dentist.** It is important for both you and your child to develop a good relationship with your pediatric dentist, particularly if your child will need to have various procedures—such as cavity filling, root canal or tooth extractions—performed. Such procedures may be scary to your child (or to you!) and you will want to know that they are being done so as to minimize pain and maximize the possibility of your child having a positive experience.

For those of you with children well beyond the first visit, it is important to feel comfortable with how your child's care is being managed, especially because for many children, braces follow shortly after the tooth fairy has paid her final visit to your child. While braces are certainly not necessary for every child, for those who have to brace themselves for braces, there is nothing like a good pediatric dentist to lead the way. In general, orthodontics start when a child's dental age is approximately 10 to 10.5 years of age, although there is a strong trend toward earlier intervention. Dental age refers to the development of the mouth and may differ from the child's chronological age.

A pediatric dentist is usually the best source for finding an orthodontist. If you are not satisfied with the referral or want a second opinion, you can get additional names from your own dentist, your pediatrician or family practitioner or other parents. Additionally, you can call the American Association of Orthodontists at 800 STRAIGHT (787-2444) for a list of practitioners in your area or 314 993-1700 for general information. You can also use the "Orthodontist Locator" feature on the affiliated website at www.braces.org. Keep in mind that you may get a different treatment plan from each orthodontist. A solid relationship with your pediatric dentist, based on your trust in his or her judgment, can help you sort through your options.

Whether or not your children are headed for the bright lights of Broadway, you will want their smiles to be bright, beautiful and healthy. So remember, start early and do not forget to floss.

Moving On

A good rapport with a medical professional is built over time. If you are unhappy with some aspect of your child's care, by all means make an effort to resolve your issues with the doctor so that misunderstandings can be cleared up or feelings aired. If you determine that it is time to move on, there is no need to be uncomfortable. You must do what you think is best for your child. When you do change doctors, you will want to have your child's records transferred to the new doctor. Typically, you will need to request in writing that your files be sent to the new doctor. By law, the doctor is required to release your child's medical records within a reasonable time (interpreted by the State Health Department, Office of Professional Medical Conduct, as 10 to 15 days). If your doctor withholds the records, you can contact the New York State Department of Health, Office of Professional Medical Conduct, Access to Patient Information Coordinator, at 518 402-0814 (for records held by physicians or health-care facilities) or 518 402-1039 (for records held by other health professions); for records held by facilities licensed or operated by the New York State Office of Mental Health, telephone 800 597-8481.

► **A final word on medical care in New York City.** We are extremely lucky to live in a city with some of the finest hospitals and medical talent to be found. There are scores of dedicated physicians in this city who help children and families every single day. Do not be disappointed if it takes more than one try to find the medical support you need for your children or the doctor to whom you and your child can relate. He, she or they are most definitely out there, and with a bit of work on your part, you will find them.

RESOURCES

Medical Care

Pediatric Care

American Academy of Family Physicians
P.O. Box 11210
Shawnee Mission, KS 66207
913 906-6000
800 274-2237
www.aafp.org

American Academy of Pediatrics
Department C
141 Northwest Point Blvd.
Elk Grove Village, IL 60007
800 434-4000
www.aap.org, www.medem.com

American Board of Family Practice
2228 Young Drive
Lexington, KY 40505
859 269-5626
888 995-5700
www.abfp.org

American Board of Medical Specialties
1007 Church Street, Suite 404
Evanston, IL 60201
847 491-9091
Certification Line 866 ASK ABMS (275-2267)
www.abms.org

American Board of Pediatrics
111 Silver Cedar Court
Chapel Hill, NC 27514
919 929-0461
www.abp.org

Society for Adolescent Medicine
1916 Copper Oaks Circle
Blue Springs, Missouri 64015
816 224-8010
www.adolescenthealth.org

American Medical Association
515 N. State Street
Chicago, IL 60610
312 464-5000
www.ama-assn.org

Manhattan Hospitals

Note: "full range of pediatric specialties" indicates that there are pediatric physicians handling a broad range of medical practice areas. Not all practice areas within each hospital are listed. If you want to know whether the hospital has specialists in a particular specialty that is not listed, contact the hospital's physician referral service or department of pediatrics. The Greater New York Hospital Association, www.gnyha.org, provides helpful links to many of the New York City hospitals.

BELLEVUE HOSPITAL, 462 First Avenue, New York, NY 10016, 562-4141
www.ci.nyc.ny.us/html/hcc/bellevue/home.html
Full range of pediatric specialties. Special pediatric programs include the Pediatric Asthma Clinic, Pediatric Emergency Department and Child Life Program, Pediatric Resource Center, Reach Out and Read (ROAR, a literacy program), Perinatal Diagnostic Unit, children's psychiatric inpatient unit and Pediatric Infectious Disease Program.

BETH ISRAEL MEDICAL CENTER
www.bethisraelny.org; www.wehealny.org
Physician Referral Service 800 420-4004
To obtain pediatric brochures 844-8300
PETRIE DIVISION, First Avenue at 16th Street, New York, NY 10003, 420-2000
SINGER DIVISION, 170 East End Avenue, New York, NY 10128, 870-9000
Full range of pediatric specialties. Special pediatric programs include the Institute for Neurology and Neurosurgery (Singer Division), the Phillips Ambulatory Care Center, Beth Israel DOCS (seven-day-a-week immediate-care facilities at the following three locations: 1555 Third Avenue, 55 East 34th Street and 202 West 23rd Street), Pediatric Music Therapy Program, Child Life Program, neonatology, medical genetics, critical and intensive care unit, cardiology, child development, asthma, endocrinology and hematology. The Continuum for Health and Healing, at 245 Fifth Avenue at 28th Street, offers integrative care, including specialties in pediatrics and adolescent medicine, by a team of conventional physicians and holistic practitioners employing conventional and complementary therapies.

Cabrini Medical Center, 227 East 19th Street, New York, NY 10003, 995-6000
Physician Referral Service 995-6600
www.cabrininy.org
Cabrini Medical Center does not treat children on an inpatient basis but does maintain two primary-care facilities (birth through geriatric) at the Cabrini East Village Family Practice at 97 East 4th Street (979-3200) and Cabrini Haven Plaza Family Medical Practice at Avenue C and 12th Street (677-2280).

Continuum Health Partners, see Beth Israel, St. Luke's-Roosevelt Hospital Center, New York Eye and Ear Infirmary, www.wehealny.org

Gouverneur Hospital Diagnostic and Treatment Center, 227 Madison Street, New York, NY 10002, 238-7000
Special pediatric programs include the walk-in clinic, adolescent clinic, Reach Out and Read (ROAR).

Harlem Hospital Center, 506 Lenox Avenue, New York, NY 10037, 939-1000
www.ci.nyc.ny.us/html/hhc/html/harlem1.html
Full range of pediatric specialties. Special pediatric programs include the Harlem Children's Own Asthma Initiative, allergy and immunology, neonatology, hematology and oncology, dentistry, surgery and ambulatory care, Pediatric Resource Center, Injury Prevention Program, Urban Youth Bike Project and the Harlem Hospital Dance Leadership Program. There are clinics for pediatric genetics, dermatology, AIDS and neurology. Harlem Hospital has strong health education, preventive services and community outreach programs (such as the Horizon Art Studio and Winter Baseball Clinic).

Hospital for Joint Diseases Orthopaedic Institute, 301 East 17th Street, New York, NY 10003, 598-6000
Physician Referral Service 888 HJD-DOCS (453-3627)
www.jointdiseases.com
www.nyuhjdcenterforchildren.org
Specialized hospital dealing with orthopedics and rheumatology, including arthritis, bone disease, Lyme disease and epilepsy. Special pediatric programs as part of the Center for Children include the Center for the Treatment of Neuromuscular Disorders, Center for Growth, Center for Pediatric Orthopedic Surgery, Center for Pediatric Bone Health, and the Institute for Limb Lengthening and Reconstruction. Other ailments treated include eating, spinal and rheumatological disorders.

Hospital for Special Surgery, 535 East 70th Street, New York, NY 10021, 606-1000
Physician Referral Service 606-1555 or 800 854-0071
www.hss.edu
Specialized hospital dealing with orthopedics and rheumatology. Special pediatric programs include specialties in Marfan's Syndrome, scoliosis, osteogenesis imperfecta, osteoporosis, familial dysautonomia, cerebral palsy and spina bifida.

LENOX HILL HOSPITAL, 100 East 77th Street, New York, NY 10021, 434-2000
Physician Referral Service 888 RIGHT-MD (744-4863) (includes Appointment Schedule Assistance Program for appointments within 24 hours)
www.lenoxhillhospital.org
Full range of pediatric specialties. Special pediatric programs include The Babies Club and The Toddlers Club (parent information sessions led by a pediatric specialist, 434-3152); the Neonatal Critical Care Unit and Neonatal Follow-up Program; Edward A. Davies, MD, Special Care Unit for acutely ill children; Pediatric Inpatient Unit; Tel-Med (a free telephone health information line, 434-3200); pediatric orthopedics; trauma; and ENT.

MANHATTAN EYE, EAR AND THROAT HOSPITAL, 210 East 64th Street, New York, NY 10021, 838-9200
Physician Referral Service 605-3793 (speech and audiology), 605-3760 (Pediatric Eye Center), 605-3735 (ENT), 605-3740 (Communication Disorders)
Specialized hospital. Special pediatric programs include the Pediatric Eye Center and pediatric practices in ENT, hearing, plastic and reconstructive surgery, communication disorders and audiology/speech.

MEMORIAL SLOAN-KETTERING CANCER CENTER, 1275 York Avenue, New York, NY 10021, 639-2000
Physician Referral Service 800 525-2225
www.mskcc.org
Specialized cancer hospital with specialties in all forms of pediatric cancers. Special pediatric programs include the Pediatric Day Hospital (to enable patients to live as normal a life as possible while in treatment).

METROPOLITAN HOSPITAL CENTER, 1901 First Avenue , New York, NY 10029, 423-6262
Physician Referral Service 423-8131
www.ci.nyc.ny.us/html/hhc/html/metropolitan.html
Full range of pediatric specialties. Special pediatric programs include pediatric infectious disease and HIV programs, developmental pediatrics, Family Centered Asthma Program and adolescent psychiatric program.

MT. SINAI MEDICAL CENTER, One Gustave L. Levy Place, New York, NY 10029, 241-6500
Physician Referral Service 800 MD-SINAI (637-4624)
www.mssm.edu
Through the Jack and Lucy Clark Department of Pediatrics, the Kravis Women's and Children's Center and the Maternal Child Health Care Center, Mt. Sinai offers a full-service children's "hospital within a hospital" unit within the Mt. Sinai Medical Center with a full range of pediatric specialties. Special programs include Meet Me at Mount Sinai Pediatric Preoperative Program, Child Life Program, Through Our Eyes (a therapeutic video production program), a family-centered care approach for families living with an ill child, Neonatal and Pediatric Intensive Care Units, Young People's Diabetes Unit, Pediatric Pulmonary Center, Cystic Fibrosis Center, Apnea Center and pediatric cardiology, gastrointestinal, liver and nutritional diseases, surgery, ENT, genetics and neurology (including a neurofibromatosis center).

New York Eye and Ear Infirmary, 310 East 14th Street, New York, NY 10003, 979-4000
Physician Referral Service 979-4000
www.nyee.edu, www.wehealny.org
Specialized hospital. In addition to specialists in ophthalmology and ENT, special pediatric programs include general care Eye Center and Pediatric Ear, Nose and Throat Center, Pediatric Glaucoma Clinic, bilingual speech therapy (English and Spanish), facial plastic and reconstructive surgery, ambulatory care and early evaluation and intervention services for children birth to three, including developmental, feeding, vision, speech, language and audiology assessments.

New York-Presbyterian Hospital (formerly Columbia Presbyterian Medical Center)

Morgan Stanley Children's Hospital of New York-Presbyterian, 3959 Broadway, New York, NY 10032, 305-KIDS (5437), Physician Referral Service 800 245-KIDS (5437)
www.childrensnyp.org
Manhattan's only comprehensive children's hospital with specialties in all practice areas, including the Pediatric Cardiac Care Center (cardiology and cardiac surgery), hematology/oncology, infectious diseases, genetics, dentistry, psychiatry, surgery, autoimmune disorders, developmental pediatrics, Sickle Cell Center, orthopedics and Pediatric Urology Services. Children's Hospital of New York-Presbyterian is at the hub of the Regional Perinatal Network and offers a Child Life program for patients.

New York Weill Cornell Medical Center, (formerly New York Hospital Cornell Medical Center), 525 East 68th Street, New York, NY 10021, 746-5454
Physician Referral Service 877 NYP-WELL (697-9355)
www.nycornell.org
Full range of pediatric specialties. Special pediatric programs include the Child Life Program; Heads Up! Children Read, Listen, and Learn; Perinatology Referral Center; Pediatric Intensive Care Unit; Pediatric Endocrinology Division; Burn Center; Healthy Steps program for new babies; pediatric allergy/immunology; child development; gastroenterology; infectious disease; mental health; neurology, hematology; cardiology; and oncology.

NYU Medical Center, 550 First Avenue, New York, NY 10016, 263-7300
Physician Referral Service 888 769-8633
www.nyuchildrens.org
Full range of pediatric specialties. Special pediatric programs include Children's Cardiology and Cardiovascular Surgery Program, Children's Brain Tumor Program, Hassenfeld Center for Children's Cancer and Blood Disorders, Children's Rehabilitation Program, Children's Craniofacial Program, Neonatal Program and Neonatal Comprehensive Continuing Care Service, Children's Cochlear Implant Program, Pediatric Infectious Disease Services, Child Study Center, Children's Epilepsy Program, Neurogenetics Program, Children's Urology Program and pediatric departments including allergy and rheumatology, endocrinology, dermatology, dysautonomia and surgery.

NYU DOWNTOWN HOSPITAL, 170 William Street, New York, NY 10038, 312-5000
Physician Referral Service 888 NYUD-DOC (888 698-3362)
www.nyudh.org
NYU Downtown is primarily an acute-care hospital. Pediatric care is mostly on an outpatient or clinic basis.

ST. CLARE'S HOSPITAL AND HEALTH CENTER, 415 West 52nd Street, New York, NY 10019, 586-1500

Physician Referral Service 265-8950 (Family Health Center)
St. Clare's does not treat children on an inpatient basis but does maintain full-service (birth to geriatric) faculty practices at the Family Health Center located at 350 West 51st Street (265-8950).

ST. LUKE'S-ROOSEVELT HOSPITAL CENTER, 523-4000
www.bethisraelny.org, www.wehealny.org
Physician Referral Service 800 420-4004
  ROOSEVELT DIVISION, 1000 Tenth Avenue, New York, NY 10019
  ST. LUKE'S HOSPITAL, 111 Amsterdam Avenue, New York, NY 10025
Full range of pediatric specialties. Special pediatric programs include the Child Life Program, St. Luke's Pediatric Outpatient Clinic, dermatology, endocrinology, gastroenterology, hematology, pulmonary medicine, neurology, sickle cell disease and HIV/AIDS. The Pediatric Emergency Room is at St. Luke's Hospital.

ST. VINCENT CATHOLIC MEDICAL CENTERS, ST. VINCENT'S HOSPITAL MANHATTAN, 153 West 11th Street, New York, NY 10011, 604-7000
www.svcmc.org
Physician Referral Service 888 4SVH-DOC (888 478-4362)
Full range of pediatric specialties. Special pediatric programs include the Cystic Fibrosis Center, Level III Neonatal Intensive Care Unit, Pediatric Emergency Room, Pediatric Intensive Care, Child Life Program, Parent Education Program, child and adolescent psychiatry, chronic disease management, cardiology, endocrinology and pediatric asthma, allergy and immunology.

Alternative and Complementary Medicine

General

American Association of Naturopathic Physicians
3201 New Mexico Avenue, NW, Suite 350
Washington, D.C. 20016
202 895-1392
866 538-2267
www.naturopathic.org

American Holistic Health Association
P.O. Box 17400
Anaheim CA 92817
714 779-6152
www.ahha.org

American Holistic Medical Association
12101 Menaul Boulevard NE, Suite C
Albuquerque, NM 87112
505 292-7788
www.holisticmedicine.org

National Center for Complementary and Alternative Medicine
National Institutes of Health
P.O. Box 7923
Gaithersburg, MD 20898
301 519-3153
888 644-6226
www.nccam.nih.gov

National Center for Homeopathy
801 N. Fairfax Street, Suite 306
Alexandria, VA 22314
703 548-7790
www.homeopathic.org

www.healthy.net
provides information and referrals in many practice areas.

Dental Care

First District Dental Society
6 East 43rd Street, 11th floor
New York, NY 10017
573-8500
www.dentalsociety.org

American Academy of Pediatric Dentistry
211 East Chicago Avenue, Suite 700
Chicago, IL 60611
312 337-2169
www.aapd.org

American Dental Association
211 East Chicago Avenue
Chicago, IL 60611
312 440-2500
www.ada.org

American Association of Orthodontists
401 North Lindbergh Blvd.
St Louis, MO 63141
314 993-1700
800 STRAIGHT (787-2444)
www.aaortho.org, www.braces.org

New York State Dental Association
121 State Street
Albany, NY 12207
518 465-0044
800 255-2100
www.nysdental.org

General Information

Children's Hospital Los Angeles
www.juniormed.com

KidsHealth
www.kidshealth.org

National Institutes of Health
9000 Rockville Pike
Bethesda, MD 20892
301 496-4000
www.nih.gov

United States National Library of Medicine
8600 Rockville Pike
Bethesda, MD 20894
301 496-4000
MEDLINE www.nlm.nih.gov/medlineplus

Office of Professional Medical Conduct
New York State Department of Health
Access to Patient Information
433 River Street, Suite 303
Troy, NY 12180
518 402-0814
800 663-6114
www.health.state.ny.us

State Education Department
Office of Professional Discipline
One Park Avenue, 6th floor
New York, NY 10016
800 442-8106
www.health.state.ny.us

State Education Department
Office of Professional Discipline
New York City Regional Office
163 West 125th Street, Room 819
New York, NY 10027
961-4369
www.op.nys.ed.gov

New York State Department of Health
Office of Professional Medical Conduct
Intake Unit Suite 303
433 River Street
Troy, NY 12180
518 402-0836
800 663-6114
www.health.state.ny.us

APPENDIX

Licensing Requirements for Professionals

The Board of Regents of the State of New York supervises the admission to and practice of the 43 professions and the special certification areas within those professions, recognized pursuant to Title VIII of the Education Law of the State of New York. Licensed professions include such practice areas as health care, psychology, social work, engineering, accountancy, dentistry, architecture, pharmacy, optometry and so forth, but not the legal or teaching professions, which are regulated separately. Individual State Boards for the Professions, each consisting of members appointed by the Board of Regents, advise the Board of Regents with respect to matters of policy and practice for the particular professions.

The Board of Regents is responsible for: (1) professional credentialing, which includes evaluating the education and training of potential licensees, developing licensing standards, assessing of applicants' credentials, and developing and administering licensing examinations and issuing licenses; and (2) dealing with matters of professional responsibility, which include handling professional discipline, regulating issues of continuing competence and operating the Professional Assistance Program to help licensed professionals with substance-abuse problems.

In New York, a professional license is effective for life unless revoked by the Board of Regents following a finding of professional misconduct or surrendered by a licensee voluntarily. All of the professions have periodic registration requirements and most of the professions have some type of continuing professional education requirements that must be fulfilled in order to keep a license in good standing.

Complaints of professional misconduct are handled by the Office of Professional Discipline for all licensed professions other than the medical profession. The main office of the Office of Professional Discipline is located at 475 Park Avenue, 2nd floor, New York, NY 10016, www.op.nysed.gov (the website contains a list of all contact information for the individual state boards for the various professions). The toll-free hotline is 800 442-8106. The New York City Regional Office for Manhattan, Bronx and Queens is located at 2400 Halsey Street, Bronx, NY 10461, 718 794-2480 and for Brooklyn and Staten Island at 195 Montague Street, 4th floor, Brooklyn, NY 11201, 718 246-3060. You can use the Office of Professional Discipline website to verify a professional's license status or see summary information of disciplinary action taken against licensees since January 1, 1994.

Allegations of misconduct by a physician, physician's assistant or specialist assistant (as defined by the Education Law) are handled by the Office of Professional Medical Conduct, New York State Department of Health, 433 River Street, Suite 303, Troy, NY 12180, 800-663-6114, 518-402-0836. You can contact the office to search a listing of physicians who have been disciplined since 1990 or look up a physician's license number or visit the website at www.health.state.ny.us/nysdoh/opmc/main.htm.

The specific credentialing requirements for doctors, dentists, psychologists, social workers, audiologists, speech therapists, occupational therapists and other professions that might be of interest to parents are as follows:

Doctor: must be at least 21 years old, either a United States citizen or otherwise authorized to work in this country, complete appropriate pre-professional and medical education in a program in an institution acceptable to the State Education Department (and/or meet additional requirements if the person attended medical school outside the United States), hold a degree of doctor of medicine or osteopathy, have a minimum of one year of postgraduate hospital training in an accredited residency program (longer for graduates of non-accredited medical schools) and pass the relevant written examinations. An applicant for a license must complete course work in identifying and reporting child abuse. All licensees must complete course work in infection control to prevent the transmission of HIV and HBV.

Dentist: must be at least 21 years old, either a United States citizen or otherwise authorized to work in this country, complete appropriate pre-professional and dental education including a degree in dentistry from a program in an institution acceptable to the State Education Department (and/or meet additional requirements if the person attended dental school outside the United States), and pass the written National Board Dental Examination and the Northeast Regional Board Examination practical examination. There are no work experience requirements. Dentists may not employ general anesthesia or certain types of sedation at other than a hospital without a special dental anesthesia certificate. An applicant for a license must complete course work in identifying and reporting child abuse. All licensees must complete course work in infection control to prevent the transmission of HIV and HBV.

Psychologist: must be at least 21 years old, have a doctoral degree in psychology from a program in an institution acceptable to the State Education Department, have a minimum of two years of supervised experience, pass the Examination for Professional Practice in Psychology of the Association of State and Provincial Psychology Boards and be proficient in English. An applicant for a license must complete course work in identifying and reporting child abuse.

Social Worker: must be at least 21 years old, have a master's degree in social work or its equivalent from a program in an institution acceptable to the State Education Department, pass the written Social Work examination administered by the American Association of State Social Work Boards and be proficient in English. There is no minimum work experience requirement except for applicants educated in foreign countries, who must have two years of supervised experience in the United States, or applicants seeking endorsement of a license issued in another jurisdiction.

Other professions:

Acupuncture: must be at least 21 years old, proficient in English, complete 60 semester hours at an accredited college or university, including nine hours in the biosciences, complete a professional acupuncture program in an institution acceptable to the State Education Department and pass the written and practical examination of the National Commission for Acupuncture and Oriental Medicine.

Audiology: must be at least 21 years old, have a master's degree in audiology or its equivalent from a program in an institution acceptable to the State Education Department, complete nine months of supervised experience, and pass the national examination administered by the Educational Testing Service.

Chiropractic: must be at least 21 years old, either a United States citizen or otherwise authorized to work in this country, complete a pre-professional and professional study program acceptable to the State Education Department, pass the written and practical examination of the National Board Examinations administered by the National Board of Chiropractic Examiners and be proficient in English. An applicant for a license must complete course work in identifying and reporting child abuse.

Dietetics-Nutrition: must be at least 18 years old, complete a bachelor's or higher degree in dietetics-nutrition in a program acceptable to the State Education Department, complete 800 hours of planned work experience and pass the written examinations administered by the Commission of Dietetic Registration and the Certification Board for Nutrition Specialists.

Massage therapy: must be at least 18 years old, complete high school and a massage therapy program acceptable to the State Education Department and pass the written New York State Massage Therapy Examination.

Occupational therapy: must be at least 21 years old, proficient in English, have a bachelor's degree or graduate certificate or degree from a program in an institution acceptable to the State Education Department (and/or meet additional requirements if the person attended school outside the United States), complete six months of supervised experience and pass an examination administered by the National Board for Certification in Occupational Therapy.

Physical therapy: must be at least 18 years old, have a bachelor's or higher degree in physical therapy in an institution acceptable to the State Department of Education and pass the National Physical Therapy Examination or its equivalent.

Speech-Language Pathology: must be at least 21 years old, have a master's degree from a program in an institution acceptable to the State Department of Education, complete nine months of supervised experience and pass a national examination administered by the Educational Testing Service.

Resources

(Note: Many of the following sites have referral services listed under "consumer information.")

Acupuncture

Acupuncture and Oriental Medicine Alliance, www.acupuncturealliance.org

Acupuncture Society of New York, www.asny.org

National Certification Commission for Acupuncture and Oriental Medicine, www.nccaom.org

Audiology/ Speech Pathology

American Speech-Language-Hearing Association, www.asha.org

Long Island Speech-Language-Hearing Association, www.lisha.org

Chiropractic

American Chiropractic Association, www.acatoday.com

Federation of Chiropractic Licensing Boards, www.fclb.org

International Chiropractors Association, www.chiropractic.org

Dentistry

Academy of General Dentistry, www.agd.org

American Dental Association, www.ada.org

New York State Dental Association, www.nysdental.org

Dietetics-Nutrition

American Dietetic Association, www.eatright.org

Massage Therapy

American Massage Therapy Association, www.amtamassage.org

New York State Society of Medical Massage Therapists, www.nysmassage.org

Medicine

American Board of Medical Specialties, www.abms.org

American Medical Association, www.ama-assn.org

Medical Society of the State of New York, www.mssny.org

New York State Academy of Family Physicians, www.nysafp.org

Occupational Therapy

American Occupational Therapy Associations, www.aota.org

Physical Therapy

American Physical Therapy Association, www.apta.org

New York State Physical Therapy Association, www.nypta.org

Psychology

American Psychological Association, www.apa.org

Association of State and Provincial Psychology Boards, www.asppb.org

New York State Psychological Association, www.nyspa.org

Social Work

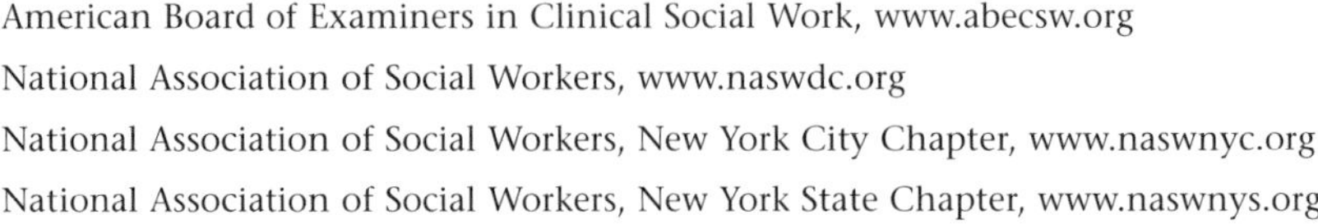

American Board of Examiners in Clinical Social Work, www.abecsw.org

National Association of Social Workers, www.naswdc.org

National Association of Social Workers, New York City Chapter, www.naswnyc.org

National Association of Social Workers, New York State Chapter, www.naswnys.org

Chapter 5

Home Safe Home and Beyond

Non–New Yorkers tend to see our fair city as a very dangerous place, with peril and temptation lurking around every corner. Those of us who have chosen to make this city our home have learned to accept the realities of living here and organized ourselves accordingly. Each of us develops our own ground rules for keeping safe in Manhattan: the neighborhoods in which we will walk at night, the hours we will ride the subway, the routes we take, the time of day we will visit the ATM and so on.

Once we become parents, however, we often see the city with new eyes. We begin to use parts of the city, such as parks and playgrounds, to which we may never have given much thought before. For those of us who are accustomed to spending business hours indoors in our places of work, we or our caregivers will be out and about with our children during those times in parts of the city where we may not usually spend much time.

As we maneuver through town with our children and their paraphernalia, we realize that we are far more encumbered and hence less able to exit a precarious situation quickly. Whatever the case, we want to protect the vulnerable new lives for whom we are totally responsible, and so we suddenly need to think about how we want our children to travel and use the city and what will be safe not only for us adults, but for Junior, too.

In this chapter, we discuss safety within and outside of the home, look at dealing with emergencies and explore talking to your children about safety and how to help your older child safely navigate the city on his or her own. At the end of this chapter, you will find a list of resources relevant to making the city as safe as possible for your family.

The City Life

From the moment your new baby crosses the threshold for the first time, your home transforms from one geared to adult living to a service center for your baby's needs. At first, the changes, though major, are relatively self contained. But whether you simply add a crib, changing table and basic baby supplies or go for all of the baby apparatus you can possibly squeeze in, you can be sure that your home will never be the same again. In a relatively short time, your baby will become mobile and your entire home will become one big playroom and field for exploration, play dates and activities.

▶ **Childproofing your home.** Childproofing your home is an important, ongoing activity for parents. You must continuously anticipate what skills your child will next master (climbing, opening doors, turning knobs, opening bottles) to prevent unnecessary accidents. Because childproofing is a process, you need to train yourself to survey your home on a regular basis and always be alert to what seemingly innocuous objects could create a hazard both for your own child and other children who visit your house. Even if your child is the most cautious, obedient child, do not underestimate his or her natural curiosity. For example, your child may know not to put things in his or her mouth, but sometimes an object looks too good, or too much like candy, to resist.

To create a child-friendly environment, you do not need to remove everything from your home and pad the walls. But you do need to address conditions that could create danger for little people. The rule of thumb is to look at things from the point of view of your child. Get down on the floor and see what each room looks like to a crawling or toddling child. What is within arm's reach or can be moved or got around to get to something interesting? Look for sharp corners and other sharp items, dangling cords and other dangling items, free-standing objects that would be unstable if your child leaned on them, objects that your child could choke on, doors that lock or slam shut, things that could be pulled off tables (including tablecloths) and counters, hinged tops that can slam on little fingers, slippery area rugs, and things that if turned on or off could be dangerous.

Some childproofing basics to keep in mind: move cleaning supplies out of reach (not just in a cabinet with a child safety lock); safeguard all poisonous, hazardous, flammable or toxic materials; keep plastic bags and electrical appliances out of reach; lock cupboards with appropriate child safety devices; carefully store scissors, knives, needles and sharp or heavy tools; safeguard windows and sliding doors; make sure you do not have poisonous plants in your home; remove matches and lighters; be alert to appliances that can burn or scald your child (including halogen lights); and plug unused electric outlets with plastic safety plugs. All nursery and baby equipment should be checked for safety features. Toys should be evaluated both for age-appropriateness and safety.

The most important aspects in childproofing your home are to pay attention to detail and to practice, and teach your children, good safety habits. To help in your endeavors, most stores selling baby supplies as well as most hardware stores offer many products developed to safeguard your home. There are also a number of catalogues that feature home safety products, which are listed at the end of this chapter. For those parents seeking a professional opinion, there are childproofing services, also listed at the end of this chapter, which will pay a house call, evaluate your home and supply and install childproofing devices.

Manhattan parents living in apartments should also be aware

that pursuant to the Multiple Dwelling Law, building owners (landlords in the case of rentals and building owner entities in the case of co-ops and condominiums) are responsible for installing and maintaining window guards at no charge to the tenants in all apartments in which children under the age of ten reside. If you do not like the standard issue window guards provided in most apartment buildings, you can purchase customized window guards that may be more decorative.

5

▶ **Fire safety in your home.** There are two elements to fire safety: fire prevention and a plan of action in the event of a fire in your home. To prevent fires, it is necessary to inspect your home for potential fire hazards. Be sure to safeguard matches and lighters, carefully store flammable materials, be careful when lighting candles (particularly if there is a tablecloth underneath lit candles that can be pulled by a child), replace frayed electrical cords, do not overload electrical outlets or run wire under rugs or over nails, safeguard halogen light fixtures, do not cook while wearing sleeves that can dangle near burners or use towels as potholders near an open flame, do not let rubbish (especially newspapers, magazines and papers) accumulate, and operate space heaters strictly in accordance with instructions. If you have a fireplace, be sure to have it professionally cleaned and checked annually and consider installing carbon monoxide detectors around your home. If you have window gates to discourage intruders on your windows, be sure to use only approved window gates and do not padlock them (which could prevent your escape from a fire).

By law, New Yorkers are required to have smoke detectors installed in our homes within 25 feet of each bedroom. If you live in a rental apartment, it is the obligation of the landlord to install smoke detectors, though you will be responsible for their maintenance (changing the batteries). If you live in a co-op or condominium, it is your obligation to install and maintain smoke detectors inside your apartment. In addition to smoke detectors, you may also want to consider heat detectors in appropriate areas, which may set off an alarm before a smoke detector would.

In the event of a fire in your home, it is crucial to have a fire-escape plan. Since many of us live in apartment buildings, it is important to locate and identify to children the fire stairs or fire escapes and to understand when it is or is not appropriate to use the building elevator. The FDNY recommends that you plan two ways out of the apartment and building. Plan your escape routes with your children and conduct periodic fire drills. It is also a good idea to post Tot Finder decals on your windows and doors to assist firefighters in rescuing your children in an emergency. If you have children old enough to follow directions, they should be taught to call 911 to report a fire and given instructions to meet at a designated meeting point in your immediate neighborhood in the event you are evacuated from your home by firefighters and become separated. See the end of this chapter for specific FDNY tips on what to do in the event of a fire.

You can obtain written materials about fire prevention and safety by calling the New York City Fire Department Fire Safety Education Program at 718 999-0321, contacting your local firehouse, or searching the www.nyc.gov website for FDNY and Fire Safety Education. You can also obtain materials (for a nominal charge) from the National Fire Protection Association at 11 Tracy Drive, Avon, MA 02322, 800 344-3555, www.NFPA.org. You can get information from the Customer Central section of Con Edison website (www.coned.com) on safeguarding your home during storms and safety in homes supplied with natural gas.

▶ **Home security.** The NYPD offers a free confidential security survey to all New York City residents. You can contact the Crime Prevention Officer in your local precinct and arrange for a survey that analyzes the present level of security at the premises and makes recommendations on how to increase it.

▶ **A healthy home.** An important step in making your home safe for your children is to eliminate environmental hazards such as lead-based paint, asbestos, excessive dust mites and other allergens, water damage or moisture conditions that facilitate the growth of molds and harmful or toxic products. While it is not necessary to bring in a SWAT team to evaluate your indoor environment, it is worth considering whether there are issues that need to be addressed.

The presence of lead-based paint can create serious problems for infants and young children because it can cause lead poisoning. Since lead-based paint was in use up until 1978, many older apartments that have multiple coats of paint on the wall and trim (particularly around windows) can have lead issues. Lead poisoning can result in learning disabilities, neurological problems and physical illness. A child does not have to eat lead paint chips to be affected; inhaling the dust from lead paint can do the damage. Lead dust can be produced not only from renovations in your home, but from any disturbance (friction, scratching or impact, opening and closing windows, flaking or peeling) of surfaces covered with lead-based paint.

The dangers of asbestos have been well documented, so it is important to be sure that there is not exposed or friable asbestos in your home. The quality of the air in your home is not only meaningful to your family's comfort but can become crucial if you have a child with allergies, asthma or respiratory problems that can be caused or exacerbated by the presence of dust mites, airborne allergens, chemical household cleaning products, pesticides or molds. It is a good idea to have ventilation systems and air-conditioning units periodically checked and cleaned by professionals.

Water quality is another area for potential investigation. Older buildings in particular may have pipes made of lead or other metals that leak impurities into your drinking water. Recent reports of bacteria contaminating the water supply have led many families to consider installing water filtration systems in their homes.

If you are contemplating, or in the midst of, renovations, your contractor, architect or other professional can help you assess what kind of inspections or evaluations (in addition to those required in connection with your building permits) you may need to ensure the environmental quality of your home. If you are not involved in renovations but are concerned and want to explore these issues, you can get information from a variety of sources, including the City Departments of Environmental Protection, Health and Sanitation, or retain a private consultant to evaluate your home. At the end of this chapter, you will find specific resources to help you in your inquiry.

The Sidewalks of New York

New York City is home to more than eight million people. As such we live in close proximity to our neighbors. When we are not walking (or running!) we travel by bus, subway and taxi. From very early on, our children are used to elevators, doormen, delivery people, public transportation and seeing many people from all walks of life throughout the day. As parents of New York children, it is incumbent upon us to teach our children age-appropriate city skills. The challenge is to do so in a way that reinforces safe and intelligent behavior without frightening them.

There are very few absolutes when it comes to safety rules. The trick is to teach your children not only specific words and actions, but also, and perhaps more important, strategies to deal with events for which they are not expressly prepared. While we want to protect our children against all harm, we cannot anticipate everything that can potentially happen. Rather, through open discussion, role playing and practice, we can help them develop good judgment and city street skills.

The development of safety rules is a process. The rules will change over time as your children become older and more capable and independent. Rules will adjust to address new concerns or in response to an incident that occurred in your home or someone else's or even as a result of a news story. When making your own safety rules, be sure to consider the age and temperament of your child and the level of responsibility he or she can handle. Balance your child's increasing need for independence against his or her level of maturity and what you believe is appropriate under the circumstances. Reinforce your rules with periodic reviews and updates, and practice, practice, practice.

The best thing you can do for your children is to teach them how to observe situations, formulate a strategy, feel confident about their decisions and take decisive action appropriate to the situation. So take a deep breath and let's get started.

▶ **Home safety basics.** Even the youngest children need to be taught the basics of home safety, such as rules for answering the telephone and doorbell and how to use the telephone. As soon as children are able, they should learn their full names, their parents' names, and their addresses and phone numbers. You can point out landmarks in the neighborhood to help them identify where they live.

Children should be instructed early on how and when to use the emergency telephone number, 911, and should be given other important telephone numbers to be used whenever needed. Teach your children your work numbers, your cellular phone or beeper numbers and the numbers for neighbors and others (relatives and friends) who can help in an emergency. If you live in a building with a doorman or superintendent, instruct the children on how to contact them.

Telephone numbers should be prominently displayed for children and caregivers in more than one location. For children who are not yet reading, you can identify phone numbers with symbols or pictures (for example, a police car or fire truck) or a photograph of the person whose number it is. If your telephone has a speed dial function, you may find it easy to use, although your child will still need to memorize certain important numbers for use outside of your home.

You will probably want to develop some specific home safety rules of your own. Such rules should be clearly communicated to all caregivers, housekeepers and babysitters who work in your home. Even very young children should be taught safety rules, because occasions may arise even when you are at home (in the shower or in the event of an emergency), where they should know what to do. At the same time, young children need to understand their limits. One curious three-year-old we know let himself out of the house while his mother went to the bathroom and took the elevator to the lobby alone. Happily the doorman stopped him at the door and safely returned him home before his mother had even realized that he had gone.

Whatever type of rules you devise, think about the kind of situations that are relevant to your children and how you want them to be prepared. Some ideas:

- Telephone. How should the telephone be answered? What information may your children give to friends or strangers (for example, who is home, when you will be home, whether you have a home security system or alarm)? Would you prefer that calls go on the answering machine rather than be answered by a child or caregiver?

- Answering the door. To whom may your children open the door? What should they say before they open the door (who is it?); what should they say if they are not going to open the door (such as, we are not expecting a visitor now)? Must visitors be announced by the doorman? What if someone rings the bell who was not announced by the doorman? What about the service door? What about delivery people? If your building has a buzzer system, under what circumstances may your children let someone into the building?

- Apartment building personnel. What employees are allowed in the apartment and when (only when you have called for a repair, if the superintendent has called in advance, during work hours)? Where in the building may your children go with an employee (bicycle room, basement, elevator, lobby, no place)?
- Leaving the house without an adult. When may the children leave and where may they go (to the garbage disposal, the laundry, the elevator, the lobby, no place)? If the children are allowed to leave the house alone, who must be told that they are leaving and for how long may they go out?
- Things children may do without direct supervision. Cooking? Using kitchen appliances? Using electrical appliances (for example, hair dryer) or tools? Taking a bath or shower? Opening windows? Climbing on a chair to reach something?

▶ **Home alone.** Sooner or later, the day will come when you agree to let your child or children stay home for some period of time without an adult in the house. The issue tends to arise when children are somewhere between eight and ten years old. Even if you do not consider it appropriate for your child to be alone in the house at that age, odds are some parents in your child's class will have deemed it so for theirs. By early adolescence, you can be sure that your child will be asking, if not demanding, the opportunity to stay home without you for some period of time.

Leaving your child home alone is a very controversial issue. We are not expressing a view as to whether or not you should do this.

While you certainly do not have to acquiesce, and we are not necessarily recommending that you do, if you do want to permit your child to be alone in the house, do so in an informed (as to both you and your child!) and deliberate manner. Remember, there is no rule that you must leave your child home alone or any prescribed age at which being left home unattended is mandated. Your decision as to when to leave your *older* child alone in the house is strictly a family matter. *It is never appropriate to leave an infant, toddler or very young child alone or in the care of another child.*

If you are ready to try leaving your child home alone, some considerations:

- Is your child ready? Consider whether your child: wants to be alone; is not afraid to be alone; has good problem solving skills; is responsible and self-motivated; can recognize a problem and take action; follows instructions and the rules; would feel comfortable seeking help (from a neighbor, by phone, calling 911).
- Make sure your child is prepared. Teach your child basic first aid; emergency procedures, what to do if there is a fire; how to reach you, another adult, building personnel, police or firefighters; how to handle phone calls, visitors or deliveries; what to do if you are late coming home. Make sure your child has one or more adults to call upon if there is a problem (neighbor, friend, doorman) and that he or she has a way to reach you (beeper, cellular phone, all your phone numbers). As you develop contingency plans, make sure to review them with your child and rehearse different scenarios. *Do not leave your child alone if you do not have adequate household security or your neighborhood or apartment is not safe for an unattended child, and do not leave a very young child alone or in the care of another child.*
- Start slowly. Get your child acclimated to staying home alone in stages. Start with very brief trial runs (about five minutes) when you are very nearby (perhaps just outside the door or in the lobby) and build up gradually. Take small steps as appropriate, talk to your child about his or her feelings and experience and modify the plan as necessary.

- If your child will be coming home from school (or other activity) to an empty house, establish procedures for your child to check in with you or another designated adult upon arrival home and how to contact you if his or her schedule will change. Make certain your child always has, and can safeguard, a key and, if he or she loses or forgets the key, how to access a spare key. Instruct your child not to enter the house if the door is open or not properly locked or (in a ground floor apartment or brownstone) if windows are open or broken.

▶ **Out and about, all-purpose safety guidelines.** Your children probably already know these things, but it is always a good idea to review them from time to time:

- Stay connected. Children should always stay with an adult or their group. On crowded streets or in places where it is easy to get separated, including a busy playground, children should not run ahead or lag behind or be out of the supervising adult's line of sight. At busy intersections, it is important that your children not turn the corner before you get to the end of the block. A good reminder is to tell your children that you must always be able to see them.
- No wandering. Children should always let an adult know where they are going. Even if they are not allowed to go far, it is good practice to get them in the habit of letting you know where they are. For example, in a store your child should not wander off to the next display but should say "I am going to look at the books."
- Pay attention. Children should always pay attention to their surroundings, look alert and self-confident and walk with purpose. Help your children by pointing out, and teaching them to take note of, landmarks and the people around them.
- Stranger danger. Help your children understand that a stranger is *any* person they do not know. This can be a very confusing subject for your children to tackle. For example, an employee at a local shop may be very helpful and even get to know your child by name, but that person is still a stranger. A

helpful approach is to teach children to be on the lookout for certain kinds of situations or actions (for example, an adult asking for a child to help find a lost puppy) rather than certain kinds of individuals.

- Help! If in trouble, a child should shout "help!" "call the police!" or "fire!" to attract attention. Knowing how to get help—calling 911 or looking for a police officer or other uniformed guard—may sound like a simple task, but without preparation, many kids faced with danger will either dissolve into tears or be paralyzed with fear. If your child is separated from you in a place of business, he or she should go to an employee—salesperson, waiter, usher, doorman—before asking for or accepting help from a patron. Help your child be comfortable asking for help from a police officer (who might be intimidating to a child) as well as saying "no" to an adult stranger.
- Lost in the crowd. It is surprisingly common for children to become separated from you, a caregiver, a group leader or other adult with whom they are supposed to be, particularly at parades, street fairs, ball parks, theaters or other crowded public events. A strategy suggested to us by a police officer for making it easier to find children lost in a crowd is to have them wear distinctive brightly colored clothing when you are expecting to go to a crowded event such as a parade. Distinguishing clothing is much easier to spot, and you can yell out "My son/daughter is missing. He/she is wearing a yellow shirt," which will get people in the vicinity focused on locating your child.
- Getting around. Children should be reminded of the basics about crossing the street, following traffic signs and rules and being alert to vehicles that cannot see them or are backing up. If your children use bicycles, skateboards, scooters or in-line skates, make sure they wear appropriate safety gear, ride safely and understand how to conduct themselves in traffic (pedestrian and vehicular).
- Elevator and bathroom safety. Children, and younger children in particular, should not go into an elevator ahead of you. Electronic doors can close very quickly and your child could end up in the elevator without you. Children need to know

never to try to stop the doors from closing by putting their arm or leg in the door, as they can easily be crushed. City parents are typically very conservative about sending children off to public restrooms on their own. A typical rule of thumb when sending your child to a bathroom that is a single room rather than a multi-stall bathroom is not to let the child go to the bathroom alone unless you can see the door (for example, from your table in the restaurant) or you stand at the door. It is always a good idea to accompany your child to a bathroom with multiple stalls. If your older child of the opposite sex needs to use a public restroom, stand by the door and make sure that your child is not in the bathroom for an unusually long time.

- Show off. City streets are not an appropriate place to count money, show others your new purchases or other valuables or loudly discuss your plans. Money and wallets should be kept out of view.
- Hello operator. Children should know how to use a public telephone and make collect or credit-card calls.

► **Out alone.** The need for independence takes root early among sophisticated city children. Your children will likely be asking for some modicum of independence somewhere around eight years old. At that age, the request may be simply to go to a public restroom without you or to take the elevator in your apartment building or wait for a friend or the school bus in the lobby alone. By the age of 11, however, your child will likely be asking to take a public bus or walk to school or even to go to a local store, coffee shop or movie with friends. Whether or not you want to let your young adolescent out without an adult, you can be sure that by sixth or seventh grade, the peer pressure will begin to build.

For most of us, letting go is one of the hardest things we will ever do. The news stories make us very aware of potential dangers to children, which unfortunately have escalated in recent times. As a result, we are naturally reluctant to send them out without our protection. On the other hand, at some time or another, we must prepare our children to fend for themselves, because eventually it will become inappropriate for us to escort them everywhere. A child with no street experience becomes an easy victim.

Regardless of our feelings on the subject, they will turn into teenagers and young adults before too long and will need to have street-smart skills. Therefore, even if we only let our children out under very limited circumstances and with very strict conditions, and even if we do not do it until they are older, we still need to think about how to prepare them, and ourselves, for that momentous occasion.

If the subject of venturing out alone has not yet arisen or if you have a very young child, it is still important for your child to be prepared for situations where an adult is not present, even if only for a moment. For example, your children should know what to do if they become separated from you, the caregiver, their teacher or other adult with whom they are supposed to be. They need to know how to conduct themselves if approached by a stranger in a store, on the street, in a crowd, at the park or anywhere else. They need to be empowered to protect themselves against potential molestation or sexual abuse. As much as we may not want to have to discuss these issues with our children, as responsible parents it is our duty to give them the tools to protect themselves.

There is a great deal of literature (for both adults and children) and a number of videos available on the topic of safety. There are even self-defense courses, videos and books for children. In talking to your children about safety, you will probably want to include these topics:

- Street safety. Children should pay attention, look alert and self-confident and walk with a purpose. They should stick to well-lit, well-traveled areas, avoid construction sites, empty or closed stores and deserted buildings and not take shortcuts through the park (stick to streets instead). Well-lit commercial streets are generally safer than quiet streets, and the park side of a street should be avoided. Lingering in a large, noisy crowd on the street can attract unwanted attention and should be avoided. Work out with them the best strategies for dealing with strangers and what to do if they are followed on foot or by a car.

- The buddy system. Going it alone is not necessarily a safe plan for a child. Traveling in small groups of two, three or four is a much better choice.

- Getting around. Review the basics about crossing the street, following traffic signs and rules and being alert to vehicles that cannot see them or are backing up.

- Transportation. Bus, subway and taxi safety are extremely important. Children riding the bus or subway alone should be instructed on specific procedures such as avoiding isolated bus stops, having extra change or a MetroCard on hand, staying clear of the platform edge and riding in the car with the motorman (usually the center car). If using the subways at other than rush hour, they should wait for the train in the area marked "Off-Peak Waiting Areas." Children using taxis should take only yellow cabs or cars from a telephone car service (making sure not to get into an unmarked car or car-service car that cannot identify by name the person it is supposed to pick up). After dark, it is advisable to take a taxi, even if only for a few blocks, rather than walk. The Parents League recommends that children riding in taxis always carry about $3.00 of "escape money" that can be quickly handed to a driver as the child exits the taxi at a traffic light if he or she is uncomfortable in the taxi.

- Dress for success. Notwithstanding your children's desire to look cool, they should not wear visible or flashy jewelry or trendy accessories. These types of sought-after items are targets for mugging or assault. If your child is approached by a mugger, the NYPD advises giving up your property rather than engaging in a fight with an assailant who may be mentally unstable, substance impaired or armed.

- Be specific. If your children are going to be out alone, it is important to set specific rules about where they are and are not permitted to go, the modes of transportation they may use and the times by which they must reach their destinations. Any deviation from agreed upon plans should require a phone call to you and specific permission.

- Communication. As cellular phones and even high-tech walkie-talkies become more available and accessible, you may want to consider using technology to remain in contact with your older child as he or she begins to be out and about without you. At the very least, it is important to institute a system of regular check-ins by telephone so that you always know where your child is.

▶ **Safety programs in Manhattan.** The Parents League has been a leader in dealing with safety issues. The Parents League produces "Safety Guidelines for Kids, Parents and Teens," a tip sheet that provides extremely useful, New York-specific advice for families, important phone numbers and resources and information on how to report a crime. *In an emergency, a crime or missing child should be reported immediately by calling 911.* In a non-emergency situation, crimes should be reported to your local police precinct (a list of Manhattan precincts can be found at the end of this chapter).

The Safe Haven Program, begun in the 1970s by the Parents League in conjunction with the East Side Chamber of Commerce, registers merchants who agree to provide a sanctuary to a child or adult who is in danger or otherwise feels threatened. Safe Haven participants display a distinctive yellow and black sticker in their window or on the door and receive training (from either the Parents League if located in the 19th Precinct or the local precinct in other areas) to assist the person in need by providing shelter, allowing or making a telephone call (either to the police or someone else) and giving help. The Safe Haven Program has expanded to include apartment buildings on routes commonly traveled by school children. It is well worth educating your children to locate Safe Havens and choose a route along which Safe Havens can be found.

There are several Safe Haven networks throughout the city. On the Upper East Side, the program is coordinated by the Parents League and has more than 500 participants. On the Upper West Side, the program is coordinated by the Westside Crime Prevention Program and has more than 300 participants. If there is not a Safe Haven Program in your area, you can start one through your local schools, neighborhood associations or local precinct. The Parents League has prepared written guidelines to help start a Safe Haven Program, which you can get by calling 737-7385. The Parents League also maintains an active Speakers Bureau, which sends speakers to talk to students, community groups and parent associations about safety. You can also contact the NYPD office of the

Deputy Commissioner Community Affairs at 646 610-5312 for more information about Safe Havens in your neighborhood.

School safety patrols play an important role in making the streets safe for our children. The public-school system, through the Board of Education, has its own security force, which includes school crossing guards and internal security guards. Some public schools supplement the security force with parent volunteers to assist at drop-off and pickup times.

The private schools tend to have very active safety-patrol networks staffed by parent volunteers. Each school handles the situation differently, but most schools maintain a daily safety-patrol force that works in conjunction with school administration and security personnel. Local police precincts work closely with parent safety-patrol organizations, via their community affairs office or other outreach personnel to address student safety issues.

A number of precincts have developed so-called safe corridors, which are designated routes commonly traveled by students from neighborhood schools and which will be specially patrolled by police during specific hours (typically before and after school and perhaps during lunch periods). Your child's school safety patrol or your local precinct can advise you whether there are any safe corridors in your neighborhood.

Your local police precinct can be another resource when it comes to safety. Precincts all have community-affairs officers and youth officers who can provide valuable information to concerned parents. These offices will send personnel to address parent and student groups, and may have written materials, about safety issues. The precinct youth officer can also provide referrals to various social services and community resources, provide information on individual programs and help parents with troubled children. The precinct can even be a resource for activities as diverse as roller hockey sports leagues and the Boy Scouts' "Explorer Program." Contact the office of the Deputy Commissioner Community Affairs at 718 834-8855 or www.nyc.gov/nypd/html or the Police Athletic League at 477-9450 or www.palnyc.org.

Most local precincts will help parents assemble a child identification package that includes fingerprints and front- and side-view photos of your child. While New York City police will not keep an identification kit in police files, you can bring your child to the station house where they will take the photos and fingerprints of your child for you to safeguard at home. Call your local precinct to see if they will assist you in putting together your kit. If you assemble an identification kit, you may also want to include a description of any identifying marks (such as birthmarks, scars, chipped tooth) or characteristics (handedness, pitch of voice, a tendency to giggle or lisp), a lock of hair, and frequently updated measurements, clothing and shoe sizes and a photo.

Every fire department in New York City is also a safe haven for children through the Firecap program. Under this program, every firehouse and fire truck is considered a safe haven for a child or adult. The Firecap decal consists of a white square bordered in black with a red helmet in the middle and two children holding hands. The decal says "If you're in trouble, or if someone's bothering you, say NO and get away. You can always go to a firefighter or firehouse for help." When someone comes to them for help, they will notify appropriate authorities and take the necessary steps to help the person in need.

▶ **It's the law.** Despite the common belief in the lawlessness of New York City, there are in fact many laws on the books that address safety issues. A sampler:

- Pedestrians. Notwithstanding the fact that native New Yorkers seem to enjoy tempting drivers to hit them by stepping into the street and crossing between lights, pedestrians can and do get ticketed for jaywalking. If you are walking, you should always stop at the corner and wait on the curb for the Walk sign. Avoid crossing mid-block or from between parked cars. It is particularly dangerous to push your stroller into the street while you are waiting to cross because your stroller can be an easy target for a car making a speedy, tight turn. It is best to give yourself the most time to cross by waiting for a newly turned green light rather than running through a blinking Don't Walk sign. Unfortunately, city drivers often regard the yellow traffic light as a signal to step on the gas rather than to slow down. Therefore, avoid the temptation to wait in the street, and remain on the sidewalk until it is safe to go. By law, cars making a turn must yield to pedestrians at the crosswalk. Drivers are required to come to a complete stop before the crosswalk for a red light or a stop sign. The New York Police Department recommends that if the sidewalk is blocked and you must walk in the road, walk facing traffic so that drivers can see you.

- Bicyclists. All bicycle riders under the age of 14 are required by law to wear a helmet. Riders 13 years or older must drive in the street and not on the sidewalk. When riding in the street, riders must ride with the flow of traffic, stop at stop signs and obey all other traffic signals and rules, including yielding to pedestrians. Cycling rules also apply on streets that run through city parks.
- Drivers. All passengers in the front seat of cars are required to wear a seat belt. All children under the age of 16 must wear a seat belt whether they are sitting in the back or front seats. Children under the age of 4 must be in a federally approved car safety seat. Drivers can receive a fine of up to $100 if a passenger under the age of 16 is not properly buckled up. (See Chapter 3 for information about using seat belts in taxis). Within New York City limits, drivers *may not* turn right on red, unless otherwise specifically advised by posted signs.

▶ **A final thought.** Preparing ourselves and our children for unpleasant or dangerous situations is a very tough thing to do. We do not even want to imagine our children in peril without us there to protect them. The reality is that we live in a very busy city where accidents can easily happen, crime is certainly not unknown and our children can be vulnerable targets. For that reason, we must help our children develop the judgment and have the tools to feel secure and help themselves. We urge every parent to spend time thinking about these issues, accessing the many available resources the city offers to aid in that endeavor and educating and working with their children to keep them as safe as possible.

Emergencies

The last thing a parent wants to think about is coping with an emergency. However, the best thing you can do in the event of an emergency is to be prepared. This does not mean that you have to live your life waiting for the moment when your lifesaving, self-defense or other survival skills are put to the test, but it does mean that you and the members of your household, which includes your children, caregivers and housekeepers, have a current working knowledge of how to handle themselves and what to do if an emergency occurs.

▶ **Medical Emergencies.** It is extremely important for you and those who take care of your children to be prepared to handle a medical emergency. At the very least, you should have a well-stocked first-aid kit in the house, a book or two about how to handle various medical emergency situations (falls, burns, wounds, nosebleeds, bites, seizures, fevers) and a list, posted at or near each telephone, containing important emergency phone numbers, such as your work and cellular numbers; the pediatrician (or any other doctor your family uses); the dentist; poison control; and a family member, neighbor or friend who should be called if you are not available. It is also wise for you and any caregiver you employ to be trained in CPR and other emergency techniques, such as how to treat a choking victim, and that such training be regularly updated.

The New York City Fire Department recommends that a basic first-aid kit contain acetaminophen, ibuprofen and aspirin; ipecac syrup and activated charcoal; elastic wraps; triangular bandages; scissors with a rounded tip; adhesive tape and two-inch gauze in pads and rolls; disposable, instant ice bags; assorted bandages; antibiotic ointment; bandage closures; tweezers; safety pins; rubber gloves (for treating open wounds); a first-aid manual; and a list of emergency phone numbers. The kit should be kept in an easily transportable tote bag and stored out of reach of children.

In the event of a medical emergency, many parents would prefer to have their regular pediatrician or family practitioner treat the child than to be taken by ambulance to an emergency room. Manhattan pediatrician Dr. Barry Stein advises that you quickly assess the situation and decide whether you have time to call your own doctor. In the case of a dire emergency, you should call 911 before anything else. If you have the choice, try to have the ambulance take your child to the hospital with which your doctor is affiliated (see below). If the situation is not dire, you can call the doctor and ask to be met or called at the emergency room or for the doctor to call ahead to the emergency room on your behalf so that you can be met by an appropriate specialist (for example, an orthopedist if a broken bone is suspected). If you are not sure how bad the situation is, do not waste time trying to decide; call 911.

Another important element of preparation is to keep an envelop in your home that contains directions to the closest emergency room and to your doctor's hospital, cab fare to get to the doctor's office or hospital and a signed consent form authorizing treatment of your child. Keep in mind that in some circumstances, the doctor or emergency room cannot administer treatment without parental consent. Your consent form should state that your child may receive treatment if deemed necessary by his or her physician or the hospital physician in the event that you cannot be reached. It should also include any pertinent information about allergies, chronic conditions, medications taken regularly by the child and medical insurance.

▶ **EMS.** The New York City Emergency Medical Service (EMS), which operates under the auspices of the City Health and Hospitals Corporation, is the primary emergency medical care provider in the city. EMS operates a fleet of more than 350 ambulances that are deployed throughout, and constantly patrol, the five boroughs. Basic and advanced life-support ambulances provide on-site medical care and transportation to hospitals. Whenever an ambulance crew requires the advice of a physician, the crew can contact a Telemetry Control Unit staffed by a physician, which can monitor, review and direct the treatment protocol of the crew.

Basic ambulances are staffed with two emergency medical technicians who can perform CPR, control bleeding, administer oxygen, deliver a baby, immobilize the spine, apply antishock trousers and use a semiautomatic defibrillator. Advanced life-support ambulances are staffed with two paramedics. In addition to the basic services, paramedics can perform more invasive procedures involving defibrillation, EKGs and the insertion of intravenous lines and endotracheal tubes.

5

When you call 911 for an ambulance, your call is routed to a high-tech EMS communications center for triage and dispatching of an ambulance. EMS will transmit information directly to a mobile data terminal located in the dispatched ambulance. The ambulance you get will either be an EMS unit, a Voluntary Hospital Unit or a Volunteer Ambulance. Voluntary Hospital Units are owned and operated by private hospitals and receive no funding from the city. The participating private hospitals have contractually agreed to be dispatched via the 911 system and be subject to EMS rules (although they can determine their own billing rates). Volunteer Ambulances are operated by unpaid volunteer ambulance corps. Volunteer Ambulances are typically called upon by EMS only during peak hours or in the event of major multi-casualty situations.

If you need an ambulance, you can call 911. Once your call is routed by the police operator to EMS, be sure to give the EMS operator all relevant information and the telephone number of the phone from which you are calling. Be certain not to hang up until the EMS operator tells you to, so that the automatic location indicator and automatic number indicator can be activated and all relevant information can be obtained. If possible, have someone meet the ambulance to lead the crew to where the patient is located. Remember to use 911 only for a true emergency.

Remember to use 911 only for a true emergency.

Once you are in an ambulance, you have a limited ability to direct EMS to the hospital of your choice. EMS is required to take you to the closest 911 Receiving Emergency Facility (an emergency room certified by EMS and relevant state authorities). You can request that EMS take you to a specific hospital, which EMS will endeavor to do only under the following circumstances: the patient is not *in extremis* and the hospital you request is *not more than* either (1) 10 minutes from the closest hospital to which you would have otherwise been taken or (2) 20 minutes from where the ambulance picks you up (that is, not more than 20 minutes of total travel time).

The decision as to the medical condition of the patient and the estimated travel time is at the discretion of EMS, not you. As an example, if the ambulance picks you up at 14th Street and Fifth Avenue, the closest hospital (within 10 minutes of travel time) would be St. Vincent's. If you requested New York University Medical Center (at 33rd and First) and it was not rush hour, your request could probably be honored if EMS determined they could get you there in under 20 minutes. If you requested Mt. Sinai Medical Center (at Madison Avenue and 100th Street), your request would be denied.

At the end of this chapter, you will find a list of Manhattan emergency rooms, New York City trauma centers, burn centers, replantation units, snakebite facilities and hyperbaric chambers.

▶ **Reporting a crime.** There are two types of situations involving crimes: emergencies and non-emergencies. In an emergency situation, the crime is in progress, or, if not actually still in progress, the person or persons who committed the crime may still be in the vicinity. In a non-emergency situation, the crime has been committed and some amount of time has elapsed.

It is important to report crimes, because police resources are allocated on the basis of reported criminal activity in the precinct. If crimes do not make it into official statistics, additional police presence or investigative resources will not be assigned or anticrime measures undertaken. From the point of view of city officials, a crime that is not reported did not happen.

You should report a crime in an emergency situation by calling 911. Patrol cars are dispatched by 911, so calling the local police precinct will delay police response. Your report should include as much information as you have about what happened, where it happened and descriptions of the perpetrator(s). The information you provide will be broadcast over the police radio. *A missing child should be reported immediately*. The responding officer will interview the victim and witnesses, if any, and file a complaint. A detective will be assigned, if appropriate under applicable police procedures.

You can report a crime in a non-emergency situation by contacting the relevant local precinct. Assaults can generally be reported by telephone, although robbery complaints must be filed in person.

The complainant will be interviewed and a detective will be assigned, if appropriate under applicable police procedures.

▶ **In case of a fire.** The New York City Fire Department recommends the following in the event of a fire in an apartment building:

- Get Help. Call 911 to report smoke, a fire or a suspected fire. If you are able, leave the area immediately and call from a safe location.
- Smoke. If you smell smoke, call 911 to reach the fire department and, if applicable, activate the building fire-alarm system. Since smoke rises, stay low. If you cannot escape, use wet towels or tape to seal the door and room vents and turn off air conditioners and fans. Open a window, but do not break it as you may need to close the window to prevent smoke from a lower floor entering through your window.
- Escape. Identify fire exits in your building and locate fire exits in any unfamiliar building. If your building has multiple apartments on the floor, count the number of doors between your apartment and the exits in case the lights go out. Fire officials recommend that you plan two ways out of the building and plan what you will do if you cannot escape. Before leaving the room, check the door with the back of your hand. If it is cool, stay low to the ground and open it slowly (be prepared to close quickly if there is smoke or fire in the hallway). Use the stairs. Do not use the elevator to escape a fire. Close the door behind you but do not lock it (or take your key) in case you need to turn back. As you move to the exit, **stay low and go;** keep low to the ground where the air is cooler. The safest escape may be to stay where you are and await help. Stay calm.
- Or Stay Put. If you cannot escape, fill the bathtub with water with which to cool down the door if it gets hot. Wave a sheet out the window to signal the fire department that you are in your apartment.
- Alarm. Do not depend on someone else to call the fire department. Always call the fire department, even if you think the

fire is out. Do not depend on the building alarm system, as it may not be directly connected to the fire department or it may not be functioning.

- Prevention. Complain to the building management if you notice blocked fire exits, locked fire doors, fire doors wedged open or trash stored in fire exits. If the building does not correct the problem, contact the Fire Department at 718 999-2541. Keep matches away from children and make sure that they know matches and lighters are tools for adults, not toys. Keep cooking areas clear of combustibles and don't leave cooking unattended. Plan and practice your family escape routes, and review and visit your chosen meeting place outside of the house. Keep flashlights in a handy place.
- If your clothes catch fire, **Stop, Drop and Roll.**

For additional information on fire safety and prevention, you can contact the New York City Department Office of Public Safety and Education at 718 999-2343 or visit www.nyc.gov/html/fdny/html/safety/firesafety.html or the U.S. Fire Administration at www.usfa.fema.gov.

▶ **Don't panic.** While there is surely a great potential for accidents to occur or for our children to land in dangerous or unsafe situations, in many ways our lives in New York City are no more or less vulnerable than anywhere else in the country. We cannot and should not scare ourselves or our children away from partaking in the fun and pleasure of living in this city. What we can and should do is take reasonable precautions at home and, when we are out, be prepared and give our children the tools and security to handle the situations we and they may encounter.

RESOURCES

Childproofing Services

All Star Baby Safety
7 Dale Lane
Levittown, NY 11765
396-1995, 877 668-7677
www.allstarbabysafety.com

Baby Proofers Plus Inc.
Summit, NJ
628-8052 (New York City office) or 908 598-0676

Childproofers Inc.
914 381-5106

HomeStep
760-5959
www.homestepsafety.com
Babyproofing, childproofing.

CPR Training

American Heart Association
661-5335, 800-877-AHA-4CPR
www.americanheart.org
AHA will direct you to hospitals and other organizations offering CPR and first-aid training. Be sure to ask for the organizations that offer training to individuals as opposed to those offering certification to medical personnel.

American Red Cross
150 Amsterdam Avenue
New York, NY 10023
787-1000, www.nyredcross.org
Health and Safety 875-2222
Greater New York course registration 800 514-5103

Babysaver CPR and Child Safety
Beth Israel Medical Center
First Avenue at 16th Street
New York, NY 10003
420-4479, www.wehealny.org

14th Street Y
Sol Goldman YM-YWHA of the Educational Alliance
344 East 14th Street
New York, NY 10003
780-0800, www.edalliance.org

Jewish Community Center in Manhattan
334 Amsterdam Avenue at 76th Street
New York, NY 10023
580-0099, www.jccnyc.org

Lenox Hill Hospital
100 East 77th Street
New York, NY 10021
434-2273, www.lenoxhillhospital.org

92nd Street Y
1395 Lexington Avenue
New York, NY 10128
996-1100, www.92ndStY.org

St. Luke's-Roosevelt Hospital Center
523-6222 (Parent/Family Education number for both divisions)
www.bethisraelny.org
www.wehealny.org
First aid and CPR classes.

St. Luke's Division
1111 Amsterdam Avenue at 114th Street
New York, NY 10025

Roosevelt Division
1000 Tenth Avenue
New York, NY 10019

St. Vincent's Hospital
Infant CPR
Maternity Education Program
153 West 11th Street
New York, NY 10011
604-7946, www.svcmc.org

Save-A-Tot
317 East 34th Street
New York, NY 10016
Infant CPR and safety course.

Tot Saver
School of Continuing Education in Nursing
Mount Sinai Medical Center
10 East 101st Street, 2nd floor
Box 1144
New York, NY 10029
241-7050
www.mountsinaihospital.org

Vanderbilt YMCA
224 East 47th Street
New York, NY 10017
756-9600, www.ymcanyc.org

West Side YMCA
5 West 63rd Street
New York, NY 10023
875-4100, www.ymcanyc.org

Emergency Rooms (ER) in Manhattan

BELLEVUE HOSPITAL (911 receiving facility), 462 First Avenue, 562-4141. ER entrance on the corner of First Avenue and 27th Street. Bellevue maintains specific pediatric emergency facilities staffed with a member of the Child Life Program. Pediatric Trauma Unit, Trauma Unit, Replantation Unit, Spinal Cord Injury Center

BETH ISRAEL MEDICAL CENTER

PETRIE DIVISION, (911 receiving facility) (downtown), First Avenue at 16th Street, 420-2000 ER entrance on 16th Street between First and Second Avenues. Beth Israel maintains specific pediatric emergency facilities.

SINGER DIVISION, (911 receiving facility) (uptown), 170 East End Avenue, 870-9000. ER entrance on East 88th Street off East End Avenue.

CABRINI MEDICAL CENTER (911 receiving facility), 227 East 19th Street, 995-6620. ER entrance on 20th Street between Second and Third Avenues.

HARLEM HOSPITAL CENTER (911 receiving facility), 506 Lenox Avenue, 939-1000. ER entrance on Lenox Avenue between 135th and 136th Streets. Harlem Hospital maintains specific pediatric emergency facilities. Trauma Unit

HOSPITAL FOR JOINT DISEASES ORTHOPAEDIC INSTITUTE, 301 East 17th Street at Second Avenue, 598-6000. Specialized hospital. ER for private ambulance only, not serviced by EMS. Entrance through main lobby. Immediate care center for broken bones, sprains, and other orthopedic emergencies.

JACOBI MEDICAL CENTER (911 receiving facility), 1400 Pelham Parkway South, Eastchester Road, Bronx, NY 10461, 718 918-5000. Hyperbaric center and snakebite center.

LENOX HILL HOSPITAL (911 receiving facility), 100 East 77th Street, 434-3030. ER entrance at 120 East 77th Street between Park and Lexington Avenues. Lenox Hill maintains specific pediatric emergency facilities.

MANHATTAN EYE, EAR AND THROAT HOSPITAL, 210 East 64th Street, 838-9200. Specialized services for eye, ear, nose or throat emergencies. ER entrance through main hospital entrance on 64th Street between Second and Third Avenues.

METROPOLITAN HOSPITAL CENTER (911 receiving facility), 1901 First Avenue, 423-6262. ER entrance on 97th Street between First and Second Avenues. Metropolitan maintains specific pediatric emergency facilities.

MT. SINAI MEDICAL CENTER (911 receiving facility), One Gustave L. Levy Place, 241-6500. ER entrance on Madison Avenue between 100th and 101st Streets. Mt. Sinai maintains specific pediatric emergency facilities staffed with a member of the Child Life Program.

NEW YORK EYE AND EAR INFIRMARY, 310 East 14th Street, 979-4000. Specialized services for eye, ear, nose or throat emergencies. ER entrance on Second Avenue between 13th and 14th Streets.

NEW YORK PRESBYTERIAN HOSPITAL (911 receiving facility)

> **COLUMBIA-PRESBYTERIAN CAMPUS** (formerly Columbia Presbyterian Medical Center), 622 West 168th Street, 305-2500. ER entrance on 168th Street between Broadway and Ft. Washington Avenue. Columbia-Presbyterian Campus maintains specific pediatric emergency facilities. Pediatric Trauma Unit
>
> **NEW YORK-WEIL CORNELL CAMPUS** (formerly New York Hospital Cornell Medical Center), 525 East 68th Street, 746-5454. ER entrance on 68th Street between York Avenue and the FDR Drive. New York-Cornell Campus maintains specific pediatric emergency facilities. Burn Center, Trauma Unit

NYU MEDICAL CENTER (911 receiving facility), 550 First Avenue, 263-5550. ER entrance on First Avenue at 33rd Street.

NYU DOWNTOWN HOSPITAL (911 receiving facility), 170 William Street, 312-5063. ER entrance at Spruce and Beekman.

ST. LUKE'S-ROOSEVELT HOSPITAL CENTER (911 receiving facility), 523-4000 (general number for St. Luke's and Roosevelt divisions)

> **ST. LUKE'S DIVISION,** 1111 Amsterdam Avenue. ER entrance on the corner of 113th and Amsterdam Avenue. St. Luke's maintains a pediatric emergency room. Trauma Unit

ROOSEVELT DIVISION (911 receiving facility), 1000 Tenth Avenue. ER entrance on West 59th Street between Ninth and Tenth Avenues. St. Luke's maintains a specific pediatric emergency department.

ST. VINCENT'S HOSPITAL AND MEDICAL CENTER OF NEW YORK (911 receiving facility), 153 West 11th Street, 604-7000. ER entrance on Seventh Avenue between 11th and 12th Streets. St. Vincent's maintains special pediatric emergency facilities. Trauma Unit

Fire Safety

5

National Fire Protection Association
11 Tracy Drive, Avon, MA 02322
www.nfpa.org (includes a list of publications), 800 344-3555

New York City Fire Department
9 Metrotech Center, Brooklyn, NY 11201
www.nyc.gov
718 999-2000 (headquarters)
718 999-2343 (fire safety education department)
718 999-2056 (public information—Fire Department and EMS)

U.S. Fire Administration
www.usfa.fema.gov

Indoor Air Quality (IAQ)

Agencies and Organizations
American Lung Association Health House Project
490 Concordia Avenue, St. Paul, MN 55103
www.healthhouse.org, 877 521-1791

Centers for Disease Control and Prevention
1600 Clifton Road, Atlanta, GA 30333
www.cdc.gov, 800 331-3435

Children's Health Environmental Coalition
PO Box 1540, Princeton, NJ 08542
www.checnet.org, 609 252-1915

Consumer Federation of America
Radon Fix-it Program
1424 16th Street NW, Suite 604, Washington, DC 20036
www.radonfixit.org, 800 644-6999

National Environmental Respiratory Center
2425 Ridgecrest Drive SE, Albuquerque, NM 87108
www.nercenter.org, 505 262-7595

National Lead Information Center
801 Roeder Road, Suite 600, Silver Spring, MD 20910
www.epa.gov/lead/nlic.htm, 800 532-3394 or 800 424-5323

National Pesticides Information Center
Oregon State University
333 Weniger, Corvallis, OR 97331
www.npic.orst.edu, 800 858-7378

National Safety Council Radon Hotline
Environmental Health Center
1025 Connecticut Avenue NW, Suite 1200, Washington, DC 20036
www.nsc.org, 800 767-7236, 800 557-2366 (info line)

U.S. Environmental Protection Agency
www.epa.gov

Indoor Air Quality Information Clearinghouse
P.O. Box 37133, Washington, DC 20013
800 438-4318

National Radon Info Line
800 644-6999

Office of Ground Water and Drinking Water
1200 Pennsylvania Avenue NW, Washington, DC 20460

Safe Drinking Water Hotline
800 426-4791

Private Consultant
Enviro Search Inc.
871 Third Avenue, Brooklyn, NY 11232
www.enviro-search.com, 718 965-6202

24-Hour Pharmacies

Police precincts maintain lists of neighborhood pharmacies that are open 24 hours.
It is best to call first as operating hours are subject to change. In some cases, the store will be open but the pharmacy may not be open.

CVS Call 800 SHOP CVS (746-7287)
First Avenue and 23rd Street 473-5750
Ninth Avenue and 59th Street 245-0611
Second Avenue and 72nd Street 249-5062
Third Avenue and 91st Street 876-7212

Duane Reade
Broadway and Houston 683-3042
Waverly Place and 6th Avenue 674-5357
Lexington Avenue and 47th Street 682-5338
Broadway and 57th Street 541-9708
Second Avenue and 63rd Street 355-5944
Third Avenue and 74th Street 744-2668
Madison Avenue and 89th Street 360-6586
Broadway and 91st Street 799-3172

Rite Aid Call 800 RITE AID (748-3243)
Grand Street and Hudson Street 529-7115
Second Avenue and 30th Street 213-9887
Eighth Avenue and 50th Street 247-8384
Lexington Avenue and 86th Street 876-0600
Amsterdam Avenue and 89th Street 787-2903
Broadway and 110th Street 663-3135

Pharmacies Containing Alternative/Natural Remedies

Statscript Pharmacy
197 Eighth Avenue 691-9050

Hickey Chemists, Ltd.
888 Second Avenue 223-6333
1258 Third Avenue 744-5944

Nutrapharm
45 East 45th Street
983-8291

Playground Safety

National Program for Playground Safety
School for Health, Physical Education and Leisure Services
WRC 205
University of Northern Iowa, Cedar Falls, IA 50614
www.uni.edu/playground, 800 554 7529
To order the SAFE playground kit, visit www.playgroundsupervision.org

New Yorkers for Parks
457 Madison Avenue, New York, NY 10022
www.ny4p.org, 838-9410

Poison Control

Poison Control Center
POISONS (764-7667) or VENENOS (836-3667)

Police Information

General information 646/718 610-5000

Child abuse hotline 800 342-3720

Civilian Observer Ride-alongs 646 610-5323

Crime victim services (Safe Horizons) 577-7777

Crimestoppers 577-TIPS (8477) or 800 577-TIPS (8477);
Spanish 888 57 PISTA (74784)

Deputy Commissioner Community Affairs 646 610-5323

Domestic violence 800 621-4673

Drug Abuse Resistance Education (DARE) 718 834-8855

Gang Resistance Education and Training (GREAT) 718 834-8855

Internship program 646 610-5323

Law Enforcement Explorers 718 834-8855

Mentoring Program 646 610-5323

Missing persons case status 646 610-6914

Police Athletic League (PAL) 477-9450

Safe Haven program 646 610-5312

Sex crime report unit 267-RAPE (267-7273)

Terrorism Hotline 888 NYC SAFE (692-7233)

Youth Leadership Program 718 834-8855

Youth Police Academy 718 834-8855

www.nyc.gov (official website of city government)

Manhattan Precincts

1st Precinct
16 Ericsson Place
334-0611

5th Precinct
19 Elizabeth Street
334-0711

6th Precinct
233 West 10th Street
741-4811

7th Precinct
19½ Pitt Street
477-7311

9th Precinct
321 East 5th Street
477-7811

10th Precinct
230 West 20th Street
741-8211

13th Precinct
230 East 21st Street
477-7411

Midtown South Precinct
357 West 35th Street
239-9811

17th Precinct
167 East 51st Street
826-3211

Midtown North Precinct
306 West 54th Street
760-8300

19th Precinct
153 East 67th Street
452-0600

20th Precinct
120 West 82nd Street
580-6411

Central Park Precinct
86th Street Transverse
570-4820

23rd Precinct
164 East 102nd Street
860-6411

24th Precinct
151 West 100th Street
678-1811

25th Precinct
120 East 119th Street
860-6511

26th Precinct
520 West 126th Street
678-1311

28th Precinct
2271 Eighth Avenue
678-1611

30th Precinct
451 West 151st Street
690-8811

32nd Precinct
250 West 135th Street
690-6311

33rd Precinct
2120 Amsterdam Avenue
927-3200

34th Precinct
4295 Broadway
927-9711

West Side Crime Prevention Program
866-8603

Product Catalogues

Baby Proofing Plus
800 683-7233
www.babyproofingplus.com

One Step Ahead
800 274-8440
www.onestepahead.com

Perfectly Safe
800 837-5437
www.perfectlysafe.com

The Right Start
www.rightstart.com

Safe N' Sound Kids
www.safensoundkids.com

Safety 1st
www.safety1st.com

Product Safety

Auto Safety Hotline
National Highway Traffic Safety Administration
U.S. Department of Transportation
Washington, DC
www.dot.gov, 800 424-9393

Center for Auto Safety
2001 S Street NW, Suite 410, Washington, DC 20009
www.autosafety.org, 202 328-7700

Consumer Federation of America
1424 16th Street NW, Suite 604, Washington, DC 20036
www.consumerfed.org, 202 387-6121

Juvenile Products Manufacturers Association
609 231-8500, www.jpma.org
Provides information on safe use of baby products

National Highway Traffic Safety Administration
SeatCheck (car safety seat inspection program)
866 SEAT CHECK (732-8243), www.seatcheck.org

U.S. Consumer Product Safety Commission
Washington, DC 20207
800 638-CPSC (800 638-2772), www.cpsc.gov

Public Services

ConEdison (gas and electric)
General Information, gas emergency, fallen power lines, damaged electrical equipment or hazardous conditions 800 75 CON ED (800 752-6633), www.coned.com

New York City Department of Environmental Protection
59-17 Junction Blvd., Corona, NY 11368
www.nyc.gov
718 DEP-HELP (337-4357) (24-hour complaint number for water, sewer, air, noise)

New York City Department of Health and Mental Hygiene
125 Worth Street, New York, NY 10013
www.nyc.gov
Central information and referrals 877 692-3647
Communicable Disease information 788-9830
Special services:
Asthma Action Line 1-877-278-4620
Heat complaints 212 824-4328
Lead hotline 226-5323
Lyme Disease Hotline 518-474-4568
Ozone alert 800 535-1345
Pest control 718 956-7107/8
Radiological health 676-1580
Tuberculosis Control Hotline 788-4162
Water complaints 718 337-4357
West Nile Virus Information 877 WNV-4692
Window falls prevention program 676-6100

New York City Department of Sanitation
Bureau of Waste Prevention, Reuse and Recycling
PO Box 156, Bowling Green Station, New York, NY 10274
646 885-4721, www.nyc.gov/sanitation
Publications on recycling and where to get rid of things you don't need (see "stuff exchange")

New York State Department of Health
Nelson Rockefeller Empire State Plaza
Albany, NY 12237
518 402-7600, www.health.state.ny.us

Metropolitan Regional Office
5 Penn Plaza, New York, NY 10001
613-4900
800 458-1158 (Center for Environmental Health Information line)

U.S. Environmental Protection Agency
Washington, DC
www.epa.gov
202 260-2090 (general number)
800 490-9198 (general number, publications)

Safety—General Information

Kid Protection Network
PO Box 516, Middlefield, CT 06455
www.kidprotectionnetwork.org

MPI
PO Box 6960, Villa Park, IL 60181
www.esafety.com
Publishes *Kids Safe and Sound* and *Home Safe and Sound* available for $1.95 each

National Center for Missing and Exploited Children
699 Prince Street, Alexandria, VA 22314
703 235-3900, 800 THE LOST (843-5678), www.missingkids.com
Report child sexual exploitation at www.cybertipline

National Safe Kids Campaign
1301 Pennsylvania Avenue NW, Suite 1000, Washington, DC 20002
www.safekids.org, 202 662-0600

New York Division of Criminal Justice Services
Missing and Exploited Children
4 Tower Place, Albany, NY 12203
www.criminaljustice.state.ny.us/missing, 518 457-6326
Missing and Exploited Children Clearinghouse 800 346-3543 (FIND-KID)

New York Public Interest Research Group
www.pirg.org, see also www.uspirg.org
Information on product and environmental safety

Parenthood.com
Safety information at www.esafety.com

Parents League of New York
115 East 82nd Street, New York, N Y 10028
www.parentsleague.org, 737-7389

West Side Crime Prevention Program
www.wcppny.org, 866-8603

Self-Defense Classes for Children

Children's Safety Project
Greenwich House
27 Barrow Street, 6th floor, New York, NY 10014
242-4140
Help for children traumatized by crime or by witnessing crimes, provides counseling and self-defense classes. Also offers safety classes and community education as part of a prevention effort.

Fighting Chance
www.kidsfightingchance.com, 800 572-7307
Produces a self-defense video, teaching techniques to thwart abduction

Prepare, Inc.
147 West 25th Street, New York, NY 10001
800 442-7273
Personal safety training classes that use realistic role play with a padded instructor.

See also martial arts programs listed in Chapter 9.

Websites/Terrorism and Emergency Preparedness

www.dhs.gov (U.S. Department of Homeland Security)

www.ready.gov (U.S. Department of Homeland Security)

www.redcross.org

Chapter 6

In Search of Mary Poppins

Arranging childcare for our families is one of the most difficult and complicated aspects of modern parenting. When we cannot be with our children ourselves, we want them to be in the care of loving, responsible and competent individuals who will take care of their needs, look out for their welfare and provide a safe, stimulating environment. Yet, when it comes to our ideas about caregivers, many of us have an image of a caretaker based on fictitious television and movie characters, such as Alice from *The Brady Bunch*, Mr. French from *Family Affair*, Maria from *The Sound of Music* and, of course, Mary Poppins. At the other end of the spectrum, today's media have left us with images of the dire consequences of selecting the wrong caregivers.

In short, we are looking for that mythical caretaker who has the patience of a saint, brilliant parenting skills, excellent judgment and a doctorate in education, is a licensed paramedic able to cope with any medical emergency and is a great friend and playmate for the kids. While most of us do of course manage to find satisfactory childcare arrangements, it is usually the result of having become more realistic along the way.

In general, there are three types of childcare alternatives available to parents. First, there is the in-home caregiver. The in-home caregiver can work on a live-in or live-out basis and is typically either a nanny, combination housekeeper/caregiver, au pair or hourly babysitter. Second, there is in-home group care, also known as family childcare. In this type of situation, the caregiver provides childcare services in her own home. Under New York law, any person caring for three or more unrelated children in her home for more than three hours per day must be registered or licensed. Third, there are day care centers, which provide care for a number of children in a group environment in a special facility. Day care centers in New York must be licensed.

In deciding what kind of childcare is most appropriate for your family, it is essential to consider several factors: your child's stage of development; the number of children needing care; your budget; your own scheduling needs and flexibility; your preferences and priorities; and the benefits and limitations of the various types of childcare. This chapter will help you to identify your needs, establish your priorities and direct you through the process of selecting the right childcare for your family. At the end of the chapter you will find a directory of resources for your easy reference.

▶ **At each stage of development, your child has different needs.** An infant is dependent on a caregiver for food, comfort, company and diaper changes. It is important to the development and sense of security of the infant that its needs be addressed promptly. As the baby gets older and develops motor skills and the beginnings of language, it becomes necessary to provide stimulation and enrichment beyond tending to physical needs and providing nurturing care. For the mobile baby and toddler beginning to explore, the safety of the environment becomes more challenging. The child needs an opportunity to walk, climb and run as well as to manipulate many types of toys, indoors and out. The preschooler must have ample opportunity for socialization with other children. School-age children have their own needs. They still need a certain degree of physical care (such as meals and baths), but they require a different type of supervision for playdates and homework and they need transportation to and from after-school activities.

If you have two or more children, it is important to acknowledge their different developmental needs and organize childcare accordingly. For example, it may not work to send an infant on the playdate of an older child or to have an older child forgo activities because of the baby's nap schedule. Evaluate your childcare alternatives and prioritize your and your child's needs on an annual basis. For example, your quiet and sweet baby nurse may not be the person who will do well chasing an active toddler at the playground. And the skills of the wonderful nanny who cared for your preschoolers may be underutilized when your children are in school all day.

▶ **What's out there?** In comparing the various types of childcare, a parent must have realistic expectations about each alternative. In-home care offers flexible hours and can be extremely convenient for parents. The children are in their own home with their own toys. If a child is sick at home, no special arrangements need be made. The parents and caregiver can organize a routine (i.e., naps, mealtimes, outings) that is specifically tailored to the child. Parents can enroll the younger child in classes attended by the caregiver to create opportunities for socialization. Parents and caregivers can also make playdates and take the child to the park or other play areas (public or private) to make the child's day active and fun. The caregiver can pick up older children from school and transport them to their after-school activities and playdates.

On the other hand, in-home caregivers are unsupervised, unregulated and unlicensed. The quality of the care is a direct function of the experience, personality and competence of the caregiver. In-home care can be more expensive than other alternatives. Because of the intimacy of having a caregiver in the home, the parent–caregiver relationship can be quite complicated. And the convenience factor becomes severely compromised when the caregiver is late for work, calls in sick, goes on holiday or quits without warning.

Group care, in the form of family care or day care centers, offers a regulated and licensed environment. Children are in a social environment that is consistent and likely to be structured. In group situations with more than one caregiver, the caregivers are supervised or at least not alone. Group care providers often have special training, or the facility may be accredited by national associations. There can be a curriculum for the children and specific activities geared to the age levels of the children. The cost can be quite reasonable.

Although the caregiver/child ratio is regulated by law, the group care option offers less one-on-one time between child and caregiver and, if care is provided by several people, the child may not have the opportunity to form a bonded relationship with a particular individual. If a child is ill and cannot be brought to day care, the parent must make other arrangements, which can be quite difficult to do on short notice. Group care usually has regular operating hours and drop-off and pickup times that are not generally flexible and rarely cover nighttime hours. There is typically a routine for meals, snack times and rest periods, which are set for the group and may not specifically accommodate a particular child's needs or schedule.

▶ **What does it cost?** The cost of childcare can be quite unexpected for the uninitiated. For full-time in-home caregivers, salaries typically range from $350 to $900 per week (plus room and board for live-ins), depending on the job description and caregiver qualifications. Average salaries range from $400 to $500. Au pairs typically cost approximately $200 per week. Family childcare and day care can cost between $100 and $350 per week. Some lucky parents have day care services provided on-site by employers at no cost or at a subsidized cost. Hourly babysitters usually get between $7 and $15 per hour plus transportation home at night, although it may be possible to hire high school students or mother's helpers at somewhat less per hour. Most of the private schools and some of the colleges and universities located in Manhattan, as well as the Parents League (a non-profit organization of parents and independent schools), maintain a registry of students interested in babysitting.

Whatever type of childcare you ultimately choose, the goal is to obtain the best quality care available to meet your needs and accommodate your budget. The person with whom you leave your children is your surrogate in your absence and so should be a valued and respected member of a parenting partnership. Childcare is not a place to find bargains. Unfortunately, in the childcare business, you really do get what you pay for. This is *not* to say that a highly paid nanny is necessarily a better quality caregiver than a lesser paid caregiver who does housework. It is to say, however, that when a caregiver or childcare facility is willing to be paid substantially below market rate, there are serious questions to be asked and reference checking to be done.

In-home Caregivers

If you have elected to hire an in-home caregiver, it is important at the outset to determine exactly what job you are attempting to fill. Although this may sound like a foolish exercise, in fact, in the realm of in-home childcare, there are a range of functions that a family may want to delegate to one or more employees. The potential employee also is likely to have a view on what tasks she is willing or unwilling to perform. (We say "she" because, according to the International Nanny Association (INA), more than 95% of in-home caregivers are women.)

In addition to caring for the children, the typical household jobs are cleaning, laundry, cooking, shopping and doing errands. The issue becomes whether the employee will do all, any or some of these tasks for just the children or for the whole family.

▶ **In-home alternatives.** As a framework for discussion, it is helpful to identify four basic categories of in-home childcare: nanny, combination caregiver and housekeeper, au pair and babysitter. These terms have no formal or legal definitions and are often used interchangeably. For our purposes however, we have based our definitions of the different types of in-home childcare on the terms most commonly used in Manhattan and the terms used by the INA.

- Nanny. The INA defines a nanny as a full-time employee who is hired to handle all tasks related to the care of children and whose duties are restricted to the domestic chores related to childcare, such as preparing meals for the children, children's laundry and cleaning children's rooms. The nanny may or may not have had formal training, but she usually has actual experience. Her work week ranges from 40 to 60 hours and she generally works unsupervised. She can live in or live out.

- Combination caregiver and housekeeper. This person provides full-time or part-time childcare and domestic help for a family. In addition to caring for the children, she is typically responsible for some level of house cleaning, laundry and cooking and may also do family errands. She usually has actual experience. She works the same range of hours as a nanny, is usually unsupervised and can live in or out.

- Parent/Mother's Helper. According to the INA, a parent/mother's helper provides full-time domestic help and full-time childcare for a family in which one parent is home most of the time. She typically works under the supervision of a parent and can live in or out.
- Au pair. An au pair is a foreign individual who works in this country under the provisions of a special one-year cultural exchange visa. Au pair programs are federally regulated by the United States Information Agency. The intention of the au pair program is to provide a young European woman or man with the opportunity to live with a host family and provide up to 45 hours per week of help with childcare and household chores in exchange for a modest stipend/salary (approximately $150 per week). The host family is required to provide the au pair with time off to attend an educational program and $500 toward its costs. The particular conditions of an au pair's employment are specified by the terms of the program with which he or she is affiliated. By law, au pairs are required to have 8 hours of child safety instruction and 24 hours of child development instruction, and they must pass a reference and criminal records check before placement with a host family. As of 2001, a new category, EduCare, was added to the au pair program. Au pairs working under the EduCare program may not work more than 30 hours per week, must complete a

minimum of 12 semester hours of academic credit during their program and are authorized only to care for school-aged children. The host family is required to provide the EduCare au pair with time off to attend an educational program and $1000 toward its costs. The average cost for an au pair, including program fees, stipend, transportation and educational expense, is between $200 and $250 per week.

- Babysitter. The INA defines a babysitter as a person who provides supervisory, custodial care of children on an irregular full-time or part-time basis. In New York, babysitters are usually paid on an hourly basis for actual time worked.

▶ **How to find an in-home caregiver.** The key to finding a caregiver is to network, network, network. The most typical methods for finding applicants are word-of-mouth recommendations, advertising and employment agencies. As will be discussed in greater detail, no matter where you find a potential employee, you must fully check her references and background before hiring her to care for your children.

◩ **Word of mouth.** Many families find their employees via word of mouth. Most caregivers have friends or relatives to recommend. Other parents can be a great source of candidates too, as can bulletin boards in pediatricians' offices, schools, the Parents League office and other facilities catering to children (for example, children's gym classes) and families. Almost any time that parents gather and talk, it is possible to generate a list of potential candidates as well as both welcome and less-than-welcome advice on getting through the search process. When relying on word-of-mouth sources, it is best to get names from people whose judgment you trust and who personally know the individuals they are proposing.

◩ **Advertising.** Another popular method is to advertise in local newspapers. Most parents who go this route have a view on which papers yield the best applicants and which papers are favorite places to list their job. The most used are the *New York Times* and the *Irish Echo*, a local newspaper that comes out every Wednesday.

The newspapers not only have listings for job opportunities but also contain sections on situations wanted. Newspapers are widely used by caregivers of all nationalities as a job source. Other possibilities include foreign language publications (Polish, Russian and Spanish), which reach specific ethnic populations.

There are three tricks to advertising for caregivers: drafting your job description, handling the volume of responses and screening applicants. Your job description must be clear and specific. Indicate the qualifications required, the number of children to be cared for, other duties included for the job, hours and salary. If, for instance, you want only someone who is legally allowed to work in this country or with a certain amount of experience, say so. The more detailed your advertisement, the fewer calls you will get from unsuitable candidates and the better the pool of applicants from which you can choose. It is helpful to peruse other advertisements for ideas before you place your own.

No matter what your ad says, be prepared for an onslaught of phone calls. You may well receive in excess of 100 responses if your ad presents an attractive job description or salary. One veteran of this process actually sets up a temporary voice mail service when she hires a new caregiver. If you plan to screen calls with an answering machine, say so in your ad, because many applicants will not leave messages on a machine. When screening calls, work up a basic telephone interview (more about this later), which an applicant must pass before being invited in for an interview. This will save you from wasting time meeting unacceptable candidates.

A concern about hiring through the newspaper is that the person comes to you totally unscreened—she has not been interviewed or her background checked, however superficially, by anyone in the employment business. Consequently, since you have no intermediary to rely on to screen the applicant, you must carefully do your own investigation and use caution before letting someone into your home. Many parents who regularly use this method arrange to meet applicants in a public place such as the lobby of the apartment building or a coffee shop for an initial screening. Others arrange to have the children out and another adult (both parents, a friend, a relative or a neighbor) present in the house for a first interview. Once you are satisfied that an applicant is an appropriate candidate, you can invite her back for a subsequent interview and to meet the children.

Agencies. This leads us to the domestic help employment agencies. The main reason a family will turn to an employment agency is that the agency will screen applicants, supply candidates that will meet your needs, check references, provide advice and guidance through the search process, serve as an intermediary in negotiating terms of employment and provide additional candidates if the placement does not work out. For this service, the typical fee is either 10% of the employee's annual salary or from one month's to six weeks' salary. Fees are not generally negotiable.

Most agencies offer a limited guarantee with respect to placements. If a placement does not work out during the guarantee period, the agency will either provide a replacement or refund all or a portion of the fee. If possible, it is advisable to have a written agreement with an agency regarding fees and guarantees.

The key to using an agency is to find a reputable one run by professionals. Wendy Sachs, the CEO of the Philadelphia Nanny Network, which places nannies in the Philadelphia area and also offers consulting services in New York City (screening, interviewing and checking references of candidates) and former president of the INA, recommends these tips for identifying a good agency:

- Investigate the reputation of the agency by asking friends, colleagues and other parents who have used that agency. Personal recommendations and referrals are very helpful. Make sure that the agency is licensed to do business in the jurisdiction. How long has the agency been in business? Has the agency had violations or citations against it? Is the agency an INA member?
- Understand the fee schedule and refund and replacement policy in the event the placement does not work out.
- Understand the screening process used by the agency and be clear about what information the agency will provide to you and in what form it will be provided. How does the agency recruit applicants, how are references checked (phone, mail,

e-mail), how far back does the agency go (age, years of employment, school records), is there a written application or report, does the agency require any health checks, is an applicant sent out for interviews before references are confirmed, does the agency do a criminal check?

- Ascertain which services the agency provides. Each agency has its own practices with respect to placement and follow-up and even training, so understand what the particular agency does.
- Check into the availability of placement staff, so important when you are in the throes of a search. Does the agency run a full-time business or will your calls be answered by a machine? Will you work with a single counselor?

While it may be difficult to get clear answers from an employment agency or to confirm independently the answers you are given, it is certainly worth initiating the dialogue and getting whatever information you can about the agency, its practices and its track record.

The INA asks that its member agencies adhere to a certain level of professional practice in order to provide the best and most reliable service to their clients. These practices include disclosing how candidates are interviewed and how their references are checked, offering a written fee agreement to parents and providing prompt refunds when the placement does not work out. Equally important, the INA recommends that agencies respect the applicants, accurately describe jobs and families so that applicants and parents are better matched, help families and caregivers develop an employment agreement and make the applicant aware of the fee policy to which the family is subject. According to Ms. Sachs, in her experience the more information made available to both applicants and families, the more likely the placement will work out for both parties.

The Alliance of Professional Nanny Agencies (APNA), a membership organization for agencies placing in-home child care providers, also offers guidelines for parents as to what to look for in a placement agency, including standards of practice and a code of ethics on its website, www.apnaonline.org. While APNA does not have many members in the New York area, a number of agencies in other parts of the country that place live-in nannies in New York are APNA members, and membership in this organization is a helpful marker of quality.

In New York, domestic employment agencies are regulated under the State General Business Law (fees, refunds), the New York City License Enforcement Law (licensing by the Department of Consumer Affairs), the Consumer Protection Law (prohibits misleading and deceptive practices) and the Human Rights Law (discrimination). The fees that an agency may charge an employer are not set by law except in the case where (1) the agency specifically recruited a domestic or household employee from outside the continental United States, in which case the fee may not exceed 11% of the employee's first full-year's wages (of which not more than 25% may be charged the employee) or (2) the agency receives a fee from the employee, in which case the fee for a placement may not exceed 10% of the first full month's salary if no meals or lodging are provided, 12% of the first full month's salary if one meal per day is provided, 14% of the first full month's salary if two meals per day are provided and 18% of the first full month's salary if three meals per day and lodging are provided.

If an agency does not receive a fee from the job applicant, the fee is determined by agreement between the employer and employment agency. Essentially, the agency is free to charge families looking for domestic help whatever the market will bear. You are not entitled by law to a refund if the placement goes awry unless the applicant also paid a fee to the agency, in which event the General Business Law has specific provisions. Since most employment agencies placing caregivers do not charge applicants and therefore have placement fees paid by the employers, your right to a refund will be a matter of contract. If the agency represented a refund policy to you and fails to live up to its promise, you may file a complaint with the City Department of Consumer Affairs at 42 Broadway, New York, NY 10004, DCA Complaint/License Hotline, 487-4444, or file your complaint online at www.nyc.gov/html/dca/html/dcacompl.html.

Agencies are not required by law to check more than one reference or to perform any other background screening of an applicant.

Agencies will vary in their screening and background checking procedures and in their vigilance in contacting references and verifying immigration status. It is therefore important to make the effort to determine what exactly the agency does and does not do and supplement its efforts with your own. No matter what any agency tells you, it is always wise to contact references and confirm other information yourself. Again, however, if an agency does represent to you that it investigated the qualifications of an applicant in any way or has done a background check, you can complain to the City Department of Consumer Affairs if you were deceived or misled by such representations.

Pursuant to the City Human Rights Law, an employment agency cannot discriminate on the basis of age, race, creed, color, national origin, gender, disability, religion, marital status, sexual orientation or alienage or citizenship status. The agency is therefore not supposed to get this type of information from applicants or honor discriminatory requests by a potential employers. This law, however, does not apply to an employer with fewer than four employees. Thus, while you are not supposed to ask an agency to send you applicants who are of a certain age, race, religion or nationality, you may reject individuals who do not meet these criteria.

To find out whether an agency is licensed in New York City, you can contact the New York City Department of Consumer Affairs, 42 Broadway, New York, NY 10004, DCA Complaint/License Hotline, 487-4444, or visit www.nyc.gov/html/dca.html. The department will not release a list of agencies with outstanding violations against them. However, you can call the department and ask whether a particular agency has outstanding violations against it.

Included at the end of this chapter for your reference is a list of a number of local agencies (licensed as of the date of this publication) that handle both live-in and live-out caregivers and agencies that handle national or regional placements (of primarily live-in caregivers). Please note that we do not recommend any particular agency and should you decide to work with an agency, we urge you to clarify its policies, procedures, fee structure and the depth of their background checks of applicants.

Au pair Agencies. If you want to hire a foreign au pair, you must go through one of the six agencies authorized by the United States Department of State Bureau of Educational and Cultural Affairs to place au pairs in this country. Because of the unique visa status granted to au pairs, you cannot hire an au pair on your own. The au pair agencies have their own recruitment personnel and a staff of local counselors to work with au pairs and their host families. The hiring and interviewing procedures followed and services offered by the agencies will differ somewhat. If hiring an au pair, it may be wise to contact more than one agency to determine which suits your preferences and standards.

You can get more information about the au pair program by contacting the United States Bureau of Educational and Cultural Affairs at 202 401-9810 or www.exhanges.state.gov or by directly contacting the au pair agencies, which are listed at the end of this chapter.

Nanny Schools. Another method for finding a caregiver is through nanny schools. As of this writing, there are very few schools and colleges offering nanny training programs that are certified by the American Council of Nanny Schools. To be certified, a program must provide 200 classroom hours and 100 "laboratory" hours in subjects such as child development, communication, family studies, nutrition, behavior and guidance, planning activities, CPR and a supervised "practicum." Nanny schools offer placement services and will provide a certificate of completion and transcript of grades to graduates. To find out more about nanny training and to obtain a current list of nanny training programs, contact Sheilagh Roth, president of the American Council of Nanny Schools, 37 South Franklin Street, Chagrin Falls, OH, 440 247-9125. At the end of this chapter you will find a list of nanny training programs (not all of which are certified by the American Council of Nanny Schools) that will help arrange placements in New York City.

Before inviting an applicant to your home, it is useful to conduct a screening over the telephone.

▶ **Interviewing basics.** Before inviting an applicant to your home, it is useful to conduct a screening over the telephone. During this call, you can describe the job (number of children, basic duties, hours/days) and salary, clarify the individual's qualifications (experience, immigration status), and confirm her availability to begin work. This is a good time to state any prerequisites you have for the job, such as swimming ability, driving licensure, cooking skills, traveling or nighttime babysitting availability. You may want to ask some open-ended questions such as "Why are you seeking a childcare job?" to get a feel for the type of person she is. If the person meets your threshold requirements, you can schedule the interview.

When interviewing, first impressions do count. Your prospective caregiver should be punctual (or have handled being late with an acknowledgment, phone call or very good excuse), be dressed appropriately, have good manners and be able to communicate in your language. The particular qualities you are seeking will depend in large part on your own priorities. Some parents prefer a high-energy, enthusiastic and jolly person while others favor a calm, steady and sensible personality. A person's age, experience, education level, household skills, sense of humor, culture and common sense are all relevant to the role this person will have in your family.

An interviewing technique we have found very effective is to prepare a written application for prospective employees to complete. The application can include basic information (name, address, driver's license, passport number, education, etc.), a health questionnaire, information about prior employment and references. Be sure to examine originals of all legal documentation. An application provides a less personal way to ask hard questions such as whether the person has been arrested or convicted or uses alcohol or drugs, and it is a good way to get information about family background and outside commitments (such as caring for her own young children or other dependents). The application is also an easy way to obtain a signed release to conduct a criminal check if you elect to do so. You can include questions about the person's philosophy about discipline, handling anger, hypothetical situations, why the person wants the job, leisure activities and long-term plans. In addition to the answers provided, you can assess the person's communication and comprehension skills. The application serves as an excellent starting place for your discussion with the applicant.

One of the most important elements of the interview is to establish an employment history of the applicant. Wendy Sachs suggests developing a timeline of the person's work experience since the age of 18. All gaps in employment should be explained and job references should be verifiable. A red flag should go up in your mind when a person has had an abundance of short-term jobs, cannot remember who she worked for (or the names and ages of the children), has long unexplained gaps in employment or cannot provide a way to contact references.

◩ **There are many qualities to seek in a caregiver.** The INA has developed a list of basic competencies for a caregiver that provides an excellent checklist for families seeking an in-home employee. While it is not possible to find the perfect nanny, it is worth seeking a person who has as many of the following characteristics as possible: is observant and consistent, can articulate a philosophy of work, maintain confidentiality, follow instructions, perform basic tasks, plan and prepare meals for the children, care for a moderately ill child, act in an emergency, create and maintain a safe and healthy environment, communicate with children, observe safety rules, provide appropriate play and learning experiences for the children, support parents' preferences and their right to privacy, maintain basic hygienic standards (bathing, washing hands, brushing teeth) and recognize her role as part of a team and the parents as the ultimate authority. She should also have a professional attitude and appearance, use decent judgment, exhibit initiative, maintain good manners, use proper language, and be able to execute appropriate management techniques (discipline, organization and supervising of activities).

On a more personal level, it is also important to find a person who expresses a similar philosophy to your own and who you think will be compatible with your family in terms of habits, neatness, flexibility, organization, food choices and style of interacting with children. There is no formula to ensure that the person you hire will meet all of your criteria, but your intuition can be a powerful tool in making a choice. If you feel comfortable and positive, by all means pursue the process. If you feel uncomfortable and negative, listen to your instincts—they probably are right.

In all cases, it is wise to meet with an applicant you are considering hiring more than once and, if at all possible, to have both parents (or any other adult whose judgment you trust or who is part of the household) present or available during one of the meetings. A call-back interview offers a useful opportunity to collect information, gain a sense of the person's disposition and confirm your original feelings.

It is also critical that you see how the individual interacts with your children, whether for a brief introduction or an extended play session. Some parents conduct the full interview with the child present, while others find this distracting and bring in the child for only a portion of the interview. Still other parents prefer to have a trial period (a weekend or several workdays) with a caregiver before making an offer to the person, the advisability of which is a function of how your children deal with strangers and handle transitions.

◩ **Checking References.** Once you have narrowed down your search, it is crucial to check completely all references given to you and confirm the specifics of the information you were given with respect to job responsibilities, length of employment and reasons for leaving. Ask the reference questions regarding the caregiver's attitude, performance and competence. Go back to your own priorities and confirm that the caregiver has the qualities you seek. It is worth asking former employers what problems they might have had with the employee and whether they would hire her again. You may also want to verify that the reference is valid and not just a friend or relative of the applicant. For example, you can confirm that the reference has the job title you were given by calling his or her office.

Current wisdom in the caregiver industry is that it is appropriate to do a background and criminal record check on a prospective caregiver before she begins work in your home. Some employment agencies will perform this valuable service as part of their own screening process, in which case you should ask for a copy of the written report. Many families hire a private investigation firm to conduct a search of the applicant's criminal, driving, and credit records, as well as a search of credit-bureau databases to determine whether a social security number is valid. The cost of a search can range from $100 to $500 or even more, depending on the number of jurisdictions involved and the depth of the search. For an additional cost, some agencies will also verify other information, such as attendance at educational institutions or foreign visa and passport information (to the extent information is public). A list of agencies that can conduct records searches can be found at the end of this chapter.

While there is no such thing as a national criminal check, in certain states it is possible to perform statewide checks, while in others, including New York, searches must be conducted at the county level. A criminal records search will reveal felony and misdemeanor convictions and must be conducted for each jurisdiction where the prospective employee has lived or worked. The driving records search, available if the applicant has a driver's license, will verify address, physical description and birth date as well as reveal license suspensions or penalties for driving under the influence or other driving-related offenses. The credit report verifies addresses (current and prior) and employment and will give you information about the applicant's behavior (excessive indebtedness, financial responsibility, collections).

When hiring an agency to do searches, be clear on how far back in time the various searches will go and the number of jurisdictions being reviewed. Remember, New York City alone has several counties, which must be searched separately. Note that neither you nor a nanny employment agency can screen a potential babysitter through the New York State Central Child Abuse and Maltreatment Registry.

The prospective employee must sign a release to enable you to arrange for a records search. The agency that you retain to do searches can provide you with a release form to be signed by the applicant. You may want to contact agencies at the start of your search so that you have the release form available during your interviews with prospective employees.

While asking for a release may feel awkward, if conducting a search will make you feel more confident in your decision, it is well worth it. If an applicant will not sign such a release, that may be an indication of a problem in her history and should be considered a warning signal. It is important to remember that searches are not fail-safe. They will not pick up crimes committed under an alias or in a jurisdiction that was not searched.

► **Health Screening.** You may want to consider requiring your new caregiver to have a physical before beginning employment in your home. If this is a precondition to employment, many parents handle the situation by sending the caregiver to the parent's doctor at their expense. For parents who elect to require a physical exam, Manhattan pediatrician Dr. Barry Stein suggests a screening for TB (and other communicable diseases) and a routine exam, which would indicate if the caregiver has any physical conditions or limitation or takes any medication that would affect her ability to do her job.

► **Becoming an employer.** Choosing to hire an in-home caregiver comes with certain legal obligations applicable to your role as an employer. Your first duty is to hire someone who is legally allowed to work in this country. This means that the person is either an American citizen, has a valid Alien Registration Card (a "green card") or has an Employment Authorization Document. You are required to verify that the employee is eligible to work here by having the employee complete the employee section of the Immigration and Naturalization Service (INS) Form I-9, Employment Eligibility Verification, which is held by the employer. You can obtain this form by calling the INS at 800 357-2099 (employer hotline) or 800 870-3676 (forms) to obtain the INS Handbook for Employers or visiting www.ins.usdoj.gov. Civil penalties for employing an illegal alien start at $2,500 and can go much higher, even resulting in criminal penalties. There are additional penalties under federal and state tax laws if the person was paid "off the books."

Because many of the applicants for in-home childcare are in fact undocumented aliens, a question frequently asked by parents is whether it is viable to sponsor a potential candidate for permanent residency in this country. While this is certainly an option, the process is time consuming, labor intensive and expensive (approximately $5,000–$15,000). For more information on the sponsoring process, see the appendix to this chapter.

▶ **Taxes.** Your next obligation is to determine whether you have to pay employment taxes. Even though many caregivers want to be paid "off the books," as an employer, you may not be able to offer them that option legally. You can learn more about your responsibility as an employer by calling the Internal Revenue Service at 800 829-1040 (24-hour information line), visiting www.irs.gov or by requesting a copy of the IRS "Household Employer's Tax Guide" by calling 800 829-3676 (forms and publications) or visiting www.irs.gov.

In addition to federal tax liability, a household employer may have state tax liability for a household employee. For state tax information, you can call 800 225-5829 or 800 972-1233, write to the NYS Department of Taxation and Finance, Taxpayer Assistance Bureau, W. A. Harriman Campus, Albany, NY 12227, or check the website at www.tax.state.ny.us. Information regarding state unemployment insurance is available from NYS Department of Labor, Unemployment Insurance Division, State Office Building Campus, Albany, NY 12240, 518 457-6339, www.labor.state.ny.us. Information regarding workers' compensation and disability insurance is available from State Insurance Fund, 199 Church Street, New York, NY 10007, 312-9000, www.nysif.com.

6

As with any matters relating to tax liability or benefits, it is wise to contact the IRS or state taxing authorities directly or consult a tax lawyer or accountant for advice and assistance with filings. You can also contact a private payroll/tax service specializing in or with expertise in domestic employment matters, a list of which you can find at the end of this chapter. For more information about taxes and domestic help, see the appendix to this chapter.

▶ **Living with your caregiver.** Congratulations. You have made it through the search and interview process and have finally hired an in-home caregiver. Whether she lives in or lives out, you must now incorporate this person into your family life and learn to be a team. You are also a manager of your household and must employ managerial skills in your role as an employer.

The employment relationship with your caregiver is unlike any you may have experienced in your working life. First and foremost, the object of her employment is what is most precious to you—

your children. You are trusting her with their welfare when you cannot be at home. Second, there are aspects of childrearing about which you may be passionate, and it is crucial that your wishes be followed. You should keep in mind that there may be some areas in which you are ambivalent or even unsure of your views, potentially affecting your ability to give clear direction. Third, the locus of employment is your home, the most personal and vulnerable place imaginable. Your caregiver will know things about your life that you may not even share with close friends. She will see you at your best and your worst, your most capable and your most confused. She must be your partner, support and trusted surrogate when you are not present. This is a huge responsibility for you to delegate and for the caregiver to accept.

With this in mind, we have compiled some thoughts on living with your caregiver, based on our own personal experience and that of our friends:

- Your relationship is first and foremost an employment relationship. Terms of employment should be clearly expressed, preferably in writing, and reviewed and updated on a regular, periodic basis. Periodic reviews are useful tools for airing out tensions and dealing with situations before they get out of hand. Open and honest communication will serve you well.
- Your caregiver is not your personal property. She is an employee and a person with her own personality, priorities and personal life. Even if she lives in your home, she is entitled to her privacy. She may become like a member of your family, but she still has her own commitments and relationships outside your home. As hard as it may be, a balance must be found between the personal and professional relationship you have with your caregiver.
- Respect and honor this line of work. Treat it professionally. It is useful to have agreed-upon benefits such as paid vacation time, paid holidays, paid sick leave, bonuses or overtime and transportation home at night. It is customary to provide two weeks paid vacation. You may want to consider having one week accrue every six months during the first year of employment. Be clear about your vacation policy and when she can or cannot take vacation time so that your caregiver can

organize her own life. Agreeing to a certain number of paid sick days and holidays per year can avoid sticky situations about when to dock pay for days off.

- Your caregiver is not superwoman either. It is hard and sometimes tedious work taking care of children and doing household chores. Be realistic about how much can really be done in a day, the rhythm of spending the day with kids and how long it takes to do things. For live-in employees in particular, because the hours tend to be long, schedule reasonable break times. Working without breaks over long periods of time leads to burnout. An overworked, stressed-out caregiver is not likely to be patient, calm or alert.

- Be clear about your expectations of conduct on the job. You may want to consider having written house rules. You cannot assume that your caregiver has exactly the same sensibilities as you do. Even the best caregiver will have different judgments from yours on various issues. Some good rules we have seen: no smoking or drinking during work hours (or in the house at any time); no meeting friends or boyfriends while on the job; dressing appropriately for work (no high heels and miniskirts in the park); no wearing headphones while with the children; rules about with whom the children may be left (no one other than the caregiver or certain named adults); rules about where the children may or may not be taken (subways, other people's cars or homes); in homes with older children, rules about whether (and under what conditions) children may be left alone in the house or are allowed to go out alone; a list of parks the children may go to and until what time; rules about food choices, computer use, video games and television; use of your telephone during work hours and for long-distance calls; and curfews and guest privileges for live-ins. Arrangements for daily household expenses (car fare, money for snacks, etc.) should be determined in advance. Be clear about how you will provide the caregiver with money for daily expenses related to the job and what receipts you expect to have for expenses.

- Work as a team. Discuss how to handle discipline, tantrums, sibling fighting and other behavioral issues as well as household basics such as snacks, television, naps, play time, playdates and such, so that your child will be given a consistent message. If you are going to have a caregiver, you must let her do her job, but you should be in agreement about the parameters of her authority. While she must support you, you must also support her, particularly in front of the children, so that your household will be harmonious.

- You are the boss, they are your children, and it is your home. You should never feel like an outsider in your own home or be made to feel by your caregiver that your parenting skills are less than adequate. While your caregiver may have excellent recommendations or input on issues relating to the children (which should surely be encouraged), and it is essential to give her the authority and opportunity to do her job, you make the final policy in your home. We have seen many high-powered, capable parents be reduced to tears and worse by caregivers who have taken over the household. When this happens, it is time to reassert yourself and take control. Even if it means saying goodbye to the caregiver, in the long run it may be a healthier choice for your family.

- Consider sending your caregiver to courses or programs to enhance her skills. Many nursery schools conduct seminars for caregivers and classes can be found at local parenting centers (see Chapter 7). Such programs are informative and eye-opening and can be very useful to the caregiver, improving her job performance. Many caregivers appreciate the opportunity to learn and enjoy being acknowledged as a relevant member of the household.

- Be a thoughtful and generous employer. Say thank you for a job well done, and, when called for, show your appreciation with appropriate raises, bonuses or intangibles (for example, time off). Remember that your children are watching how you treat people. The person at issue here is someone to whom they are probably very connected. It can be a great opportunity to teach your children about kindness and respect.

6

▶ **Surveillance cameras.** In recent years, there has been a growing trend to use surveillance cameras in the home to monitor job performance of caregivers. This is a subject about which many people have strong opinions and about which the law is not terribly clear. For some, cameras offer the only way to really "know" what happens when parents are not home, in terms of the caregiver's interaction with her charges and her time-management skills. For others, camera surveillance without the knowledge or consent of the caregiver is considered an unacceptable invasion of privacy.

Parents wishing to use a surveillance device may want to consider notifying the caregiver that they may use a hidden camera from time to time without advance notice. Certain caregivers will be willing to accept this, but others may become irate at the thought of being "spied on" and resign.

While a tape showing negligent or abusive treatment of a child provides obvious cause for termination, a tape that shows nothing outrageous or upsetting does not necessarily mean all is well either. Even though a hidden camera can indeed reveal a great deal of information, parents should use it as a tool for monitoring a situation and not as a substitute for their own intuition and vigilance. Surveillance tapes, when used, should be one element of a full evaluation of your caregiver. Moreover, if your instincts tell you that there is a problem, do not wait for evidence, but take action as soon as possible.

For information on renting or buying a surveillance camera for your home, see the resource list at the end of this chapter.

▶ **Breaking up is hard to do.** The impetus to change your child-care arrangement can come from many different directions. The decision is often clear, such as needing to let go of a caregiver who is unqualified or not performing up to par. Sometimes, however, the situation is more complicated. Perhaps the children are older and the job description has changed. Perhaps the relationship is tense or uncomfortable or has become too familiar. Perhaps the caregiver's personal life is interfering with her work. Or perhaps the relationship has simply soured and no one is happy anymore.

In any such situation, it is time to review the situation, sit down with your caregiver and act on your decision. In some cases, it may be possible to rework the job description to accommodate changes in the family (new baby, children attending school full-time, parent going back to work or leaving a job, moving), resolve disputes or otherwise set the relationship back on course. When the situation cannot be rectified, or if the caregiver is endangering the children in any way, it is time to move on and end the relationship as amicably as possible.

Many parents are reluctant to make a change, preferring the known, however unsatisfactory, to the unknown. Other families are anxious about disrupting their children's lives or their own schedules or forcing their children to lose a caregiver to whom they are attached. Unfortunately, there is never a convenient or optimal time for a transition. However, prolonging a situation that is not working out is probably more detrimental to the family than letting a caregiver go. Whatever your situation, if you treat the relationship and the caregiver respectfully, you will likely find that irreconcilable differences do not always have to end in an ugly divorce.

The experts agree that, in general, a child can well tolerate saying goodbye to a caregiver as long as the parents are sensitive to the feelings of the child and handle the situation appropriately. Remember that no matter how unsatisfactory the caregiver was in your eyes, your child may, at least in the beginning, miss the caregiver with whom he or she spent a great deal of time.

Much of how to orchestrate a departure has to do with the circumstances of the caregiver's leaving, the relationship between the caregiver and child and your own personal style. While some families give a caregiver departing on good terms a party and a gift and encourage an ongoing relationship, others prefer a farewell with less fanfare and limit subsequent contact. However you choose to arrange things, keep in mind that your child and caregiver may have a strong bond and that the child's feelings need to be considered. If a new caregiver will be on the scene, the family needs to give her a chance to integrate into the family without undue interference from the former caregiver.

Group Childcare

If you have decided that group childcare is the right choice for your family, there are two alternatives: in-home care, known as family childcare, where the caregiver provides childcare services for several children in her own home; and group day care, known as day care centers, where childcare services are provided in a special facility.

The New York City Department of Health, Bureau of Day Care is responsible for the regulation and licensing of all group care facilities that care for children up to the age of six. There are also private organizations that provide additional accreditation, and sometimes support and training services, to licensed facilities. While unlicensed facilities do exist, particularly with respect to family care services, it is recommended that parents avoid these situations.

▶ **Prioritizing your needs.** Before you get on the phone or start visiting day care facilities, it is worth spending some time thinking about what you want out of a group care facility. Some considerations:

- During what days and hours do you need care? What about holidays?
- Does the facility have flexible or fixed drop-off or pickup times? Can you commit to an exact time or do you need a contingency capability if you must work late or go to work early?
- Do you need the facility to be within walking distance, on a public transportation route, near home or near your workplace?
- What are your feelings about the number of children being cared for and the number of caregivers present?
- Do you prefer a more school-like setting or a homey feeling? More professional or more nurturing? Educational or custodial?
- Do you want your child to be with children of mixed ages or in a group with less age range?
- Can the group accommodate siblings of different ages?
- Do you want the caregivers to have the type of educational training that is required in day care centers but not family care facilities?
- Do you want a setting that is structured or one that is more laid-back? Do you want there to be a curriculum or more free play?
- Do you have a preference for a facility that is part of a network or a community agency?
- Do you want the caregivers and children to be multilingual?
- What preferences do you have about the methods of working with children? Scheduled or demand feeding for infants? Food choices? Access to television, computers or videos during the day? Discipline?

Naps? Outdoor play? Toilet training? Reading? Field trips? Independent play or one-on-one activities with an adult?

- Is your child more comfortable in small groups or large groups? With one adult or several adults? In large open spaces or more intimate spaces?
- Is your child very active, needing a lot of opportunity for outdoor activities, or does your child prefer more quiet play? Is your child sensitive to noise? Does your child need a lot of adult stimulation or does he or she prefer to play independently or with other children with minimal adult intervention?

Having developed a checklist of your basic priorities, you can decide whether you are more interested in family care or a day care center.

▶ **Family Day Care.** Individuals caring for more than two unrelated children in their homes for more than three hours per day must register with the New York City Department of Health as family day care providers. Family day care providers care for children in their own homes. By law, family day care providers can take care of up to six children, including their own, of at least six weeks of age and under the age of 12. If there are no children under the age of two, the provider can care for six children. If there are any children under the age of two, the provider may only care for five children. If the provider receives special approval and passes an inspection by the Department of Health, she may care for an additional two children of school age. The provider may not care for more than two children under the age of two at any one time.

Another category of family day care is group family day care. In this case, the provider may provide care in her home for seven to 12 children, including her own, of at least six weeks of age and under the age of 12, provided that she has at least one assistant. If there are no children under the age of two, the facility can accommodate 12 children. If there are any children under the age of two, it can have a maximum of ten children. No more than four children under two years old and no more than six children under three years old can be cared for at the facility at any one time.

Under New York law, to become a registered family care provider, an individual must be at least 18 years old, complete 10 hours of health and safety training given by an approved program, have at least one year of childcare experience, be fingerprinted and screened through the New York State Central Child Abuse and Maltreatment Register (as must all assistants, emergency coverage personnel and other adults in the home), complete a comprehensive written application and medical form and certify that she has never been convicted of a felony. Although the facility must meet certain safety requirements before registration, note that registered family care homes are thereafter inspected only on a random basis. Providers are also required to receive 15 hours of training during the first sixth months of operation and 30 hours of training every two years thereafter.

6

In addition to meeting the registration requirements for a family care provider, a group family care provider must comply with additional regulations regarding the specific location of the facility and means of ingress and egress. The facility must pass an inspection by the New York City Department of Health, an educational consultant and a fire safety inspector.

Family day care offers a more intimate environment and may be less expensive than a day care center. Because the provider is working out of her home, there is a greater possibility for flexibility in organizing pickup and drop-off times. With the right provider (a loving person with great time-management skills) and a small number of children, there may be opportunity for developing a bonded relationship between caregiver and child. The children can have ample opportunity for socialization and interaction in a home-like environment.

There are potential drawbacks to consider. If the provider is ill or has her own emergency, how is coverage handled? If the caregiver works alone, she is unsupervised. It may be difficult to arrange for outdoor play or activities (and transportation to and from activities) outside the home. The caregiver may have limited resources for providing play materials or separate areas for rest and play. Because the facility is in her home, her own household obligations may need to be attended to during her workday. Depending on the age range of children in the facility, it may be difficult to organize and monitor age-appropriate activities, meals and schedules for each child. If the caregiver does not have any assistants, it is important to consider the effects of the isolation and stress associated with caring for many children on the caregiver's patience, alertness and ability to be creative.

▶ **Group Day Care.** All out-of-home day care programs caring for more than six children under six years old must be issued a permit by the New York City Department of Health. An initial permit is issued for a six-month period, at the end of which the facility is evaluated and a subsequent permit is issued. One-year permits are issued for programs that include children under the age of two. Two-year permits are issued for programs for children between the ages of two and six years old. Licenses must be displayed at the facility. The relevant regulations cover facilities known as childcare centers, day nurseries, day care agencies, nursery schools, kindergartens, play schools or any other facility that meets the definition, whatever its name.

To obtain a permit, the program must meet minimum requirements for physical space, equipment and teacher–child ratios. The premises must pass an inspection by the New York City Fire Department, Buildings Department and Public Health Sanitarian. The director and teaching personnel must be either New York State certified teachers or have other specified training, education and experience. The staff and children must supply evidence of certain health screenings and immunizations. There are also permit requirements pertaining to food service, snacks, rest periods, admissions policies and transportation. All personnel must be fingerprinted and screened for criminal convictions and pending criminal actions and screened with respect to the New York State Central Child Abuse and Maltreatment Register. Each prospective employee's three most recent employment references must be checked.

Because the permit criteria are more stringent for group care facilities than for family day care facilities, the group care facilities may offer families a higher level of service, feeling of security and professionalism. Caregivers must have professional training or education in the field of child development. With more personnel on the premises, caregivers are supervised and do not handle all situations alone. Physical premises are likely to be larger and contain more play materials, perhaps even an outdoor play space. Depending on the facility, there may be a curriculum for the older children and more structured activities for the younger set. If a particular caregiver cannot come to work, there is staff available to cover her duties and the overall operation of the facility is not disrupted. Since group care centers care for a larger number of children than family day care providers, there is ample opportunity for your children to socialize with other children of their own and other ages, and siblings can generally be accommodated.

On the other hand, the group care facility may have specific operating hours and be less flexible for parents. Facilities may be closed for holidays or vacation periods, leaving parents without day care coverage during those times. Because of the number of children being tended, there may be less opportunity to accommodate the specific needs of an individual child and the environment may be less personalized. There may be several adults responsible for caring for young babies so that your own baby may not have a close relationship with a particular person. If there are a large number of children being cared for at the center, it may be overwhelming or too stimulating for your child.

▶ **How to find a day care facility.** If you have decided on family day care or a day care center or you would like to look at both before making a final decision, you must set about finding a facility that meets your needs and where you feel comfortable leaving your child. A first course of action is to ask friends, colleagues, neighbors or your pediatrician for recommendations. To obtain a list of registered and licensed facilities or family day care providers and group care centers, you can contact the Bureau of Day Care at 676-2444 or visit www.nyc.gov (under the Department of Health). The Bureau will generate a list by zip code. If you want to know whether a particular facility has any outstanding violations, you can make a specific request by writing to the Secretary, New York City Department of Health, 125 Worth Street, Room 604A, Box 31, New York, NY 10013. Unfortunately, you cannot receive a list of all facilities with pending violations.

If you are interested in getting personalized assistance in finding a facility, you can contact a Child Care Resource and Referral Agency (CCRR). CCRRs are private community organizations that provide a variety of services to parents in connection with childcare services. They are funded in part by the New York State Office of Children and Family Services. In general, a CCRR will provide detailed information, usually from a computerized database, about the childcare and early education providers and programs in the community. CCRRs have trained counselors who provide advisory services (for free or at a nominal cost) for parents seeking childcare services.

While a CCRR does not actually place the child, the counselors can provide lists of registered and licensed providers, direct families to the type of care that will meet their needs, provide information on choosing a facility and assist in sourcing social services, financial aid and services for families with special needs. CCRRs will make referrals but not recommendations.

CCRRs are involved in providing training and other services or technical support to childcare providers and creating networks of providers with the intent of generally upgrading the childcare services in the community. They may be involved in conducting research, developing childcare public policy and exploring public and private funding sources to expand the availability of childcare services. The CCRRs provide excellent written materials in the form of brochures, checklists, tip sheets and websites to help parents evaluate and select a facility.

Most CCRRS are members of the National Association of Child Care Resource & Referral Agencies (NACCRRA). Its mission is to promote and develop a high quality national CCRR system and offer guidance to policymakers on improving childcare services. NACCRRA provides members with technical support, professional education and conferences; develops a policy agenda; and engages in advocacy activities. NACCRRA also publishes various brochures and other materials, which can be obtained by contacting NACCRRA at 1319 F Street NW, Suite 500, Washington, DC 20004, 202 393-5501, or visiting www.naccrra.org.

The CCRRs that service Manhattan are listed at the end of this chapter. The Administration for Children's Services Agency for Child Development, which also administers publicly funded day care in New York City, can provide you with information regarding eligibility for publicly funded day care services and Head Start programs.

Another excellent resource in the search for quality childcare is Child Care Aware, a program of NACCRRA. Child Care Aware is committed to "helping parents find the best information on locating quality childcare and childcare resources" in their communities. By calling Child Care Aware's parent hotline, 800 424-2246, or checking their website at www.childcareaware.org, you can receive, at no cost, a referral to the CCRRs in your region, brochures and other materials to help you find and choose a facility and tools for evaluating childcare services.

Other potential sources for locating day care services are the UJA Federation of New York Resource Line at 753-2288 (www.ujafedny.org/Get-Help), which provides free and confidential information about day care, camps and other programs, and the Catholic Charities of the Archdiocese of New York, Family and Children Services at 371-1000 (www.catholiccharities.org), which will direct you to services offered by Catholic charities.

► **Selecting a quality childcare facility.** Once you have developed a list of potential childcare providers, a telephone screening is in order. You can establish that the facility has openings and get basic information about the number of children enrolled, their ages and the age distribution, the ratio of caregivers to children, how long the facility has been in operation, the hours during which care is available and the cost. This initial screening will assist you in deciding which facilities warrant a visit.

It is essential that you observe several facilities in order to develop a basis for comparison. It is best to visit when children are present. The bottom line is to find a facility that is safe, has a sufficient number of appropriate caregivers, will provide an environment with adequate stimulation for your child and lets you feel comfortable leaving your child. During your visit you should observe the caregivers and children, see the entire facility and any outdoor play areas and be shown a copy of the license or registration certificate. If possible, meet with the particular personnel who will be caring for your child.

In evaluating a childcare provider, you may want to consider the following:

- Is the facility part of any networks or does it have any other accreditation or affiliations? Accredited facilities voluntarily meet quality standards developed by national organizations. The caregivers in these facilities usually are required to attend continuing education programs, which can raise the level of services provided to your child. Day care centers may be accredited by the National Association for the Education of Young Children (NAEYC). You can obtain a list of accredited facilities by contacting the NAEYC at 1509 16th Street NW, Washington, DC 20036, 202 232-8777, or visiting www.naeyc.org. Family care providers may be accredited by the National Association for Family Child Care (NAFCC). You can contact the NAFCC for information at 5202 Pinemont Drive, Salt Lake City, UT 84123, 801 269-9338, or www.nafcc.org.
- Ask for parent references and check them. Talking with other parents who have children at the facility is a great way to check out the quality of the care.
- Ask how drop-off and pickup are handled and how caregivers deal with separation issues. Ask about procedures for visiting your child during the day. Under New York law, parents must be able to see their children or take them out of the center at any time. Determine how security issues are handled. To whom will the provider release your child? Who has access to the facility during the day?
- Determine whether the provider has scheduled conferences or is available to meet with you at your request. Are parents involved in the facility? Do the caregivers report to parents about the child's activities daily or weekly? The willingness of the provider to meet with parents can be a good indicator of the philosophy of the caregivers and the level of communication to which they aspire.
- Does the facility provide meals or do parents send in meals? What foods are served and what happens if your child does not want what is offered?
- Is the physical facility clean, bright, cheerful, organized and well ventilated? Are there a variety of toys and materials as well as areas for

different types of play? Where do children play outdoors? Where do children rest or relax? What is the typical day for the children? What is the noise level?

- Are any personnel trained in CPR and first aid? Where are fire exits? What are fire procedures (escape routes, fire drills)? Are there window guards, gates or doors at stairwells; are there safety plugs on electrical outlets? Could a child leave the facility unobserved? What are the procedures for handling a sick child?
- Do the children seem busy and happy? Do the caregivers seem engaged and happy? Do they seem to enjoy the children? Are children held or comforted? Are caregivers talking and playing with the children? Is the atmosphere nurturing and relaxed? How is discipline handled? What about toilet training? Assess the program through your child's eyes. Does this seem like a fun and interesting place to spend your days? The CCAC suggests avoiding a facility where children seem to be wandering around or run to any adult who comes into the room.

- What is the training and background of caregivers? How long have employees been at the facility? Is there much employee turnover? What is the ratio of caregivers to children? In general, the fewer children a single adult has to care for, the better for your child. Experts in the industry suggest that for each adult, there should be no more than three to four infants or toddlers or four to six two-year-olds or seven to eight three-year-olds, or eight to nine four-year-olds or eight to ten five-year-olds or ten to 12 school-age children.

▸ **Once your child is in day care.** No matter what your level of due diligence in selecting a facility, there is no absolute guarantee that the situation will work out as you hoped. Accordingly, keep up your vigilance by visiting the facility as much as possible, perhaps by arriving early for pickup or making surprise visits when you have the chance. Talk with the caregivers as much as possible and ask for feedback about your child. Keep up a dialogue with parents of the other children being cared for and find out about their feeling about the level of care and the experience of their children.

Be sensitive to your child's behavior. Is he or she happy to be dropped off? What is he or she like when you pick him or her up?

If your child can talk, ask about his or her day and listen to what he or she says. Does he or she like going to day care, has he or she made friends, does he or she bring home projects or sing songs learned during the day? Be alert to changes in your child's behavior and look into the reasons for the change.

If you feel it is warranted, you can file a complaint against the childcare provider by calling the New York City Department of Health, Bureau of Day Care at 676-2444.

As with any other types of childcare, reassess your needs on an annual basis to make sure that the choices you have made continue to be appropriate.

▶ **Summer Care and Before- and After-School Care.** When seeking resources for summer or before- and after-school care, the CCRRs can often direct you to programs in your neighborhood. Child Care Aware has tip sheets and booklets to help you get started in your search and provide information in helping you select an appropriate program. You can contact Child Care Aware by calling the parents' hot line at 800 424-2246 or accessing its website at www.childcareaware.org. The Parents League (www.parentsleague.org, 737-7385) is a good source for summer programs, and your child's school may be able to direct you to early-morning and after-school programs.

When evaluating programs for school-age children, use the same criteria as for other day care programs. You may also want to consider whether the program arranges field trips, the type of time allocated and supervision available for doing homework, how snacks are handled and the availability of transportation to and from school if the program is not at your child's school.

RESOURCES

In-Home Childcare

Alliance of Professional Nanny Agencies (APNA)
Annie Davis, President
P.O. Box 391026, Solon, OH 44139
206 784-8462, www.apnaonline.org
Membership organization that upholds a code of ethics and sets standards of practice for member agencies.

American Council of Nanny Schools (ACNS)
Sheilagh G. Roth, President
37 South Franklin Street, Chagrin Falls, OH
440 247-9125

International Nanny Association (INA)
900 Haddon Avenue, Suite 438, Collingswood, NJ 08108
856 858-0808, www.nanny.org
Membership organization that upholds a code of ethics and sets standards of practice for member agencies. Publishes the International Nanny Association Directory (contains information on nanny training programs, placement agencies and special services) and other brochures and material on in-home caregivers.

Parents League of New York, Inc.
115 East 82nd Street, New York, NY 10028
737-7385, www.parentsleague.org

Au Pair Programs

United States Department of State
Office of Exchange Coordination and Designation
ECA/EC/ECD SA-44, Room 734
301 4th Street SW
Washington, DC 20547
202 401-9810
www.exchanges.state.gov

Au Pair Care
San Francisco, CA
800 428-7247
www.aupaircare.com

Au Pair in America
Stamford, CT
800 928-7247
www.aupairinamerica.com

EF Au Pair
Cambridge, MA
800 333-6056, 617 619-1000
www.efaupair.org

EurAuPair Intercultural Child Care Programs
Laguna Beach, CA
800 333-3804, 949 494-5500
www.euraupair.com

Go Au Pair
Salt Lake City, UT
800 574-8889, 801 255-7722
www.goaupair.com

Interexchange Au Pair
New York, NY
800 287-2477, 924-0446
www.interexchange.org

Government Resources

Immigration and Naturalization Service
800 357-2099 (employer hotline), 800 870-3676 (forms), 800 375-5283 (customer service center), www.ins.usdoj.gov

INS New York City District Office
26 Federal Plaza, New York, NY 10278

Internal Revenue Service
800 829-1040 (24-hour information line), 800 829-3676 (forms and publications), www.irs.gov.

New York City Department of Consumer Affairs
42 Broadway, New York, NY 10004
487-4221 (Complaint/License Hotline), 487-4444,
www.nyc.gov/html/dca.html (see Consumer Affairs)

New York State Department of Labor
Unemployment Insurance Division
State Office Building Campus, Albany, NY 12240
518 457-6339, www.labor.state.ny.us

New York State Department of Taxation and Finance
Taxpayer Assistance Bureau
W. A. Harriman Campus, Albany, NY 12227
800 225-5829 or 800 972-1233, www.tax.state.ny.us

State Insurance Fund
199 Church Street, New York, NY 10007
312-9000, www.nysif.com.

Nanny Background Searches (B) and Surveillance Services (S)

Babywatch Corporation (S)
Spring Valley, NY
800 558-5669

Babywatch Murray Hill (B, S)
New York, NY
889-1494
Also screens and interviews job candidates.

Care Check, Inc. (B)
1056 Fifth Avenue
New York, NY 10028
360-6640
Rents and sells video surveillance equipment; sells webcam hookups. Also screens, interviews and checks references of job candidates as well as helps structure nanny positions.

HomeStep (S)
760-5959, www.homestepsafety.com
Video surveillance, nanny-cams.

InfoMart's NannySearch (B)
1582 Terrell Mill Road
Marietta, GA 30067
800 800-3774
www.backgroundscreening.com

Innovative Personnel Strategies (psychological screening)
Napa, CA
888 477-8378

Kid View, Inc. (S)
Great Neck, NY
800 339-7146

Know Your Nanny (S)
Toms River, NJ
888-692-2291
www.knowyournanny.com
Hidden video surveillance equipment sales and rental.

Mind Your Business, Inc. (B)
Warren, NJ
888 869-2462, 732 302-9102
www.mybinc.com
Also checks references and arranges for psychological and drug screening of candidates.

Nanny Track (S)
828-9070, www.nannytrack.com
Childcare surveillance outside the home.

PFC Information Services, Inc. (B)
Oakland, CA
510 653-5061
www.pfcinformation.com

Philadelphia Nanny Network (B)
New York Office
717-0446, www.nannyagency.com
Offers consulting services in Manhattan to screen, interview and check references of job candidates as well as help structure nanny position.

Nanny Employment/Placement Agencies

New York City:

A Choice Nanny (INA member)
850 Seventh Avenue, Suite 305
New York, NY 10019
246-5437, www.achoicenanny.com

Adele Poston Agency (INA member)
16 East 79th Street
New York, NY 10021
879-7474
www.adelepostonagency.com

All Home Services
2121 Broadway
New York, NY 10023
799-9360

Austin Agency, Inc.
71-09 Austin Street
Forest Hills, NY 11375
718 268-2700

Babysitter's Guild
60 East 42nd Street, Suite 912
New York, NY 10165
682-0227
www.babysittersguild.com

Best Domestic Services Agency, Inc. (INA member)
10 East 39th Street, Suite 1126
New York, NY 10016
685-0351, www.BestDomestic.com

Elite Nannies, Inc. (INA member)
120 West 57th Street, Suite 1214
New York, NY 10107
212 489-3900
www.elitenanny.com

Fox Agency
30 East 60th Street
New York, NY 10022
753-2686

Frances Stewart Agency
1220 Lexington Avenue
New York, NY 10028
439-9222
www.francesstewart.com

London Agency
767 Lexington Avenue
New York, NY 10021
755-5064

My Child's Best Friend Nanny Services (INA member)
44 East 32nd Street, 11th floor
New York, NY 10016
206-9910
www.nynannyservice.com

Pavillion Agency, Inc. (INA member)
15 East 40th Street, Suite 400
New York, NY 10016
889-6609
www.pavillionagency.com

Phillipino Placement Agency, Inc.
104 East 40th Street, #106
867-8558

Pinch Sitters (places temporary or occasional sitters)
799 Broadway, Suite 204
New York, NY 10003
260-6005

Professional Nannies Institute (INA member)
501 Fifth Avenue, Suite 908
New York, NY 10017
692-9510, www.profnannies.com

Robin Kellner Agency (INA member)
2 West 45th Street
New York, NY 10036
997-4183, www.robinkellner.com

Sterling Domestics, Inc.
633 Third Avenue, 8th floor
New York, NY 10017
661-5813, www.sterlingny.com

Town & Country
162 West 56th Street, Suite 207
New York, NY 10019
245-8400

Working Solutions, Inc. (INA member)
51 East 42nd Street, Suite 1511
New York, NY 10017
922-9562
www.workingsolutioninc.com

www.sittercity.com
888 211-9741
Database of college student babysitters

Regional or National Services:

Advance Nannies
800 874-6717

A Mother's Resource
Larchmont, NY 10538
914 834-7353

All American Nanny, Ltd. (INA member)
Virginia Beach, VA
800 362-6697
www.allamericannanny.com

America's Nannies (INA member)
Paramus, NJ
201 262-2400
www.americasnannys.com

An Extra Pair of Hands
800 756-0567

Beacon Hill Nannies, Inc.
(INA member)
Newton Centre, MA
800 736-3880
www.beaconhillnannies.com

Child Care Services of Wisconsin
(INA member)
Wauwatosa, WI
414 543-1612; 800 795-7440
www.childcareservicesofwi.com

The Choice Care Agency (INA member)
Tucson, AZ
866 878-8274; 520-322-6966

Heartland Caregivers
(INA member)
Missoula, MT
406 542-0241
www.heartlandcaregivers.com

Larchmont Employment Agency, Inc.
Larchmont, NY
866 287-2477
www.thelarchmontagency.com

Midland Nanny Placement
(INA member)
Grundy Center, IA
319 824-6158
www.midlandnanny.com

Nannies of Nebraska
(INA member)
Norfolk, NE
402 379-2444
www.nanniesofnebraska.com

Nannies Plus, Inc. (INA member)
Chester, NY
845 469-5130; 800 752-0078
www.nanniesplus.com

The Nanny Authority, Inc.
16 Ferry Street, Newark, NJ 07105
973 466-2669
www.nannyauthority.com

NannyBank.com, Inc.
South San Francisco, CA
www.nannybank.com

Neighborhood Nannies, Inc.
(INA member)
Haddonfield, NJ
800 590-5437

New Age Nannies, Inc.
(INA member)
Smithtown, NY
866 306-2669; 631 979-3484
www.newagenannies.com

New York Nanny Center
(INA Member)
Port Washington, NY
516 767-5136

Oregon Nannies, Inc.
(INA member)
Eugene, OR
541 343-3755
www.oregonnannies.com

Plaza Domestic Agency
Lynbrook, NY
466-1662

Professional Nanny Care Solutions, Inc.
877 776-6266
www.pronannycare.com

Nanny Health Insurance
Nanny Health Insurance Services
Richard A. Eisenberg Associates
Newton Centre, MA
800 777-5765, www.eisenbergassociates.com

Nanny Professional Development
American Red Cross
Various Locations
800 514-5103, www.nyredcross.org
Childcare classes, including New York State Healthy Child Course and infant and child CPR.

The Language Exchange
889-5362
English language classes for nannies and au pairs.

LifeWork Strategies
800 777-1720, www.lwsonline.com
Sells the Nanny Essentials Training kit, a stand-alone resource guide that forms the basis of a nanny-training curriculum. Check the website to locate a trainer near you. Alternately, you can purchase the kit to offer the course to your nanny at home.

NannyWise/Amy Hatkoff
19 East 88th Street, New York, NY 10128
628-7124
A six-hour training program covering child development and behavior, positive discipline and CPR.

Workshops for Caregivers
92nd Street Y, 1395 Lexington Avenue, New York, NY 10128
415-5500

Nanny Training Programs that may place graduates in New York City
American Council of Nanny Schools (ACNS) (provides a list of accredited programs)
Joy Shelton, President
Office A74
Delta College
University Center, MI 48710
517 686-9417

Boston's Best Baby Sitters/Nannies
12 Roseclair Street
Boston, MA 02125
617 268-7148
www.bostonsbestbabysitters.com

English Nanny & Governess School, Inc. (ACNS Accredited)
37 South Franklin Street
Chagrin Falls, OH 44022
216 247-0600

Hocking College Nanny Academy (ACNS Accredited)
3301 Hocking Parkway
Nelsonville, OH 45764
740 753-3591 ext. 2204

Lake Land Community College
5001 Lakeland Blvd.
Mattoon, IL 61938
217 234-5426

Northeastern Oklahoma A & M College (INA member)
Child Development Department
200 I Street, NE
Miami, OK 74354
918 540-6265

Northwest Nannies, Inc. (ACNS Accredited)
11830 SW Kerr Pky. #100
Lake Oswego, OR 97035
503 245-5288, www.nwnanny.com

Southeast Community College (INA member)
Professional Nanny Diploma, Early Childhood Education Program
8800 O Street
Lincoln, NE 68520
402 437-2455, www.southeast.edu

Sullivan University (ACNS Accredited)
Professional Nanny Program
3101 Bardstown Road
Louisville, KY 40205
800 844-1354 ext. 327

6

Tax and payroll information and services

Internal Revenue Service
800 829-1040 (24-hour information line)
800 829-3676 (forms and publications)
www.irs.gov

NYS Department of Labor
Unemployment Insurance Division
State Office Building Campus
Albany, NY 12240
518 457-6339
www.labor.state.ny.us

NYS Department of Taxation and Finance
Taxpayer Assistance Bureau
W. A. Harriman Campus
Albany, NY 12227
800 225-5829 or 800 972-1233
www.tax.state.ny.us

State Insurance Fund
199 Church Street
New York, NY 10007
312-9000, www.nysif.com

Breedlove & Associates, Inc.
Golden, CO
800 723-9961
www.breedlove-online.com

GTM Payroll Services
Albany, NY
800 929-9213, www.4easypay.com

Home/Work Solutions, Inc.
Sterling, VA
800 626-4829
www.4nannytaxes.com

Nanny Tax, Inc.
50 East 42nd Street #2108
New York, NY 10017
867-1776, www.nannytax.com

Group Care

New York City Administration for Children's Services
150 William Street, 18th floor, New York, NY 10038
543-7692, Head Start Services 718 260-7080 or 718 361-6758
www.nyc.gov (see Children's Services)

New York City Department of Health
Bureau of Day Care
2 Lafayette Street, 22nd floor, Box 68, New York, NY 10007
676-2444, www.nyc.gov (see Department of Health)

New York City Department of Health
125 Worth Street, Room 604A, Box 31, New York, NY 10013
877-692-3647, www.nyc.gov (see Department of Health)

New York State Child Care Coordinating Council, Inc.
130 Ontario Street, Albany, NY 12206
518 463-8663, www.nyscccc.org/nysc4.htm

New York State Council on Children & Families
Head Start—State Collaboration Office
5 Empire State Plaza, Suite 2810, Albany, NY 12223
518 474-6297, capital.net/com/council/headstart.html

New York State Department of Family Assistance
Office of Children and Family Services
Bureau of Early Childhood Services
52 Washington Street 3N, Rensselaer, NY 12144
518 474-9454; 800 345-5437 to order Think About Child Care
www.ocfs.state.ny.us

U.S. Department of Health and Human Services
Administration for Children and Families (ACF)
370 L'Enfant Plaza Promenade SW, Washington, DC 20447
www.acf.hhs.gov (see Head Start Bureau to find a local program)
ACF Regional Office
26 Federal Plaza, Room 4114, New York, NY 10278
264-2890

Child Care Resource and Referral Agencies (CCRRs)

Child Care, Inc.
275 Seventh Avenue, 15th floor
New York, NY 10001
929-4999, www.childcareinc.org

Child Development Support Corp.
1213 Fulton Street
Brooklyn, NY 11216
718 398-6738

Chinese American Planning Council
365 Broadway, ground floor
New York, NY 10013
941-0030

Committee for Hispanic Children and Families
140 West 22nd Street, Suite 301
New York, NY 10011
206-1090, www.chcsinc.org

Day Care Council of New York, Inc.
10 East 34th Street, 6th floor
New York, NY 10016
206-7817, www.dccnyinc.cs.com

Other Resources
Catholic Charities of the Archdiocese of New York
Family and Children Services
1011 First Avenue, New York, NY 10022
371-1000, www.catholiccharities.org

Child Care Aware
Parent Hotline 800 424-2246, www.childcareaware.org

Citizens' Committee for Children of New York, Inc.
105 East 22nd Street, New York, NY 10010
673-1800, www.kfny.org
Advocacy organization

National Association for the Education of Young Children (NAEYC)
1509 16th Street NW
Washington, D.C. 20036
202 232-8777, www.naeyc.org

National Association of Child Care Resource & Referral Agencies (NACCRRA)
1319 F Street NW, Suite 500
Washington, DC 20004
202 393-5501, www.naccrra.org

National Association of Family Child Care (NAFCC)
5202 Pinemont Drive, Salt Lake City, UT 84123
801 269-9338, www.nafcc.org

National Child Care Information Center
243 Church Street, NW, 2nd floor, Vienna, Virginia 22180
800 616-2242, www.nccic.org

United Jewish Appeal-Federation of New York Resource Line
130 East 59th Street , New York, NY 10022
753-2288, www.ujafedny.org
Among its many resources are daycare, preschool, school and special needs referrals.

To report known or suspected child abuse or neglect by a caregiver call the NYS Child Abuse and Maltreatment Register at 800 342-3720

APPENDIX

In-home Employees

▶ **Sponsoring an undocumented immigrant.** The process for sponsoring a domestic employee (e.g. nanny, housekeeper, governess) for a green card is complicated and time consuming. Since many individuals working in domestic positions are undocumented and will not be eligible for sponsorship because they have been living in the U.S. without valid immigration status, a thorough analysis of the prospective employee's immigration situation should be undertaken before considering sponsorship. As a prospective employer, you should retain an experienced immigration lawyer specializing in this type of situation.

If the situation of the family and the prospective employee make it feasible to begin the process, the first step is an application for Labor Certification with the Department of Labor (DOL). That application requires that the family agree to pay the applicant a prevailing market wage (currently deemed to be $379 per week for a live-out nanny in Manhattan). Additionally, the applicant must have written references showing that she has at least one year of paid prior employment for the same type of work for which she is being sponsored. Processing of the application at the DOL can take two years or more and requires that the family advertise in the newspaper to fill the position, interview applicants and prove that there are no qualified U.S. candidates to fill the position. If the application is not rejected, a Labor Certification will be issued. Once the Labor Certification is issued, there is a two-part petition process (including an application for adjustment of status) at the Immigration and Naturalization Service (INS). This stage can take an additional two years or more.

It is important to point out that during the sponsorship period, the applicant for a green card is not supposed to work for the family that is sponsoring her. Additionally, if she does not have valid, unexpired, non-immigrant visa status (in other words, if her status is illegal), she is not supposed to be living in the United States. Undertaking the sponsorship process does not change this. Families who decide to take the risk and employ the nanny during the sponsorship process face the possibility of significant penalties. Indeed, with the recent attention to illegal immigration and to political appointees who hired illegal aliens, this course of action cannot be recommended. It should be discussed thoroughly with an immigration lawyer who is acting in the best interests of the family, which may not be the same interests as those of the employee.

Some parents may attempt to sponsor a caregiver as a cook, butler or other "skilled" job category, since DOL considers nannies and housekeepers to be "unskilled" workers and treats the unskilled categories differently. Others attempt to hire the person to be an employee of a family-owned business rather than as an employee of the individual family. Needless to say, the laws are strict, and sponsoring an individual under misleading or fraudulent conditions can subject the employer to serious civil and even criminal penalties.

Keep in mind that laws and procedures are frequently changing, and current information should be obtained and an immigration attorney consulted before considering sponsorship. You can contact the INS at 800 357-2099 (employer hotline), 800 870-3676 (forms), 800 375-5283 (customer service center) or www.ins.usdoj.gov. See www.aila.org for information about immigration matters or to find an immigration lawyer.

▶ **Taxes.** It is important to ascertain whether you are responsible for paying taxes with respect to your in-home employees. If you pay the employee wages of $1,400 (this is the amount for 2003 and may change in the future) or more in the calendar year, you are required to pay Social Security and Medicare taxes. The employer is responsible for payment of both the employer's and employee's share of these taxes; however, the employee's share can either be withheld from her wages or paid from the employer's own funds. The share of taxes for the employer and employee is 7.65% (6.2% for Social Security and 1.45% for Medicare) each, for a total of 15.3% in the aggregate.

If you pay the employee wages of $1,000 or more in any calendar quarter, you must also pay federal unemployment tax. This tax is not withheld from the employee's wages. It is paid from the employer's own funds. An employer is not required to withhold federal income tax from a household employee's wages but may agree to do so. If your employee is eligible for an earned income credit (available to certain workers who have a child or children living with them), you may have to make special advance payments of her earned income credit along with her wages.

You will need to obtain a federal employer identification number (which is different from your social security number) in order to process tax filings and report federal household employment taxes (Social Security, Medicare and unemployment) with your individual federal tax return on Schedule H – Form 1040. You can learn more about your responsibility as an employer by calling the Internal Revenue Service at 800 829-1040 (24-hour information line) or requesting a copy of the IRS's Publication 926, "Household Employer's Tax Guide," by calling 800 829-3676 (forms and publications) or visiting the website at www.irs.gov.

In addition to federal tax liability, a household employer may have state tax liability for a household employee. As under federal law, you are not required to withhold New York State or New York City taxes, but you may agree to do so. Unlike federal law, however, New York still has quarterly filing requirements. If you pay your employee wages of $500 or more in any calendar quarter, you must also pay state unemployment tax. Finally, if you employ a domestic employee who works 40 or more hours per week for you, you are subject to the Workers Compensation Law and Disability Benefits Law and must provide each eligible employee with these benefits.

For state tax information, you can call 800 225-5829 or 800 972-1233, visit www.tax.state.ny.us or write to the NYS Department of Taxation and Finance, Taxpayer Assistance Bureau, W. A. Harriman Campus, Albany, NY 12227. Information regarding state unemployment insurance is available from NYS Department of Labor, Unemployment Insurance Division, State Office Building Campus, Albany, NY 12240, 518 457-6339, www.labor.state.ny.us. Information regarding workers' compensation and disability insurance is available from State Insurance Fund, 199 Church Street, New York, NY 10007, 312-9000, www.nysif.com.

Surprisingly, if your caregiver is not legal, even though it is illegal for you to employ her, you are still supposed to make the necessary filings and pay employment taxes with respect to her employment, and your employee is required to file a tax return. The IRS will assign your caregiver a taxpayer identification number (different from a social security number) to process her return. The IRS claims not to share this information with the INS. Needless to say, if this is your situation, you should consult a tax professional.

Notwithstanding the foregoing, there are certain situations where you may not have to pay taxes with respect to your domestic help. If an individual is not an employee but is a bona fide independent contractor (as defined in the tax law and regulations) you will not have payment obligations although in some cases you will still have filing obligations. You should consult with a tax advisor to determine whether your situation meets the technical requirements for this tax treatment.

Not all the news about taxes is bad. You may be eligible for a child-and-dependent-care tax credit if you incur expenses to care for a child under the age of 13 so that you can work or look for work. Also, your employer may have a flexible spending arrangement (or reimbursement account) pursuant to which you can receive certain tax-free reimbursements for dependent care or a cafeteria plan that allows employees to receive dependent-care assistance benefits from the company.

As with any matters relating to tax liability or benefits, it is wise to contact the IRS or state taxing authorities directly or consult a tax lawyer or accountant for advice and assistance with filings. You can also consult a tax service specializing in or with expertise in domestic employment matters.

Chapter 7

The Enlightened Parent

Each generation is subject to historical factors that make its parenting experience unique. For this generation of parents, technological advancements, the increase in the number of dual-career households, the explosion of information and the change in our culture's general attitude toward children all affect the way in which children are raised today. Things simply are not as they were when the parents of today were kids being raised by their parents.

Certainly more is known about child development and the processes of how little people become adults. Never has information about parenting been so plentiful, accessible and potentially conflicting. Parent organizations, professional groups and individuals in private practice disseminate information through lectures, workshops and discussion groups. There are radio and television shows, videos, magazines, books, computer software and websites dedicated to the topic of parenting. The abundance of theories, strategies and general advice has translated into a new business category, and today the business of parenting is big business.

Big business, however, is not necessarily a bad thing. Information can be a great comfort to new parents adjusting to their changing lifestyles as well as to seasoned parents moving through the different stages of parenthood. Attending programs and joining support groups can be both interesting and informative. The opportunities for parents to gain perspective and understanding, as well as to connect with others, can truly enhance the ability to parent lovingly and productively while making it more fun in the process.

Most parents today look beyond traditional avenues of support to the new world of knowledge, packaged and marketed to an audience accustomed to having the answers. Whether you are an information junkie or just an occasional user, the mere existence of the information around us has made parenting a more intellectual endeavor and potentially an enlightening experience.

Keep one thing in mind as you seek out all that there is to know: the ultimate parenting manual or authority does not exist, no matter where you look for it. There simply is no absolutely right way to parent. Our society defines, through the many laws we have created to protect children, what we cannot do to our children. But no one can spell out exactly what we must do to help them grow to be balanced, healthy and happy people.

Our only advice: be an educated consumer. Almost any point of view can be validated by an "expert," so make sure to use your good judgment when evaluating the information you receive and the credibility of the source. If you are uncomfortable with the advice you get or if a recommendation proves ineffective, even if it came from a highly respected source, have faith in yourself and continue your search.

Following is a list of some of the parenting resources available in Manhattan. The list includes individuals and organizations that offer group-oriented programs rather than individual counseling (although some on the list may offer individual sessions). Note that we do not recommend specific individuals, businesses or services, nor have we attempted to check or validate their credentials for the services they offer. Good luck!

RESOURCES

The following resources offer lectures, seminars, workshops and/or group programs. Some organizations listed offer groups for caregivers as well. Call for information on the specific kinds of programs each organization provides.

Central Synagogue Parenting Center
123 East 55th Street, 838-5122

Child's Play
236 West 73rd Street between Broadway and West End Avenue in the Rutgers Presbyterian Church, 877-8227
165 West 86th Street in the West Park Presbyterian Church, 838-1504

The Early Childhood Development Center/Rebecca Myers Thomas, M.S.
163 East 97th Street, 360-7803

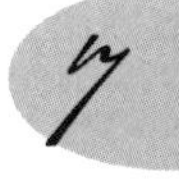

Elizabeth Bing Center for Parents
164 West 79th Street, 362-5304

Elizabeth Seton Childbearing Center
222 West 14th Street, 367-8500, www.birthcenter.org

14th Street Y
Sol Goldman YM – YWHA of the Educational Alliance
Parenting and Family Center
344 East 14th Street, 780-0800 ext. 239, www.edalliance.org

Groups for Mothers/Dr. Beverly Amsel
165 West End Avenue, #1E, 362-5903

Jewish Board of Family and Children's Services/Child Development
120 West 57th Street, 582-9100

Jewish Community Center in Manhattan
334 Amsterdam Avenue, 646 505-4380, www.jccmanhattan.org

McBurney YMCA
215 West 23rd Street, 741-8729, www.ymcanyc.org

The New Center for Modern Parenthood
Dr. Eleanor Morin Davis, Psychologist/Psychoanalysis
3 Rutherford Place, 982-7733

The Pacella Parent Child Center/New York Psychoanalytic Society
247 East 82nd Street, 879-6900, www.theparentchildcenter.org

Parenting Center - 92nd Street YM-YWHA
1395 Lexington Avenue, 415-5611, www.92ndStY.org

Parenting Development Resource, Inc./Virginia Stowe, M.S.N.
1088 Park Avenue, Suite 16F, 423-0532

Parenting for Success/Ronnie Grosbard, M.S. and Kathleen Cochran, Ed. M.
875-1030

Parent Guidance Workshops/Nancy Samalin
180 Riverside Drive, 787-8883, www.samalin.com

Parenting Horizons/Julie A. Ross, M.A.
405 West 57th Street #1F, 765-2377, www.parentinghorizons.com

ParentWise/Amy Hatkoff
Multiple locations, 628-7124

The Rhinelander Center
350 East 88th Street, 876-0500, www.rhinelanderchildrenscenter.org

Sackler Lefcourt Center for Child Development
17 East 62nd Street, 759-4022

The SoHo Parenting Center
568 Broadway, 2nd floor, 334-3744

Vanderbilt YMCA
224 East 47th Street, 756-9600, www.ymcanyc.org

West Side YMCA S
5 West 63rd Street, 875-4100, www.ymcanyc.org

These hospitals offer a variety of prenatal, sibling, parenting, toddler and family programs. Call for details.

Bellevue Hospital Parent Resource Center
First Avenue and 16th Street, 562-4141
www.ci.nyc.ny.us/html/hcc/bellevue/home.html

Beth Israel Medical Center Parent Education Center
First Avenue at 16th Street, 420-2999, www.wehealny.org/familyed

Lenox Hill Hospital
100 East 77th Street, 434-2160, www.lenoxhillhospital.org.
(Refers new parents to outside resources offering new parent classes.)

Mount Sinai Medical Center
Maternal Child Health Care Center/Parent Education Program
1 Gustav Levy Place, 241-8909, www.mssm.edu

New York Medical College Center for Comprehensive Health Care
163 East 97th Street, 360-7872

New York-Presbyterian Hospital
Columbia-Presbyterian Campus
622 West 168th Street, Parent Education 305-2040, www.childrensnyp.org

New York-Presbyterian Hospital
New York Weill Cornell Medical Center
525 East 68th Street, Preparation for Parenthood 746-3215
www.nycornell.org

New York University Medical Center
Parenting Institute at NYU Child Study Center
550 First Avenue, 263-6622, www.nyuchildrens.org

St. Luke's-Roosevelt Hospital Center
523-6222 (Parent/Family Education number for both St. Luke's and Roosevelt divisions)
www.bethisraelny.org, www.wehealny.org

Saint Vincent's Hospital & Medical Center of New York
Parenting Education Program
153 West 11th Street, 604-7646, www.svcmc.org
(Programs for children under three only)

The following are specialized resources:

Ametz Adoption Program, Jewish Child Care Association
Workshops at multiple locations
425-3333, www.jccany.org
How-to workshops, support groups and educational programs for parents at all stages of adoption (domestic and international). Referral service.

Child Abuse Hot Line
800 4-A-Child
24-hour advice and referral service

Children's Rights Council/Fathers Help Hotline
6200 Editors Park Drive, Suite 103
Hyattsville, MD 20782
431-7724, www.gocrc.com
Non-custodial parent groups. New York chapter meets at the McBurney YMCA.

Dads and Daughters
34 East Superior Street, Suite 200
Duluth, MN 55802
888 824-DADS, www.dadsanddaughters.org

Family Support America
Chicago, IL, 312 338-0900, www.familysupportamerica.org

Fatherhood Project/Families and Work Institute
465-2044, www.fatherhoodproject.org

Gilda's Club
195 West Houston Street, 647-9700, www.gildasclubnyc.org
Support groups for families with children, parents or other family members living with cancer.

Mocha Moms
www.mochamoms.org
Organization for women of color who have chosen to stay home to raise their children.

National Association of Mothers' Centers
www.motherscenter.org
Information and support to mothers by decreasing isolation, promoting good health and recognizing the importance of good mothering.

National Organization of Mothers of Twins Club and Higher Order Multiples
P.O. Box 438, Thompsons Station, TN 37179-0438, www.nomotc.org
Check the website for information, web resources and local chapters in Queens, Staten Island and nearby suburban counties.

The New Mommies' Network
East and West Side locations, 769-3846
New mothers support group.

New Mothers Luncheon/Ronni Soled
Upper East and West Side locations, 744-3194
New mothers support group.

New York City Parents In Action
426-0240, www.parentsinaction.org
Conducts programs through various schools and independently.

Parenting Coalition International, Inc.
1025 Connecticut Avenue, NW, Suite 415, Washington, DC 20036,
202 530-0849, www.parentingcoalition.org
Advocacy organization of parenting professionals.

Parents Anonymous, Inc.
Claremont, CA, (909) 621-6184

Parents Committee of New York City
718 259-7921

Parents without Partners
800 637-7974, www.parentswithoutpartners.org

Single Mothers By Choice
988-0993, www.singlemothersbychoice.com

Single Parent Resource Center
31 East 28th Street, New York, NY 10016, 951-7030
Offers programs for the single parent, conducts seminars and has support services.

Single Parents Group
14th Street Y/Sol Goldman YM – YWHA of the Educational Alliance
Parenting and Family Center
344 East 14th Street, 780-0800 ext. 239

Stepfamily Foundation Resources
333 West End Avenue, 877-3244, www.stepfamily.org

24-hour Parent Helpline/NY Foundling Crisis Nursery
472-8555
Crisis intervention for families and children.

Other Parent Resources:

Family Resources
800 641-4546, www.familyresourcesofpa.org

PIRC-Parent Information Research Center
800 342-7472

National Parent Information Network
800 583-4135, www.npin.org

The National Parenting Center
800 753-6667, www.tnpc.com

Websites for parents to browse:

www.abcparenting.com (the index lists and links to hundreds of parenting websites)

www.daughters.com

www.family.com (Disney)

www.hbwm.com (Home Based Working Moms)

www.ivillage.com

www.parenthood.com

www.parenthoodweb.com

www.parentsoup.com

www.zerotothree.org

Chapter 8

From ABC to ERB

Contrary to popular belief, it is neither necessary nor possible to sign your child up for school at birth, and there is no direct track from preschool to the Ivy League. Facing the process of enrolling your child in the school of your choice does, however, create some interesting challenges for even the most sensible parent. Finding the right school for your child can be daunting, but the difficulty has more to do with the learning curve involved in the application process than it does with how competitive Manhattan schools truly are.

School today is quite different from the institutions we attended as kids. School administrators have applied current educational theory to their curricula and day-to-day operations in surprisingly different ways. Private schools have worked hard to differentiate themselves from one another and thus offer a wide range of educational options. The New York City public school system also contains many alternative school models and programs to consider.

The diversity of educational opportunities available for city kids is such that long before it is time for school, parents need to become familiar with the ABCs of education today.

In addition to understanding how schools differ, Manhattan parents must work through an admissions process that is unique to this city and must become familiar with a system that appears to be arbitrary, complicated and at times incomprehensible. We are here to help you do your homework.

This chapter is organized into sections on preschool, ongoing private school and ongoing public school. The sections cover the general procedures and timetables for admissions, information on the application process and recommendations for getting through this exhausting process and maintaining your perspective. Sample checklists are included, which are designed to assist you in organizing your efforts. A list of resources and references is included at the end of the chapter.

The Bottom Line

Deciding where to send your child to school can feel overwhelming. Very few of us come to the process fully informed or even totally clear about what we want. We all want to send our children to the best school possible. At the very least, we want to find a safe place with qualified individuals in charge who will provide a rich, stimulating social and academic environment. But we may want more, a lot more. We may want a school that espouses values similar to our own or with a family community with which we feel we can connect. We may have particular interests that we want reflected in the curriculum: foreign languages, technology, athletics, the arts, ethnic diversity, community service, gender equity or religious affiliation. We may have specific views about traditional versus progressive education and public versus private schools.

There is probably no school that can fulfill every item on your wish list, so you will need to prioritize. When you visit schools, as you inevitably will, observe carefully and ask questions. Here are some factors you may want to consider when visiting and reading about schools and talking with parents about the schools their children attend. This list was culled from parents, educators, nursery school directors, principals and ongoing school admissions officers and can be helpful when looking at programs from toddler groups to middle schools.

- Location. To what extent do you want the school to be located near your home or workplace? How will your child get to and from school? Is busing available and, if so, commencing at what age? Who monitors the busing process? If you have more than one child, can you manage the logistics of getting children to and from different schools? Will you be able to attend school programs and teacher conferences conveniently or pick up your child in an emergency or if your regular arrangements fall through?
- The physical plant. Is the school orderly, neat, clean and cheerful? Do classrooms have age-appropriate activities and equipment in a stimulating environment? Is the children's work displayed? Are classrooms child friendly? Do children have easy access to restrooms (and for little ones, can they go to the bathroom alone or do they need to be accompanied)? Are there opportunities for outdoor play and indoor physical activity? Do the children need to leave the building to get to other parts of the school? Is the building in good repair?

- Faculty. What is the child/teacher ratio? How many children are in a typical class? What kind of professional qualifications do teachers and administrators have? Do teachers have professional development opportunities? What is teacher turnover like? How do teachers interact with children?
- Security. What kind of security measures are employed around the school building and grounds? How are drop-off and dismissal of children handled? Is play equipment safe and well-maintained? Do the children use public playgrounds and parks and, if so, how are they supervised and transported back and forth? Does the school accommodate early drop-off or late pickup?
- The classroom. Do children seem happy and engaged? Do children seem well supervised? How is a child's progress measured? How many times during the year do parents have formal teacher conferences

and written reports? What forms of enrichment and remediation are offered on-site? Are classes grouped by age or is there some mixing of age groups? For the younger set, how does the school handle the separation process, and what kind of transition schedule is used to allow children to become familiar with the classroom, teachers and other students (home visits, phasing into a full schedule)? If meals or snacks are served, are they nutritious? What kind of extras are offered: music, art, swimming, dance, cooking, woodworking, etc.? For ongoing schools, when do the children begin getting homework, grades and tests? How is the school day structured?

- Philosophy. Is the school's stated philosophy evident in its environment? Does the school's style or ambiance feel comfortable to you? Is the school formal or informal? Does the school welcome parent involvement and in what ways? Is there an active parents' association? Are parents expected to do fund-raising for the school? Is the school responsive to the needs of individual children? Is the school culturally diverse? How does the school accommodate children with special needs? How are disciplinary issues handled? Is there a specific policy? What is the student population and what is the projected growth of the school? For older children, is there a school code of ethics, a dress code or school uniform, and is community service part of the curriculum? How does the director relate to parents? What kind of extracurricular and after-school activities are offered by or at the school? For schools with a religious affiliation, how is religious training integrated into daily activities?

- Curriculum in ongoing schools. Does the school prepare a written curriculum guide or other materials to explain the curriculum? How much time is dedicated to social studies, language arts and reading, math, science, "specials" (music, art, movement, etc.), foreign language, library periods and gym. To what extent do children move among different classrooms and teachers during the day? How does the school teach reading and what is expected of students? What percentage of students are tutored? What types of extracurricular activities are offered (for example, athletic teams, school publications, orchestra or singing groups, clubs) and for what age children? When and how is technology used in the classroom?

- Cost. With respect to nonpublic school, what is the tuition and what payment plans or schedules are available? Are parents expected to contribute to an annual fund to support operating budgets or a capital campaign? Does the school offer financial aid or accept students whose tuition is paid via non-profit organizations? What percentage of children receive financial aid? Is the school committed to maintaining a financial assistance program?

When looking at schools, keep notes on your impressions from your tours and meetings with school officials and compare them with written materials prepared by the schools to see whether they are consistent. It is also interesting to observe drop-off and dismissal of children to see how the system works. Follow your instincts. Schools have different personalities and will likely evoke a response from you on more than just an intellectual level. You want a place where you believe your child will fit in as well as grow and a program you believe can meet its stated goals. Since school becomes a family affair when you have young children, it is also important that you feel the school creates a community of which you would like to be a part. You will find that some places just feel right or can be eliminated because they feel so wrong.

You will probably have other concerns that you will want to explore as you gather information about and visit schools. Remember, the schools want to attract new students as much as you want to find a place for your child. Feel free to ask your questions and do your research as thoroughly as you feel is necessary in order for you to make an informed and reasoned choice.

Preschool

Applying your child to preschool in Manhattan can be a time of great anxiety, especially if this is your first child. There is a lot of hype about the competition and the need to be well connected and rich. Horror stories make the rounds each year about how you and your children will be arbitrarily judged by sadistic school directors and how failure to get into the best preschool will ruin your child's chances of going to a fine ongoing school as well as label you as a social pariah. You will get advice, solicited or not, from many self-proclaimed experts on planning your strategy. Depending on your personal fortitude, you may stay calm or be anxious until notification dates, or you may experience periodic bouts of both.

It is true that the process can be competitive and that there are certain popular schools (which change from year to year!) that are highly sought after. Particularly for toddler programs, there may be more applicants than places. However, there are many excellent programs in the city, and in due course your child will be happily settled into preschool, the application process a distant memory. With this in mind, the most important thing to remember is to keep the focus on what makes sense for your family and child. Remember, first steps are always awkward but are mastered quickly.

▶ **Is it time for school yet?** This is really a question of your personal preference and what you want for your child. Preschool provides an opportunity to develop socialization and separation skills and, depending on the particular preschool program, varying degrees of more academic skills. Attending preschool, however, is not legally mandated, so the decision to attend, or when to attend, is yours. By law, you are not required to have your child attend school until first grade. Most city kids, however, are school veterans by then, having attended one to three years of preschool and kindergarten. Generally, by age three-and-a-half, many city kids are involved in some kind of preschool program.

In Manhattan, the terms preschool and nursery school are used interchangeably and refer to programs for children between the ages of three and five. Toddler or so-called "two's" programs refer to programs that require that the child be two years old before September of the school year in which the child starts school. The exact date by which the child must have turned two years old will vary among programs, but generally, to be considered a toddler program, the children attending will be less than three years old by December of the year in which they begin school. Many, but certainly not all, preschools offer toddler programs. Many children do not attend toddler programs. Even with respect to the preschools that do offer toddler programs, a child is not required to have attended the toddler program in order to get into a preschool class for an older age group.

Toddler programs are designed to accommodate the developmental needs of the very young child and are best for children who are somewhat verbal and comfortable separating from a parent or caregiver. Toddler groups tend to focus on socialization skills, playing and other activities such as singing and arts and crafts. Nursery schools offer many of the same activities but add in activities for older children and may introduce other academic skills such as work with numbers and letters.

There are two typical entry points for preschool: the child either turns three sometime during the school year or the child has already turned three before the school year starts. Depending on where their birthdays lie, the former group will either be in a toddler program or the youngest class in a preschool program. Your decision about when to apply a child to preschool has to do with what age you determine makes the most sense for your child and family.

Planning for a child just leaving infancy, whose needs are constantly changing and whose personality you are just getting to know, is tricky. Be honest with yourself about what you want, what you think your child can handle and will enjoy, and how your family can accommodate the logistics of getting a young child to school in the morning and home at the end of the school day. Remember, there is no right answer, and not every child goes to a toddler group or even nursery school. No matter what you may hear, you need only do what you believe is best for your particular circumstances.

No matter what you may hear, you need only do what you believe is best for your particular circumstances.

▶ **When do I have to start thinking about applying to schools?** The general rule of thumb is that you must apply to a preschool the autumn before the September you want your child to begin school. For example, if you want your child to begin school in September 2004, you start the application process in September 2003. So if you want to apply your child to a toddler program, you will need to start thinking about this when your child is between 12 and 18 months old. To people outside of New York City, it seems ludicrous to have to plan a year ahead for a toddler, but for better or worse, that is the system we have here.

In order to gear up for the application season, you need to begin your own information gathering in advance so that when the time comes, you are ready to roll. Applications for preschool are made available in September of each year for the school year commencing the following September. The application scramble begins the day after Labor Day. Literally. To a large extent, it is this mad dash for applications that causes the most craziness in the process.

Each school handles the distribution of applications differently, although many limit the total number of applications given out in a particular year. As unfair as this may appear, it has become a necessary practice to make the process manageable for the schools due to the large number of families who apply to multiple schools. Schools that limit applications have devised different ways of dealing with the situation. Some schools have a lottery system, others distribute to a limited number of first callers and others give out applications only until a certain date. Still others schedule parents for a limited number of parent open houses at which applications will be distributed.

As a result, parents start working the phones the first Tuesday in September to be sure to get applications to the schools they want to see. For this reason, you and every other interested parent will have to block out a period of time that day or that week to make your request for applications. You may well get a busy signal, but be persistent and you will eventually get through. Schools will be receiving literally hundreds of phone calls, so do not be surprised if they are curt with you. There will be plenty of opportunities to ask questions, so choose your inquiries for this initial contact thoughtfully.

If you are applying to a particular school for a sibling or other type of legacy (for example, the child of a graduate or a child in a family who belongs to the congregation with which the school is affiliated), the application process may be somewhat different. You should clarify the policy and the timetable for obtaining your application, which may be different from that of people with no relationship to the school.

Consequently, we urge you to prepare for the September frenzy by using the spring and summer before you are planning to apply to start your research and think about where you might want to apply. If you have identified schools, you may want to contact them in the spring or over the summer (some have summer camp programs) to ask how they distribute applications so you can be prepared. You do not need to speak to the director to get this information and it is not appropriate to ask to tour the school or meet the director before September.

▶ **Where to begin.** Figuring out what preschools you may want to apply to involves a fair amount of research on your part. Preschools can vary widely in terms of philosophy and implementation of educational concepts. In investigating schools, you will hear terms such as developmental, Montessori, academic and cooperative to describe a school's approach. Finding out what the different labels mean will help make your search easier. As you start to think about beginning this project, it is worth paying a visit to the library or bookstore to do some basic reading on the subject to get yourself comfortable with what is available. The Early Childhood Resource and Information Center (ERIC) - Division of New York Public Libraries has an extensive collection of materials on education as well as other topics related to young children and sponsors seminars and other free programs. It is located at 66 Leroy Street, 2nd floor, New York, NY 10014, 929-0815, or see www.nypl.org/branch/man/ecc.html.

Having mastered the jargon, or at least having become familiar with what to expect in general, it is time to go shopping. Manhattan offers scores of programs, so your next step is to identify preschools in which you think you might be interested.

Most of the preschool programs in Manhattan are private. In Manhattan, certain private schools are also referred to as independent schools. An independent school is a not-for-profit, racially nondiscriminatory institution that has its own board of trustees and is chartered by the New York State Board of Regents. Most independent schools in New York City are members of the Independent Schools Admissions Association of Greater New York (ISAAGNY). ISAAGNY is a not-for-profit organization of admissions directors and heads of schools that, among other things, sets guidelines and coordinates dates for notification of admission to member schools. Independent schools may also be accredited by the New York State Association of Independent Schools or the Middle-States Association of Colleges and Schools.

The term private school can have several meanings. A private school can refer to an independent school that is or is not a member of ISAAGNY or to a school that is owned and operated by an individual or group and is managed as a business enterprise for profit. Knowing whether a school is run as a for-profit or not-for-profit organization is important for evaluating the basis on which schools will be making decisions on everything from curriculum to operating budget. Finally, the term private school is used by many people to refer generically to any school that is not public school.

There are very few public preschools in Manhattan, although pursuant to New York State's Universal Pre-Kindergarten initiative, more public programs are being developed. To find out whether there is a public preschool or toddler program in the school district in which you reside, you can contact your local school district for information. This issue is more fully discussed in the section of this chapter on ongoing public schools.

One of the best places to begin your investigation of private preschool options is with the Parents League of New York, a non-profit organization of parents and independent schools. Each year the Parents League produces two books, *The Toddler Book* and the *New York Independent Schools Directory* (in cooperation with ISAAGNY), which list toddler and preschool programs available in Manhattan. *The Toddler Book* lists not only preschool-style toddler programs and nursery schools that offer toddler programs, but other types of individual classes and programs for all children under the age of three. The *Independent Schools Directory* lists all preschools that are members of ISAAGNY, including those that offer toddler programs. The books contain basic information about the programs included, as well as a brief description of the school prepared by the school itself. In order to purchase these books and gain access to a wealth of additional information and services, you must be a member of the Parents League. You can join the Parents League by calling 737-7385 or writing The Parents League, 115 East 82nd Street, New York, NY 10028 or visiting www.parentsleague.org. Annual dues are a very well spent $85 (or $225 for three-year dues). Note that the Parents League is closed during the summer.

Another written source is *The Manhattan Directory of Private Nursery Schools* by Victoria Goldman and Marcy Braun (Soho Press, 2002). This book contains a description of each school included as well as other useful general information about schools and the application process. It includes a listing of preschools (including both members and non-members of ISAAGNY) and therapeutic and special needs facilities.

The Parents League offers an advisory service to members free of charge. You can meet with a volunteer counselor who can help to focus or narrow your search or sort through information. Advisors are extremely knowledgeable. Although they cannot get your child into a particular school and will not recommend programs, advisors can help you identify schools that address your priorities and needs. The Parents League also offers a number of seminars and lectures on the preschool application process in both the spring and fall, which are enormously valuable for reducing your stress level, providing an opportunity to meet other parents and offering useful information.

The proverbial park bench is always an interesting, albeit relatively unreliable, place to get information on preschools. By keeping your ears open and talking with people who have been through the process, you can gain a great deal of information. But beware. While you might get good tips, you may also get a lot of misinformation, gossip or old news. You simply have to keep in mind that you cannot believe all that you hear. Park bench information is most reliable when it comes from people you know and trust. Even then, however, remember that no matter how much you think you share the same values with another parent, a preschool setting that is terrific for one family can be a disaster for another, or vice versa.

Information you get from other parents is usually subjective, opinionated and often based on hearsay rather than fact. What is specific to one school can be interpreted by the park bench as a general truth for all schools. Conversely, what applies to most schools may not apply to a particular school. As long as you edit what you hear, you will be fine.

What can be useful, however, is to talk to other parents whose children attend a school in which you are interested. Answers to specific questions, such as how many children are in a class, how often parents meet with teachers and how discipline is handled, can typically be relied upon as accurate. If the information is consistent with what you have otherwise learned about the school, then you will have a pretty good idea about how the school operates.

What can be useful, however, is to talk to other parents whose children attend a school in which you are interested.

Another source for finding out about schools is the National Association for the Education of Young Children (NAEYC). NAEYC sponsors an independent, nationwide accrediting system that has been conducted by the National Academy of Early Childhood Programs since 1985. While toddler programs and nursery schools are not required to be accredited in order to operate, those that undertake this step are making a commitment to maintain quality standards and are willing to have an outside body come in and review their program against objective criteria. The process of accreditation takes from 9 to 12 months to complete, so a relatively new program may not be accredited but may still be a very good program. You can get a list of accredited early childhood programs in New York City as well as information on the accreditation process either by visiting www.naeny.org or by contacting NAEYC at 1509 16th Street NW, Washington, DC 20036-1426, 202 232-8777, fax 202 328-1846. NAEYC also publishes materials on what to look for in an early childhood program, which are available free of charge.

There are also a number of private educational consultants who can be hired to help with the application process and advise parents on the various options. Consultants can minimize much of the legwork by supplying information on the different schools and opinions as to their personalities and reputations. The most important service they provide is to help identify the schools that will best meet the family's priorities and the child's needs. The fee for this service can be substantial, but for some families, such as those moving to the city from out of town, it can be the most expedient way to dive into the process. You can obtain a list of consultants in the New York City area by contacting the Independent Educational Consultants Association (IECA), 3251 Old Lee Highway, Suite 510, Fairfax, VA 22030, 703 591-4850 or 800 808-4322, or visiting www.educationalconsulting.org. A number of educational consultants also advertise in the various local parent publications referenced at the end of Chapter 2.

You can obtain lists of early childhood programs licensed by the New York City Department of Health and Mental Hygiene, Bureau of Day Care, by contacting the New York City Department of Health, 2 Lafayette Street, 22nd floor, New York, NY 10007, 676-2444, or www.nyc.gov (see Department of Health/Bureau of Day Care). Note that the programs in this list will include both preschool programs and day care centers. The Department of Health will not separate out a list of preschool programs only.

Using these resources should help you to develop a preliminary list of schools that sound interesting. After making your list and checking it twice, you can relax until September.

▶ **The application process.** Once you have made your September calls to obtain applications, there is nothing to do until the applications begin to arrive. There are no uniform application forms, fees or procedures among preschools, so you need to review each application carefully and make a checklist of what you need to do for each school. Included for your reference is a sample checklist at the end of this chapter. Most applications are due by the end of November and require an application fee (on average between $25 and $60) unless you are applying for financial aid.

Each school will provide some opportunity for you to tour the school, usually with a group of other parents. Some schools have open houses or parent tours for interested parents who have not yet decided whether to apply. Other schools will not schedule a parent tour until an application (with a paid fee) has been filed. At first glance this may seem unfair. However, for many schools it is the only way to limit classroom disruptions for their children and limit the number of shoppers who are more curious than actually serious about applying.

Most, but not all, schools will meet with your child as part of the application process. Meetings will not be arranged until you have submitted your application and fee. Some schools arrange playgroups of several applicants, while others will meet with you and your child individually. When you set up your appointment for a child visit, it is worth asking how the time will be organized so that both you and your child can be prepared.

Parents often ask to how many schools should they apply. While there is no magic formula, nursery school directors observe that for the past several years, six to nine has been the average. The exercise of whittling down your list is useful in working out your priorities.

For schools that are members of ISAAGNY, the application process is completed in late winter. ISAAGNY schools are required to mail admissions decisions on the same date. Parents then have a prescribed time (one week) in which to return a signed contract to the school. During the response period, as parents make their choices, waiting lists are drawn upon. Parents are urged to notify schools as soon as possible of their decisions so that families on the waiting list can be given a place. Schools that are not members of ISAAGNY each have their own notification procedures, which should be confirmed by parents during the application process.

The key to managing the process is organization. Once you have collected applications, done your homework, cut down your list to a reasonable number, filed your applications and scheduled the necessary appointments with each school, you will feel much better—at least until February, when you will start to wonder if there was anything else you could or should have done and did not.

▶ **The inside scoop.** On its face, the process seems relatively straightforward: you investigate, get applications, send in your paperwork, tour the schools, have your child visit the schools and wait for a decision. Then why does applying to nursery school have such a bad rap?

First of all, people are intimidated by the numbers. A typical toddler class has 10 to 15 children. Nursery school classes tend to be between 15 and 24 children (depending on the number of teachers). After accounting for siblings, legacies and, if applicable, congregants, a given school may have very few spaces available.

Second, New Yorkers are competitive by nature. There is a perception that there are certain schools that are better than others. It may be because a school seems to have a lot of celebrity, socialite or wealthy families or to be the first step on the path to elite ongoing schools and even universities. It may be that everyone at the playground you frequent is looking at the same cluster of schools in the neighborhood, which makes it appear that your child is one of multitudes. It may be that people you talk to are bragging about the "ins" they have at various schools, which leaves you feeling like a total outsider.

Third, it may seem that decisions are being made about you and your child on what you may feel is very little information. Your school visit with your child may be less than half an hour in a room with ten other children. You may not have a chance to speak personally to the director for more than a few minutes. You may feel as if you have no impact on the outcome of your child's application.

Fourth, you may feel that you are making an important decision based on too little or confusing information. You will hear that certain schools demand a pedigree while others are more inclusive, that some accept only brilliant children while others are little more than day care centers. It may be hard to reconcile what you see at the school with what you read or hear on the street. You may feel unsure about what would be the best environment for your child.

If you get through the process without being intimidated at least once, you are in the minority. Just remember that you are not the only one living through this—there are many who have gone before you and survived. Weeding through the information you are exposed to during the process, separating fact from fiction, is an art. We can give you a head start by setting the record straight on a few key issues.

◩ **All toddler and preschool programs must be accredited.** False. Toddler and preschool programs must be licensed to do business by the New York City Department of Health and Mental Hygiene's Bureau of Day Care but do not have to either be chartered by the State University of New York Board of Regents, accredited by any independent professional organization such as NAEYC or belong to ISAAGNY.

◩ **Without the right nursery school director, it is impossible to get into an ongoing private school.** False. Nursery school directors are important for a lot of reasons. Most are very helpful when the time comes to apply to another school. However, the degree of involvement of the director in out-placement differs among directors. In nursery schools that are affiliated with ongoing schools, the nursery program director may have a very small role in your search for a new school other than completing a school report that is included in your child's application to another school. At the other end of the spectrum, more proactive directors will actively guide you through the admissions process and school selection.

There is a view that a well-connected director can get your child into the school of your choice. In reality, if a child is not well suited for a particular school but is foisted on that school by the nursery school director, only for the experience to be disastrous later, clearly no one is well served. Certainly the director's recommendation would not hold much credit with future applications. So, despite the appearance that some directors "get" children into certain schools, what you are really seeing is a director who is a good matchmaker. To accomplish that, the director has to know the child and a great deal about the different schools, their philosophies and environments. If hands-on guidance through the application process for ongoing schools is an important issue for you, ask about it during your school tour or interview.

8

◩ **Do feeder schools really exist?** No. Feeder schools were at one time an important tool used by ongoing schools to preselect candidates, but that is no longer the case. Except with respect to some ongoing schools that have preschool or pre-kindergarten programs that feed directly into the ongoing schools, preschools do not have feeder arrangements. Most preschool programs are represented in ongoing schools all over the city. This is not to say that you will not find that several students from the same nursery end up in certain schools each year, which may give the appearance that there is a feeder relationship.

Each spring, schools offer admission to candidates who have been selected for a variety of reasons. Families in turn accept the offered spots based on their own priorities. What often happens is that parents are attracted to particular ongoing schools because of the similarities to their preschool or because they know many families from their preschool who have moved on to that school. Such things as the school's location, familiar philosophy and the desire to have siblings and friends attend the same school can influence families from a preschool to attend certain ongoing schools.

Additionally, there are preschool directors who have developed relationships with many of the ongoing schools and can be relied on by admissions directors to identify appropriate candidates for their schools. While nursery school directors do not determine who will be admitted to kindergarten, they can provide a comprehensive picture of an applicant that the ongoing school can assume, based on experience, is an accurate assessment of the child. This historical perspective provided by the nursery school allows the ongoing admissions director better to determine whether or not the child is a good match for the school.

◩ **Children are given intelligence tests during their visits.** False. There is no end of speculation as to what the school staff could possibly be looking for during a child's visit. Most people are convinced that their child is being administered some version of an IQ test. Each school is different, but basically what really goes on, you will be relieved to hear, has little to do with intelligence testing. Some schools do look for developmentally and age-appropriate skill levels, but for the most part the emphasis is on the following: the ability to engage in activities, verbal ability, interaction between parent and child and the general level of comfort of the child when dealing with adults other than a parent.

◩ **A disastrous interview means your chances are shot.** Not necessarily. You bring your bright, adorable, loquacious child to the interview. He or she drops to the floor, dissolves into screams, refuses to take off his or her coat and spits at the teacher. Alternatively, your otherwise outgoing child holds on to your leg for dear life and does not say a word or lift a crayon. You see your child's opportunity to get into this school evaporate. Do not despair. Whatever your child does, it is probably not the first time the teachers or directors have seen it. They are well trained and can usually read the situation objectively. If there are any extenuating circumstances (ear infection, a parent out of town on a business trip, a sleepless night), be sure to explain them. If possible, ask whether you can try again. You may want to send a note to the director about the incident. Do not be defensive, just be honest. It is sometimes possible to avoid a disaster by preparing your child for the visit by explaining in advance what will happen. Also, if your child is ill, reschedule the interview. Finally, the more relaxed you are, the more relaxed your child will be in a new environment.

◩ **Do you need connections to get into preschool?** No. There is no dearth of connected people in Manhattan. But who you know is not necessarily an ace in the hole when it comes to applying to preschool. When using connections, use the ones that matter when they matter. If connections are used well, they can have a positive impact. First, do not ask some VIP who has little relationship to your child or family to write or call on your behalf. In this context, your connection will have little influence, and the effort may do little more than entertain the staff. It is more meaningful to have a person who knows your family well and who is very connected to the school support your application, even if the person is not a luminary. Second, do not ask someone to "put in a good word" for you unless you are really interested in the school. It is awkward for everyone involved if the individual, perhaps a board member, recommends your child and then you decline the offer of a spot.

For those of you without connections, panic not. Nursery schools consider many things when putting together classes. The next best thing to a connection is a sincere, genuine letter that lets the director know the school is your first choice. Remember though, first choice is first choice. Sending more than one such letter is likely to reduce your options, not secure one.

◩ **Chaos is creativity.** False. The type of school environment that you find appealing is a matter of personal preference. According to NAEYC, a good program "provides appropriate and sufficient equipment and play material and makes them readily available" and is "spacious enough to accommodate a variety of activities and equipment. Most importantly, the facility should be safe for all children and adults." Many adults have a hard time understanding how children play, so when they see chaos, they interpret it as an expression of free-flowing creativity. While small children are by nature not very neat when they play and while many activities certainly leave their impression behind on faces, hands and clothing, a classroom that appears to be a scene from a natural disaster is probably not a well-organized room. The major task for preschoolers is to make sense of the world around them and learn to get along with others. Without a routine, consistent rules gently applied, a safe environment and nurturing, interested adults around them, it is a difficult task to achieve.

Getting on a waiting list is the same as being rejected. False. If the admissions process were perfect, everyone would get into their first choice school. Since it is not perfect, there will be families who find themselves with limited or perhaps no choices and for whom the result of months of work and worrying is disappointment and despair. The prospect of such an outcome is what creates all of the anxiety in the first place.

So, where do you turn? How do you regroup? Understand that the wait lists exist because there is a lot of movement in the period between the notification date and the date by which parents must return a signed contract. Your first step should be to call and notify schools that have waitlisted your child as to whether or not you want to remain on the wait list. If not, your spot can be given to someone else. For those schools where you want to stay on the wait list, discuss with the director your options and how to proceed. Schools will let you know when to call back, the anticipated timeframe for giving you an answer and the likelihood that there will be movement on their list. As crazed as you may feel, make sure to stay calm This is definitely the time when being a squeaky wheel does not help the situation. An attentive, cooperative parent is appreciated. Let the director know, by phone or in writing, your level of interest in the school.

If your child has not been accepted or waitlisted by any school, you might consider consulting the Parents League advisory service.

Advisors can be very helpful. The Parents League keeps a list of ISAAGNY schools that still have openings at the conclusion of the formal admissions process. Parents League advisors can also assist families that move to the city after the admission process has been completed. Keep in mind that you must join the Parents League to use the advisory service and that the Parents League offices are closed during July and August.

Though not every family is offered a spot at its first choice school, very few find themselves without any alternatives. For many families, the wait list is the answer to finding a place at the first choice school. You simply have to have patience and nerves of steel.

▶ **On to nursery school you go.** Come that first day, when you and your child head off to school, the memory of the prior year's tribulations will fade. Not to worry though, you will have the opportunity to do it all again when it is time for kindergarten.

Ongoing Private Schools

There are many nonpublic elementary schools from which to choose in Manhattan. There are coeducational and single-sex schools, schools that emphasize foreign languages, schools with religious affiliations, schools that end at sixth, eighth or twelfth grades, schools with campuses outside the city, large and small schools, schools for children with disabilities and schools with every imaginable type of philosophy.

If you have already survived preschool applications and your child is attending a preschool program, the process of applying to ongoing schools is somewhat familiar. You probably know many more families with children in different schools and have some ideas, even if only vague ones, about some schools. You also know a lot more about your child and may have some views as to the type of school you think might suit him or her.

Unfortunately, even with a few more years of parenting experience, the process is no less threatening, because for some reason the stakes seem higher. Because private schools require some testing and an interview as part of the admissions procedure, parents often become anxious over their child's performance and worry that the child will not qualify for admission to a school of their choice.

Ongoing school seems much more serious than preschool. The decision feels more monumental—you are making a commitment to a school potentially for 13 years. While your child is there, he or she will be building foundational skills for a lifetime, not to mention developing social skills and friendships and going through adolescence.

It is important to remember throughout the process that while you are making an important decision for your child when you choose a school, it is not an irrevocable one. Many students change schools during the elementary school years; in fact, there is a great deal of movement at middle and upper school entry points (sixth, seventh and ninth grades). If the school your child starts at turns out to be the wrong choice or becomes inappropriate over time, it is more than possible to transfer to another school. So take a deep breath and dive in.

Applying to ongoing schools is a major undertaking, but as with preschool applications, there are three keys to getting through application season intact: do your research early and thoroughly, submit your applications and complete your school visits in a timely fashion, and stay organized. Though the process may seem overwhelming, and your child's future seems to be dependent on how well you perform this task, in the end your efforts will pay off and you will find an acceptance to school in the mail come March.

▶ **Getting Started.** Applications for ongoing schools become available in September for admission for the following school year. Unfortunately, whereas the post–Labor Day frenzy experienced for getting nursery school applications did not used to apply to the ongoing school application process, application mania has now spread to ongoing schools as well. As the number of applicants for kindergarten spots has increased in recent years, ongoing school applications can no longer be requested on a more relaxed timetable during the early autumn. In fact, the mad dash for applications begins in the first days of September (in some cases even before Labor Day) and some schools, faced with a deluge of requests, have begun to limit the number of applications sent out to families (or the number of applicants given interviews).

For parents applying their children for kindergarten, a tricky issue is making sure that your child is eligible to apply under the birthday cutoff for the school. In general, most private schools require that the child be five years old sometime between September 1 and December 1 of the year he or she begins kindergarten. Each school will have an exact cutoff date.

Notwithstanding the official birthday cutoff, some schools hesitate to accept children who will turn five on the eve of the cutoff date, preferring that children with birthdays close to the cutoff wait another year before entering kindergarten. For such children, it is vital to consider the child's developmental readiness for kindergarten in addition to technical cutoff dates before proceeding with an application. This is an area where a good nursery school director can guide you well.

Another wrinkle in the process develops if you are interested in an ongoing school that has a preschool or pre-kindergarten class. Such schools tend to draw their kindergarteners primarily from their preschools and so may have very few spaces for children applying from elsewhere. If you have think you may be interested in one of these schools, you may want to consider moving your child during preschool so that he or she can continue on at the ongoing school. In such a case, you would have to time your application so that you are applying to the school for the final year(s) of preschool rather than for the kindergarten year.

As a general rule, you will begin looking at ongoing schools in September of the school year in which your child: is four and turns five if he or she will do so after December 1 of such school year (so that your child will begin kindergarten at age five+); or turns four if he or she will do so prior to December 1 of such school year (so that your child will turn five before December 1 of the kindergarten year). Children in the latter group often wait a year before applying to kindergarten so that they will turn six during the first semester of kindergarten.

As with the preschool application process, it is worth spending some time over the spring or summer before you begin applying to gather information about schools and identify schools to which you might want to apply. You may want to contact school admissions offices in the spring to find out whether the school offers spring tours and to clarify when applications will be available, so that when September arrives you do not miss the chance to get one. Be aware, too, that schools do have application deadlines, some as early as the end of October, so it is important to pay attention to the calendar. Once applications are in, you will have the opportunity to visit the schools and the schools will have an opportunity to meet and observe your child.

▶ **Reading, writing and research.** To review, a private school can refer to any of the following institutions: an independent school that is not-for-profit, racially nondiscriminatory, has its own board of trustees and is chartered by the New York State Board of Regents; a school with a religious affiliation; or a privately owned for-profit institution. Most, but not all New York City independent schools are members of ISAAGNY. Private schools are not required to be chartered by the New York State Board of Regents to operate.

An easy place to begin your research is with a good book or two. Doing some reading early on will help you get the lay of the land and create a list of schools that are worth further investigation. The *New York Independent Schools Directory* is an annual publication of ISAAGNY with the cooperation of the Parents League and is available from the Parents League. Each member school prepares a brief statement about itself for inclusion in the book, which also contains general information about the application process for ISAAGNY schools.

The Manhattan Family Guide to Private Schools, Fourth Edition, by Catherine Hausman and Victoria Goldman (Soho Press, 2001), is another guide to private schools. This book contains basic information about the application process, testing and financial aid, as well as descriptions prepared by the authors of more than 70 private schools. This book looks at ISAAGNY member schools as well as non-ISAAGNY schools. It also discusses educational consultants, lists special needs schools and provides information about certain public school options.

The Parents League is a valuable general resource, hosting an annual forum in the early fall (open to the general public) at which the application process is discussed. The Parents League also sponsors Independent School Day at which you will have the opportunity to speak with admissions directors from ISAAGNY schools as well as to pick up brochures and application materials. Although Independent School Day, usually held in a school gymnasium, is hectic and crowded with anxious parents, it is an easy way to pick up literature about different schools, ask basic questions about admissions (deadlines, birthday cutoff, etc.), find out about open houses and arrange to get applications if they are not available at the event.

The Parents League also offers a school advisory service to members free of charge. You can meet privately with a volunteer advisor who can provide unbiased and accurate information about schools and help guide you through the process.

Early Steps, a program whose goal is to promote racial diversity within ISAAGNY schools, can be another resource for learning about schools for families of color. To fulfill its mission, Early Steps offers informational workshops and seminars on issues related to students of color attending independent schools and provides counseling, referrals and assistance to families of color throughout the independent schools admissions process. Each autumn, Early Steps sponsors a school fair at which families can meet admissions directors from participating schools. You can reach Early Steps at 540 East 76th Street, New York, NY 10021, 288-9684.

If your child is in preschool, the preschool director is likely to be a major source of assistance through the process. Most directors are available in the fall to discuss ongoing schools and provide direction and suggestions. Many preschools arrange individual conferences to discuss the application process, help you with your application strategy, review your child's test results and recommend schools where the director feels your child will fare well and has a good shot of getting admitted. The degree of involvement, however, differs from director to director, and especially if your preschool is part of an ongoing school program, the director may not get actively involved in your search.

Whatever his or her approach, the nursery school director will be required to prepare a confidential school report about your child, which will constitute a portion of his or her application to ongoing school. Although a copy of this report is not made available to parents, its contents are relevant to your child's application, and, accordingly, most directors will discuss its general thrust with parents.

Attending open houses and tours conducted by individual schools is another excellent way to learn about schools. Open houses are often held in the evening and consist of a presentation by admissions directors with a question and answer period. Some schools have parents, principals and/or the headmaster either speak or be available to answer questions at the event. Tours are conducted either in conjunction with an open house or at separate times. Some schools require that an application be filed before you can tour the school. Most schools do not offer opportunities to visit until the autumn, although some schools do arrange spring tours for families interested in applying during the next school year.

You can also get a great deal of information from other parents who have first-hand knowledge about particular schools. As we discussed in the context of the preschool application process, you may as well listen to all the park bench talk, but do not take it as gospel. Schools evolve and change over time, but reputations are often slower to change and old stories can remain in circulation long after the facts have changed. More important, most families tend to be happy where they are and promote their schools, while families who have had negative personal experiences with a school may be hard pressed to find anything good to say about it.

Some parents elect to use private educational consultants to assist them with the application process. Fees can be hefty, and if you have a good preschool director and no anticipated or unusual problems with your child's application, you do not need this service. You can obtain a list of educational consultants from the Independent Educational Consultants Association, 3251 Old Lee Highway, Suite 510, Fairfax, VA 22030, 703 591-4850 or 800 808-4322, www.educationalconsulting.org. A list of educational consultants can be found in *The Manhattan Family Guide to Private Schools*, and a number of consultants advertise in the local parent publications referenced at the end of Chapter 2.

Private consultants can be enormously useful if your child has not attended preschool, if you are applying to schools outside of the mainstream timetable, if you are coming to Manhattan from out of town and do not know where to start or if you are conducting your search from outside the city.

Once you have done your homework, you will begin to submit applications and proceed through the process. While it used to be a rule of thumb for families to apply to between four and six schools, in recent years there has been a dramatic increase in the number of schools to which families apply, to between eight and ten schools. The reasons behind this increase are not entirely clear. Some admissions directors note that the absolute number of applicants has grown due to a confluence of demographic factors, including a purported bulge in the population of young children (while the number of school places has remained constant), an increase in the number of families choosing to stay in the city (rather than heading for the suburbs) and a lack of spaces in premiere public school programs. It is best to consult with your preschool director for a recommendation as to an appropriate number of schools to which you should apply. Whatever the final number, you can be certain that you will likely have looked at many schools to come down to your final list.

▶ **Applications 'R' Us.** Although each school designs its own application process, there are some basic similarities among private schools. Each school will have a written application and application fee (on average, around $50–60); require your child to be tested (the infamous ERBs, more about this later!); require either an interview with or observation of your child; give parents an opportunity to visit the school; and require a school report from the preschool(s) attended by your child.

◩ **Written Applications.** The application may simply require basic data about your child and family such as address, birthdays, parents' educational background and occupations, ages and schools of siblings and names of preschools attended by your child. Some parents ask whether applications should be typed. The answer to this is simple: whatever feels more like you. If you choose not to type, make sure to print clearly. The application fee is typically required in order to proceed with the process unless you are applying for financial aid, in which case the fee may be waived or reduced.

Some schools require you to write essays about your child and/or submit letters of recommendation. If an essay is required, the school is looking for a picture of your child that is consistent with other aspects of his or her application (school report, test results) as well as your personal impressions. It is important to communicate your understanding of the school, its philosophy and why you think it would work for your child. Do not try to fake this. Make sure to read the school brochure or review the notes of your tour or school visit carefully.

Recommendations, when required, should be from someone who knows you and your family. A letter from the president of the United States is impressive, but unless the letter communicates a relationship with your family and knowledge about your child, it does not serve its purpose. The best letters are well written and present an objective and detailed view of the child. Obviously, it is also helpful if the writer has some connection to the school.

◩ **Testing.** ERB. How can three letters make so many so nervous? ERB does not actually refer to a test, but to the Educational Records Bureau, a not-for-profit national organization that administers and interprets many types of testing for children in the United States and abroad. Since 1966, ERB has been the testing agency for ISAAGNY. ISAAGNY schools have agreed to use the WPPSI-R (the Wechsler Preschool and Primary Scale of Intelligence test, pronounced "whip-see") for pre-K, kindergarten and first grade applicants and other specific tests for applicants to higher grades. The cost of the test is $315, although financial aid is available. Non-ISAAGNY schools may require a different or additional test, which may or may not be administered by ERB. Be sure to get exact requirements for testing from each such school to which you apply.

The WPPSI-R is divided into two components, verbal and nonverbal. The former looks at general knowledge, vocabulary, comprehension and simple math skills. The latter looks at block design, assembly, and completion of mazes and pictures. The test takes about one hour and is scored in percentiles against a national sample of children of the same age. Most educators agree that the test is not accurate in predicting long-term academic success but is useful as providing a snapshot in time of development. The test is administered by psychologists, either on-site at certain nursery schools, at the ERB offices or at other authorized test sites.

Most children take the ERBs in the fall of the school year in which they are applying (for example, the test is taken between September and November 2003 for application to kindergarten for September 2004). However, there has been a recent trend, encouraged by the ERB, for children to take the ERBs in the prior spring or summer (for example, the test is taken between May and August 2003 for application to kindergarten for September 2004). Since the test is scored on a developmental scale in which a child is compared with his or her exact age group within the general population, there is no advantage to waiting until the child is older to take the test. The ERB notes that test appointments are easier to book in the spring and that there is less postponement of testing due to fall colds and flu. It is best to confer with your nursery school director for guidance on timing your child's test.

While professionals insist that it is not necessary to prepare or coach your child for the ERBs, many parents and some nursery schools work with their children in advance of the test. Note, however, that extreme or intensive coaching for the test may be obvious to a tester, who will so indicate in the test report, potentially compromising the child's test results in the eyes of an ongoing school admissions director. Whatever path you follow, the most important thing is for your child to feel comfortable and natural during the testing period. The more relaxed you are, the more relaxed your child will be. Be careful not to send your child the message that something major is at stake for which you feel he or she is responsible or not prepared. However your child does on the ERB, remember that these scores are not etched in stone and may indeed change substantially over time. If you are anxious, you can schedule a private consultation with ERB to discuss your child's test at a cost of $250. You can contact ERB at 220 East 42nd Street, New York, NY 10017, 672-9800, www.erbtest.org.

◩ **Interviews.** There is no standardized procedure for interviews. Each school has its own system. Some schools meet with your child individually, while others have several children together at the same time with more than one school representative, faculty or admissions personnel in the room. While your child is having his or her interview, you may be meeting individually or in a group with other parents with an admissions officer or having a school tour. In some cases, the school will send an admissions officer or teacher to observe your child at his or her nursery school.

To some degree the method chosen may tell you something about what the school thinks is important. For example, a school that meets the parents of each family separately and interviews the children in groups might feel that knowing a bit more about the parents helps round out their picture of the child. On the other hand, some schools are less focused on the parents, touring them in groups and spending quality time with each child. Whatever the case, do not read too much into the system, as it may have more to do with the size of the admissions staff or school tradition than anything else.

Most parents are very curious as to what the school is interested in finding out during the child's interview. Some schools simply observe the child in a social setting. Others provide children with different tasks to complete, and some administer their own skills assessment test. The school also is looking at whether its impression of the child is consistent with other parts of the application, especially the nursery school report and test results. Regardless of what specifically is being looked at, you have to place some faith in the fact that each school is trying to make a successful match between school and student.

Parents tend to become very anxious about interviews. It is crucial to stay calm and not scare your child. Here are some tips to keep in mind. If your child is fussy about clothing, make sure he or she wears something comfortable and that he or she likes. There is no point putting on party clothes if your child will be miserable. Find out what will happen and prepare your child, especially if your child will be required to separate from you. Make the process interesting rather than serious. Depending on what your child can handle, you can let your child understand that you are looking at schools, but try not to make him or her feel that you will be angry if he or she does not perform well.

One last thought on the subject. As much as you want to present your family in the best light to the admissions personnel, they truly want you to walk away liking their school. Both sides are under a lot of pressure to make the experience a good one.

◩ **Parent visits.** Again, there is no formula for how parent visits are handled. Some schools have open houses early in the fall that are open to the public. These are worth attending because the information provided and the atmosphere at an open house can offer you a sense of the school that cannot be conveyed in printed materials. Some schools have full-blown tours for parents who are deciding whether to apply as well as those who have applied. Individual or group tours may be given by admissions personnel or parent volunteers. Finally, aside from tours or open houses, some schools arrange private meetings with parents, which may be informational or more in the nature of an interview. Your child's visit may occur at the same time as your visit or at a totally separate time. We advise that you take every opportunity available to go back to schools in which you are interested. At each visit you may see something different or hear information, or other parents' questions answered, that may help form your opinion about the school.

◩ **Nursery school report.** The report provided by your nursery school director to ongoing schools will contain a checklist of social, emotional, cognitive and physical achievements of your child. It will also contain information about the parents, such as your tuition payment record, issues that may have arisen while your child was at the school, and your financial support of the school. The report is confidential so as to preserve the director's ability to speak freely. Although you will not get a copy of the report as filed, most directors will review their report in general terms because what the report says about your child is relevant to your choice of schools. Most directors will alert you to issues about your child raised in the report that may affect an application.

▶ **Keeping track.** The application process has a number of steps and deadlines, so it is necessary to keep organized. You may want to carve out some shelf or file space or buy an accordion folder or notebook with pockets to keep your information on each school in order, designating one calendar to be used to note deadlines and appointments. Some suggestions on keeping track:

◩ **Important dates.** Make sure to note application deadlines. Most schools have deadlines in October, November or December for filing a written application, which includes the fee and any parent essays. Typically, letters of recommendation, school reports and ERB scores follow under separate cover, with the completion of the entire package, including any requisite interviews, required by the end of January or early February. Make sure to consult each school's materials to confirm all deadlines.

◩ **ERBs and interviews.** If the ERB is administered at your nursery school, consult the director about any scheduling or timing issues. You will not need to schedule the appointment but you will have to send in your check to ERB before the test can be administered. If your school does not arrange testing on-site, contact ERB to schedule an appointment.

You will need to call each school to which you have applied to arrange tours and interviews as required by that school. Be sure to confirm the time and date and who is expected to attend (one or both parents). If you need to send your child to an appointment with a caregiver, make sure that this will not be a problem, as schools expect to see parents whenever possible. As soon as you become aware of a scheduling conflict, call to reschedule. Changing your appointment on a whim is not recommended, but if you must reschedule, do it as early as possible as appointments get filled very quickly.

There is some debate about how to time ERBs and school interviews. By and large, strategies are not terribly meaningful, absent extenuating circumstances. For example, you would not want to schedule for the week you expect to bring home a new baby or are settling into a new apartment. It is best not to pick a week when you or your spouse will be out of town or returning from a trip (if this is upsetting to your child), have houseguests or expect any other life-disrupting event to occur. If at all possible, try to arrange appointments for times of day when your child is at his or her best, even if it means missing a day of preschool, and try to avoid scheduling during an activity your child loves and will resent missing (such as a favorite gym class). If an appointment is scheduled for a meal or nap time, try to feed your child or carve out rest time before the appointment.

◩ **A complete application.** A completed application consists of the written application, recommendations if required, ERB scores, school report, and interviews. For your files, you should retain a photocopy of all materials you send to each school so that anything lost in the mail or at a school is easily replaced. It is also wise not to leave to chance any piece of the application sent independently of the written form. Give the nursery school a list of the schools to which you are applying and make sure to confirm that reports have been sent to each school. You will need to provide a written list to ERB as to where to send scores. There is no charge for sending out scores to five schools. There is a $3 charge for each additional report. You should then confirm with each ongoing school that it has received a school report and ERB report as well as anything else it is to receive from third parties.

In advance of the final application deadline, be sure to call the school to confirm that there is nothing outstanding. You may want to consider writing a thank you note to the admissions person with whom you met during your visit to the school. A note provides an opportunity to reflect on what you saw and your impressions. If you really have one, you may also want to write a sincere letter to your first choice school indicating that it is your first choice. Such letters are taken seriously by the schools and are best when written from the heart, expressing your reasons for making such a decision.

◩ **The waiting game.** Once you have reviewed your checklist not once but twice, you can take a deep breath and know that you have done all that could have been done. ISAAGNY schools must mail out admissions decisions on the same date. Families receiving an acceptance have a certain period (currently one week) to return a signed contract to the school. During this period, the wait lists move and many spaces open up. We urge parents who receive multiple acceptances to contact schools as early as possible so that other families have an opportunity to get a place before the end of the decision period. You should confirm notification dates with non-ISAAGNY schools.

If you have the good fortune to have a choice of schools, you may well find yourself in a quandary when it comes time to pick. Most schools have an open house for parents whose children have been accepted right after the notification date. At these events you will have a chance to meet other parents and school personnel. At some schools the kindergarten teachers are available to answer questions. If you are still unsure, you can usually arrange to meet with an admissions officer and visit kindergarten classes. This is the time to rely on your instincts about what you think will be the best match.

While you are waiting to find out where your child will be going the next school year, your anxiety level may rise. Keep in mind the following. No one piece of the application is inherently more important than the others. Schools are looking for a consistent picture of your child. If the school report, ERB and interview all present the same story, so much the better. If one piece of the picture is out of whack, do not panic. Many outstanding students had meltdowns on their interviews or ERBs that were not up to their usual levels of performance and still got into their first choice schools. With the myriad choices in Manhattan, there is almost always a place for every child whose family is looking for one.

▶ **Other Stuff.** There are a few other items worthy of mention regarding the admissions process. Some may apply to you; others will not. Keep in mind that if you have questions during the process, you should contact admissions personnel at the schools directly. The admissions office should not be considered untouchable. If you have a question, call. More often than not you will be addressed by a warm and approachable individual. If you have the misfortune to reach someone within the department who is less than enthusiastic, basically uninformative or otherwise seems bothered by you, keep in mind that the person is fielding many calls, is not superhuman and can have a bad day too.

◪ **Siblings and legacy applicants.** Siblings of current students and legacies (relatives of an alumnus or persons with another relationship to the school) may have different application procedures. ISAAGNY schools have an early notification policy for legacies under which families will be notified about a month in advance of the regular notification date. If you accept a place under the early notification policy, you are required to withdraw applications pending at other ISAAGNY schools. Participation in the early notification program is optional.

◪ **Transferring schools.** The decision to transfer your child from one school to another can be very smooth or very rough, depending on the situation. Where the decision was reached by mutual agreement on the best course of action for the child, school administrators at the school the child currently attends can be helpful in selecting a school that would be more appropriate.

If you have initiated the move because of problems with the school, the situation may be awkward. Because the current school must send a school report to other schools to which you are applying, your search cannot be kept secret for very long. If the school has initiated the move, you may feel angry, frustrated and resentful. However, in order for you to find another school for your child you need to be as objective as possible while remaining your child's advocate.

Whatever the impetus for a transfer, you can make it less complicated by maintaining a professional relationship with your child's current school and taking advantage of whatever resources—principal, faculty, psychologist, admissions office—the school can offer you in finding the right place for your child.

If you are applying to transfer to a new school where your child will attend first grade, ISAAGNY schools follow the same procedures as for kindergarten admissions, including a common notification date and response period. For transfers into second grade and up, ISAAGNY schools will use tests administered by ERB, but notification dates are at the schools' discretion, with a common outside date for responses. Many schools have rolling admissions for transfers. Because available spaces in higher grades may be filled quickly, it is advisable to begin the process as soon as possible in the school year.

Applying to schools on a different timetable. If you find yourself scheduled to move to New York City without sufficient notice to go through the standard admissions process timetable, do not fear. You will still be able to find a place for your children to go to school. Though to a certain extent there is something to be said for bypassing the six-month admissions experience and finding a school on an abbreviated schedule, not having an acceptance in hand can make a big move more stressful.

How to proceed is dependent on several factors: where schools are in the admissions process when you begin your search, when you will actually be moving into the city (mid-year is the hardest), and how easily you can bring your children into town for interviews and/or testing. Your knowledge of the schools is important, so if you are unfamiliar with New York City schools, it is wise to get the books describing the different schools so you have an idea of where you want to focus your efforts. You can contact the Parents League for assistance and advisory services. The Parents League can usually tell you which ISAAGNY schools have open spaces.

You may want to call upon a professional consultant, who can often be very helpful in directing your search, finding out which schools have places available and making all of the calls and appointments for you. These services can be well worth the money, particularly when you are under a time constraint and out of town. In some situations, your employer may pick up the fees of a school consultant as part of a relocation benefits package. Before you hire a consultant, clarify what services are included in the fee. Remember, no one can legitimately promise you a spot in an independent school.

If you elect to proceed on your own, contact any school to which you want to apply. The admissions director can tell you whether there are any spaces and how to proceed with an application. It is essential to keep accurate notes because each school will have a different procedure. This task is not impossible, but it is hard work.

Financial Aid. Admission to independent schools is made without regard to a family's financial situation. However, an admission is not automatically accompanied by a financial aid package. You must separately apply to each school for assistance where decisions will be made by a scholarship committee.

If you are applying for financial aid in connection with an application to an independent school, the school will send you a Parent Financial Statement (PFS), which is prepared by the School and Student Service (SSS), a organization that is affiliated with the National Association of Independent Schools and that is administered by the Educational Testing Service (ETS) in Princeton, New Jersey. Although you will receive a PFS from each school, you need complete only one. The PFS is comprehensive and requires you to submit certain backup information, so follow directions carefully. You will need to provide ETS with a list of schools to which your report should be sent. Be sure to include yourself on the list of recipients, as this will be your only opportunity to review the information for accuracy.

The SSS will process your PFS according to national guidelines for families sending children to independent schools. The report will include a recommendation as to what SSS determines the family can pay in tuition. Schools receiving the report may adjust the recommendation to account for the local cost of living. The SSS may see your financial situation very differently from how you do. You may consider sending a personal account of your circumstances to individual schools to assist them in evaluating your situation and how you expect your needs to change over time (e.g., a parent who expects to return to work).

Although the financial aid application process is somewhat simplified by use of the PFS, individual schools may ask for additional information, and each will have its own deadlines. A school will also have its own philosophy for awarding scholarships and allocating funds available for this purpose. There may appear to be little rhyme or reason to a school's decision process, but if your efforts pay off and you receive a much-needed scholarship, consider the sacrifices you make for your child to receive a private education well rewarded.

◪ **Connections.** Connections can be of significance or they may not have any influence on an application. There is no denying that if a school board member has a niece or nephew applying to the school, a call to the admissions director will be meaningful. In some cases children will be admitted on this basis. However, when the school does not select a child on the basis of the criteria it has established to ensure a good match between school and child, no one is well served. For this reason, few schools allow connections to be the paramount determining factor. This is not to say that if there are two candidates of equal merit and one has a letter or call supporting the application from a person important to the school that that child will not have an advantage. So what kind of connection is a good one? A family member, alumnus, teacher, board member or anyone else affiliated with the school who knows you and your child well. A letter or call from such a person can sometimes make a difference.

Ongoing Public School

The New York City public school system serves in excess of one million children. Unfortunately, within the system there are individual schools where children pass through metal detectors to be taught in overcrowded classrooms by underqualified teachers. But that is only part of the story. In addition to many fine, clean and decently equipped neighborhood schools, the public school system also contains schools and programs that are on the cutting edge of what is exciting and modern in education. You may be among the lucky families zoned for one of the better schools or you may have to do some digging to find one, but in either case, public school is certainly a viable educational alternative. And you cannot beat the price.

▶ **A system in transition.** Upon taking office in 2002, Mayor Michael R. Bloomberg began the process of effecting major educational reform and transforming the public school system. With the administration of the entire system now lodged in the Department of Education of the City of New York (DOE), which is under the jurisdiction of the Mayor's office, a wholesale overhaul of the organization and structure of the educational bureaucracy has commenced. The intention behind the reorganization is to create a "single, coherent system-wide approach" to instruction, unify and streamline the management of the school system and institute new parent support systems.

To implement the plan, some basic changes have been made to the structure of the system, the most important of which is the consolidation of the 40 existing community school districts into 10 Instructional Divisions, each of which is led by a Regional Superintendent. While the Regional Superintendents will be based primarily in the DOE headquarters in downtown Manhattan's Tweed Building, there will also be offices in 10 newly created Learning Support Centers located in 13 different sites (some Instructional Divisions will have more than one Learning Support Center) throughout the city. The Learning Support Centers will house both instructional leadership teams and Parent Support Offices. Some offices will also house Operations Centers.

In connection with this reorganization, the 40 existing community school district superintendents and boards have been eliminated and the office space that they occupied within various school buildings is being converted to classroom space. Although the district governance structure is essentially gone, for organizational purposes, there will continue to be school "districts" covering the same geographical regions as before the reorganization, although they will now be under the jurisdiction of the Instructional Divisions. It is also contemplated that some type of "parent engagement boards" will probably be created to replace the old community school boards.

Please note that as of the date of this writing, administrative regulations sorting out the details of the new structure have not been finalized, and the exact locations and contact information (office addresses and phone numbers) for the Regional Superintendents, Learning Support Centers and other new entities and divisions have not been released to the public. What is known thus far however, is that Manhattan will be within Instructional Divisions 9 (covering community school districts 1, 2, 4 and 7) and 10 (covering community school districts 3, 5, and 6). It is expected that final information will be available to the public on the DOE website, www.nycenet.edu by the summer of 2003.

In addition to local changes to the public school system, New York City public schools are also subject to the provisions of the federal No Child Left Behind Act of 2001 (NCLB). Under this law, parents whose children attend schools that have been identified as needing improvement have the right either to send their children to better performing public schools or to remain where they are and receive supplemental educational services. For New York City parents, this means that children requiring placement under NCLB must have priority over all other students with respect to transfers to schools within the system. Also, in response to NCLB, DOE has centralized the transfer process (more about this below) for the entire school system to the Office of Zoning and Student Placement.

▶ **The basics.** As of the date of this printing, the six school districts in Manhattan are still in place but are now under the jurisdiction of Instructional Divisions 9 and 10. Each district contains approximately 15 to 20 schools on the elementary and junior high school levels. Each school serves a specifically bounded geographical area called a zone (formerly known as a catchment area). By law you are entitled to send your child to the school closest to your home that is in your school zone. On occasion, the school nearest to your home may not actually be in the school zone in which you live. If the school for which you are zoned does not have space for your child, the DOE is responsible for finding a place in another school that is within an acceptable distance from your home.

Students typically enroll for school the spring before the September that they will begin attending school. If your child will be attending the school in your zone, there is no application process, you simply register your child. The birthday cutoff for kindergarten in public schools is December 31. In other words, your child must turn five by December 31 of the year he or she is in kindergarten.

Under a school choice policy (sometimes referred to as the parent choice policy), parents have the opportunity to seek to transfer their child from the school for which the child is zoned to a school that is either outside of the zone but within the same district or outside of the district altogether. Note that students entitled to transfers under NCLB have priority over students seeking transfers under the school choice policy. You can get specific information about the transfer policy (and copies of Regulations A-101, A-180 and A-181, which set forth the policy) by contacting the Office of Zoning and Student Placement at 374-5426 or visiting www.nycenet.edu.

Depending on the school or particular program within a school to which you are applying, the application process can range from filing the right paperwork to requiring the testing of your child or an interview with you or your child.

In order to take advantage of the school choice policy, you must apply to the school (or program within a particular school) or schools in which you are interested. Depending on the school or particular program within a school to which you are applying, the application process can range from filing the right paperwork to requiring the testing of your child or an interview with you or your child.

This is where things get complicated, because the application and admission process for the various programs and schools is not uniform. Worse still, there is no handbook or other publication that lists all of the schools that accept students from outside the zone or district or explains their application procedures or admissions policies, although some districts do have written material about programs within the district. Each district, and in many cases each school, has its own rules, deadlines, procedures and admissions criteria. Unlike the admissions process for ISAAGNY schools, public schools have no common notification dates and response periods for acceptances, although programs for gifted and talented students often time their notification to that of ISAAGNY schools. Because there are no citywide timetables for admissions and a great deal happens on a first come, first served basis, it is wise to begin your investigations early in September of the year before your child will begin kindergarten.

If you have opted to apply to a school outside of your zone, once your child has been accepted, you need to effect the "transfer" out of the school for which your child was zoned (even if your child never attended the zoned school) and into the school of choice. For a transfer to another school within your district or to a school in another district, you must obtain a "variance" (see below). If your child attends a public school outside of your school zone, the city does not provide transportation, although your child is entitled to a city bus pass that will allow him or her to ride New York City buses for free during certain hours. Therefore, factor into your decision to apply out of your school zone the logistics for getting your child to and from school.

▶ **The alternatives.** Before embarking on a search for a public school, it helps to become familiar with the possibilities. There are alternative schools; gifted programs (also known as TAG for "talented and gifted"); magnet programs that implement special projects such as bilingual education, liaison with cultural institutions and development of new curricula; and charter schools.

◩ **Alternative schools.** An alternative school (sometimes referred to as an "option school") is a specialized program that has a distinctive philosophy and vision. Such programs tend to be educationally progressive and may be supported in part by private sector grants. Alternative schools are often housed within another school's building, sometimes on a designated floor, but they operate totally independently of their immediate neighbors. While each program is unique, they typically have small classes, teachers hired directly by the program administrator and a high level of parent involvement. To be successful, these programs require a serious commitment by families to the school. Alternative programs are not considered gifted programs and so do not require entrance testing, but many do require a meeting with the child, the parents, or both. Alternative schools are not zoned for a particular neighborhood, but rather accept students from either a particular district or the entire city.

◩ **TAG programs.** Every district has programs for gifted and talented children. Generally, such programs operate within a public school open to all children. There are, however, a few schools operated solely for gifted children, Hunter Elementary School probably being the best known. As a prerequisite to admission, most gifted programs require the applicant to have a minimum score on a standardized IQ test. Unlike the ERB, which is accepted by all ISAAGNY schools, there is no single test that is accepted by all public school gifted programs. When applying to programs for gifted children, it is necessary to clarify the specific test used and obtain a list of authorized test centers.

◩ **Magnet schools.** There is no common theme to magnet programs built around special projects. On the contrary, these programs are one-of-a-kind and are intended to implement a particular educational philosophy or pursue a curriculum built around certain academic subjects (such as science or the arts) and to draw families interested in the program. They typically receive special governmental funding. Such schools are often, but not always, progressive.

◩ **Charter schools.** Charter schools are autonomous, publicly funded schools that operate independently of the local school district. In accordance with the Charter Schools Act of 1998, charter schools must be non-sectarian, tuition-free, open to all students eligible for admission to other public schools and operated by a self-selecting board of trustees. They operate under five-year licenses. You can get more information about charter schools and a list of New York City charter schools from the Office of Charter Schools at 374-6500 or www.nyucenet.edu/charterschools/charter.profiles.html.

▶ **Getting educated about public education.** The first order of business is to find out for which school you are zoned. This can be accomplished by calling the DOE Office of Zoning at 374-5426 or visiting www.nycenet.edu. A list of the Manhattan school districts as of the date of printing can be found at the end of this chapter, but be aware that this information is likely to change by the summer of 2003. If you want to look beyond your zoned school, you will need to do a lot of legwork, make scores of phone calls and be prepared to spend a lot of time on hold. Stamina, patience and organization will keep you going through this process.

Because each community school district develops its own guidelines regarding transfers, in the past the DOE has not necessarily been the best place to begin your research. As the new system evolves, this may change. One way you can start is to visit the DOE website or call the community school district offices for districts in which you are interested and request a list of the schools, including the names of the individuals in charge of gifted, option/alternative, magnet or special programs. Some districts have compiled this information in a single source book, but most likely you will receive a list of numbers and addresses. Depending on the detail provided to you by the district office, you will probably have to call individual schools to obtain program details and admissions and tour information. Again, this may change as the function of the district offices evolves.

Though there is no way to avoid the laborious step of calling schools directly, there are additional sources of information worth tapping. The Center for Educational Innovation–Public Education Association (CEI-PEA) is dedicated to ensuring a quality public education for every child in the system. The CEI-PEA publishes various pamphlets regarding public education and charter schools in New York City that can be extremely helpful in your search. These can be accessed on the website at www.cei-pea.org.

You can also check the Annenberg Institute for School Reform website at www.annenberginstitute.org or www.annenbergchallenge.org/sites/nynsr.html to obtain a list of the schools that receive funds from various programs supported by the Annenberg Institute for School Reform, which awards grants to innovative school programs.

New York City's Best Public Elementary Schools: A Parents' Guide, by Clara Hemphill (Teachers College Press, 2002), is an excellent guide to over 140 public school programs in the five boroughs. The author reviews and describes the various programs and provides a great deal of information on learning about public school programs and the admissions process.

As you develop your list of schools, keep in mind that public schools do not have uniform admissions procedures, so deadlines for applications and timing of admissions decisions will vary. Your best strategy is to call schools as early in the fall as possible to clarify application procedures and to schedule appointments for school tours, testing for your child if necessary, and interviews with school officials if required. If you are applying to more than one program for gifted children and your child will be required to take several tests in connection with those applications, remember that testing can become expensive, so balance the decision to apply to multiple schools against the prospect of putting your child through multiple evaluations.

▶ **Evaluating public schools.** The CEI-PEA recommends that when you look at a public school, you should look for the following characteristics: schools that are small or are subdivided into small units; collaborative schools administered with the participation of staff, students and parents; schools that have interactive, challenging, activity-based methods and curricula to engage students fully in their learning; and schools that reach out to the community to provide necessary social supports for students and their families.

To assess how effective a school is at teaching its curriculum, you can review the scores received on city-administered reading and math tests (upper grades are also evaluated on additional subjects) in an annual report published by the DOE, which appears in most city newspapers. When analyzing test scores, be aware that the scores of the students in gifted programs within individual schools are not reported separately, so these scores will bring up the school average. Test scores also may reflect the energy the school has devoted to preparing students for the test and not necessarily the totality of academic achievement.

The DOE Division of Assessment and Accountability can also provide certain specific information about schools, in the form of Annual School Report Cards, which can assist you in your evaluations. The Annual School Report Card provides information about student/teacher ratios; expenditure per pupil; the number of hours available for enrichment activities such as gym, computer lab, art, music and other specialties; and information on the building, programs and staff. You can access school report cards at www.nycenet.edu or submit your request for a School Report Card directly to the Division of Assessment and Accountability by calling 374-3990.

If you are interested in a school, you may want to contact the head of its Parents Association to discuss particular issues about the school that may be of concern to you. Some possibilities: opportunity for parent participation, how effective the school is in implementing the curriculum, quality of teaching, amount of school work and so forth.

▶ **The waiting game.** Once you have selected schools and programs of interest, submitted the necessary paperwork, taken your child to required interviews and, for programs where testing for eligibility is part of the admissions procedure, had your child's scores forwarded to the relevant schools, you are left with nothing more to do than sit and wait. The schools and programs for gifted children, including Hunter, tend to follow the ISAAGNY schedule for notification of admission, since the independent schools are their biggest competitors for talented students. Other public schools follow their own notification policies. Some schools notify parents on a rolling admissions basis while others do not make decisions until the spring.

It is important to be aware of the context in which public school admissions decisions are made. For citywide school budget allocations, all public schools must submit pupil projections for the following year by May of the current school year. With the exception of last minute enrollments within the school zone, once projections are submitted, the school cannot readily increase the student population above the budgeted enrollment. While choice is, to a certain extent, a reality and not simply propaganda, in most districts your choice can be effectively limited due to overcrowding, a lack of optional schools and the placement of students under NCLB. In addition, students who are zoned for a school must be given first priority, followed by students who do not live in the zone but who do live in the same district.

▶ **What is a "variance" and how do you get one?** Once your child has been accepted by a school or program, there is still a bit more work to do before you can congratulate yourself on a job well done. A variance is the documentation required to permit your child to attend a school other than the one for which he or she is zoned. In the past this piece of paper, which allows the accepting school to place your child on its register, was generated by the district office in the district where the school to which your child has been accepted (the "receiving school") is located.

Under the new structure of the public school system, the details of effecting transfers, which now must all be processed through the Office of Zoning and Student Placement, are, as of the date of this printing, not finalized. However, what is certain is that specific paperwork will need to be filed with both the receiving school, the school for which your child is zoned (the "sending school") and the relevant district offices or Instructional Divisions. If you are intending to seek a variance, be sure to contact all relevant officials at both the receiving and sending schools, the Instructional Division and the Office of Zoning and Student Placement and check www.nycenet.edu for the latest information on this subject.

The basic policies regarding transfers, as of the date of this printing, seem to be intact. Districts are required to accept students who apply from out of the district, provided that there is room in the chosen school. Districts are not allowed to set requirements for out-of-district students that are different from those they set for district students. Students living within the school zone or district are given priority over out-of-district applicants. If a school does not have specific admissions requirements, such as test scores required by gifted programs, then after students from within the zone and district are placed, admission is determined by random lottery. A district is not permitted to refuse to allow a student to transfer to a school in another district, and the home district is responsible for forwarding records once a variance is been granted. A transferring student is required to stay in the new district for at least a year and a student cannot be sent back to his or her home district for truancy or disciplinary reasons.

▶ **If your application for a variance is denied.** As of the date of this printing, if you are denied a variance, you can appeal to Office of the Chancellor of the New York City school system. Appeals should be directed to the attention of the Deputy

Chancellor for Operations and Communications, Office of Parent Outreach, 52 Chambers Street, New York, NY 10007, 374-6000. Be aware that this, too, may change as the new regulations and procedures are fleshed out.

▶ **A note about home schooling.** Parents who are interested in home schooling their children must inform the district for which the children are zoned of the intention to home school. The district must respond by providing the text of the law governing home schooling in the state and requesting from the parents an Individualized Home Instruction Plan (which must include required quarterly academic progress reports and annual assessment). Once the plan is approved by the district, the parents are notified and the children are registered in the district as home-schooled students. See www.nycenet.edu for more information.

In Conclusion

Gone are the days when you simply sent your child to school with the secure feeling that by graduation, somehow, some way, your child would have acquired the knowledge and skills necessary to succeed in life. The plethora of available options, both public and private, compels us to investigate as many alternatives as we can before committing to a particular school. The bad news is that it is a time-consuming, complicated project for parents who are already juggling family and professional lives. The good news is that by going through the process, we are more likely to make the kind of informed and reasoned choices that will best support our children. At least we hope so.

RESOURCES

General Resources

Commission on Secondary Schools—Middle States Association of Colleges and Schools
3624 Market Street
Philadelphia, PA 19104
215 662-5603
www.css-msa.org

Educational Resources Information Center
2277 Research Boulevard, MS 6M
Rockville, MD 20850
800 538-3742
www.eric.ed.gov

Educational Testing Service
Rosedale Road
Princeton, NJ 08541
609 921-9000
www.ets.org

Independent Educational Consultants Association
3251 Old Lee Highway, Suite 510
Fairfax, VA 22030
703 591-4850, 800 808-4322
www.educationalconsulting.org

Independent Schools Admissions Association of Greater New York (ISAAGNY)
www.isaagny.org.
Produces the Independent Schools Directory (see below)

National Association of Independent Schools
1620 L Street NW, Suite 1100
Washington, DC 20036
202 973-9700
www.nais.org

National Parent Information Network
www.npin.org

National PTA
1090 Vermont Avenue NW, Suite 1200
Washington, D.C. 20005
202 289-6790
www.pta.org

New York State Association of Independent Schools
12 Jay Street
Schenectady, NY 12305
518 346-7390
www.nysais.org
See www.nysais.org/schools/sss.cfm for information on financial aid and the School and Student Service for Financial Aid

Parents League of New York, Inc.
115 East 82nd Street
New York, NY 10028
737-7385
www.parentsleague.org

University of the State of New York
State Education Department
Education Building
Albany, NY 12234
518 474-3852
www.usny.nysed.gov
New York State Board of Regents, www.regents.nysed.gov

Preschool

Center for Early Care and Education
www.ceceny.org

Child Care, Inc.
275 Seventh Avenue, 15th floor, New York, NY 10001
929-7604, www.childcareinc.org

Early Childhood Resource and Information Center (ERIC)
Division of New York Public Libraries
66 Leroy Street, 2nd floor, New York, NY 10014
929-0815, www.nypl.org/branch/man/ecc.html

The Manhattan Directory of Private Nursery Schools by Victoria Goldman and Marcy Braun (Soho Press, 2002)

National Association for the Education of Young Children (NAEYC)
1509 16th Street NW
Washington, D.C. 20036-1426
202 232-8777
www.naeyc.org

New York City Department of Health and Mental Hygiene
Bureau of Day Care, 2 Lafayette Street, 22nd floor, New York, NY 10007
676-2444, www.nyc.gov (see Department of Health/Bureau of Day Care)

Schuyler Center for Analysis and Advocacy
150 State Street, 4th floor, Albany, NY 12207
518 463-1896, www.scaany.org

The Toddler Book, published annually by the Parents League

Ongoing Independent/Private School

Early Steps
540 East 76th Street, New York, NY 10021
288-9684

Educational Records Bureau (ERB)
220 East 42nd Street, Suite 100, New York, NY 10017
672-9800, www.erbtest.org

The Manhattan Family Guide to Private Schools, Fourth Edition, by Catherine Hausman and Victoria Goldman (Soho Press, 2001)

New York Independent School Directory, published annually by ISAAGNY and the Parents League

Prep for Prep
328 West 71st Street, New York, NY 10023
579-1390, www.prepforprep.org
Admits talented 5th- and 6th-grade students and prepares them for 7th-grade placement in independent schools. Prep 9 admits 7th-grade students and prepares them for 9th-grade placement in independent schools.

Ongoing Public School

Advocates for Children
www.insideschools.org

Annenberg Institute for School Reform/Annenberg Challenge
Brown University
Box 1985, Providence, RI 02912
401 863-7990, www.annenberginstitute.org, www.annenbergchallenge.org

Center for Arts Education School Partnership Program
www.cae-nyc.org/projects.htm

Center for Educational Innovation–Public Education Association (CEI-PEA)
28 West 44th Street, Suite 914, New York, NY 10036
868-1640, www.cei-pea.org

Department of Education of the City of New York (DOE)
Tweed Building
52 Chambers Street, New York, NY 10007
374-5110, www.nycenet.edu
- Chancellor's Customer Service Center 718 482-3777
- Division of Assessment and Accountability 374-3990
- Office of Charter Schools 374-6500
- Office of the Chancellor 374-6000
- Office of Parent Outreach and Leadership Development 718 935-5202
- Office of Zoning and Student Placement 374-5426

New Visions for Public Schools
96 Morton Street, New York, NY 10014
645-5110, www.newvisions.org

New York City's Best Public Elementary Schools: A Parents' Guide, by Clara Hemphill (Teachers College Press, 2002)

New York City's Best Public Middle Schools, by Clara Hemphill (Soho Press, 1999)

New York State Board of Regents
www.regents.nysed.gov

Community School Districts (www.nycenet.edu/dist_sch/)
(expected to change as of summer 2003)

District 1
80 Montgomery Street
New York, NY 10002
District Office: 602-9701
School Board: 602-9765

District 2
333 Seventh Avenue
New York, NY 10001
District Office: 330-9400
School Board: 330-9418

District 3
154 West 93rd Street
New York, NY 10025
District Office: 678-2880
School Board: 678-2845

District 4
319 East 117th Street
New York, NY 10035
District Office: 828-3500
School Board: 828-3501

District 5
433 West 123rd Street
New York, NY 10027
District Office: 769-7500
School Board: 769-7601

District 6
4360 Broadway, 4th floor
New York, NY 10033
District Office: 917-521-3600
School Board: 917-521-3740

Sample Checklist for Nursery School Applications
(one per school)

- ❑ School name
- ❑ Call to obtain application
- ❑ Application due date
- ❑ Submit Application:
  - ❑ Return completed application form
  - ❑ Fee
  - ❑ References if required
- ❑ Schedule Appointments:
  - ❑ Open house or tour
  - ❑ Parent appointment (note who is required to attend)
  - ❑ Child appointment (who has to bring child)
- ❑ Thank you note to admissions officer or director (optional)
- ❑ Recommendation if you requested one
- ❑ If applicable, first choice letter

Sample Checklist for Ongoing School Applications
(one per school)

- ❑ School name
- ❑ Call to obtain application
- ❑ Application due date
- ❑ Schedule ERB on-site at nursery school or at a testing center
- ❑ Pay ERB fee
- ❑ Submit Application:
  - ❑ Return completed application form
  - ❑ Fee
  - ❑ References if required
  - ❑ Arrange for ERB report to be sent to school
  - ❑ Arrange for nursery school report to be sent to school

- ❑ Schedule Appointments:
    - ❑ Open house or tour
    - ❑ Parent appointment (note who is required to attend)
    - ❑ Child appointment (who has to bring child)
- ❑ Financial aid: Obtain and complete all required forms, including PFS
- ❑ Confirm that school has received application, ERBs, nursery school report, PFS (if applicable), references
- ❑ Thank you note to admissions officer or director (optional)
- ❑ Recommendation if you requested one
- ❑ If applicable, first choice letter

Sample Checklist for Ongoing Public School Applications (one per school)

- ❑ School name
- ❑ Register in home district
- ❑ Contact districts for lists of schools
- ❑ Contact each school for its application materials, procedures and information
- ❑ Contact district for information/procedures on applying to school within the district and obtaining a variance
- ❑ Application due date
- ❑ Submit application
- ❑ Schedule testing if required
- ❑ Schedule appointments if required:
    - ❑ open house or tour
    - ❑ meeting with principal, director or admissions officer
    - ❑ parent appointment
    - ❑ child appointment
- ❑ Confirm that school has received all necessary paperwork and test scores
- ❑ Confirm decision date, process for notification and amount of time you have to make a decision whether to accept a place if offered
- ❑ Apply for variance
- ❑ Effect transfer from home zone or district

Chapter 9

Steppin' Out with My Baby

As New York has become increasingly child friendly, the number and variety of entertainment options created especially for children has burgeoned. Almost everywhere you go there is something for children to do or, at the very least, something to intrigue them. At times, even the most sensible parents can feel overwhelmed by the sheer volume of kid stuff that is available. From professional performances to special cultural events, there is no end of opportunities for our children to experience theater, dance, music, film or other arts.

Having worked through all the options and settled on a day's or evening's entertainment, the true New Yorker will then focus on dining possibilities, since a day or night on the town almost always includes a meal out. In this foodie capital, even the youngest New Yorkers have their favorite restaurants.

There is no magic to finding entertainment or restaurants in New York City that will be suitable for the kids and pleasant for you. Like most other aspects of orchestrating city life, the answer lies in doing your research and being realistic about what you and your children can tolerate and will enjoy. Whether you are considering taking your child to a Broadway show, a museum exhibition, a cruise around Manhattan, a day of shopping, a top restaurant or the local coffee shop or some other event or activity not entirely geared to children, your child will most likely be welcome (or at least tolerated!) as long as you are respectful and considerate of others.

In this chapter, we will discuss making the most of your family leisure time and direct you to a variety of arenas for theater, dance, music, film, seasonal attractions, circuses and other performances. What is not included in this chapter is information about sporting events, museum programs, arcades and other attractions and "boredom busters," all of which can be found in Chapter 10. We will also offer some thoughts and ideas on dining out *en famille*.

Out on the Town

Organizing an outing with the children takes some planning. Whether your contemplated activities are completely child oriented or will include something for the adults, too, the most important thing is to be realistic about what you think your child can handle and how hard you are prepared to work to make the outing pleasant for both you and your child. It is no fun to spend your leisure time listening to your children whine about having to sit through a ballet, chasing your kids through an exhibit you really wanted to see or stuffing them with cookies so you can have five minutes to whiz through an auction preview, and it is no fun for your child to be yelled at for doing what kids do. Even an activity that is family oriented, such as a cruise on the Circle Line, can feel like a voyage across the Atlantic if the children get bored.

Deciding how to spend your leisure time with your kids in the city involves a reasonable assessment of the various attention spans, energy levels and interests of the kids and adults involved and, if the children are old enough to express a point of view, a major negotiation among all parties and points of view to come to a viable decision.

Some ideas:

- Keep it short. There is an old adage that it is best to leave a party while you are still having fun. The same is true for a family outing. Children generally do not have the ability to spend hours focusing on cultural activities. By the same token, parents generally do not have the ability to spend hours at a children's attraction (think hours of arcade games). A good rule of thumb is to allocate one to two hours to a particular place, leaving room to stay longer if it is going well. Your family will have a better time loving half of the exhibits at a museum than dragging itself through every last gallery.
- Do different kinds of things in a day. The best way to keep the group happy is to keep the day varied. For example, organizing your day to include a stop in a playground for some physical activity (not to mention the ability to make a lot of noise) or some shopping will take the pressure off a day of "inside voices" and "museum manners."
- Divide and conquer. The whole family does not have to be together 24/7. Splitting up throughout the day or even for an entire day allows everyone to get to do the things he or she wants to do. If you find yourself grappling with uncooperative kids, the grownups can take turns alternately minding the kids and going through the exhibit or attraction.

- Check it out first. Whenever possible, do a little research before heading out to see if your planned activity is suitable for or will be at all interesting to your children. If you are in doubt, call ahead to find out whether it is appropriate to bring children at all.
- One from column A... Engage the family in the planning process by working out a schedule of weekend (and other free time) activities that includes everyone's top choices over a period of time (shows, sporting events, exhibits, time in the park). This exercise in negotiation and deal making will not only ensure that everyone gets to do what is most valued, but it will provide a hands-on experience in cooperation, collaboration and respecting the wishes of others.
- Keep moving. If you get to a place and it is a complete bust for your family, move on. Particularly if your child is becoming disruptive and unhappy, it may be best to leave and try again another time.

- Bring distractions. It is always worth packing a small bag with a variety of distractions in the form of food, toys, books, electronic games, drawing materials, workbooks or anything else your child will enjoy that will buy you some time, provided that the distraction is not prohibited in the facility and will not disturb other patrons.
- Bribery. Most parents balk at the concept of outright bribery, but in some instances, a modest bribe can be a good thing. For example, if you really want to get see the New York City Ballet and your kids are whining about seeing another performance, perhaps the offer of a fast-food meal or an hour of television may create a little more cooperation.
- Gear. Make sure to bring a stroller, baby backpack or other baby carrier for an overtired or sleepy child.
- Shopping. While shopping may be fun for adults, unless you are shopping for toys or candy, most kids couldn't care less. One way to make a visit to a department store with a small child more tolerable is to make your first stop at a cosmetic counter to get a few samples in a small bag that the child can carry him or herself. And no, it's never too early to expose boys to a little grooming or styling advice. Make sure to have a morning or afternoon of shopping conclude with something your child wants to do. It is much easier for children to withstand the torture of shopping boredom with an activity they enjoy to follow.

To improve the quality of your "out on the town" experiences with children, you have to keep in mind that as wonderful, amazing and charming as your child may be, no one will ever think your child is as adorable and clever as you do. It is often hard for us to realize our children's physical and emotional limitations, to enforce limits on their behavior or to contain an active, curious child or keep his or her interest during an activity not inherently interesting to children. However, if you respect that others may not have children of their own and therefore may not be very accommodating or patient with your children or that others may actually be escaping their own responsibilities of parenthood for a few hours, there really is not a place you cannot take children in New York.

Performances, Concerts, Theater and More

New York City has a huge selection of shows performed by professionals and geared for audiences of children, presenting wonderful opportunities to expose children to the arts. There is a vast array of alternatives, including puppet shows, plays, dance performances, storytelling, films, all kinds of music, mime and even stand-up comedy by and for children. In addition to providing an introduction to cultural pursuits, taking your children to a performance provides a wonderful opportunity to introduce them to many new concepts, such as being in a dark theater, focusing on a performance, listening and observing, doing without food and drink for a period of time, keeping quiet and, when they need to talk, remembering to whisper.

New York has an abundance of talented performers who mount children's productions. The beauty of these performances is that they are created to appeal to the younger set. They are typically short, the stories are not too complex, they are scheduled at child-appropriate times, and they often include elements of audience participation or interaction. While children's shows are not always the most interesting to parents (especially when you are seeing productions that you have already seen with your older children), they are usually very interesting to your children and provide a great introduction to various forms of performing arts.

In addition to the performances created specifically for children, there are many other performances put on by the major adult-oriented cultural institutions of the city (such as opera and dance companies) exclusively arranged for children. Sometimes, productions that are otherwise primarily directed at adult audiences may offer tickets to dress rehearsals or other less formal previews that are suitable for children to attend. These options represent a perfect transition from the purely child-oriented performances to big-time city culture, which can otherwise often create culture shock for your children. Generally the harsh reality of grownup show protocol and the length of grownup performances can be quite difficult for kids and parents alike without some advance preparation.

Among the entertainment options for grownups are many which are appropriate also for children. Older children and teenagers in particular will both enjoy and understand a wide variety of performances that are primarily geared to adults. Younger children on the other hand, who may enjoy being taken to a performance, especially if it is in the evening and will extend their bedtimes, may not actually appreciate the content of what they are attending and become bored and cranky.

Happily, there is something for everyone in New York City. In addition to Manhattan's 39 Broadway theaters, there are at least 125 Off-Broadway performance venues and countless Off-Off-Broadway performance spaces hosting more than one-thousand annual productions. From marathon esoteric performance art happenings to 20-minute puppet shows for the pre-verbal, if it can be done on stage, on film or outdoors, it is probably here.

▶ **Theater etiquette for kids.** Gone are the days when children were to be seen and not heard. In those times, a conversation about children's behavior at a performance was academic as there were so few performances at which children were permitted. Today, however, we have become quite accustomed to introducing our children to the arts ever earlier, and more and more performances are accessible to the younger set.

That said, it is important to make sure that when children attend performances they know the basics, such as not talking during the performance, using the restroom before the show begins or during intermission, not eating in theaters where food is not permitted and so forth. Adults taking children to performances should also try to remember to be considerate of other audience members and deal with noisy, unhappy, scared, tired, crying or overly fidgety children by promptly taking them out of the theater. While of course it is difficult to deal with an unhappy child you have brought to a show, your audience neighbors are far less likely to be tolerant if their own enjoyment of the show is disrupted.

The best way to insure a successful trip to a performance is to be sensitive to the suggested age recommendations. Your preschool child may indeed enjoy pieces of *A Midsummer Night's Dream*, but the attention span of a three-year-old rarely holds for the number of hours required to sit through the entire performance. Even a child who seems mature is not likely to understand or appreciate a performance that is above his or her head. It is useful to familiarize yourself with the content of a performance you plan on attending so that you do not end up at a show that is not appropriate for your child.

While age-appropriate children's programming is the most likely to provide a positive experience for adult and child alike, if you are considering taking your child to an event or performance not particularly geared to children, your child will most likely be welcome as long as you are respectful and considerate of others. While it requires a lot of effort to keep an active, busy, and perhaps bored child quiet and calm during showtime, it is not fair to others to let your child run wild in an adult environment.

Be realistic about your child's capabilities and stamina.

So what do you do when you want to take your child to something more adult? Be realistic about your child's capabilities and stamina. Forcing your child to conform to behavior requirements that are out of reach invites frustration for both you and your child. Even a performance that is specifically intended to appeal to children, such as the circus, can make you feel as if you are being fed to the lions if the children get tired or restless.

You can call in advance of attending a performance to find out whether it is appropriate to bring children at all, and if you are told no, listen to that advice. If your child cannot make it through the entire performance, the grownups in the group can take turns watching the show while one takes the children outside. You can also bring distractions, in the form of food, toys, books, or anything else that will divert your child's attention, provided that they are permitted in the theater and will not disturb others. If your child is not doing well and is becoming disruptive and unhappy, be prepared to leave, regroup and try again another time.

When you do venture beyond the kid-oriented selection of performances to bring your child to a grownup show, a few tricks may keep potential disaster at bay. Children under eight usually do not last more than an hour and a half, so be prepared to leave at intermission. Unless your children are quite used to staying up late, when possible get tickets for a matinee rather than an evening performance. If you must go in the evening, try to avoid Friday and Saturday nights. Try to get aisle seats so that if you have to get up, you can escape without requiring the entire row to get up with you. Bring lifesavers or other "quiet" candy that can buy you some time until intermission or the end of the show.

Parents often ask whether children need to dress up when attending live performances. When attending children's shows, your kids will definitely find informal, casual dress appropriate. When taking children to Broadway shows, evening performances or other special events, it is always nice to recognize the occasion by having the children dress in other than play clothes. While there are typically no official dress codes for theaters and other performance spaces, it helps children understand that there is a standard of behavior and attention required at performances if they dress for the event.

A final word—do not forget to turn off your cell phones and beepers during the performance!

► **How to find out what is going on around town.** Finding entertainment in New York City that will be appropriate for the kids and pleasant for you does not have to be difficult. The key is to do your research and be realistic about what truly works for your family. To find out about concerts, theater, and other performances or cultural activities geared to children, the best sources are the local newspapers, *New York* magazine, *Time Out New York*, the city's other weekly magazines and the local parenting publications (see the list at the end of Chapter 2). The museums frequently organize children's programs, as do other metropolitan cultural institutions (for example, Carnegie Hall, Lincoln Center, City Center). Some programs are single-performance events and others are part of longer series. *The Parents League Guide to New York and Calendar* also contains a great list of organizations and locations that have children's programming. See Chapter 10 for a listing of city museums.

Other sources:

- Special events in the city's parks. City Parks and Recreation Special Events Hotline at 888 NY-PARKS (888 697-2757) or 360-3456 or www.nyc.gov/parks.
- Jazz. Jazzline (presented by the Jazz Foundation of America) at 479-7888 or www.jazzfoundation.org.
- Broadway and off Broadway. The Broadway Line at 888-BROADWAY (888 276-2392) from outside Manhattan or 302-4111 within Manhattan, www.broadway.org (the website of Live Broadway), www.offoffbway.com, www.playbill.com and www.nytheatre.com
- Lincoln Center. Lincoln Center Information Hotline at LINCOLN (546-2656), www.lincolncenter.org.
- Other institutions. www.nyckidsarts.org, the website of the Alliance for the Arts, a not-for-profit organization that gathers and publishes information about the arts in New York City. The Alliance also publishes the *Kids Culture Catalog*, which contains comprehensive listings of things cultural for kids.

▶ Broadway, Off-Broadway, Off-Off-Broadway and beyond. Broadway theater generally refers to the major theaters located in the Times Square vicinity, from 42nd Street to around 56th Street and between Broadway and Eighth Avenue. Broadway theaters are denominated as such in theater listings and connote more a state of mind than an actual Broadway address. Broadway shows are typically the blockbuster, celebrity-studded, big-ticket musicals and plays.

Off-Broadway theaters, which can be located anywhere around the city (including in the Broadway theater district), tend to seat 500 patrons or fewer. Productions may be less mainstream and casts may contain lesser known actors, although many major performers like to do more "artistic" or less mainstream work in Off-Broadway shows. Off-Off-Broadway performances typically feature "non-equity" (non-union) actors and are held in much smaller venues. It is to Off-Off-Broadway you head when you are interested in more experimental theater.

For music, dance, opera and theater, Lincoln Center is a great destination. The Lincoln Center complex, located on Manhattan's West Side on Broadway between 62nd and 66th Streets, includes several theaters and recital halls, an opera house and an outdoor band shell. Avery Fisher Hall is home to the New York Philharmonic. The Metropolitan Opera House is home to the Metropolitan Opera and American Ballet Theatre. The New York City Opera and New York City Ballet reside at the New York State Theater. Alice Tully Hall hosts the Lincoln Center Chamber Music Society and the annual International Film Festival. The New York Film Festival and other films are featured at the Walter Reade Theater. The Repertory Company of Lincoln Center, Wynton Marsalis' Jazz Orchestra, the Chamber Music Society, and a variety of additional programming can also be found at Lincoln Center. In addition, the Vivian Beaumont Theater and the Mitzi Newhouse Theater stage plays of all types. The plaza to the rear of the complex hosts various arts-and-crafts shows and the Big Apple Circus.

Carnegie Hall, located at 57th Street and Seventh Avenue, is an architectural landmark as well as the host to musical performances of all types. Another important concert hall is the Brooklyn Academy of Music (BAM), which hosts the Brooklyn Philharmonic, concerts and performances of all types as well as cutting-edge performance festivals.

Venues for dance include City Center, the Joyce Theater and the Sylvia and Danny Kaye Theater. Musical performances can be found at the Juilliard School located at Lincoln Center and The Tisch Center at the 92nd Street Y. The 92nd Street Y also hosts many performances specifically geared to or otherwise appropriate for children.

Madison Square Garden, which serves as the home court for several athletic teams, is also a major venue for pop-music concerts and the ever-popular ice shows. The Theater at Madison Square Garden hosts many children's shows (including *Sesame Street Live* and *A Christmas Carol*).

▶ **Getting tickets.** You do not have to have special connections to get tickets to a performance in New York. You can purchase full-price tickets to most performances with your credit card through one of the ticket agencies serving New York City or at the theater box office.

The ticket agencies are:

- CenterCharge—721-6500 for Lincoln Center events only (www.lincolncenter.org)
- CityTix—581-1212 and 581-7907 for City Center events only (www.citycenter.org/information/citytix.cfm)
- Madison Square Garden—465-MSG1 (465-6741) or www.thegarden.com for Madison Square Garden events only
- NYC/On Stage—768-1818 to hear recorded listings of various performances and have your call transferred to the ticket agency handling the tickets for that event
- Tele-charge—800 432-7250 from outside the Tri-State area, 239-6200 or 563-2929 (Broadway Inner Circle) within New York City or www.telecharge.com
- Ticket Central—279-4200 or www.ticketcentral.org
- TicketMaster—800 755-4000 from outside New York City, 307-4100 or 307-7171 within New York City or www.ticketmaster.com

If you are unable to get tickets for a particular show through the usual routes, it is sometimes possible to get what are known as "house seats." House seats refer to tickets that are reserved by the theater to be used for VIPs or other special guests of the production. Often, these tickets will be released to the public for sale. House seats can be released at any time from weeks before a performance to the day of. When checking with one of the ticket services for tickets, be sure to inquire whether there are any house seats or "released" tickets available. You can also get house seats from Care-Tix (840-0770, ext. 229 or 230), run by Broadway Care/Equity Fights AIDS, www.broadwaycares.org. Tickets can be purchased from Care-Tix at twice their face value, but 50 percent is donated to charity and is therefore tax deductible.

For smaller productions and many of the children's productions, tickets are generally purchased directly from the box office. In most cases, you can call the box office and either reserve tickets, which are picked up and paid for at the time of the performance, or pay for tickets in advance by credit card over the phone.

You can also purchase same-day theater tickets at TKTS, a discount ticket seller. Tickets to most shows are half-price, but some shows are discounted by only 25 percent, and you will pay a $3 surcharge per ticket. TKTS does not accept credit cards but takes only cash or travelers checks. Information concerning the tickets available for the day is posted on a board. You must go in person to get the tickets, and you should be prepared to stand in line. Visit www.tdf.org for more information.

The TKTS outlet is located at 47th Street and Broadway on a little traffic island called Duffy Square. It is open from 3 p.m. to 8 p.m. Monday through Saturday, from 10 a.m. to 2 p.m. on Wednesday and Saturday (matinee days) and 11 a.m. to 7 p.m. on Sunday. There is also a downtown location at the corner of John and Front Streets at the South Street Seaport. It is open from 11 a.m. to 6 p.m. Monday through Saturday and 11 a.m. to 3 p.m. on Sunday. At the downtown location, matinee tickets can be purchased one day in advance.

If you are willing to pay a premium for tickets, you can usually purchase tickets, particularly hard-to-get ones, from tickets brokers (also known as ticket resellers). Some ticket brokers are Theatre Direct International at 800 334-8457 (outside New York) or 541-8457 (in New York), www.theaterdirect.com; Prestige Entertainment at 800 243-8849, www.prestigeentertainment.com; Manhattan Entertainment at 382-0633; Applause Theatre & Entertainment Service at 307-7050, www.applause-tickets.com; or check the listings in the Yellow Pages of the telephone book under Tickets. By law, ticket brokers are not supposed to sell tickets for the greater of 10 percent or $5 more than their face value, but this law is routinely flouted. If you elect to buy through a ticket broker, it is wise to get price quotes from more than one broker.

Ticket brokers should not be confused with "scalpers." Scalpers are individuals offering tickets to theaters, concerts, sporting events and other performances, who typically hawk their tickets in front of or near the entrance to the theater or arena. Scalpers are not licensed or authorized to sell their tickets and usually charge a big premium above the price of the tickets. Beware of purchasing tickets from scalpers, because the tickets they hand you may very well be counterfeit; if so, you will have no recourse.

It is also possible to get tickets for certain productions on eBay and other auction websites. Your credit card company can also be a good source for ticket purchases. American Express offers its Playbill Online service at www.americanexpress.com, and Gold or Platinum Card holders may also be able to get tickets to special events from the AmEx special-events program (visit www.americanexpress.com/gce). Visa cardholders can visit www.visa.com to explore their ticket-purchase opportunities. MasterCard also offers ticket-purchase opportunities on its website at www.mastercard.com. Gold and Platinum MasterCard holders may have special access to various performances through MasterCard's Preferred Seating program.

Some theaters and the major cultural institutions offer discounts for children, students and senior citizens for certain performances. Be sure to bring identification for students and seniors.

Junior high school and high school students can purchase special discounted tickets to performances (and discounted museum admissions) through the High Five Tickets to the Arts programs. Participating arts organizations donate tickets to the program. The tickets are then sold to students for $5.00 each. Tickets can be purchased at Ticketmaster and some can be purchased on the High Five website. Students must show valid student identification to purchase tickets. For more information and listings of events for which High Five tickets are available, you can call HI5-TKTS (445-8587) or visit the website at www.high5tix.org. High Five also sponsors special Teen Scene events.

If your preferred form of family entertainment is going to the movies, you can avoid standing in line and get guaranteed admission to the film of your choice by ordering advance tickets from Moviefone at 777-FILM (777-3456), www.moviefone.com; or Fandango at 800-555-TELL (8355), www.fandango.com. Tickets are available over the phone or Internet for credit-card purchase, and some theaters even offer reserved seating. If you are not sure whether a film is kid friendly, visit the family movie guide at www.nytoday.com.

▶ **A word about subscriptions.** You may want to consider theater subscriptions or series tickets for various venues or companies.

Besides potentially saving you some money on tickets (many subscriptions feature a discount) and supporting a performance center or group, you may be guaranteed advance notice of and tickets to popular performances.

Dining Out

With more than 18,000 eating establishments, New York's varied and flavorful gastronomic landscape provides an opportunity for the adventurous to embark on an international culinary tour. The younger members of your group may not yet have the palate to appreciate the diversity, but for the curious—or simply willing—epicure, new taste buds may be born. And for the recalcitrant, there are always chicken nuggets!

▶ **Where and when to go.** There are basically two ways to approach dining out: feeding the troops or destination dining. In the case of the former, the goal is simply to get food into the group in the most expedient manner. In the latter case, dining is an end in itself. The restaurant is chosen for the cuisine, the atmosphere or the entertainment value. Whether you elect to go for fast food, a diner or pizza joint, a family restaurant, a grownup restaurant or a true gastronomic experience, there is no magic answer to creating a positive family-dining experience. However, you can maximize the potential for a good time by giving some thought not only to your choice of restaurant but to the timing of the meal.

Until your youngster has moved beyond a staple of hamburgers, chicken nuggets and pasta, avoid more sophisticated restaurants unless they either specifically cater to kids or offer something your children will eat (even if it is just plain rice). Your best bet may be a restaurant with a children's menu. Try to select a restaurant where the noise level will camouflage the potentially loud noise coming from your own table rather than choosing a very formal adult restaurant.

Theme restaurants are always a popular family-dining destination. While they do provide a certain level of entertainment for the kids, they often offer somewhat mediocre, but very expensive, food. Also, you can pretty much count on a long wait to be seated. Be prepared for an onslaught of pricey souvenirs your children will beg to bring home. If theme restaurants are on your list, be sure to review your visiting-the-gift-shop policy in advance.

Many restaurants bend over backward to attract families. These restaurants tend to be decorated in a playful way, providing an atmosphere that interests most kids. They usually have a children's menu, provide crayons or other table activities and are very busy and noisy. These types of restaurants lend themselves to family dining. Be forewarned that even though a restaurant may have entertainment of some kind, it may not offer the diversion needed to get through a whole meal. Some kids have a hard time keeping themselves in control either because of the noise or the level of activity.

As you make your restaurant choices, do not feel compelled to linger in the fast food or diner categories, though they certainly have their place in the eating repertoire. Trying different types of restaurants with your children can expand both their palates and their view of the world. As long as you are realistic about what the group can handle and are mindful about your destination, you can have a delicious adventure.

To maximize the chance to be seated quickly and receive prompt service, choose an early dinner time, especially on Friday and Saturday nights, and avoid the prime lunch hour by eating before it begins or when the rush is over. Additionally, try to streamline your meal. Most children are not prepared to sit through a two-hour dinner starting at 8:30 p.m. A night out with young children is not the night to have a four-course meal.

Dining with children may not be a relaxing experience, but it is a family one, and that is reason enough for undertaking such an effort.

If you are going to be dining at a restaurant that requires reservations and that would typically not be host to New York's youngest dining set, let the maitre d' know (in advance if possible) that your party includes a child or children. Generally, a table can be selected that will present the fewest distractions to others. With advance notice, the restaurant may be able to provide you with a child seat.

In general, it is best to avoid peak times so that the staff will be less harried and the restaurant less crowded, noisy and busy. It is amazing what a difference 30 minutes can make for your dining experience. Whenever possible, make a reservation, particularly if you are dining with a large party.

▶ **You are the ringmaster.** Wherever you dine *en famille*, it may seem as if you are running a three-ring circus. In many respects you are. That being said, you still can exercise authority over a disintegrating situation and keep things not only in perspective but under control. The key is to remain calm and be flexible.

To more fully enjoy your restaurant experiences with children, it is important to acknowledge your children's physical and emotional limitations and to place appropriate limits on your children's behavior. Just as children need to be taught to use "indoor voices" in a museum, so too must they learn about "restaurant manners" and the level of kid's conduct that passes muster at different types of restaurants.

While we have all had the opportunity to witness, in horror, someone else's dining disaster, we have also been in the parental hot seat and had to manage one of our own. When faced with a table of unruly kids, keep your cool and try not to salvage your meal at the expense of the other patrons. Dining with children may not be a relaxing experience, but it is a family one, and that is reason enough for undertaking such an effort. Some basics:

- Keep your child at the table. To allow children to wander among tables unattended is dangerous for both children and waiters carrying hot food and inconsiderate to other diners.
- Outlaw food fights and other disruptive behavior and stick to your position.
- Be prepared to leave or take your child outside for a little walk in case of meltdown during the meal. If all else fails, order dessert early, buy everyone a round of drinks and tip well.

▶ **Let's hear it for distractions and other strategies.** A key strategy against long waits, slow service or lack of interest in the table conversation is distraction. Distractions come in many forms. Some are edible (crackers, candy) and some consist of activities for the kids to do with you or on their own. Stickers, drawing materials, cards, trading cards, electronic hand-held games, books, Mad Libs and magazines help direct your child's energy and usually provide just the distraction necessary to buy the time you need to get in and out of the restaurant.

Some other ideas:

- Younger kids sometimes benefit from an adult-supervised walk either in an open area or outdoors between the time you order and the time the meal is served. This tactic can help to postpone a child's limited table-time attention span to the time when you need it the most—while you're eating.
- Keep it short. Skip the appetizer, order the kids' food immediately and let the children eat dessert while you have your entrée.
- Don't try to enforce a balanced meal in a restaurant. Eating in a restaurant marks a departure from regular meals and can be a good time to relax your rules. Letting a child have a coveted soft drink or dessert can be much more pleasant than spending the entire meal trying to get the greens down. A wise pediatrician once told us that a child's nutritional needs should be balanced over time, not necessarily at each meal or over a particular day. Your children will fondly remember the time they had candy for lunch (which may have bought you the cooperation to get through an exhibit at the Met!).
- If your child is an especially picky eater, or mealtime is running late and it is likely your child will hit the wall before food can be ordered and served, consider giving him or her a healthy snack before you get to the restaurant or bringing something with you to supplement the meal.

▶ **Have it your way.** Children are notoriously choosy when it comes to their food. We have all seen tears shed because the vegetables touched the pasta and tantrums thrown because the food was served with a garnish of icky "green stuff" that has to be removed piece by verdant piece. As a result, if the food ordered does not meet expectations, a child is likely to reject it (and if you are lucky, without much fanfare).

The best way to make sure that what is ordered actually has a chance of being eaten is to ask questions before you order and to be clear about any specific requests you may have regarding how it is prepared. For example, in a funky retro diner, a grilled cheese may come on fluffy fresh-baked bread rather than "regular" bread. A hamburger may be oversized or served on an English muffin. Gourmet pizza may be garnished with herbs and not cut in triangles. Having that information will help your child decide what to order or how to modify the order to make it edible.

One last tip if you have young children who cannot manage well on an empty tummy: It is always a good idea to have the server bring the children's food as soon as it is prepared rather than waiting until everyone's meal is ready to be served.

▶ **Practice makes perfect.** The table manners emphasized at home are more likely to show up when you're out on the town than those that are not. Napkins on laps, elbows off the table, staying in one's seat, no horseplay and passing instead of reaching for items across the table are just a few of those basic rules of etiquette that make children seem less primitive.

However, even if your kids are usually civilized at the table at home, the excitement of being at a restaurant or on a special outing or the cumulative effects of a day on the move may challenge even the most polite child. What to do? Be realistic. Do not expect your kids to be perfect and hold it together at every meal. After all, they are still children—drinks will spill, napkins will be on the floor, noise will be made. What you can prevent is silverware flying, standing on chairs and food fights.

You can help your children with restaurant readiness by role-playing at home. You can practice ordering, rehearse what to do if the food that arrives is different from what was expected and learn how to excuse yourself to go to the bathroom. You can review the basic place setting and your own restaurant rules. Most important, do not expect your kids to be suddenly transformed into grownups. With realistic expectations, clearly spelled out before you sit down to eat, you will enjoy many meals out with your children while they practice their way to dinner at Lutèce.

RESOURCES

Dining Out

Manners

Barnes, Bob, and Emilie Barnes. *A Little Book of Manners for Boys* (Harvest House Publishers, 2000). Most appropriate for ages 9–12.

Barnes, Emilie. *A Little Book of Manners: Courtesy and Kindness for Young Ladies* (Harvest House, 1998). Most appropriate for ages 4–8.

Hoving, Walter. *Tiffany's Table Manners for Teenagers* (Random House, 1989). Most appropriate for young adults.

Samuel, Catherine, and Maggie Swanson. *Elmo's Good Manners Game (Sesame Street)* (CTW Books, 1999). Most appropriate for preschool children.

Restaurant guides

Grimes, William, and Eric Asimov. *The New York Times Guide to New York City Restaurants 2003* (New York Times, 2003).

Time Out New York Eating and Drinking Guide 2003 (Time Out New York, 2002). Updated annually.

Zagat Survey 2003: New York City Restaurants. An annual compilation of surveys completed by local restaurant "consumers," this guide to one of the world's most dynamic and varied restaurant scenes provides valuable information on dining options. Available in bookstores and specialty shops or by calling 800 333-3421.

Tickets

Ticket brokers

Applause Theatre & Entertainment Service
307-7050
www.applause-entertainment.com

Manhattan Entertainment
382-0633

Prestige Entertainment
800 243-8849
www.prestigeentertainment.com

Theatre Direct International
800 334-8457
www.theaterdirect.com

Ticket and special event information

City Parks and Recreation
Special Events Hotline
888 NY-PARKS (888 697-2757) or
360-3456

Jazzline (presented by the Jazz
Foundation of America)
479-7888

League of American Theatres &
Producers
www.broadway.org

Lincoln Square Business
Improvement District
www.lincolnbid.com

New York Theatre Experience
757-7200
www.nytheatre.com

Off Broadway Theater
Information Center
251 West 45th Street
575-1423
www.offbroadway.com

Off-Off Broadway information
www.offoffbway.com

www.broadway.com

www.broadwaynewyork.com

www.dealsonbroadway.com

Ticket services

American Express
www.americanexpress.com/gce

Broadway Hotline
888-BROADWAY (888 276-2392)
outside NYC
302-4111 within NYC

Care-Tix
840-0770
www.broadwaycares.org

CenterCharge
721-6500 Lincoln Center events only

CityTix
581-1212 City Center events only

Fandango
800 555-TELL (800 555-8355)
www.fandango.com

High Five Tickets to the Arts
HI5-TKTS
www.high5tix.org

Lincoln Center Information Hotline
LINCOLN (546-2656)
www.lincolncenter.org

Madison Square Garden
465-MSG1 (465-6741)
www.thegarden.com

MasterCard
www.mastercard.com

Moviefone
777-FILM (777-3456)
www.moviefone.com

NYC/On Stage
768-1818

Tele-charge
800 432-7250 outside NYC
239-6200 or 563-2929 within NYC
www.telecharge.com

Ticket Central
279-4200

Ticketmaster
800 755-4000 outside NYC
307-4100 and 307-7171 within NYC
www.ticketmaster.com

Ticketweb
269-4TIX (269-4849)
www.ticketweb.com

TKTS
47th Street and Broadway on Duffy Square
South Street Seaport
www.tdf.org

Visa Card
www.visa.com

Websites

www.allny.com

www.citidex.com

www.cityguideny.com

www.citysearch.com

www.cuisinenet.com

www.culturefinder.com

www.digitalcity.com

www.go-newyorkcity.com

www.kerrymenu.com

www.metronewyork.com

www.museumstuff.com

www.newyorkled.com

www.nyc.com

www.nyc.gov (official website of New York City)

www.nyc-arts.org

www.nyckidsarts.org

www.nyctourism.com

www.nycvisit.com

www.nymuseums.com

www.nytimes.com

www.nytoday.com

www.timeoutny.com

www.zagat.com

Entertainment Listings

Aaron Davis Hall
West 135th Street and Convent Avenue (on the campus of City College of New York), 650-6900, www.aarondavishall.org or www.ccny.cuny.edu/aboutus/campus/aarondavis00.htm
This performing-arts center in the heart of Harlem, located on the campus of The City College of New York, is the host to a variety of programming throughout the year. For more than 15 seasons, the multicultural International Series has presented 20 to 30 performances per year featuring music, dance, theater and film from African, Caribbean, Asian, Latino, African American and European cultures. Some performances are part of the Dialogue Series where the artists speak with the audience after the show. Performances are on weekdays at 10:30 a.m. and 12:30 p.m. The Saturday afternoon Family Series, which usually runs approximately five times each year, features programming for children and their parents and often includes ancillary programs connected to the performance.

Abrons Arts Center
Henry Street Settlement at Pitt Street, 466 Grand Street, 598-0400, www.henrystreet.org
This multifunctional arts center boasts three professional theaters as well as classrooms, art studios and gallery space and hosts professional and student theater and music performances for all ages. Throughout the school year, the Abrons Arts Center offers an Arts for Families series (usually one weekend a month), featuring a variety of performances for children. Reservations are recommended, and do not forget to check the age recommendation for the show.

Alvin Ailey American Dance Theater
767-0590, www.alvinailey.org
This renowned modern dance troupe is in residence for six weeks during December and early January at City Center. While most of its work is geared to mature audiences and young adults, during the New York City season they schedule several Family Matinee performances. The junior company, Ailey II (formerly the Alvin Ailey Repertory Ensemble), is in residence at Aaron Davis Hall for a brief season during March or April. Students from the Ailey School usually perform in May.

American Ballet Theatre
Metropolitan Opera House at Lincoln Center, 477-3030, www.abt.org
ABT is in residence in New York for an eight-week season April through July at Lincoln Center. Though its repertoire is geared to mature audiences and young adults, your young ballet fan (age 10+) may be able to sit through a portion of a regular program. For the past several years, ABT has had an annual Saturday matinee Family Day gala once each spring. ABT also conducts a unique Family Series program once each fall and each spring during which you and your child can attend studio visits, tours, education workshops and performances over a two-afternoon period. Although the Family Series is an expensive proposition, it may be appropriate for a serious ballet fan or student.

Apollo Theatre
253 West 125th Street, 531-5305; events hotline 531-5301, www.appollotheatre.com
This legendary theater in the heart of Harlem showcases a variety of musical performances, amateur shows, and standup comedy featuring African American performers. Call ahead to determine whether the programming for your dates is age appropriate. Every Wednesday evening at the Apollo is Amateur Night and children are very welcome. The Apollo also hosts a Free Films for Kids program that features many first-run G-rated movies. Tours of the theater are available.

ArtsConnection
520 Eighth Avenue, Suite 321, 3rd floor, 302-7433, www.artsconnection.org
Housed in a historic landmark building in the theater district, ArtsConnection operates its Saturdays Alive! Program from October through May, hosting performances, readings and hands-on arts workshops. The Family Performance series features dance, theater and music from cultures all around the world. The Family Workshop series allows children and parents to participate in projects led by professional artists. The Books Alive! series includes readings by, and activities with, children's authors. Artsplay! Performances for Preschoolers features performances for children between the ages of three and five.

Big Apple Circus
Lincoln Center, 268-2500, www.bigapplecircus.org
This popular one-ring circus sets up its heated tent at Lincoln Center each year (from October through January). The Big Apple Circus, a not-for-profit performing-arts institution that is committed to children and families, is unusually child friendly and manages to thrill and delight young audiences with a variety of clowns, acrobats, jugglers, animals large and small and other annual surprises. No seat is more than 50 feet from the action. Fun for the parents, too.

Bronx Arts Ensemble
Bronx, 718 601-7399, www.bronxartsensemble.com
The Bronx Arts Ensemble, in residence at Fordham University, features music from many cultures and styles, including classical, salsa and jazz. The Ensemble features an annual children's performance series and includes family-friendly programming in its general performance schedule. The Music Circus Children's Concerts are part of the Ensemble's regular season.

Brooklyn Academy of Music (BAM)
30 Lafayette Avenue, Brooklyn, 718 636-4100, www.bam.org
BAM is one of the oldest performing arts centers in the U.S. and is host to a variety of performing arts throughout the year, including contemporary and classical dance, theater, performance art, repertory and first run films, music performances (including the resident Brooklyn Philharmonic and BAM Opera) and theater for young people. While often associated with avant-garde performances, BAM showcases many traditional and contemporary works as well. BAM features BAMfamily music and theater performances for the entire family.

Brooklyn Center for the Performing Arts at Brooklyn College
Flatbush Avenue and Avenue H, Brooklyn, 718 951-4500, www.brooklyncenter.com
This performing-arts complex in the heart of Brooklyn contains the 2,450-seat Walt Whitman Hall, the 500-seat Gershwin Theatre as well as several

other performance and rehearsal venues. The Center hosts an array of music, dance and theater performances as well as film events and the Jewish Gems (Yiddish theater), Music Masters, World of Dance and Caribbean Celebrations series. The Family Fun Sunday matinee series offers several annual productions (between October and May) especially for children and a Nutcracker each December.

Carnegie Hall
57th Street and Seventh Avenue, 247-7800, www.carnegiehall.org
World-class musicians look forward to performing in this landmark concert hall. From the top orchestras of the world to contemporary singers, there is a variety of programming throughout the year. While much of the programming is not specifically child friendly, there is a great deal that would be appropriate for older or more mature children and particularly for young (10+) musicians. In addition, Carnegie Hall hosts occasional Saturday matinee Family Concerts, which are accompanied by pre-performance family activities, and weekday CarnegieKids concerts for preschoolers. Carnegie Hall also sponsors an annual series of Neighborhood Concerts in various locations throughout the five boroughs. Tours of the facility are available.

Chamber Music Society of Lincoln Center
Alice Tully Hall at Lincoln Center, 875-5775, www.chambermusicsociety.org
The Chamber Music Society of Lincoln Center performs chamber music of all periods during its annual concert season. The Meet the Music! series features three short concerts per year to introduce children to chamber music.

City Center
130 West 55th Street, 581-1212, 581-7907, www.citycenter.org
Since 1943, City Center has been a venue for music, dance and theater. Companies that perform annually at City Center include Alvin Ailey, American Ballet Theatre, American Dance Theater and Paul Taylor Dance Company. City Center also houses Manhattan Theatre Club and City Center Encores! Great American Musicals in Concert. Others who have recently performed at City Center include the Australian Ballet, Ballroom Fever, the Dance Theatre of Harlem and the Moscow Chamber Orchestra. Although the general productions are not aimed at children, particular performances may be appropriate for your older (10+) child. For over ten years City Center's Young People's Dance Series has brought professional artists into city schools.

City Lights
300 West 43rd Street, Suite 402, 262-0200, www.clyouththeatre.org
This non-profit educational organization provides quality theater-arts programs for children ages 7 to 18. Performances are held at various locations throughout the city.

Colden Center for the Performing Arts
65-30 Kissena Boulevard (Queens College of the City University of New York) Flushing, Queens, 718 544-2996, www.coldencenter.org
The Colden Center for the Performing Arts has hosted many of the world's leading artists in music, dance, theater and other performing arts as well as innovative and entertaining children's programming. Especially for kids are the KidsClassics and Family Theater series, many of which feature audience participation or interaction. Different series will have age recommendations. In addition, there are many special events that are appropriate for children of all ages.

Community Works Theater Connections
459-1854
This not-for-profit community arts organization brings a rich variety of affordable, multicultural performing arts events to more than 65,000 students per year (grades K–12) via its Theater Connections program. Their four major presenting sites are Hostos Center for the Arts & Culture (Bronx), Pace University Downtown Theater (lower Manhattan), Marcus Garvey Park Amphitheater (Harlem) and LaGuardia Mainstage Theatre (Queens). Performances are primarily geared to school groups, held on weekdays during school hours and generally open to the public.

Czechoslovak–American Marionette Theatre
777-3891, www.czechmarionettes.org

Since 1990, this company has produced traditional and original puppet plays for adults and children (generally 5+) using a troupe of antique marionettes. The Czechoslovak–American Marionette Theatre performs in various venues in New York as well as nationally and internationally. Reservations recommended.

Dance Theater Workshop
219 West 19th Street, 924-0077, www.dtw.org
Dance Theater Workshop is a not-for-profit organization that provides artist sponsorship programs, production facilities and support services to independent artists in New York City and across the country. Dedicated to identifying and nurturing contemporary artists working in diverse cultural contexts, DTW offers a Family Matters series of performances for children ages 5 to 12 and their parents on selected weekend afternoons at its Beside Schoolbag Theater. Artists who have worked with DTW include Mark Morris, Bill Irwin, Bill T. Jones and Whoopi Goldberg.

Dance Theatre of Harlem
466 West 152nd Street, 690-2800, www.dancetheatreofharlem.org
This world-famous multicultural dance company has an exciting repertory of many works. Though the performances are not specifically geared to children, your older dance fan (10+) will find a lot here to enjoy. For families, the Dance Theatre of Harlem offers an Open House Series on the

second Sunday of each month between November and May. Open House performances feature a variety of performers, such as jazz and gospel musicians, other dance companies and Dance Theatre of Harlem students. Performances are followed by a reception.

Film Society of Lincoln Center
Walter Reade Theater at Lincoln Center, 875-5610; ticket orders at 496-3809, www.filmlinc.com
The Film Society of Lincoln Center hosts Movies for Kids intermittently throughout the year. The Reel to Real series, offered over several weekends spaced out over the school year, features "silver screen classics on double bills with dynamic live performances and audience participation." A true New York experience.

Growing Up with Opera
Metropolitan Opera Guild, 362-6000, www.operaed.org
Growing Up With Opera, presented by the Metropolitan Opera Guild (769-7022), the organization behind the Metropolitan Opera, is a unique program that introduces children (and adults, too!) to opera. Classic works are sung in English and performed in child-friendly venues. Backstage tours of the Opera House are available for children nine and older (769-7020).

Hostos Center for the Arts & Culture
450 Grand Concourse (at the Hostos Community College of the City University of New York), Bronx, 718 518-4455, www.hostos.cuny.edu/culturearts

Containing an art gallery, theater and concert hall, this facility showcases drama, folk arts, dance and music, including strong Spanish-language theater programming and works from cultures from around the world. For children, there are performances including everything from puppets, merengue, poetry readings and a rhythm-and-blues Christmas concert. Performances reflect the concerns and traditions of the local Latino and African American communities.

Ice Theatre of New York
929-5811, www.icetheatre.org
This professional skating group, which is the nation's first not-for-profit artistic ice dancing ensemble, is the "PBS of figure skating." Not to be confused with ice extravaganzas, the Ice Theatre of New York performs original choreographed pieces every year between October and May. You can catch their unique works in October at the Chelsea Piers Skyrink and can watch for free at Rockefeller Center on the third Wednesdays of January, February, March and April at 1:00 p.m. and at Riverbank State Park on the third Thursdays of January, February and March. Ice Theatre is great for any child who loves skating and dance.

Jazz at Lincoln Center
Alice Tully Hall, Lincoln Center, 258-9800, www.jazzatlincolncenter.org
Jazz at Lincoln Center features a series of jazz concerts, films, lectures and other programming under the artistic direction of Wynton Marsalis. The Jazz for Young People series, offered several times between October and May, is a unique series of one-hour concerts led by Wynton Marsalis exploring different forms of jazz. It is fun for the kids and educational for the grownups, too, but it is not recommended for children under six.

Joyce Theater
175 Eighth Avenue, 242-0800, www.joyce.org
Founded in 1982, the Joyce Theater was created by dancers as a home for all types of dance, from contemporary to the avant-garde. The Joyce Theater building was converted from a 1941 movie house into an intimate theater seating 472. The Joyce's Family Matinee Series consists of six to eight family-oriented performances followed by Meet the Artists gatherings each year. The Joyce Junior Membership Program offers children (ages 6 to 14) who see three Family Matinees a 40-percent discount on the price of their tickets as well as discounts at local restaurants and bookstores.

Lenny Suib Puppet Playhouse
Mazur Theater at Asphalt Green, 555 East 90th Street, 369-8890
Every Saturday at 10:30 a.m. and noon from September to April, the Lenny Suib Puppet Playhouse stages a puppet show for children between the ages of two and seven in the intimate Mazur Theater. Stories are drawn from fairy tales, folk tales and original pieces and are very kid friendly. Plays usually last about 45 minutes. Performances are diverse and can include hand, shadow and rod puppets, marionettes, magicians, clowns, storytellers and more. There is a different show each weekend.

Lincoln Center
70 Lincoln Center Plaza, 875-5000; customer service 875-5456,
Hotline LIN-COLN (546-2656), www.lincolncenter.org
Situated on 15 acres on Manhattan's Upper West Side, Lincoln Center is one of the world's largest cultural complexes, offering an array of programming for all ages and tastes. Through its Department of Programs and Services for People with Disabilities, Lincoln Center has made a major commitment to providing access to patrons, visitors and artists with disabilities (875-5375). Lincoln Center consists of Alice Tully Hall (875-5050), Avery Fisher Hall (875-5030), The Juilliard School (799-5000), Lincoln Center Theater (362-7600), Metropolitan Opera House (362-6000), New York Public Library for the Performing Arts (870-1630), New York State Theater (870-5570) and the Walter Reade Theater (875-5601).

At Lincoln Center, you can find

- American Ballet Theatre, 477-3030, Metropolitan Opera House, www.abt.org (see listing above)

- The Chamber Music Society of Lincoln Center, 875-5775, Alice Tully Hall, www.chambermusicsociety.org (see listing above)
- The Film Society of Lincoln Center, 875-5610, Walter Reade Theater, www.filmlinc.org (see listing above)
- Jazz at Lincoln Center, 258-9800, www.jazzatlincolncenter.org (see listing above)
- Juilliard School, 799-5000, www.juilliard.edu
  This famed college invites the public to the school's free public recitals by advanced students on Saturdays during the academic year. A treat for your aspiring musician.
- Lincoln Center Theater, 362-7600, www.lct.org
  The Vivian Beaumont and Mitzi E. Newhouse Theaters have a year-round schedule of programming. While not particularly geared to children, certain of the productions may be appropriate for older children (10+) or teenagers.
- Metropolitan Opera, 362-6000, www.metropera.org (and see www.operaed.org, Growing Up with Opera listing above)
- New York City Ballet, 870-5570, New York State Theater, www.nycballet.com (see listing below)
- New York City Opera, 870-5600, New York State Theater, www.nycopera.org (see listing below)
- New York Philharmonic, 875-5656, www.newyorkphilharmonic.org (see listing below)

Little Orchestra Society
971-9500, www.littleorchestra.org
For the past 50 years, the Little Orchestra Society has been introducing the youngest audiences to orchestral music in a delightful, fun-filled way. For three- to five-year-olds, the weekend Lollipop Concerts, three of which are offered in the fall, winter and spring, use friendly characters, each representing a section of the orchestra, to teach the ABCs of music at the Sylvia and Danny Kaye Playhouse at Hunter College. Happy Concerts for 6- to 12-year-olds are offered at Avery Fisher Hall at Lincoln Center three times a year (including a rousing *Amahl and the Night Visitors*, complete with live animals!). A New York tradition.

Los Kabayitos Puppet & Children's Theater
Society of the Educational Arts (SEA), CSV Cultural & Educational Center, 107 Suffolk Street, 260-4080 ext. 14, www.sea-ny.org
Voted one of the "10 Best Latino Theater Companies in New York," the Society of the Educational Arts, Inc./Sociedad Educative de las Artes, Inc. is a not-for-profit Hispanic/Bilingual Arts in Education organization founded in Puerto Rico in 1985. In addition to an array of community- and school-based programming, Los Kabayitos Puppet & Children's Theater offers year-round general audience performances in both Spanish and English.

Their original productions explore educational themes as well as Latino arts and culture.

Madison Square Garden
Seventh Avenue between 31st and 33rd Streets, 465-MSG1 (465-6741), www.thegarden.com
More than five million fans pass through the turnstiles every year at Madison Square Garden. Located in the heart of Manhattan above Pennsylvania Station, this newly renovated landmark sports-and-entertainment complex is home to the NY Knicks, Rangers and WNBA and hosts ice shows, Ringling Brothers Barnum & Bailey Circus, horse shows, dog and cat shows, rock concerts and more. The facility consists of the 20,000-seat Arena, the 5,600-seat Theater and the 40,000-square-foot Expo Center. Annual favorites at the Theater include *Sesame Street Live* and *A Christmas Carol*. Tours of the facility are available.

Manhattan Children's Theatre
380 Broadway, 4th floor, 252-2840, www.manhattanchildrenstheatre.org
This not-for-profit organization is committed to producing "affordable, high-quality theatrical experiences for children and families" by offering "professional writing, compelling stories and exceptional production values" in its brand new, family-friendly space located in the heart of Tribeca. Audiences will also have the ability to see the production and technical teams do their magic. Some productions will offer activities after the performance.

Marionette Theater
Swedish Cottage in Central Park (Near 81st Street), 988-9093, www.centralpark.org
Originally built as a schoolhouse in 19th-century Sweden, the cottage made its way to Central Park via the 1876 Philadelphia Centennial Exposition. Marionette performances run between October and June and are at 10:30 a.m. and noon on weekdays and 1:00 p.m. on Saturdays. Each autumn, a new production of a classic fairy tale is presented. Performances last about an hour and are great for children between the ages of 4 and 11. Reservations are recommended.

New Victory Theater
209 West 42nd Street between Seventh and Eighth Avenues, 646-223-3020, www.newvictory.org
This gem of a theater located in the heart of Times Square is totally dedicated to children's programming and education. The VicTeens program allows 13- to18-year-olds to mingle with cast members and theater professionals, check out behind the scenes, and learn about the biz. Throughout the year, the New Victory hosts an incredible array of high quality and often unique performances by artists from around the world, including circuses, mime, plays, music, puppeteers, dance and even performance art for the younger set. All programs have specific age recommendations

(which are very accurate) and are reasonable in length. Should not be missed!

New York City Ballet
New York State Theater at Lincoln Center, 870-5570, www.nycballet.com
This world-renowned ballet company highlights works by George Balanchine, Jerome Robbins, Peter Martins and new choreographers. While not particularly geared to young children, your older ballet fan (10+) will enjoy this wonderful dance company. For children ages eight and older, NYCB offers Family Insights, a pre-performance program (usually offered four times a year) designed to enhance the ballet experience for young audience members and their families. The NYCB's Nutcracker is an institution.

New York City Opera
New York State Theater at Lincoln Center, 870-5600, www.nycopera.com
This company is decidedly more accessible than the Met, without any diminution in quality. Foreign-language operas are presented with supertitles projected above the stage. For children ages 6 to 12, the New York City Opera offers hour-long programs designed to introduce various aspects of opera performance and production. Prior to selected matinees during the regular season, there are also several pre-performance young people's workshops during which a City Opera teaching artist conducts a brief interactive program introducing audience members to the opera being performed that day.

New York Philharmonic
Avery Fisher Hall at Lincoln Center, 875-5656, www.newyorkphilharmonic.org
Under the direction of Lorin Maazel, this world-famous orchestra, the oldest in the United States, presents numerous concerts each year. Its famed Young People's Concerts (usually four per year on Saturday afternoons between September and June) introduce children ages 6 to 12 to orchestral music. Concerts are preceded by an hour-long Children's Promenade where children are invited to meet members of the Philharmonic and make their own music. Children from 12 to 17 can participate in Phil Teens and attend a Rush Hour Concert (6:45 to 7:45 p.m.) preceded by a pre-concert event at 5:30 p.m. The youngest music lovers (ages three to six) can attend a free half-hour musical storytime with members of the Philharmonic at Barnes & Noble at Broadway and 66th Street.

92nd Street Y
1395 Lexington Avenue, 415-5500, www.92ndstY.org
The 92nd Street Y, located on Manhattan's Upper East Side, offers a full range of performance programming and activities for families. The "Y" has a long history of serving as a community cultural center presenting concerts, dance performances, lectures, films and other special events and family activities throughout the year. The Bronfman Center for Jewish Life (415-5765) offers a variety of programming for adults and families.

Paper Bag Players
362-0431, www.paperbagplayers.org
Since 1958, the award-winning Paper Bag Players has been delighting young audiences with their rousing songs, freewheeling dances and sets and props fashioned from cardboard boxes and paper bags. Perfect for children ages four to eight. They can be found at the Sylvia and Danny Kaye Playhouse at Hunter College from January through March and at other locations during the rest of the year.

Poets House, Children's Room
72 Spring Street, 431-7920, www.poetshouse.org
This downtown literary center and poetry archive is a "home for all who read and write poetry," houses 40,000 volumes of poetry and offers public programs and hosts events and readings throughout the city. The Children's Room, open on Saturdays from 11 a.m. to 1 p.m., is designed for kids ages four to ten and "features poetry books for children and a whimsically designed setting in which to read them." The Children's Room hosts poetry readings and workshops throughout the year.

Poppy Seed Players
Elaine Kaufman Cultural Center, Merkin Concert Hall, 129 West 67th Street, 501-3330, www.ekcc.org
Since 1990, the Poppy Seed players have been staging family musicals with Jewish cultural themes. Professional actors perform about five productions per year. Productions are based on various stories, including those of Isaac Bashevis Singer. There are also special holiday productions during Chanukah, Passover and Purim, all of which feature a children's chorus comprising students from the Lucy Moses music school. Performances are usually at 11:00 a.m. on Sunday. Recommended ages vary based on productions, although the holiday shows are fine for kids four and up.

Puppetworks
338 Sixth Avenue, Brooklyn (Park Slope), 718 965-3391, www.puppetworks.org
The Puppetworks Company stages weekend afternoon performances with hand-carved wooden marionettes. These original productions are based on children's literature, folk and fairy tales and other familiar stories. Perfect for children between the ages of 5 and 12.

Radio City Music Hall
1260 Sixth Avenue at 50th Street, 247-4777; for tickets 307-7171, www.radiocity.com
This dazzling landmark Art Deco masterpiece, located in the heart of Rockefeller Center and having the largest proscenium stage in the world, is a must-see for all visitors. Radio City is perhaps best known for the annual Radio City Christmas Spectacular featuring the famed Rockettes (seen by more than one-million people each year), but it is also the venue for concerts, television events and other special events. You can find live family

entertainment shows such as Barney and family movie premieres. Tours of Radio City are available.

Ringling Brothers and Barnum & Bailey Circus
Madison Square Garden, 800 755-4000, www.ringling.com
The Greatest Show on Earth comes to New York every spring (usually sometime in March) for a six-week run at Madison Square Garden. With three rings, clowns, daring tumblers, aerialists, live animals and a menagerie, the circus is bound to delight and thrill your children. Be advised that your littlest ones may be overwhelmed by the action, so plan accordingly.

Shadow Box Theater
YWCA of Brooklyn, 30 Third Avenue, Brooklyn, 724-0677, www.shadowboxtheatre.org
This award-winning, not-for-profit company has been presenting "puppet and people" musicals and storytelling performances for more than 30 years. Its mission is to reach children "with important messages of multicultural awareness, self-esteem, preservation of the earth's environment, health and safety and the simple joy of artistic expression." Shadow Box Theater is the resident children's theater of the YWCA of Brooklyn. It also performs at various venues in the other four boroughs. Performances are on weekdays, usually at 10:30 a.m., between November and May.

Sony IMAX Theatre
Broadway and 68th Street, 800 555-8355
Feel as if you are in the movie when you experience a 3D IMAX film in this theater with an eight-story-high screen. The kids will love the cool headgear they wear to get the full 3D effect. Films typically run about one hour. IMAX may be a bit much for kids under five or six.

Symphony Space
Broadway at 95th Street, 864-5400, www.symphonyspace.org
This Upper West Side performing-arts center features a broad array of diverse music, dance, film, theater and other arts programming. One Saturday per month from November through April, Symphony Space presents Just Kidding, a series intended to introduce children between the ages of 5 and 12 to the arts and excite them about its possibilities. Performances tend to be lively and often interactive. A great opportunity to get a taste of the Upper West Side!

Tada! Theater
15 West 28th Street, 3rd floor, 252-1619, www.tadatheater.com
This not-for-profit youth theater company presents original musicals, plays and dance productions performed by the multiethnic members of the TADA! Company, all of whom are between the ages of 8 and 17. Your kids will love seeing kids perform.

Theater for a New Audience
229-2819, www.tfana.org
Since 1978, TFANA has been staging the works of Shakespeare and other works from the world's classic repertoire and has been committed to "bonding the diverse community of New York to the language, pleasures and issues of classical drama." While the performances are not particularly geared to children, your older child (10+) and your teens will enjoy these works. At certain performances, TFANA features a pre- or post-performance event with the actors that will give your older child a window into the production. The Sunday afternoon New Deal events (offered several Sundays during the year) bring a scholar or person involved with the production to meet with the audience about the day's show.

Theatreworks/USA
647-1100, www.theatreworksusa.org
Theatreworks/USA is the nation's largest professional not-for-profit theater company for children performing all over the U.S. and reaching an annual audience of almost four million people. In New York, Theatreworks/USA presents its October–April weekend series at the Equitable Tower (787 Seventh Avenue between 51st and 52nd Streets). Theatreworks mounts approximately 14 shows each season from a body of work of more than 90 plays and musicals that fall into three categories: history and biography, literary adaptations and "issue" shows. The shows feature such themes as discrimination, peer pressure, friendship, illiteracy and perseverance. While Theatreworks entertains children from pre-school through high school, each show has a (very accurate) recommended age level. Note that Theatreworks/USA has recently added Teenworks, a series intended to draw older kids and teens. All of these high quality and entertaining shows should not be missed.

Thirteenth Street Repertory Company
50 West 13th Street, 675-6677, www.13thstreetrep.org
For the past 28 years, this Greenwich Village repertory company has been delighting young audiences with original children's theater. Throughout the year, the Thirteenth Street Theater offers entertaining shows for the younger set on Saturday and Sunday at 1:00 p.m. and at 3:00 p.m. The early show is usually for kids three and up and the later show is for kids five and up. Audience participation is definitely part of the program!

Tribeca Performing Arts Center
199 Chambers Street, 220-1460, www.tribecapac.org
This downtown performing arts center produces a variety of multicultural dance, theater and music programming. For children, it offers a popular weekend Family Folk and Fairy Tale series from October to June. Works are performed by American and international companies.

UniverSoul Big Top Circus
Downing Stadium, Randalls Island, www.universoulcircus.com
This unique and exciting circus brings hip-hop, rhythm and blues, jazz and gospel to traditional circus acts performed by people of color from around the world. UniverSoul is usually in New York during April and May each year.

Vital Theatre Company
43 West 42nd Street, 3rd floor, 592-4508, www.vitaltheatre.org
Since 1999, Vital Theatre Company has worked to "build a sense of community by offering affordable, educational entertainment for young audiences" and has provided a home for emerging theater artists. The Vital Children's Theatre brings five original plays a year to children of all ages.

Wave Hill
675 West 252nd Street, Bronx, 718 549-3200, www.wavehill.org
This picturesque public garden located in the Riverdale section of the Bronx offers a variety of performing arts (primarily concerts) in addition to spectacular views of the Hudson River and Palisades, green lawns and magnificent gardens. For children, Wave Hill hosts Nature Stories and Songs for Families between October and March. A great break from the hustle and bustle of the city.

Weekend Family Films
Metropolitan Museum, 1000 Fifth Avenue, 570-3932, www.metmuseum.org

In conjunction with the Museum's Look Again! and Hello, Met! family programs (sketching and discussion programs conducted at the Museum for children between 5 and 12 with accompanying adults), short films are presented in the Museum's Uris Auditorium on Saturdays and Sundays from 12:30 p.m. to 1:00 p.m. and Tuesday through Friday from noon to 12:30 p.m.

World Financial Center Arts & Events Program
The Winter Garden, West Street, Battery Park City, 945-2600, www.worldfinancialcenter.com
This vaulted glass and steel dome overlooks the Hudson River from the heart of the World Financial Center (WFC), which was severely damaged by terrorist attacks on September 11, 2001. It has been painstakingly restored and features an "innovative series of free performances and visual and sound installations created to showcase emerging as well as established artists." Summer events are frequently staged on the outdoor Plaza on the Hudson River. Since 1988, the program, which is one of the largest privately funded ongoing free performing- and visual-arts programs in the country, has hosted more than 800 performances, including works commissioned for the WFC and previews of works headed for the city's major cultural venues.

Long Running Shows

Beauty and the Beast
Lunt-Fontanne Theatre, 205 West 46th Street, 575-9200
A big musical stage version of the Disney movie about the beautiful Belle, the scary Beast (really a handsome prince under a wicked spell), the enchanted castle (where the Beast's loyal staff have been turned into household objects) and a happy ending. (2 hours, 30 minutes)

Blue Man Group: Tubes
Astor Place Theatre, 434 Lafayette Street, 254-4370, www.blueman.com/ticketinfo/nyc.shtml
Three guys painted blue, a lot of noise, a lot of silliness and a lot of fun. Since 1991, Blue Man Group has been entertaining audiences with its own brand of irreverent performance art and physical and intellectual comedy. While some of the humor is above kids' heads, the show is so entertaining that everyone has a good time. Audience members in the front row risk getting wet or "goo-ed." The grand finale involves a lot of toilet paper. OK for kids over five, but note, there are a few "bad" words in the show. (1 hour, 45 minutes)

Les Miserables
Imperial Theatre, 249 West 45th Street, 239-6200
Based on the epic novel by Victor Hugo, "Les Mis" tells the stories of Jean Valjean, the policeman Javert and a host of other memorable characters set in the backdrop of 19th-century France. Beautiful music and some amazing theater moments (particularly the barricade scene) create a special theater outing for the family (as well as a chance to discuss good and evil and some history). Best for older kids. Closing in 2003. (3 hours, 10 minutes).

The Lion King
New Amsterdam Theatre, 214 West 42nd Street, 282-2900
Based on the Disney movie, "The Lion King" tells the story of Simba, Mufasa, Scar and Nala. Notwithstanding the underlying issues of fratricide, greed and the like, this is still a show for kids. What distinguishes this show from others are the incredible costumes, masks, puppets and staging. The opening scene is truly unforgettable and pure magic. For kids four and older. (2 hours, 40 minutes)

The Phantom of the Opera
Majestic Theatre, 247 West 44th Street, 239-6200
The story of a young beautiful opera singer and the disfigured Phantom who haunts the Opera House makes for a romantic tale set to a wonderful score. With lavish costumes and sets, including a very realistic chandelier that descends over the audience to crash onstage, this is a spectacle your older children will enjoy. (2 hours, 30 minutes)

Rent

Nederlander Theatre, 208 West 41st Street, 921-8000

Set in New York's East Village and loosely based on "La Bohème," this energetic rock musical explores love and friendship in the age of AIDS. This show is definitely not for kids, but your teen will not forgive you if you do not at least try to get tickets. (2 hours, 45 minutes)

Seasonal Events

Big Apple Circus

October through January.

A Christmas Carol

The Theater at Madison Square Garden. November and December.

The Nutcracker

New York City Ballet. Christmastime.

Radio City Holiday Shows

Christmas Show—November, December and the beginning of January. Spring Spectacular—April.

Ringling Brothers Barnum & Bailey Circus

Six-week run usually commencing in March.

ENTERTAINMENT INDEX

New Victory Theater
New York City Ballet
92nd Street Y
Symphony Space
Tada! Theater
Tribeca Performing Arts Center

Films

Aaron Davis Hall
Brooklyn Academy of Music (BAM)
Brooklyn Center for the Performing Arts at Brooklyn College
Film Society of Lincoln Center
Jazz at Lincoln Center
92nd Street Y
Lincoln Center
Radio City Music Hall
Sony IMAX Theatre
Symphony Space
Weekend Family Films

Folk Arts and Multicultural Events

Aaron Davis Hall
ArtsConnection
Bronx Arts Ensemble
Brooklyn Center for the Performing Arts at Brooklyn College
City Center
Community Works Theater Connections
Czechoslovak–American Marionette Theatre
Dance Theater Workshop
Dance Theatre of Harlem
Hostos Center for the Arts & Culture
Los Kabayitos Puppet & Children's Theater
92nd Street Y
Poppy Seed Players
Shadow Box Theater
Tribeca Performing Arts Center
UniverSoul Big Top Circus

Ice Shows

Ice Theatre of New York
Madison Square Garden

Music

Aaron Davis Hall
Abrons Arts Center
Apollo Theatre
ArtsConnection
Bronx Arts Ensemble
Brooklyn Academy of Music (BAM)
Brooklyn Center for the Performing Arts at Brooklyn College
Carnegie Hall
Chamber Music Society of Lincoln Center
City Center
Colden Center for the Performing Arts
Growing Up with Opera
Hostos Center for the Arts & Culture
Jazz at Lincoln Center
Lincoln Center
Little Orchestra Society
Madison Square Garden
New Victory Theater
New York City Opera
New York Philharmonic
92nd Street Y
Radio City Music Hall
Symphony Space
Tribeca Performing Arts Center
Wave Hill

Poetry

Poet's House

Puppet Shows

Czechoslovak–American Marionette Theatre
Hostos Center for the Arts & Culture
Lenny Suib Puppet Playhouse
Los Kabayitos Puppet & Children's Theater
Marionette Theater
New Victory Theater
Puppetworks
Shadow Box Theater

Readings

ArtsConnection
Wave Hill

Special Events

Colden Center for the Performing Arts
Madison Square Garden
92nd Street Y
Radio City Music Hall
World Financial Center Arts & Events Program

Theater

Aaron Davis Hall
Abrons Arts Center
ArtsConnection
Brooklyn Academy of Music (BAM)
Brooklyn Center for the Performing Arts at Brooklyn College
City Center
City Lights
Colden Center for the Performing Arts
Community Works Theater Connections
Hostos Center for the Arts & Culture
Lincoln Center
Los Kabayitos Puppet & Children's Theater
Madison Square Garden
Manhattan Children's Theatre
New Victory Theater
Paper Bag Players
Poppy Seed Players
Shadow Box Theater
Symphony Space
Tada! Theater
Theater for a New Audience
Theatreworks/USA
Thirteenth Street Repertory Company
Tribeca Performing Arts Center
Vital Children's Theatre

Chapter 10

Keeping the Kids Busy and Yourself Sane

There are some children who never want to leave their homes and others who champ at the bit to get up and out by dawn. While some quite literally never stop moving, others can sit quietly focused for hours. Wherever your children may fall in the spectrum, as parents we try to direct their activity so that their seemingly endless stream of energy and their vivid imaginations have healthy and productive outlets.

Manhattan is home to some of the world's great museums, zoos, parks and libraries as well as a thriving creative community in almost any discipline you can imagine. This bounty affords Manhattan's youngest set the opportunity to explore almost anything their hearts desire, in many instances under the direction of some of the greatest talents of our time. However, as resourceful as most city parents are, we often find ourselves drawing a big blank when it comes to deciding on something to do. Like the child standing in front of a closet full of toys complaining that there is nothing to play with, the abundance of choices at our fingertips can render even the most competent parent helpless.

Mastering the **ABC**s of juvenile entertainment and enrichment does not have to be the first step on the road to insanity, although we can guaranty that the number of things kids can do in Manhattan is indeed mind boggling. This first step to keeping the kids busy and yourself sane is to get a handle on what is actually out there for children to do. In this chapter, we have endeavored to do just that by providing an extensive listing of the possibilities.

Our ABC guide to children's activities includes **A**ctivities, which covers classes, programs and workshops offered for children; **B**oredom Busters, which covers various drop-in activities, excursions, parks, public libraries, attractions and sporting events; and **C**ultural institutions, which covers galleries, gardens, historical houses, museums and zoos. A subject index has been created for our **A**ctivities section, but don't forget to look through our **C**ultural section for additional opportunities to explore art, music, performances, science, history, gardening and much more. This information will, we hope, assist you in making choices for and with your children. We have omitted such specifics as class schedules, operating hours and costs and fees, because that sort of information tends to change frequently (and sometimes seasonally). We urge you to call for and confirm details for all programs and facilities in advance.

10

As you peruse the ABCs of keeping the kids busy and yourself sane, we hope that the listings in this chapter spark your imagination and provide options for how your children (and family!) can spend time in ways that prove both meaningful and fun. As for your sanity, we guarantee nothing.

Activities and Classes

Manhattan has an abundance of classes and programs to meet the needs of curious, active and accomplished children. We are fortunate to have an incredible number of talented individuals who are drawn here to pursue their professions, particularly in the arts. As a result, our children frequently have the opportunity to be taught by amazing teachers. As if that was not enough, there really is something for everyone. From your basic mommy-and-me class to learning how to garden in the asphalt jungle, you can probably find a class for it, or find someone who will teach you privately, in Manhattan.

The fact that a class or program exists, however, does not mean that it is right for your child. For an experience to be positive, it is important to match your child's interests and abilities with age-appropriate activities. Introducing a child to something (for example, playing an instrument) before he or she is ready (physically, socially or even emotionally) can turn him or her off to an activity or skill acquisition that later on would be perfectly fine. We must fight off the impulse to give our children a too-early head start on developing abilities or skills and instead make realistic determinations about their capabilities as well as what they actually enjoy.

Additionally, not all classes or facilities are the same. Each facility has a unique philosophy, a particular physical plant and specific instructors, all of which create a certain atmosphere. It is up to you to decide whether that atmosphere will suit your child. For example, some children can tolerate a gym where several classes are conducted at the same time, while others become overwhelmed by too much noise and activity. Some children love large classes, while others may find them intimidating. It is a good practice to visit the facility, meet the head of the program or even observe a class before signing up for an activity. Many facilities offer a free trial class, so by all means take advantage of this benefit if available.

Be aware, too, that what is supposedly the "best" class or program is not always the best for everyone. A class is only the best if your child is having a positive experience and learning what he or she is there for while having some fun.

▶ **Choices, choices, choices.** Some of the things you may want to consider when selecting an activity:

- Younger children. Does your child need to be accompanied by an adult? If so, is the class mostly attended by parents or caregivers (very important to know if you are looking for playdates too)? How does the schedule fit with your child's naps, meals, other activities, schedules of siblings and so on? If the child will attend without you, how is separation handled?

- Your child's interests. Make sure the activity makes sense for your child's age, skill level, physical ability and attention span. For older children in particular, be sure that your child is interested and committed to the program. There is nothing like spending several hundred dollars for a class only to find yourself forcing your child to go each week. Depending on the age of your child, it might be helpful to have him or her participate in the decision to take the class. It is hardly a guaranty that he or she will stick with it, but at least you can answer a protest by pointing out that he or she made the decision.
- Cost. Look at the per-class fee rather than the overall cost. A program can seem like a bargain until you realize it only meets for 10 45-minute sessions as compared to another which meets for 15 90-minute sessions.
- Program basics. Before signing up, it is worth inquiring about dropout policies, refunds, make-up classes, continuity of staff (will your child have the same instructor throughout the series), the range of ages of the children in the class and the number of children taking the class. If the program is a drop-off program or children will be bused there directly from school, make sure to inquire about the facility's security and supervision procedures (who meets children at the bus, are they accompanied to the locker room or bathrooms and so on) and, if applicable, whether an adult will wait with them until they are picked up. Visit the facility to be sure it is clean, safe and secure. If the program involves potentially dangerous physical activity (such as advanced gymnastics or hockey), inquire as to how the participating children are safeguarded against injury and what happens if a child is injured.
- Transportation. How will your child get to and from the class? In good weather walking or taking the bus may be a breeze, but in bad weather taxis may be required. Is the facility easy or hard to get to and home from? Some programs offer bus service (pick up from school, drop off at home) which can be a blessing. If busing is offered, be sure to find out how long the bus trip will be. Busing may not be so great if your child is going to have a major rush-hour commute.

- Over-scheduling. Consider the number of programs that make sense for your child. With all the interesting classes available around town, it is often hard to resist signing up for everything that sounds good. However, while a busy week may be a good thing, a too-busy week can become difficult to maintain. It is all too easy for a heavy schedule of enrichment programs to become a stressing experience. Sometimes it is better to plan light with ample down time and fill in with drop-in activities, time in the park and playdates.
- How serious? There are classes designed to expose children to an activity and those designed to immerse them in it. The age and personality of your child can help you decide which is the better direction. Younger children generally enjoy classes as much for the socializing as they do for the activity, and some may be more interested in taking a class with a friend than in concerning themselves with what they will be taking. Other children have a natural talent, genuine curiosity or focus that is best satisfied with a class that really gets into the meat of the subject.

As you embark on the ongoing process of enrolling your children in various classes and programs, we encourage you to call places for details and class schedules, ask questions, visit the locations that interest you and your child and, when appropriate, involve your child in the decision. It is up to each of us to establish our own comfort levels and to gauge what is likely to be a positive experience and what is not worth the effort. Each child deserves to find and develop a love of something, and in this city there is certainly plenty of opportunity to do so.

The classes and programs are listed in alphabetical order and include the location, phone number, ages served and program offerings. At the end of this section you will find an index of classes and programs by category (swimming, dance, music, sports and so on). A geographical code follows each facility listed under a particular category, so that you can determine its general location and look up only those facilities most convenient to you. Because class times and seasonal schedules change frequently, we cannot list such program details.

There are quite a few organizations that offer a full range of classes catering to many different interests and age levels. In those instances the indication for ages may not apply to all courses offered by a particular facility. Finally, names can be deceiving, so be aware as you use this resource that nothing can replace your inquiry. For example, there are many programs referred to as "mommy-and-me" classes. The term "mommy-and-me" has become a generic phrase for classes, typically geared to the under-three-year-old crowd, at which the child is accompanied by an adult during class time. In many cases, the adult can be either parent (mommy or daddy) or caregiver, but some classes strictly limit the adults to parents. We recommend contacting organization directly for specifics.

Many, if not most, of the listed facilities, programs and activities host birthday parties or have summer programming (including anything from full camp to special summer workshops) or school vacation programs held during school breaks throughout the year. We have not specifically indicated whether such offerings are made because the offerings are very facility-, program- or activity-specific and tend to change frequently. For example, birthday parties can mean anything from space rental to a soup-to-nuts party package, a vacation program can mean anything from a one-day event to a full two-week all-inclusive program, and a summer program can mean a full day of camp or a one-hour class offered once a week. If you are interested in organizing a party or looking for programming beyond after-school activities, it is best to contact the facility, program or activity for more information.

▶ **Summer in the city?** As the end of the school year approaches, parents of school-age kids are faced with decisions about summer plans for the family. Some families leave the city for all or part of the summer, but the vast majority remain in town, at least during the work week. Without the proverbial backyard or local town swim or recreational program to fall back on, once children get beyond the toddler stage, most city parents opt to put their kids in some type of summer program for all or part of the day. Fortunately for Manhattan parents, there are many programs from which to choose both within, or within a reasonable bus ride from, the city.

By the time the kids reach the latter part of elementary school, many families begin to look beyond day programs to resident camping, travel or academic experiences.

As you begin to consider organizing your child's summer plans, the first step is to determine what type of program you are looking for. Note that within the following categories, many programs can be further classified as co-ed or single sex and that some will have a particular religious or other affiliation.

- Day camp. Day programs can range from the traditional camps, which offer a wide range of sports, arts and social activities during the day, to specialty programs (all-sports, a particular sport, drama, computer, dance, etc.). Depending on the facility, the program may involve leaving the premises for field trips or for certain activities (bowling, tennis, swim).
- Resident camp. Also referred to as sleepaway or overnight camp, again programs can range from traditional all-activity programs to specialty programs. Resident camps usually offer sessions ranging from one week to seven- or eight-week programs. Traditional camps in the Northeast tend to offer either four-week or full summer sessions. Specialty programs tend to offer weekly sessions.
- Travel or adventure camps. These programs take older children on various themed trips such as outward-bound experiences, camping trips, "teen tours," hiking, horseback riding, community service experiences and so forth.

- Educational camps. These programs typically focus on particular academic pursuits such as foreign languages, science or math, remedial tutoring, enrichment, computer/technology or test preparation (such as SAT preparation).
- Special needs camps. Special needs programs are designed around particular issues such as learning or behavioral issues, physical disabilities, health issues, weight loss and so forth. The programs generally provide specific support (including therapeutic support) that addresses the needs of the particular population.

With more than 10,000 day, resident and travel programs available in the U.S., finding a camp can be a daunting task. As with most other things, the key is to do your research thoroughly and well in advance of the time you need to make your plans. The best source is the recommendations of friends and family. You can also refer to the local parenting publications, which usually run one or more issues about summer camp (generally during the winter) that highlight local and resident programs. There are many websites (some of which are listed at the end of this chapter) to peruse which list camps by region, specialty and so forth. In addition, there are quite a few private consultants in the tri-state area (most of whom advertise in the local parenting publication) who specialize in helping families find summer programs. Finally, be on the lookout for camp fairs, usually advertised in local publications, which are generally held in malls and schools, at which many camps will have on-site representatives and materials about their programs.

As you evaluate summer programs, it is always recommended that you visit the camp facility (many offer off-season tours, or try to tour the camp during the summer for programs you are considering for the following year) and be sure to speak with the director of the program before signing up. Some other things to consider:

- What kind of experience are you or your child seeking: learning or improving certain skills or knowledge (such as sports, performing, playing an instrument, swimming); leadership opportunities; enhancing social skills or building friendships; being outdoors; an "old-fashioned" camp experience?

- What are the logistics of the program: what are the camp hours; is transportation provided; is lunch provided or served; how is security handled; is the camp accredited by any camping association or organization; how many campers are there, what is the age range of participants and what is the staff/camper ratio; how are activities scheduled and how is the day paced; how are the children supervised; are the physical facilities clean, well-maintained and safe; how are medical or other emergencies handled?
- What is the camp philosophy and how is that philosophy reflected in the program?
- Who runs the camp and what are the director's qualifications? How is staff selected and what are their qualifications (particularly important with respect to instructors in specialty programs)?

- When looking at resident programs, consider whether your child is ready (physically, emotionally and psychologically) to be away from home and how the camp handles issues of separation and homesickness.

▶ **One from Column A....** We wish you luck in organizing your children's schedules, the stamina required to keep the ball rolling, the patience to keep up with their ever-changing interests and the sense of humor you will need when they say "I don't want to do that anymore."

Activities and Classes

ABC Language Service 5+
135 West 29th Street, between Sixth and Seventh Avenues, Suite 1204, 431-9101, www.abclang.org
Group (either existing or form your own) and private lessons in Spanish, French, Italian, German, Portugese, Russian, Chinese, Japanese and more.

ACE-IT Junior Development Tennis Program 6+
East River Tennis Club, 44-02 Vernon Blvd., Long Island City, Queens, 718 937-2381 ext. 28, www.ace-it.net
Tennis instruction for all levels. Pee Wee tennis for younger kids. Transportation available.

ACT Programs at Cathedral of St. John the Divine 18 months–13 years
Amsterdam Avenue between 111th and 112th Streets, 316-7530
Toddler classes. After-school program.

Acting Creatively 6–16
122 West 26th Street between Sixth and Seventh Avenues, 2nd floor, 646 336-7985, www.actingcreatively.com
Acting workshops and classes. Private coaching and industry showcases.

Acting Works 8+
80 West 40th Street between Fifth and Sixth Avenues, 9th floor, 721-2255, www.actingworks.com
Arts and crafts, breath and voice work, improvisation, sound and movement, theater games, writing.

Actors Workshop 5+
757-2835 or 877-4899
Individual coaching and teaching by appointment with Flo Salant Greenberg. Classes for teens.

After School Workshop on Madison 5–13
45 East 81st Street between Madison and Park Avenues (in P.S. 6, but an independent program), 734-7620
Arts and crafts, ballet, computers, homework help, languages, sports and tennis.

Aikido, New York Aikikai 5–12
142 West 18th Street between Sixth and Seventh Avenues, 242-6246, www.nyaikikai.com
Martial arts instruction.

Alfred E. Smith Recreation Center 6+
80 Catherine Street between Madison Avenue and South Street, 285-0300, www.nyc.gov/parks
Arts and crafts; break dancing; chess; computer room with an Internet-for-kids program; gardening; karate; co-ed sports, including baseball, basketball and soccer; and teen video production club. Movie night, video game night and Saturday rollerblading.

All City Junior Tennis 5+
Roosevelt Island Racquet Club, 281 Main Street next to Tram
Manhattan Plaza Racquet Club, 450 West 43rd Street at Tenth Avenue
Columbus Tennis Club, 795 Columbus Avenue at 98th Street
935-0250, www.rirctennis.com
Tennis instruction for all levels. Transportation available.

Alvin Ailey American Dance Center 3+
211 West 61st Street between Amsterdam and West End Avenues, 3rd floor, 767-0940 ext. 242, www.alvinailey.org
Creative movement, pre-professional track in ballet and other dance forms by audition and a Saturday sampler multi-disciplinary dance program.

The American Academy of Dramatic Arts 8+
120 Madison Avenue between 30th and 31st Streets, 686-9244, www.aada.org
Saturday morning acting, movement, speech/voice classes. Summer program for individuals 15 years and older.

The American Youth Dance Theater infant+
434 East 75th Street between First and York Avenues, Suite 1C, 717-5419, www.americanyouthdancetheater.com
Ballet, Isadora Duncan, jazz, Kindermusik, modern dance, mommy-and-me movement, preschool ballet/creative movement and tap.

Antonia Arts, Inc. 8–16
Multiple locations, 800 799-5831
Theater workshops and show-dancing programs.

Applause Theatrical Workshop 5+
Multiple locations, 439-9050, www.applauseny.com
Weekend musical theater workshops. After-school classes.

Art Farm 6 months–5 years
419 East 91st Street between First and York Avenues, 410-3117, www.theartfarms.org
Classes with animal guests followed by art, baking, cooking and music activities.

Art 'n' Orbit 18 months+
Multiple locations, 646 366-9771, www.artnorbit.com
Invention-oriented classes combining science and art. After-school programs.

Art Safari, Inc. 3–11
2 Fifth Avenue at Washington Square, 529-1484
Art program including painting, puppet-making, mask-making, museum tours and sculpture. Special-needs classes available.

Art Students League of New York 8+
215 West 57th Street between Broadway and Seventh Avenue, 247-4510, www.theartstudentsleague.org
Saturday and Sunday art programs.

Arts Gate Center 3.5+
70 Mulberry Street between Canal and Bayard Streets, 2nd floor, 349-0126, www.htchendance.org
Ballet, martial arts (wusu), modern dance, piano, pre-ballet, traditional Chinese dance.

Asphalt Green infant+
555 East 90th Street at York Avenue, 369-8890, www.asphaltgreen.org
Art and recreation, basketball, chess, dance and movement, fine and graphic arts, football, gymnastics, hip-hop, inline skating, jazz, lifeguard training for teens, martial arts, mommy-and-me, soccer, softball, swimming, and yoga. Private lessons available in swimming and gymnastics. Community sports leagues. Gymnastics and swim teams. Swimming with disabilities program.

Asser Levy Recreation Center 18 months–12 years
East 23rd Street and FDR Drive, 447-2020, www.nyc.gov/parks
After-school program, kids karate and Rhythmic Tots.

Baby Aqua 5 months–3 years
East and West Side locations, 744-6622, www.aquamom.com
Baby swim classes during the warm months.

Baby Fingers 1 month–4 years
Multiple locations, 874-5978, www.mybabyfingers.com
Sign language classes designed for hearing children. Mommy-and-me classes teach sign language through music. Drop-off nursery program incorporates sign language with the arts and social play. Deaf and hard-of-hearing children welcome.

Ballet Academy East 2–16
1651 Third Avenue between 92nd and 93rd Streets, 410-9140
Ballet instruction for all levels. Classes in jazz, modern dance, mommy-and-me movement and tap.

Ballet Hispanico 4+
167 West 89th Street between Columbus and Amsterdam Avenues, 362-6710, www.ballethispanico.org
Ballet, Flamenco, jazz and modern.

Basketball City 6+
Pier 63 on West 23rd Street and Twelfth Avenue, 924-4040 exts. 106 and 115, www.basketballcity.com
Basketball instruction, clinics, leagues and tournaments. Open playtime.

Berlitz Kids 3+
40 West 51st Street between Fifth and Sixth Avenues, 765-1000, www.berlitz.com
Individual, semi-private, and group instruction in all languages at various locations.

Big Apple Sports Club grades 1–9
Multiple locations, 987-9865, 987-9853
Youth basketball league. Summer sports training camp.

biz Kids NY 8+
125 Barrow Street at Washington Street, 646 336-9101
Professional training for commercial, film and TV. Acting workshops and conservatory classes.

Bloomingdale School of Music 6 months+
323 West 108th Street between Broadway and Riverside Drive, 663-6021, www.bsmny.org
Classes in guitar, keyboard, music/movement and violin. Private instruction in all instruments. Suzuki piano, violin and cello. Some ensemble groups.

Body and Spirit Program of Rutgers Presbyterian Church 6 months+
236 West 73rd Street between Broadway and West End Avenue, 877-8227 ext. 212, www.rutgerschurch.com
Art, creative movement, music, musical theater, sports, tap. Toddler program. After-school program

Boys Choir—Church of the Transfiguration 9–11
One East 29th Street between Fifth and Madison Avenues, 684-6770
Boys choir by audition only.

Boy Scouts of America 6+
350 Fifth Avenue (office), 242-1100, www.bsa_gnyc.org
Call to locate the den closest to you or start your own.

Bridge for Dance 3+
2726 Broadway between 104th and 105th Streets, 3rd floor, 749-1165, www.bridgefordance.org
Ballet, creative movement, hip-hop, jazz, modern dance, and tap.

Broadway Babies 6 months–5 years
184 East 76th Street between Third and Lexington Avenues in St. Jean's Community Center, 472-0703
142 West 81st Street between Amsterdam and Columbus Avenues in Mt. Pleasant Baptist Church, 787-2704
www.applauseny.com
Unique mommy-and-me and drop-off classes, each using a different Broadway musical to combine drama, dress-up, movement and singing. Live music accompaniment. Instructors are Broadway actors.

Broadway Dance Center 3+
221 West 57th Street at Broadway, 5th floor, 582-9304 ext. 25, www.broadwaydancecenter.com
Ballet, creative movement, hip-hop, jazz, pre-dance, tap, and triple threat.

The Calhoun School 4+
160 West 74th Street between Amsterdam and Columbus Avenues
433 West End Avenue at 81st Street
877-1700, www.Calhoun.org
After-school program open to all.

Campbell Music Studio 18 months+
436 East 69th Street between First and York Avenues
2095 Broadway at 73rd Street
305 West End Avenue at 74th Street
496-0105, www.campbellmusicstudio.com
Preschool music includes creative movement and singing. Classes are non-instrumental up to age five. Music history and theory for advanced students. Private piano instruction beginning at age 3.

Carlos Oliveira Soccer Academy 4+
Astroturf field at 101st Street and Riverside Drive, 718 743-9402, www.cosacademy.com
Soccer skills training programs for all levels.

Carmine Recreation Center 3–12
One Clarkson Street below Seventh Avenue South, 242-5228 or 242-5418, www.nyc.gov/parks
After-school program, basketball, flag football, swimming classes, drop-in recreation opportunities.

CATS, Children's Athletic Training School 1–12
235 East 49th Street between Second and Third Avenues, 832-1833
109 East 50th Street at Park Avenue in St. Bart's Church house, 751-4876
131 West 86th Street between Columbus and Amsterdam Avenues at the Jewish Center, 877-3154
Basketball, dance (ballet, creative movement, hip-hop/jazz, tap and theater dance) martial arts, multi-sports, swimming, yoga.

Cavaliers Athletic Club 4+
Multiple locations, 865-4300
Seasonal sports program and summer sports day camp. Transportation available.

Central Park Youth Hockey 6–13
Wollman and Lasker Rinks, 439-6900 ext. 14, www.wollmanskatingrink.com
Hockey, power skating, girls' hockey development.

Champs Sports Club 4–10
Multiple locations, 996-7646
Gymnastics, ice skating, team sports, after-school programs. Transportation available.

Chelsea Piers infant+
23rd Street and the Hudson River, 336-6666, www.chelseapiers.com
Aggressive skating, basketball, batting, bowling, dance, figure skating, golf, gymnastics, in-line skating, ice hockey, ice skating, indoor soccer, martial arts, mommy-and-me, outdoor soccer, rock climbing, roller hockey and skateboarding.

Childhood Memories 6 months–7 years
Upper East Side locations, 717-1853
Group music classes. Private flute and piano instruction.

Children and Art 7+
747 Amsterdam Avenue at 96th Street in the Claremont Children's School, 917 841-9651, 917 447-1562
After-school art classes.

Children of Today 1–5
131 West 72nd Street between Columbus and Amsterdam Avenues, 799-7810, www.childrenoftoday.baweb.com
Classes blending art and craft, dance, dramatic play, movement, and music.

Children's Acting Academy 5+
East and West Side locations, 860-7101
Acting classes, starting with creative drama for young students. Casting director invited to spring performance.

The Children's Aid Society—Greenwich Village Center 10 months+
219 Sullivan Street between West 3rd Street and Bleecker Street, 254-3074, www.childrensaidsociety.org
After-school program, arts and crafts, chorus, cooking, dance and movement, Kindermusik, martial arts, performing, photography, visual arts and toddler time.

Children's Tumbling 2–12
9-15 Murray Street between Broadway and Church Street, 10th floor, 233-3418, www.childrentumbling.com
Mommy-and-me, circus arts, creative movement and gymnastics.

Child's Play 9 months–4 years
236 West 73rd Street between Broadway and West End Avenue in the Rutgers Presbyterian Church, 877-8227
165 West 86th Street in the West Park Presbyterian Church, 838-1504
www.westparkchurch.org
Parent and child playgroups (no caregivers) organized by age. Homeschooler program at West Park location.

China Institute in America 4+
125 East 65th Street between Park and Lexington Avenues, 744-8181 ext. 142, www.chinainstitute.org
Weekend classes in Chinese language and culture.

Chris Porté's After School Junior Tennis 5+
Multiple locations, 288-4005
Tennis instruction for all levels.

Church Street School for Music & Art 16 months+
74 Warren Street between West Broadway and Greenwich Street, 571-7290
Art Express and classes for brass ensembles, flute, folk and rock guitar, music and movement, Dalcroze eurythmics, piano, recorder and visual arts. Private instruction in most instruments.

Circus Gymnastics 6 months+
2121 Broadway between 74th and 75th Streets, 799-3755
Gymnastics instruction for all levels, mommy-and-me classes.

City Lights Youth Theatre K+
300 West 43rd Street at Eighth Avenue, Suite 402, 262-0200
Year-round workshops in acting, musical theater, playwrighting and productions.

Claremont Riding Academy 6+
175 West 89th Street between Columbus and Amsterdam Avenues, 724-5100, www.potomachorse.com
Private horseback riding instruction for all levels.

The Collective 10+
541 Avenue of the Americas between 14th and 15th Streets, 741-0091, www.thecoll.com
Instruction in bass, drum, guitar, keyboard and voice. Private lessons for all ages. Hand drumming classes available.

Columbus Gym 1–12
606 Columbus Avenue at 89th Street, 721-0090
Gymnastics classes.

Corbin's Crusaders 4–14
Multiple locations, 875-8174, www.corbinscrusaders.com
Afternoon and Saturday programs in baseball, basketball, soccer, softball, lacrosse, roller hockey, tennis, touch football and swimming. Transportation provided.

Core Fitness 5+
12 East 86th Street between Fifth and Madison Avenues, 327-4197, www.corefitnessinc.com
Self-defense classes combining boxing, kick boxing, and tae kwon do. Individual instruction available.

Creatability 2+
500 East 88th Street between York and East End Avenues, 535-4033, www.creatability.us
Arts and crafts center and playspace. Both drop-in projects and scheduled classes available.

Crosstown Tennis 5+
14 West 31st Street between Fifth Avenue and Broadway, 2nd floor, 947-5780, www.crosstowntennis.com
Tennis instruction for all levels.

CYO (Catholic Youth Organization) Manhattan Youth Baseball K+
Multiple locations, 924-7001
Co-ed youth baseball program. All-girls teams for fourth graders and older.

Dance! Dance! Dance! 18 months–16 years
220 East 86th Street between Second and Third Avenues, 439-9528
Arts and crafts, dancing, mommy-and-me singing, theater.

Dance Theater Workshop 5+
219 West 19th Street between Seventh and Eighth Avenues, 691-6500, www.dtw.org
Modern dance, improvisation and composition.

Dance Theatre of Harlem School 3+
466 West 152nd Street between St. Nicholas and Amsterdam Avenues, 690-2800, www.dancetheatreofharlem.org
Ballet and tap.

Developing Artists Acting School 8+
48 West 21st Street between Fifth and Sixth Avenues, 4th floor, 929-2228, www.developingartists.com
Acting, improvisation, writing. Youth theater company.

Dieu Donne Papermill, Inc. 5+
433 Broome Street between Broadway and Crosby Street, 226-0573, www.papermaking.org
Papermaking classes and workshops.

Diller-Quaile School of Music 1+
24 East 95th Street between Fifth and Madison Avenues, 369-1484, www.diller-quaile.org
Comprehensive music program. Individual instrumental and voice instruction available.

Discovery Programs Inc. 6 months+
251 West 100th Street between Broadway and West End Avenue, 749-8717
Art, art and science (Young Leonardos), ballet, gymnastics, music and movement, musical theater, pre-ballet, tae kwon do. Alternative toddler and preschool programs.

Djoniba Dance & Drum Center 3+
37 East 18th Street between Broadway and Park Avenue, 7th floor, 477-3464, www.djoniba.com
African dance, African drums and ballet.

Drama Kids International 5+
Various Upper West Side locations, 268-0054, www.dramakids.com
This drama program is the exclusive U.S. provider of the Helen O'Grady Children's Drama Program.

The Early Ear Music Program 4 months–5 years
48 West 68th Street between Central Park West and Columbus Avenue
353 East 78th Street between First and Second Avenues
110 West 96th Street between Amsterdam and Columbus Avenues
877-7125, www.theearlyear.com
Early childhood music classes.

Earthworks and Artisans 6+
2182 Broadway at 77th Street, 2nd floor, 873-5220
Pottery instruction.

East Side Creative Arts Studio 6 months+
317 East 89th Street between First and Second Avenues, 369-9492, www.eastsidecas.com
Individual instruction in guitar, percussion and piano, art therapy, drama therapy and music therapy.

East Village Dance Project 4–12
536 East 5th Street between Avenues A and B, 982-5751
Ballet, creative movement and modern dance. Run and Jump (for boys) and Tai Chi (for girls).

Ellen Robbins Modern Dance 5+
219 West 19th Street between Seventh and Eighth Avenues, 254-0286, www.dtw.org
Modern dance technique, improvisation and composition.

Empire Dance 7–17
127 West 25th Street, between Sixth and Seventh Avenues, 11th floor, 645-2441, www.empiredance.com
Hip-hop, salsa, swing, tango.

Ethics for Children 4–13
New York Society for Ethical Culture, 2 West 64th Street at Central Park West, 874-5210, www.nysec.org
A non-theistic program involving discussions, music, art and dramatics, all of which provide the context for developing moral reasoning.

The Family Music Center 6 months–4 years
864-2476
Kindermusik Musikgarden classes and individual piano instruction for all levels and ages.

First Impression 7+
472-1270
Group and private etiquette classes for children, teens, and families held at a fine East Side restaurant.

14th Street Y infant+
Sol Goldman YM-YWHA of the Educational Alliance, Inc.
344 East 14th Street at First Avenue, 780-0800, www.edalliance.org
Arts, basketball, dance, gymnastics, martial arts, mommy-and-me, music, performing arts, soccer, swimming and theater/creative dramatics. Programs in Jewish life and learning and a Japanese Parenting and Family Center.

Fred Astaire Dance Studio 6+
127 West 25th Street between Sixth and Seventh Avenues, 475-7776
303 East 43rd Street between First and Second Avenues, 697-6535
2182 Broadway at 77th Street, 2nd floor, 595-3200
157 East 86th Street between Lexington and Third Avenues, 3rd floor, 348-4430
www.fredastaire.com
Private ballroom dancing lessons. Form your own group for group lessons.

French–American Conservatory of Music at Carnegie Hall 3+
154 West 57th Street at Seventh Avenue, Suite 136, 246-7378, www.facmusic.org
Kindermusik. Instruction for children's choir, flute, piano, string instruments and voice for all levels.

French Institute/Alliance Française 4+
22 East 60th Street between Park and Madison Avenues, 355-6100, www.fiaf.org
Saturday morning language classes.

Frozen Ropes Baseball Center 2+
202 West 74th Street between Broadway and Amsterdam Avenue, 362-0344, www.frozenropesnyc.com
Private lessons and team training. After-school program. Batting and pitching practice. Indoor and outdoor leagues.

Futurekids 3+
1628 First Avenue between 84th and 85th Streets, 717-0110, www.nycfuturekids.com
Computer learning center for kids.

German American School 4+
Multiple locations, 787-7543, www.german-american-school.org
After-school German language classes.

Girl Scout Council of Greater NY, Inc. 5+
43 West 23rd Street at Fifth and Sixth Avenues, 7th floor, 645-4000, www.girlscoutsnyc.org
Call to locate the troop closest to you or start your own. Summer camping.

Global Enrichment & Discovery Classes 3.6–10
1287 Madison Avenue between 91st and 92nd Streets, 410-4767
Hands-on activities in art history, earth science, geography, language, literature, math, science, writing and zoology.

Goddard-Riverside Community Center 6–10
647 Columbus Avenue between 91st and 92nd Streets, 799-9400, www.goddard.org
After-school program, including computers, environmental education, homework help, performing and visual arts, sports and fitness.

Goodson Parker Wellness Center infant+
30 East 76th Street, 4th floor, 717-5273, www.yogababy.com
Yoga for babies and children.

Gramercy Park School of Music 2.6+
9 East 36th Street between Fifth and Madison Avenues, 683-8937, www.gramercyparkschoolofmusic.com
Private instruction for piano, recorder, voice and other instruments.

Greenwich House Music School 1+
46 Barrow Street between Seventh Avenue and Bedford Street, 242-4770, www.gharts.org
Art, ballet, and music. Private instruction for most orchestral instruments.

Greenwich House Pottery 2.6+
16 Jones Street between Bleecker and West 4th Streets, 242-4106, www.gharts.org
All levels of clay instruction using both hand work and potter's wheel.

Gym Time 6 months+
1520 York Avenue at 80th Street, 861-7732
Gymnastics instruction for boys and girls at all levels. Age-appropriate developmental fitness classes, including floor hockey, soccer, tae kwon do, tennis and tiny tot fitness. Location shared with Rhythm and Glues, an arts-and-crafts program, allowing parents to schedule coordinating classes.

Gymboree 1 month–3 years
64 West 3rd Street between LaGuardia Place and Thompson Streets
50 Lexington Avenue at 24th Street
30 West 68th Street between Central Park West and Columbus Avenue
401 East 84th Street at First Avenue
165 West 86th Street at Amsterdam Avenue
877-496-5327
Gymagination, Gymboree play, and Gymboree music.

Hands On! 4 months–4 years
19 Warren Street between Church Street and Broadway, 227-7375
1356 First Avenue between 73rd and 74th Streets, 628-1945
529 Columbus Avenue between 85th and 86th Streets, 496-9929
Music classes featuring songs from Broadway musicals and the American folk tradition as well as classical music.

Harbor Conservatory for the Performing Arts 6+
One East 104th Street between Fifth and Madison Avenues, 427-2244 ext. 573
African dance, ballet, hip-hop, jazz, modern dance and tap. Private lessons in most instruments. Specializes in Latin music and Latin percussion.

Harlem School of the Arts 4+
645 St. Nicholas Avenue near 141st Street, 926-4100 ext. 304, www.harlemschoolofthearts.org
Dance, theater and visual arts. Private lessons in musical instruments and voice. Percussion, violin and vocal ensembles. Jazz band. Audition-only college prep programs.

HB Studio (Herbert Berghof Studio) 9–17
120 Bank Street between Greenwich and Washington Streets, 675-2370, www.hbstudio.org
Acting, movement, musical theater and speech. During the school year, children's classes are offered only on the weekend.

Henry Street Settlement Abrons Arts Center infant+
466 Grand Street at Pitt Street, 598-0400, www.henrystreet.org
Dance, drama, music, theater, visual arts and voice. Parent–toddler classes for music and art.

Herard Center of Multimedia 9–teen
47 West 34th Street between Fifth and Sixth Avenues, Suite 543, 268-0915, www.hcm-ny.com
Computer instruction and program developing computer and entrepreneurial skills.

Hi Art 2–12
Mid-town and Lincoln Center Studios, 362-8190, www.hiartkids.com
Parent and child workshops, which offer an introduction to "Hi Art." "Culture Bugs" offered during the summer.

Hippo Family Club infant+
Midtown location, 800 315-4387, www.lexlrf.org
Language classes for families and individuals. Weekly club meetings introduce members to up to six different languages through songs and games.

Hola 18 months–4 years
Various downtown locations, 917 648-5006
Mommy-and-me playgroups conducted in Spanish (including arts and crafts, games and music) for children who have one or two hispanic parents, a hispanic caregiver or just want to learn Spanish.

Ice Hockey in Harlem 4+
Lasker Rink in Central Park and Ice Rink in Riverbank State Park, 722-0044, www.icehockeyinharlem.org
Saturday clinics, after-school program, intramural leagues.

Imagine Swimming 18 months–10 years
Upper East Side and Gramercy Park locations, 253-9650, www.imagineswimming.com
Swimming classes and private lessons.

Improvisational Theatre for Children 7–15
East and West Side locations, 874-5054
A program that encourages children to express themselves creatively through the language of movement and theater.

In Grandma's Attic 2–12
48 West 68th Street at Studio Maestro and other locations, 726-2362
A fantasy-based creative dance program, guiding students through story, dance, dress-up and pretend.

Institute of Culinary Education 8+
50 West 23rd Street between Fifth and Sixth Avenues, 847-0770, www.iceculinary.com
Single-session cooking classes include pizza-making, baking and others. Three-day cooking camps with each day focusing on a different cuisine. Gingerbread house-making parent–child class for younger children offered in December.

Instituto Cervantes 5+
122 East 42nd Street, 661-6011 ext. 6, www.institutocervantes.org
Spanish language and culture classes.

The InterSchool Orchestras of New York 6–19
Multiple locations, 410-0370, www.isorch.org
Five orchestras for young instrumentalists at all levels. Opportunities to participate in The Brooklyn Wind band, percussion and chamber music ensembles. Two beginner orchestras require no audition.

Jack & Jill Playgroup 20–30 months
61 Gramercy Park North between Lexington and Park Avenues, 475-0855
Mommy-and-me program.

Jams infant+
165 West 91st Street, 595-0563, www. jamsnet.com
Music literacy, music appreciation and pre-instrumental classes.

Janet Nixon teens
779-3018
Group etiquette lessons and private workshops focusing on self-respect and respect for others.

Jeff Nerenberg Tennis Academy 7+
Manhattan Plaza Racquet Club, 450 West 43rd Street at Tenth Avenue and other locations, 718 549-9391
Tennis instruction for all levels. Kinder Tennis, an introductory tennis program. Grand prix travel team, USTA national player development program. Transportation available.

Jewish Community Center in Manhattan infant+
334 Amsterdam Avenue at 76th Street, 580-0099 ext. 213, www.jccnyc.org

Art, baby massage, ballet, baseball, boxing, capoeira, clay, clowning, ceramics, cooking, creative movement, community service programs for preteens and teens, family programs, gymnastics, jewelry making, Jewish culture, karate, mommy-and-me, multi-sports, musical theater, painting, photography, playwriting, pottery, science, swimming, yoga. Special-needs classes available. All-afternoon clubhouse program for children taking an after-school class. Evening and weekend teen programs.

Jodi's Gym 6 months–12 years
244 East 84th Street between Second and Third Avenues, 772-7633
Gymnastics for all levels.

Joe Espinosa's Sports Club 6–14
Multiple locations, 662-8807, 800 556-6154
After-school co-ed baseball and basketball leagues. Transportation provided.

Joffery Ballet School 3+

434 Sixth Avenue between 9th and 10th Streets, 254-8520, www.joffreyballetschool.com

Graded classes in creative movement, pre-ballet, ballet, character and jazz.

Judy Lasko Modern Dance 3+

165 West 86th Street in the West Park Presbyterian Church
124 West 95th Street in the Studio School
864-3143

Co-ed modern dance. Teen company.

Juilliard Pre-College Division 5+

60 Lincoln Center Plaza between Broadway and Amsterdam Avenue, 799-5000 ext. 241, www.juilliard.edu

Saturday music program for gifted children.

Just Wee Two 14 months–3.5 years

Upper West Side location, 800 404-2204, www.justweetwo.com

Arts and crafts, creative movement, music, stories.

Karen's Performing Arts 5–11

331 West 25th Street between Eighth and Ninth Avenues, 243-5192

Multi-disciplinary program includes on-camera training, dance, drama, vocalization, sports and art. Regular performances for children. Other classes include African dance, musical theater, clowning and hip-hop.

Karma Kids Yoga 3–12

104 West 14th Street between Sixth and Seventh Avenues, 646 638-1444, www.karmakidsyoga.com

Yoga classes for children plus mother/infant and parent/child classes.

Kid City Theater Company 6–12

50 West 13th Street at the Thirteenth Street Theater, 604-0502

Musical theater. Classes stage performances at the end of each semester.

Kids at Art 2–11

1349 Lexington Avenue between 89th and 90th Streets, 410-9780, www.kidsatartnyc.com

Art classes including drawing, painting and sculpture.

Kids Co-Motion in Soho 1+
280 Rector Place in Battery Park City
579 Broadway between Prince and Houston Streets
37 West 26th Street between Sixth Avenue and Broadway in the Stepping Out Studio
165 West 86th Street at Amsterdam Avenue in the West Park Presbyterian Church
431-8489, www.rebeccakelly.com
Beginning ballet, choreography, creative movement, dance movement, beginning modern dance, mommy-and-me and music classes.

Kids in the Kitchen (renamed **The Mixing Bowl**) 2.5–9
243 East 82nd Street between Second and Third Avenues, 585-2433, www.kidsinthekitchennyc.com
Cooking classes.

Kids 'N Comedy Workshop 8–15
34 West 22nd Street in Gotham Comedy Club, 877-6115, www.kidsncomedy.com
Monthly workshops. Stand-up shows by invitation.

Kids on Wheels Joel Rappelfeld's In-line Skating 5+
Multiple locations, 744-4444
In-line skating programs offered after school and weekends. Private and group instruction and family programs available.

Kids Pilates 11+
Multiple locations, 627-5852, www.powerpilates.com
Pilates for children and teens.

Knickerbocker Greys 7–15
643 Park Avenue at 67th Street in the Seventh Regiment Armory, 683-3154
This organization dates back to 1881 and continues to teach leadership skills in a military context.

Kokushi Budo Institute of New York 6+
331 Riverside Drive between 105th and 106th Streets, 866-6777
Aikido, jiujitsu, judo, karate and self-defense.

Kumon Math and Reading Centers 3+
1582 First Avenue between 82nd and 83rd Streets, 717-1644, 861-8007
165 West 86th Street between Columbus and Amsterdam Avenues, 749-2931
Downtown location, 532-1365
800 ABC-Math (800 222-6284), www.kumon.com
With more than 1,300 locations in the U.S., these popular math and reading centers use a curriculum based on timed tests to promote progressive skill-building.

Kyokushin Karate 4+
284 Fifth Avenue at 30th Street
131 West 72nd Street between Columbus and Amsterdam Avenues
947-3334, www.kyokushinkarate.com
Karate.

La Croisette Language Center 6 months+
Multiple locations, 861-7723
After-school programs for children ages 2–13. In-home instruction available.

La Mano Pottery 5+
237 West 18th Street between Seventh and Eighth Avenues, 627-9450, www.lamanopottery.com
Classes in handbuilding with clay and mosaics. Teen wheel class.

Language Garden 2.6–5
888-3594
Mommy-and-me and nannies speech and language enrichment program focusing on vocabulary, speech, social skills and other activities that facilitate language development.

Language Workshop for Children 6 months–12 years
888 Lexington Avenue between 65th and 66th Streets, 396-1369, 800 731-0830, www.thibauttechnique.com
Language for tots, after-school and Saturday language classes in French and Spanish.

Lasker Rink and Pool 2+
Central Park at 110th Street, 534-7639
Outdoor private and group skating and ice hockey instruction available from November to March. From the end of June to Labor Day, the Rink is converted back into a swimming pool and is available for swimming with summer programs run by the Department of Parks and Recreation.

Lee Strasberg Theatre Institute 7–17
Young People's Program, 115 East 15th Street between Union Square and Irving Place, 533-5500, www.strasberg.com
Acting for the camera, basic acting and technique as well as dance instruction, Young Actors & Company production.

Lenox Hill Neighborhood House 4–14
331 East 70th Street, 744-5022 ext. 24
Karate, scuba diving, soccer, swimming.

Lezly Skate School 11+
Multiple locations, 777-3232, www.skateguru.com
Group and private in-line and traditional skating instruction.

Life Sport Gymnastics 2+
165 West 86th Street at Amsterdam Avenue in the West Park Presbyterian Church, 769-3131
Gymnastics instruction for all levels.

The Lion and the Lamb 6+
1460 Lexington Avenue between 94th and 95th Streets, 876-4303
Knitting, beading, needlepoint. Private and semi-private instruction available.

Little Cooks, Ltd. 4+
Multiple locations, 888 695-2665, www. littlecooks.com
Private and group instruction in your home. After-school programs, scout sessions and camps.

Little League Baseball 7+
860 585-4730, www.littleleague.com
Call this general number for referral to local administration affiliates for specific information. Teams are co-ed.

Loco-Motion Dance Theater for Children 6+
West Village location, 979-6124
All styles of dance and theater.

The Loft Kitchen 7+
551 West 22nd Street between Tenth and Eleventh Avenues, 924-0177
Form your own group for cooking instruction.

Lucy Moses School 18 months+
129 West 67th Street between Amsterdam Avenue and Broadway, 501-3360, www.ekcc.org
Art, chorus, Dalcroze eurythmics, dance, music and theater. Musical theater workshops.

Madison Square Boy's and Girl's Club 6+
477-2200, www.madisonsquare.org
After-school program begins with the Paine Weber power hour for homework. Other programs include sports education, computer lab and poetry workshop. Youth Employment Program.

Manhattan Babe Ruth League, Cal Ripken Division 5–11
www.nycbaberuth.org
Baseball league. Plays in Central Park. Travel teams play other local Babe Ruth League teams.

Manhattan Ballet School, Inc. 3+
149 East 72nd Street between Lexington and Third Avenues, 535-6556
Classical training in ballet, pre-ballet through professional. *Nutcracker* and spring performances.

Manhattan Treehouse infant–14 years
148 West 83rd Street between Columbus and Amsterdam Avenues, 712-0113
Animated storytime, art, ballet, cooking, dance, gymnastics, karate, mommy-and-me, Pilates, Spanish, storytime, yoga. Drop-in art and singalong classes. Day, after-school, evening and weekend classes.

Mannes College of Music—Preparatory Division 4+
150 West 85th Street between Columbus and Amsterdam Avenues, 580-0210 ext. 224
Pre-instrumental instruction. Training in chamber ensembles, chorus, orchestra and theory. Private and group instruction. Musical theater workshops.

Martha Graham School of Contemporary Dance 3.6+
316 East 63rd Street between First and Second Avenues, 838-5886, www.marthagrahamdance.org
Creative movement and modern dance.

Mary Ann Hall's Music for Children 1–7
2 East 90th Street at the Church of the Heavenly Rest, 800 633-0078
Children explore music through fantasy play, eurhythmic movement, singing, dancing and piano.

McBurney YMCA 2+
215 West 23rd Street between Seventh and Eighth Avenues, 741-8729, www.ymcanyc.org
Exercise and play classes, gymnastics, me-and-my-grownup, nursery program. After-school classes in aikido, arts and crafts, basketball, dance, game sports, photography.

10

Medieval Workshop at the Cathedral of St. John the Divine 4+
1047 Amsterdam Avenue at 112th Street, 932-7347, www.stjohndivine.org
Brass rubbing, clay gargoyle sculpture, medieval lettering, limestone carving, stained-glass collage, weaving.

Metropolis Fencing School/Club 5+
114 West 26th Street between Sixth and Seventh Avenues, 463-8044, www.metropolisfencing.com
Private and group instruction.

Midtown Karate Dojo 6+
465 Lexington Avenue between 45th and 46th Streets, 2nd floor, 599-1966
Karate.

Midtown Tennis Club 4+
341 Eighth Avenue between 26th and 27th Streets, 989-8572, www.midtowntennis.com
Junior development program for all levels and munchkin tennis for tots.

The Mixing Bowl
see Kids in the Kitchen

Mozart for Children 2.6–7
East and West Side locations, 942-2743, www.mozartforchildren.com
Classes introducing young children to classical music. In-home group instruction available.

Museum Adventures 3–8
200 East 66th Street, Suite 1505, and museum locations throughout Manhattan, 794-2867
After-school classes combining exhibition tours and art classes.

Music for Aardvarks and Other Mammals 6 months–5 years
440 Lafayette Street at Astor Place, 718 858-1741, www.musicforaardvarks.com
Parent–child music classes.

Music Together 6 months–Kindergarten
Various locations, www.musictogether.com
Downtown East MT, 491-7222
MT of Lower Manhattan/Murray Hill, 358-3801
Music Together of Manhattan, 539-8459
City Music Together, 613-6155
MT Morningside Heights, 592-4627
MT of Columbus Circle/Midtown West, 244-5772
Eastside Music Together, 244-3046, www.eastsidemusic.com
West Side Music Together, 219-0591, www.westsidemusictogether.com

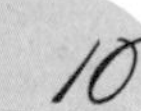

A nationwide program for infants through kindergartners of music education through movement, songs and rhythmic rhymes. Some of the various locations also offer additional classes such as baby massage.

Musical Kids 6+
East and West Side locations, 996-5898, 721-4400
Music and movement.

Neighborhood Playhouse Junior School 6+
340 East 54th Street between First and Second Avenues, 688-3770
Theatrical training including acting, dance and voice.

New Dance Group Arts Center 8+
254 West 47th Street between Broadway and Eighth Avenue, 719-2733, www.ndg.org
Times Square Kidz performing group. Audition required.

New Federal Theatre, Inc. 13+
292 Henry Street, 353-1176, www.newfederaltheatre.org
Drama workshops. Program conducted out of The Henry Street Settlement.

New Media Repertory Company, Inc. 4+
512 East 80th Street between East End and York Avenues, 734-5195
Theatrical classes.

New York Health & Racquet Club 2–10
Various locations, www.nyhrc.com
Swimming instruction.

New York Junior Tennis League 6+
Multiple locations, 24-16 Queens Plaza South (office), Long Island City, Queens, 718 786-7110, www.nyjtl.org
Tennis instruction for all levels.

New York Kids Club 6 months–12 years
265 West 87th Street, 721-4400
Acting, art instruction, baby classes, cooking, dance, gymnastics, music, rock climbing.

New York Road Runners Club 2+
9 East 89th Street between Fifth and Madison Avenues, 860-4455, www.nyrrc.org
Junior Road Runner's Club Series. Children's track and field program run by City Sports for Kids (914 366-4175).

New York Sailing School 8+
22 Pelham Road, New Rochelle, 914 235-6052, www.nyss.com
Learn to sail program.

New York Sports Club 7+
151 East 86th Street between Lexington and Third Avenues, 860-8630, www.nysc.com
Junior squash for kids.

10

New York Swims 5 months+
75 West End Avenue at 63rd Street in All Star Fitness Center, 265-8200
Private and group lessons in swimming and water safety.

New York Theater Ballet 3+
30 East 31st Street between Madison and Park Avenues, 679-0401, www.nytb.org
Pre-ballet through advanced instruction in ballet.

Next Generation Yoga newborn+
200 West 72nd Street, Suite 58, 595-9306, www.nextgenerationyoga.com
Yoga classes for all ages.

92nd Street Y infant+
1395 Lexington Avenue at 92nd Street, 415-5500, www.92ndStY.org
Classes for children up to age 4 and their parents or caregivers include arts, baby massage, cooking, mommy-and-me, movement, music, Park Bench, science. After-school program with transportation available. Classes for other ages include athletics/sports, arts and crafts, boxing/self-defense, circus arts, cooking, dance and movement, educational enrichment, gymnastics, martial arts, music, tennis, swimming and theater arts. Private music instruction. Other programs include basketball leagues, gymnastics and swim teams, ensemble performance companies, Jewish culture. Programs for children with developmental disabilities.

NYC Elite Gymnastics, Dance, and Yoga 18 months+
100 Sixth Avenue, enter on Thompson between Watt and Grand Streets, 334-3628
Dance, gymnastics, mommy-and-me, yoga.

Oishi Judo Club 5+
79 Leonard Street between Broadway and Church Street, 966-6850
Judo.

Once Upon a Baby newborn–18 months
769-3670
Classes for parent/infant pairs focusing on reading to infants, choosing books and developing a love for reading.

The Origami Workshop 7+
645-5670
In-home origami instruction available year round.

Parent's Cooperative Playgroup at St. Bartholomew Community Preschool 12 months–2.6
109 East 50th Street between Park and Lexington Avenues, 378-0238, www.stbarts.org
A professionally facilitated, parent-orchestrated playgroup.

Parsons School of Design 8+
2 West 13th Street at Fifth Avenue, 229-8933, www.parsons.edu
Art and design classes on Saturdays.

PeriChild Program 18 months+
132 Fourth Avenue at 13th Street, 505-0886, www.peridance.com
Ballet, creative movement, hip-hop, jazz, modern dance, Tae Kwon Do and tap.

Peter Westbrook Foundation 10+
119 West 25th Street between Sixth and Seventh Avenues, 459-4538
Saturday morning fencing instruction.

Poppyseed Pre-Nursery infant–3 years
424 West End Avenue between 80th and 81st Streets, 877-7614
Art, arts and crafts, dance, free play, mini gym, mommy-and-me and music.

Prepare, Inc. 5+
147 West 25th Street between Sixth and Seventh Avenues, 255-0505, 800 442-7273, www.prepareinc.com
Personal safety training classes that use realistic role play with a padded instructor.

Randy Mani Tennis Academy 3+
Sutton East Tennis Club at 60th Street and York Avenue
914 674-6060
Tennis instruction for all levels and Pee Wee tennis.

Reebok Sports Club/NY and Sports Club/LA 10 months+
45 Rockefeller Plaza, 218-8600 (Sports Club)
160 Columbus Avenue at 67th Street, 362-6800 (Reebok)
For Kids Only childcare program for members and guests. Fun N' Fit programs in sports, teen and fit kids, multi-sports, kick-boxing, swimming dance, art, music, drama available to members and non-members. Karate provided by HarmonyByKarate and computer instruction provided by Techno Team.

Rhinelander Children's Center infant–12 years
350 East 88th Street between First and Second Avenues, 876-0500, www.rhinelandercenter.org
Mommy-and-me. Nursery school program with classes in art, cooking, computer, dance, martial arts, movement, music and theater arts. Kinder Club. After-school program for K–second grade with transportation from some locations. Private instrumental and vocal instruction.

10

Rhythm and Glues 1–8
1520 York Avenue at 80th Street, 861-7732
Arts and crafts, cooking, dance, drama, music and movement and science. Adult and child preschool format class. Location shared with Gym Time gymnastics program, allowing parents to schedule coordinating classes.

Richard Chun Martial Arts School 3+
220 East 86th Street between Second and Third Avenues, 772-3700, www.chunmartialarts.com
Tae Kwon Do, Kick Start for pee-wees, Kicking for Kids for ages 6–9, weapons training, chi-gung, tai chi and meditation.

The Rink at Rockefeller Plaza Rink 3+
Fifth Avenue between 49th and 50th Streets, 332-7654
Private, semi-private and group ice skating instruction during winter months. Skate rentals available.

Riverdale Equestrian Center 5+
West 254th Street and Broadway in Van Cortland Park, Riverdale, Bronx, 718 548-4848, www.riverdaleriding.com
Private English riding instruction at all levels; semi-private and group lessons for advanced levels.

Robert Quackenbush's Workshops 6–13
223 East 78th Street between Second and Third Avenues, 744-3822, www.rquackenbush.com
After-school art classes.

Rodeph Sholom School 3–12
10 West 84th Street between Central Park West and Columbus Avenue, 362-8800
After-school program open to all.

St. Bartholomew's Choristers Grades 1–12
109 East 50th Street at Park Avenue, 378-0220, www.stbarts.org
By audition only, with optional karate program. Singing tours and recordings.

Saturday Art School at Pratt Institute 3+
200 Willoughby Avenue, Brooklyn, 718 636-3654, www.pratt.edu
Parent and child classes for pre-schoolers and a variety of art classes for school-aged children.

The School at Steps 2.6+
2121 Broadway at West 74th Street, 874-2410, www.stepsnyc.com
Ballet, jazz, modern dance, pre-ballet and tap.

School for Strings 16 months+
419 West 54th Street between Ninth and Tenth Avenues, 315-0915
Early childhood program for very young children. Suzuki cello, piano and violin. String orchestra and chamber music.

School of American Ballet 8+
70 Lincoln Center Plaza on 65th Street between Broadway and Amsterdam Avenue, 877-0600
Ballet. By audition only.

School of Visual Arts Kindergarten–9th grade
209 East 23rd Street between Second and Third Avenues, 592-2560, www.schoolofvisualarts.edu
Saturday art programs.

Seido Karate 4+
61 West 23rd Street between Fifth and Sixth Avenues, 924-0511, www.seido.com
Japanese style karate.

74th Street Magic 6 months+
510 East 74th Street at York Avenue, 737-2989, www.74magic.com
Art, ballet, cooking, gymnastics, hip-hop, mommy-and-me, music, musical theater, rhythmic gymnastics and science. Preschool alternative program available.

Shuffles 3.6+
Studio Maestro on 68th Street between Central Park West and Columbus Avenue , 877-6622
Tap-dancing classes for all levels, musical theater program for ages eight and older, end-of-program mini-musical recital.

Singers Forum 7+
39 West 19th Street between Fifth and Sixth Avenues, 366-0541, www.singersforum.org
Private and group instruction in voice technique and speech, summer musical theater workshops.

Skating Club of New York 5–16
West 23rd Street at Chelsea Piers, 646-638-0030
Second oldest membership club of the United States Figure Skating Association. Children can join at various levels to skate in a club atmosphere and represent the club at competitions.

Soho Children's Acting Studio 6+
345 West Broadway between Grand and Broome Streets, 219-8688
Acting program.

Sokol 3+
420 East 71st Street between York and First Avenues, 861-8206
Dance, gymnastics and martial arts instruction for all levels.

10

Sol Goldman YM-YWHA of the Educational Alliance, Inc.
See 14th Street Y.

Spanish Institute 6+
684 Park Avenue at 68th Street, 628-0420, www.spanishinstitute.org
Spanish language classes.

Spence School—Second Act Kindergarten–5th grade
22 East 91st Street between Fifth and Madison Avenues, 289-5940
After-school program open to all, co-ed.

Sports & Fitness for Children 4–14
Lenox Hill Neighborhood House, 331 East 70th Street, 744-5022, ext. 24
Skill deveopment and fitness workouts for kids ages 4-14. Swimming (group or private lessons) and karate classes available.

Sports Club/LA
See Reebok Sports Club/NY

Stadium Tennis 6+
Stadium Racquet Club, 11 East 162nd Street, Bronx, 718 588-0077, www.nytennis.net
Tennis instruction for all levels. Junior development and tournament training available. Transportation available.

Stella Adler Conservatory of Acting 10+
419 Lafayette Street near Astor Place, 6th floor, 260-0525
Movement, theater and voice.

The Studio 8+
Upper East Side location, 737-6313
Art classes, workshops and portfolio development.

The Sunshine Kids Club 6 months–4 years
230 East 83rd Street between Second and Third Avenues, 439-9876
Parent–child music and art classes. Year-long program.

Super Soccer Stars 3–12
Multiple locations, 877-7171, www.supersoccerstars.com
Soccer skills.

Supermud Pottery School 5+
2744 Broadway between 105th and 106th Streets, 2nd floor, 865-9190, ww.supermudpotterystudio.com
Classes in pottery for both hand and wheel work, paint bar.

Sutton East Tennis Club 3–16
488 East 60th Street at York Avenue, 751-3452
Pee Wee tennis. Private and group lessons for older children.

Sutton Gymnastics and Fitness Inc. 18 months+
533-9390, www.sutton-gymnastics.com
Baby gymnastics and gymnastics instruction for all levels. Sutton Gymnastics is seeking a new location and expects to reopen in 2003.

Swim Jim 6 months+
Multiple locations, 749-7335
Swimming lessons.

TADA! 5+
16 West 28th Street between Fifth Avenue and Broadway, 627-1732
Acting and musical theater.

Take Me to the Water 6 months+
Multiple locations, 828-1756 or 888 SWIM NYC, www.takemetothewater.com
Private and small-group swimming instruction in heated indoor pools for all levels. Baby-and-me. Swim team.

The Techno Team provided by Radicel Education Technology Services 3+
160 Columbus Avenue between 67th and 68th Streets, level 1 at the Reebok Sports Club, 501-1425, www.thetechnoteam.com
Educational Technology Specialist teaches platforms, programs and academic developmental skills through individualized computer classes.

Theatrical Workshop for Children 7–13
Multiple locations, 978-0079
Theater games, creative dramatics, improvisation, monologue and scene study. Final performances at end of each session.

Third Street Music School Settlement 21 months+
235 East 11th Street between Second and Third Avenues, 777-3240, www.thirdstreetmusic.com
Early childhood program. Suzuki program. Individual and group instruction in most instruments, ballet, creative movements, dance and visual arts, Spanish dance and tap.

Thomas Jefferson Recreation Center 6–15
2180 First Avenue at 112th Street, 860-1383
After-school arts and crafts, game room, homework help, soccer, softball and karate. Fencing on Saturdays.

Tiger Schulmann's Karate Clubs 3+
39 West 19th Street between Sixth and Seventh Avenues, 727-0773, www.tsk.com
Karate.

Topspin Tennis and Sports 5+
Multiple locations, 465-2520
After-school tennis clinic. Tennis instruction for all levels, competitive drills, match play and video analysis. Transportation available.

The Training Floor 10+
428 East 75th Street between First and York Avenues, 628-6969
Physical-fitness training, boxing and kick-boxing year round.

Tumble Town 6 months–6 years
17 Lexington Avenue at 23rd Street, located in Baruch College, 802-5632
Music and gym combination classes. Pre-kindergarten gymnastics.

Turtle Bay Music School 18 months–8 years
244 East 52nd Street between Second and Third Avenues, 753-8811 ext. 14, www.tbms.org
Suzuki, Orff Schulwerk, Tuneful Tots, chamber music ensemble, jazz, teen flute ensemble. Private traditional instruction in instruments and music theory. Suzuki piano, violin, cello and flute.

Union Square Ceramics Center 4+
7 East 17th Street, between Fifth Avenue and Broadway, 8th floor, 633-2026
Wheel throwing and hand building.

Uptown Athletic Club 4+
Multiple locations, 917 699-4583
After-school instructional sports program. Transportation from most schools and drop off at home.

USA Oyama's Karate 6–12
350 Sixth Avenue between West 4th Street and Washington Place, 2nd floor, 477-2888, www.oyamakarate.com
Karate.

USTA National Tennis Center 4+
Corona Park, Flushing Meadows, Queens, 718 760-6200, www.usta.com
Tennis instruction for all levels.

Vanderbilt YMCA 6 months+
224 East 47th Street between Second and Third Avenues, 756-9600, www.ymcanyc.org
New mom and baby class. Early childhood center programs including swimming and gym. Adventure programs including art, dance, gymnastics and swimming. After-school programs including basketball and karate. Additional programs include a teen center, leadership club, youth and government club, earth services corps and youth theater. Scholarships available. Virtual Y—a literacy-based after-school program.

Village Community School 5+
272 West 10th Street between Greenwich and Washington Streets, 691-5146, www.vcsnyc.org
After-school program open to all.

Weist Barron Studios 5+
35 West 45th Street between Fifth and Sixth Avenues, 840-7025
Acting conservatory with an emphasis on film and TV. Programs include "Kids Love Acting" and "ACTEEN." Commercial, film and TV acting classes.

West Park Presbyterian Church infant+
165 West 86th Street, 864-2476, www.westparkchurch.org
Integrated arts program exploring relationships between visual arts, music, and movement. Music classes. Spiritual programs, parenting programs, playgroups for home-schooling families

West Side Soccer League 5+
AYSO Region 611, 946-5102, www.wssl.org
West Side Soccer League is a member of the American Youth Soccer Organization (AYSO). Call or visit the website for registration materials. Note that parents are expected to volunteer, and league games are played in the fall and spring.

West Side Tae Kwon Do 3+
661 Amsterdam Avenue between 92nd and 93rd Streets, 663-3998, www.westsidetkd.com
Martial arts

West Side YMCA 3 months+
5 West 63rd Street at Central Park West, 875-4100, www.ymcanyc.org
Art, basketball, general sports, gymnastics, jazz, martial arts, mommy-and-me, music, musical production, theater arts and swimming. After-school program operates out of P.S. 166, on-site program for P.S. 87 and P.S. 199.

Wollman Rink 3+
Mid-Central Park at 62nd Street, 439-6900 ext. 12
Parent and tot class, figure skating and hockey. During the winter months the rink is used for ice skating. In the late spring, summer and early fall the rink is used for in-line skating. In-line skating and hockey instruction available.

Yorkville Youth Athletic Association Kindergarten–8th grade
Multiple locations, 570-5657
Co-ed Little League baseball program. Other sports leagues include basketball, tennis and volleyball. Call for specific age requirements.

The Young People's Chorus of New York 8+
Lexington Avenue at 92nd Street in residence at The 92nd Street Y, 415-5579
A vocal ensemble of 150 boys and girls by audition only.

Young Plaza Ambassadors 6–16
Plaza Hotel, Fifth Avenue at Central Park South, 546-5377, www.plaaypa.com
Classes in etiquette and cooking.

YWCA of the City of New York 6 months+
610 Lexington Avenue at 53rd Street, 755-4500, www.ymcanyc.org
Swimming instruction and swim team.

ACTIVITIES INDEX

Neighborhood Locator

es	East Side, East 23rd Street through and including 60th Street
lm	Lower Manhattan, below 23rd Street
mul	Multiple locations
out	Outside the borough of Manhattan
ues	Upper East Side, East 61st Street up to 110th Street
um	Upper Manhattan, 110th Street and above
uws	Upper West Side, West 61st Street up to 110th Street and Central Park
ws	West Side, West 23rd Street through and including West 60th Street

Body and Spirit Program of Rutgers Presbyterian Church **uws**
The Calhoun School **ues, uws**
Carmine Recreation Center **lm**
Champs Sports Club **mul**
Children and Art **uws**
The Children's Aid Society—Greenwich Village Center **lm**
Chris Porté's After School Junior Tennis **mul**
Frozen Ropes Baseball Center **uws**
Goddard-Riverside Community Center **uws**
Jewish Community Center in Manhattan **uws**
Kumon Math and Reading Centers **lm, ues, uws**
Madison Square Boy's and Girl's Club **ws**
Manhattan Treehouse **uws**
Museum Adventures **ues**
92nd Street Y **ues**
Rhinelander Children's Center **ues**
Rodeph Sholom School **uws**
Spence School—Second Act **ues**
Village Community School **lm**
West Side YMCA **uws**

Art including Arts and Crafts, Ceramics, Drawing, Painting, Sculpting and Visual Arts
Acting Works **ws**
After School Workshop on Madison **ues**
Alfred E. Smith Recreation Center **lm**
Art 'n' Orbit **mul**
Art Farm **ues**
Art Safari, Inc. **lm**
Art Students League of New York **ws**
Asphalt Green **ues**
Body and Spirit Program of Rutgers Presbyterian Church **uws**
Children and Art **uws**
Children of Today **uws**
The Children's Aid Society—Greenwich Village Center **lm**
Church Street School for Music & Art **lm**
Creatability **ues**
Dance! Dance! Dance! **ues**
Discovery Programs Inc. **uws**
Earthworks and Artisans **uws**
East Side Creative Arts Studio **ues**
Ethics for Children—New York Society for Ethical Culture **uws**
14th Street Y **lm**
Global Enrichment & Discovery Classes **ues**
Goddard-Riverside Community Center **uws**
Greenwich House Music School **lm**
Greenwich House Pottery **lm**
Harlem School of the Arts **um**
Henry Street Settlement Abrons Arts Center **lm**
Hi Art **uws**
Jewish Community Center in Manhattan **uws**
Just Wee Two **uws**
Karen's Performing Arts **ws**
Kids at Art **ues**
La Mano Pottery **lm**
The Lion and the Lamb **ues**
Lucy Moses School **uws**
Manhattan Treehouse **uws**
McBurney YMCA **ws**
Medieval Workshop at the Cathedral of St. John the Divine **um**
Museum Adventures **ues**
New York Kids Club **uws**
92nd Street Y **ues**
Parsons School of Design **lm**
Poppyseed Pre-Nursery **ues**
Rhinelander Children's Center **ues**
Rhythm and Glues **ues**
Robert Quackenbush's Workshops **ues**
Saturday Art School at Pratt Institute **out**
School of Visual Arts **es**
74th Street Magic **ues**
Sol Goldman YM-YWHA **lm**
The Studio **ues**
The Sunshine Kids Club **ues**
Supermud Pottery School **uws**
Third Street Music School Settlement **lm**
Thomas Jefferson Recreation Center **um**
Union Square Ceramics Center **lm**
Vanderbilt YMCA **es**
West Park Presbyterian Church **uws**
West Side YMCA **uws**

Basketball
Basketball City **ws**
Big Apple Sports Club **mul**
Carmine Recreation Center **lm**
CATS, Children's Athletic Training School **es, uws**
Chelsea Piers **ws**

Corbin's Crusaders **mul**
14 Street Y **lm**
McBurney YMCA **ws**
Sol Goldman YM-YWHA **lm**
Vanderbilt YMCA **es**
West Side YMCA **uws**

Chess
Alfred E. Smith Recreation Center **lm**
Asphalt Green **ues**
92nd Street Y **ues**

Circus Arts
Children's Tumbling **lm**
Jewish Community Center in Manhattan **uws**
Karen's Performing Arts **ws**

Computer Classes/Training
After School Workshop on Madison **ues**
Alfred E. Smith Recreation Center **lm**
Futurekids **ues**
Goddard-Riverside Community Center **uws**
Herard Center of Multimedia **ws**
Madison Square Boy's and Girl's Club **ws**
Reebok Sports Club/NY and Sports Club/LA **ws, uws**
Rhinelander Children's Center **ues**
The Techno Team provided by Radicel Education Technology Services **uws**

Cooking
Art Farm **ues**
The Children's Aid Society—Greenwich Village Center **lm**
Institute of Culinary Education **ws**
Jewish Community Center in Manhattan **uws**
Kids in the Kitchen **ues**
Little Cooks, Ltd. **mul**
The Loft Kitchen **lm**
Manhattan Treehouse **uws**
The Mixing Bowl **ues**
New York Kids Club **uws**
92nd Street Y **ues**
Rhinelander Children's Center **ues**
Rhythm and Glues **ues**
74th Street Magic **ues**

Dance including Ballet, Ballroom, Creative Movement, Hip-Hop, Isadora Duncan, Jazz, Tap and other forms
After School Workshop on Madison **ues**
Alfred E. Smith Recreation Center **lm**
Alvin Ailey American Dance **uws**
The American Youth Dance Theater **ues**
Antonia Arts, Inc. **mul**
Arts Gate Center **lm**
Asphalt Green **ues**
Ballet Academy East **ues**
Ballet Hispanico **uws**
Body and Spirit Program of Rutgers Presbyterian Church **uws**
Bridge for Dance **uws**
Broadway Dance Center **ws**
CATS, Children's Athletic Training School **es, uws**
Chelsea Piers **ws**
Children of Today **uws**
The Children's Aid Society—Greenwich Village Center **lm**
Church Street School for Music & Art **lm**
Dance Theater Workshop **lm**
Dance Theatre of Harlem School **um**
Dance! Dance! Dance! **ues**
Discovery Programs Inc. **uws**
Djoniba Dance & Drum Center **lm**
East Village Dance Project **lm**
Ellen Robbins Modern Dance **lm**
Empire Dance **ws**
14th Street Y **lm**
Fred Astaire Dance Studio **es, ues, uws, ws**
Greenwich House Music School **lm**
Harbor Conservatory for the Performing Arts **ues**
Harlem School of the Arts **um**
Henry Street Settlement Abrons Arts Center **lm**
In Grandma's Attic **uws**
Jewish Community Center in Manhattan **uws**
Joffery Ballet School **lm**
Judy Lasko Modern Dance **uws**
Just Wee Two **uws**
Karen's Performing Arts **ws**
Kids Co-Motion in Soho **lm, ws, uws**
Loco-Motion Dance Theater for Children **lm**
Lucy Moses School **uws**
Manhattan Ballet School, Inc. **ues**

Manhattan Treehouse **uws**
Martha Graham School of Contemporary Dance **ues**
McBurney YMCA **ws**
Neighborhood Playhouse Junior School **es**
New Dance Group Arts Center **ws**
New York Kids Club **uws**
New York Theater Ballet **es**
92nd Street Y **ues**
NYC Elite Gymnastics, Dance, and Yoga **lm**
PeriChild Program **lm**
Poppyseed Pre-Nursery **ues**
Reebok Sports Club/NY and Sports Club/LA **ws, uws**
Rhinelander Children's Center **ues**
Rhythm and Glues **ues**
The School at Steps **uws**
School of American Ballet **uws**
74th Street Magic **ues**
Shuffles **uws**
Sokol **ues**
Sol Goldman YM-YWHA **lm**
Third Street Music School Settlement **lm**
Vanderbilt YMCA **es**
West Park Presbyterian Church **uws**

Fencing
Metropolis Fencing School/Club **ws**
Peter Westbrook Foundation **ws**
Thomas Jefferson Recreation Center **um**

Gardening
Alfred E. Smith Recreation Center **lm**
92nd Street Y **ues**

Gymnastics including Rhythmic and Tumbling
Asphalt Green **ues**
Champs Sports Club **mul**
Chelsea Piers **ws**
Children's Tumbling **lm**
Circus Gymnastics **uws**
Columbus Gym **uws**
Discovery Programs Inc. **uws**
14th Street Y **lm**
Gym Time **ues**
Gymboree **es, lm, ues, uws**
Jewish Community Center in Manhattan **uws**
Jodi's Gym **ues**
Life Sport Gymnastics **uws**
Manhattan Treehouse **uws**
McBurney YMCA **ws**
New York Kids Club **uws**
92nd Street Y **ues**
NYC Elite Gymnastics, Dance, and Yoga **lm**
74th Street Magic **ues**
Sokol **ues**
Sol Goldman YM-YWHA **lm**
Sutton Gymnastics and Fitness Inc.
Tumble Town **es**
Vanderbilt YMCA **es**
West Side YMCA **uws**

Homework
After School Workshop on Madison **ues**
Goddard-Riverside Community Center **uws**
Madison Square Boy's and Girl's Club **ws**
Thomas Jefferson Recreation Center **um**

Horseback Riding
Claremont Riding Academy **uws**
Riverdale Equestrian Center **out**

Ice Skating including Figure Skating and Hockey
Central Park Youth Hockey **uws**
Champs Sports Club **mul**
Chelsea Piers **ws**
Ice Hockey in Harlem **uws**
Lasker Rink and Pool **uws**
The Rink at Rockefeller Plaza Rink **ws**
Skating Club of New York **ws**
Wollman Rink **uws**

In-Line Skating
Alfred E. Smith Recreation Center **lm**
Asphalt Green **ues**
Chelsea Piers **ws**
Corbin's Crusaders **mul**
Kids on Wheels Joel Rappelfeld's In-line Skating **mul**
Lezly Skate School **mul**
Wollman Rink **uws**

Languages
ABC Language Service **ws**
After School Workshop on Madison **ues**
Baby Fingers **mul**
Berlitz Kids **ws**
China Institute in America **ues**
French Institute/Alliance Française **es**

German American School **mul**
Global Enrichment & Discovery Classes **ues**
Hippo Family Club
Hola **lm**
Instituto Cervantes **es**
La Croisette Language Center **mul**
Language Garden
Language Workshop for Children **ues**
Manhattan Treehouse **uws**
Spanish Institute **ues**

Martial Arts
Aikido, New York Aikikai **lm**
Alfred E. Smith Recreation Center **lm**
Arts Gate Center **lm**
Asphalt Green **ues**
Asser Levy Recreation Center **es**
CATS, Children's Athletic Training School **es, uws**
Chelsea Piers **ws**
The Children's Aid Society—Greenwich Village Center **lm**
Core Fitness **ues**
Discovery Programs Inc. **uws**
14th Street Y **lm**
Gym Time **ues**
Jewish Community Center in Manhattan **uws**
Kokushi Budo Institute of New York **uws**
Kyokushin Karate **ws, uws**
Lenox Hill Neighborhood House **ues**
McBurney YMCA **ws**
Midtown Karate Dojo **es**
92nd Street Y **ues**
Oishi Judo Club **lm**
PeriChild Program **lm**
Reebok Sports Club/NY and Sports Club/LA **ws, uws**
Rhinelander Children's Center **ues**
Richard Chun Martial Arts School **ues**
Seido Karate **ws**
Sokol **ues**
Sol Goldman YM-YWHA **lm**
St. Bartholomew's Choristers **es**
Thomas Jefferson Recreation Center **um**
Tiger Schulmann's Karate Clubs **lm**
USA Oyama's Karate **lm**
Vanderbilt YMCA **es**
West Side Tae Kwon Do **uws**
West Side YMCA **uws**

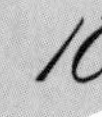

Music
Art Farm **ues**
Arts Gate Center **lm**
Bloomingdale School of Music **uws**
Body and Spirit Program of Rutgers Presbyterian Church **uws**
Boys Choir—Church of the Transfiguration **es**
Campbell Music Studio **ues, uws**
Childhood Memories **ues**
The Children's Aid Society—Greenwich Village Center **lm**
Church Street School for Music & Art **lm**
The Collective **lm**
Diller-Quaile School of Music **ues**
Discovery Programs Inc. **uws**
The Early Ear Music Program **ues, uws**
East Side Creative Arts Studio **ues**
Ethics for Children—New York Society for Ethical Culture **uws**
The Family Music Center
14th Street Y **lm**
French–American Conservatory of Music at Carnegie Hall **ws**
Gramercy Park School of Music **es**
Greenwich House Music School **lm**
Hands On! **lm, ues, uws**
Harlem School of the Arts **um**
Henry Street Settlement Abrons Arts Center **lm**
The InterSchool Orchestras of New York **mul**
Jams **uws**
Juilliard Pre-College Division **uws**
Just Wee Two **uws**
Kids Co-Motion in Soho **lm, ws, uws**
Lucy Moses School **uws**
Mannes College of Music—Preparatory Division **uws**
Mary Ann Hall's Music for Children **ues**
Mozart for Children **es, ws**
Music for Aardvarks and Other Mammals **lm**
Music Together **mul**
Musical Kids **es, ws**
New York Kids Club **uws**
92nd Street Y **ues**
Poppyseed Pre-Nursery **ues**
Rhinelander Children's Center **ues**
Rhythm and Glues **ues**
St. Bartholomew's Choristers **es**
School for Strings **ws**
74th Street Magic **ues**

Singers Forum **lm**
Sol Goldman YM-YWHA **lm**
The Sunshine Kids Club **ues**
Third Street Music School Settlement **lm**
Tumble Town **es**
Turtle Bay Music School **es**
West Park Presbyterian Church **uws**
West Side YMCA **uws**
The Young People's Chorus of New York **ues**

Parent/Child, Mommy-and-me or Pre-Nursery Programs

ACT Programs at Cathedral of St. John the Divine **um**
The American Youth Dance Theater **ues**
Art 'n' Orbit **mul**
Asphalt Green **ues**
Asser Levy Recreation Center **es**
Baby Aqua **es, ws**
Baby Fingers **mul**
Ballet Academy East **ues**
Bloomingdale School of Music **uws**
Broadway Babies **ues, uws**
Chelsea Piers **ws**
Children's Tumbling **lm**
Child's Play **uws**
Circus Gymnastics **uws**
Dance! Dance! Dance! **ues**
Discovery Programs Inc. **uws**
14th Street Y **lm**
Henry Street Settlement Abrons Arts Center **lm**
Hi Art **uws**
Hippo Family Club
Hola **lm**
Jack & Jill Playgroup **es**
Jewish Community Center in Manhattan **uws**
Kids Co-Motion in Soho **lm, ws, uws**
Language Garden
Manhattan Treehouse **uws**
McBurney YMCA **ws**
Music for Aardvarks and Other Mammals **lm**
92nd Street Y **ues**
NYC Elite Gymnastics, Dance, and Yoga **lm**
Parent's Cooperative Playgroup at St. Bartholomew Community Preschool **es**
Poppyseed Pre-Nursery **ues**
Rhinelander Children's Center **ues**
Rhythm and Glues **ues**
Saturday Art School at Pratt Institute **out**
74th Street Magic **ues**
Sol Goldman YM-YWHA **lm**
The Sunshine Kids Club **ues**
Take Me to the Water **mul**
Vanderbilt YMCA **es**
West Side YMCA **uws**
Wollman Rink **uws**

Personal Enrichment Skills

First Impression **es**
Janet Nixon
Knickerbocker Greys **ues**
Young Plaza Ambassadors **ws**

Programs for Children Under 18 Months

The American Youth Dance Theater **ues**
Art Farm **ues**
Asphalt Green **ues**
Baby Aqua **es, ws**
Baby Fingers **mul**
Bloomingdale School of Music **uws**
Body and Spirit Program of Rutgers Presbyterian Church **uws**
Broadway Babies **ues, uws**
Chelsea Piers **ws**
Childhood Memories **ues**
Children of Today **uws**
Child's Play **uws**
The Children's Aid Society—Greenwich Village Center **lm**
Church Street School for Music & Art **lm**
Circus Gymnastics **uws**
Columbus Gym **uws**
Diller-Quaile School of Music **ues**
Discovery Programs Inc. **uws**
The Early Ear Music Program **ues, uws**
East Side Creative Arts Studio **ues**
The Family Music Center
14th Street Y **lm**
Goodson Parker Wellness Center **ues**
Greenwich House Music School **lm**
Gym Time **ues**
Gymboree **es, lm, ues, uws**
Hands On! **lm, ues, uws**
Henry Street Settlement Abrons Arts Center **lm**
Hippo Family Club
Jams **uws**
Jewish Community Center in Manhattan **uws**

Jodi's Gym **ues**
Just Wee Two **uws**
Kids Co-Motion in Soho **lm, ws, uws**
La Croisette Language Center **mul**
Language Workshop for Children **ues**
Manhattan Treehouse **uws**
Mary Ann Hall's Music for Children **ues**
Music for Aardvarks and Other Mammals **lm**
Music Together **mul**
New York Kids Club **uws**
New York Swims **uws**
Next Generation Yoga **uws**
92nd Street Y **ues**
Once Upon a Baby
Parent's Cooperative Playgroup at St. Bartholomew Community Preschool **es**
Poppyseed Pre-Nursery **ues**
Reebok Sports Club/NY and Sports Club/LA **ws, uws**
Rhinelander Children's Center **ues**
Rhythm and Glues **ues**
School for Strings **ws**
74th Street Magic **ues**
Sol Goldman YM-YWHA **lm**
The Sunshine Kids Club **ues**
Swim Jim **mul**
Take Me to the Water **mul**
Tumble Town **es**
Vanderbilt YMCA **es**
West Park Presbyterian Church **uws**
West Side YMCA **uws**

Science
Art 'n' Orbit **mul**
Global Enrichment & Discovery Classes **ues**
Jewish Community Center in Manhattan **uws**
92nd Street Y **ues**
Rhythm and Glues **ues**
74th Street Magic **ues**

Special Needs
Art Safari, Inc. **lm**
Asphalt Green **ues**
Baby Fingers **mul**
Jewish Community Center in Manhattan **uws**
92nd Street Y **ues**

Sports and Athletics including Gym and Mini Gyms
After School Workshop on Madison **ues**
Alfred E. Smith Recreation Center **lm**
Asphalt Green **ues**
Basketball City **ws**
Big Apple Sports Club **mul**
Body and Spirit Program of Rutgers Presbyterian Church **uws**
Carlos Oliveira Soccer Academy **uws**
Carmine Recreation Center **lm**
CATS, Children's Athletic Training School **es, uws**
Cavaliers Athletic Club **mul**
Champs Sports Club **mul**
Chelsea Piers **ws**
Corbin's Crusaders **mul**
CYO (Catholic Youth Organization) Manhattan Youth Baseball **mul**
14th Street Y **lm**
Frozen Ropes Baseball Center **uws**
Goddard-Riverside Community Center **uws**
Gym Time **ues**
Jewish Community Center in Manhattan **uws**
Joe Espinosa's Sports Club **mul**
Karen's Performing Arts **ws**
Lenox Hill Neighborhood House **ues**
Little League Baseball **mul**
Madison Square Boy's and Girl's Club **ws**
Manhattan Babe Ruth League, Cal Ripkin Division
McBurney YMCA **ws**
New York Road Runners Club **ues**
New York Sports Club **ues**
92nd Street Y **ues**
Poppyseed Pre-Nursery **ues**
Reebok Sports Club/NY and Sports Club/LA **ws, uws**
Sol Goldman YM-YWHA **lm**
Sports and Fitness for Children **ues**
Super Soccer Stars **mul**
Thomas Jefferson Recreation Center **um**
Uptown Athletic Club **mul**
West Side Soccer League **ws**
West Side YMCA **uws**
Yorkville Youth Athletic Association **mul**

Swimming
Asphalt Green **ues**
Baby Aqua **es, ws**

Carmine Recreation Center **lm**
CATS, Children's Athletic Training School **es, uws**
Corbin's Crusaders **mul**
14th Street Y **lm**
Imagine Swimming **es, ues**
Jewish Community Center in Manhattan **uws**
Lasker Rink and Pool **uws**
Lenox Hill Neighborhood House **ues**
New York Health & Racquet Club **mul**
New York Swims **uws**
92nd Street Y **ues**
Reebok Sports Club/NY and Sports Club/LA **ws, uws**
Sol Goldman YM-YWHA **lm**
Swim Jim **mul**
Take Me to the Water **mul**
Vanderbilt YMCA **es**
West Side YMCA **uws**
YWCA of the City of New York **es**

Tennis
ACE-IT Junior Development Tennis Program **out**
After School Workshop on Madison **ues**
All City Junior Tennis, **out, ws, uws**
Chris Porté's After School Junior Tennis **mul**
Corbin's Crusaders **mul**
Crosstown Tennis **ws**
Gym Time **ues**
Jeff Nerenberg Tennis Academy **ws**
Midtown Tennis Club **ws**
New York Junior Tennis League **mul**
92nd Street Y **ues**
Randy Mani Tennis Academy **es**
Stadium Tennis **out**
Sutton East Tennis Club **es**
Topspin Tennis and Sports **mul**
USTA National Tennis Center **out**

Yoga
Asphalt Green **ues**
CATS Children's Athletic Training School **es, uws**
Goodson Parker Wellness Center **ues**
Jewish Community Center in Manhattan **uws**
Karma Kids Yoga **lm**
Manhattan Treehouse **uws**
Next Generation Yoga **uws**
NYC Elite Gymnastics, Dance, and Yoga **lm**

Other
Alfred E. Smith Recreation Center—gardening, teen video production **lm**
Art Safari, Inc.—museum tours **lm**
Asphalt Green—lifeguard training for teens **ues**
Baby Fingers—sign language for hearing and deaf children **mul**
Boys Scouts of America—scouting **mul**
Chelsea Piers—rock climbing, skateboarding **ws**
The Children's Aid Society—Greenwich Village Center—Photography **lm**
Child's Play—home schoolers group **uws**
Dieu Donne Papermill, Inc.—papermaking **lm**
Djoniba Dance & Drum Center—African drums **lm**
East Side Creative Arts Studio—art therapy, drama therapy, music therapy **ues**
Ethics for Children—New York Society for Ethical Culture—ethical development **uws**
14th Street Y—Jewish life and learning, Japanese Parenting and Family Center **lm**
Girl Scout Council of Greater NY, Inc.—scouting **mul**
Global Enrichment & Discovery Classes—multi-disciplinary program **ues**
Goddard-Riverside Community Center—environmental education **uws**
Jewish Community Center in Manhattan—baby massage, boxing, capoeira, clay, community service programs for pre-teens and teens, jewelry making, Jewish culture, photography **uws**
Just Wee Two—stories **uws**
Kids 'N Comedy Workshop—comedy **lm**
Kids Pilates—Pilates **mul**
Lenox Hill Neighborhood House—scuba diving **ues**
The Lion and the Lamb—knitting, beading, needlepoint **ues**
Madison Square Boy's and Girl's Club—poetry workshop, Youth Employment Program **ws**

Manhattan Treehouse—animated storytime, fencing, Pilates, story-time, singalong classes **uws**
McBurney YMCA—exercise and play classes, nursery program, photography **ws**
Medieval Workshop at the Cathedral of St. John the Divine—brass rubbing, clay gargoyle sculpture, medieval lettering, limestone carving, stained glass collage, weaving **um**
Museum Adventures—exhibition tours **ues**
New York Kids Club—baby classes, rock climbing **uws**
New York Sailing School—sailing out
92nd Street Y—baby massage, boxing/self-defense, educational enrichment, Jewish culture **ues**
The Origami Workshop—origami **nl**
Poppyseed Pre-Nursery—free play **ues**
Prepare, Inc.—personal safety training **ws**
Reebok Sports Club/NY and Sports Club/LA—kick-boxing **ws, uws**
Sol Goldman YM-YWHA—Jewish life and learning, Japanese Parenting and Family Center **lm**
Thomas Jefferson Recreation Center—game room **um**
The Training Floor—boxing **ues**
Vanderbilt YMCA—teen center, leadership club, youth and government club, earth services corps and youth theater, Virtual Y **es**
West Park Presbyterian Church—spiritual programs, parenting programs, playgroups for home-schooling families **uws**

Boredom Busters

Boredom Busters consist of the wide range of everyday drop-in activities and in-and-around-town adventures. So whether you are looking to provide some cabin-fever relief or trying to plan something for that upcoming day off from school, Boredom Busters will provide just the inspiration needed to help you keep them busy.

Entries are listed in alphabetical order and include the activity name, location, phone number, ages best served and a brief description. For some entries, such as the one for Central Park, we follow a different format to better provide you with the full range of possibilities. We recommend calling for detailed information and, when appropriate, making reservations.

Asphalt Green All ages
555 East 90th Street at York Avenue, 369-8890, www.asphaltgreen.com
Open swimming sessions in Olympic and Delacorte (smaller and warmer) pools. Call for hours and rates.

Basketball City 6+
Pier 63 at West 23rd Street and Twelfth Avenue, 924-4040, www.basketballcity.com
Open playtime weekdays and weekends.

Beaches

The City Parks & Recreation Department operates 14 miles of public beaches in four boroughs as well as 53 public outdoor and a number of indoor swimming pools.

- GENERAL PARKS & RECREATION DEPARTMENT INFORMATION: Manhattan, 718 408-0243; Bronx, 718 430-1858; Brooklyn, 718 965-8941; Queens, 718 520-5936; Staten Island, 718 390-8020; www.nycparks .completeinet.net
- BRONX: Orchard Beach and Promenade (Long Island Sound), 718 885-2275
- BROOKLYN: Brighton Beach and Coney Island (Atlantic Ocean), 718 946-1350, www.coneyislandusacom; Manhattan Beach (Atlantic Ocean), 718 946-1373
- QUEENS: Rockaway Beach and Boardwalk (Atlantic Ocean), 718 318-4000; Jacob Riis Beach and Boardwalk (Atlantic Ocean), 718 318-4300
- STATEN ISLAND: South and Midland Beaches and Franklin D. Roosevelt Boardwalk (Lower New York Bay), 718 816-6804, 718 987-0709; Wolfe's Pond Beach (Raritan Bay), 718 984-8266
- The United States National Park Service operates Gateway National Recreation Area, a 26,000-acre recreation area extending through Brooklyn, Queens, Staten Island and New Jersey, which includes several beaches. 718 338-3688, www.nps.gov, www.rockaway chamberofcommerce.com
- Jones Beach State Park, Wantagh, Long Island, 516 785-1600. Located 33 miles from Manhattan, this famous local beach offers 6.5 miles of ocean beach, a bay beach, two swimming pools, a boardwalk, deck games and miniature golf.

10

Bowlmor Lanes 4+

110 University Place between 12th and 13th Streets, 225-8188, www.bowlmor.com

Bumper bowling for beginners, regular bowling for older children and adults.

Broadway City 4+

241 West 42nd Street between Seventh and Eighth Avenues, 997-9797, www.broadwaycity.com

Arcade with pinball, basketball and video games with prizes. Best to visit before 5 p.m.

Bryant Park All ages

42nd Street and Sixth Avenue, 719-3434

Various activities for kids during the summer months. Call for details.

Carl Schurz Park All ages
86th Street and East End Avenue
Beautiful park overlooking the East River with a playground, dog run and areas for biking and rollerblading.

Carnegie Hall Individual Tours 4+
57th Street at Seventh Avenue, 247-7800 (box office), 903-9765 (tour schedule), www.carnegiehall.org
Weekday tours available of behind-the-scenes Carnegie Hall. Note that tours are not offered during the summer. Visit the small museum on the second floor to see changing exhibits of mementos. Carnegie Hall also holds a number of educational events, including concerts for families.

Central Park All ages
From 59th Street (or Central Park South) to 110th Street and from Central Park West to Fifth Avenue, 360-3444; Emergencies 570-4820, Urban Park Rangers 988-4952, www.centralparknyc.org
Covering over 840 acres in total, with many playgrounds and special spots within it, the park is available to visitors for most activities with the exception of barbecuing. To find out more about the park, programs and events, pick up a free copy of the Central Park Conservancy's quarterly publication, "Central Park Views," at any of the park's visitor centers: The Charles A. Dana Discovery Center, The Dairy, Belvedere Castle and The North Meadow Recreation Center (locations listed below). Copies of "Central Park Views" are also mailed to Central Park Conservancy members free (call 310-6641 for membership information or visit www.centralparknyc.org).

Some of the special spots in Central Park of particular interest to children:

- Alice in Wonderland Sculpture. Near Fifth Avenue at 75th Street.
- Balto the Sled Dog Statue. East side of the park at 67th Street.
- Belvedere Castle. Mid-park at 79th Street. A 19th-century stone castle, it houses the Henry Luce Nature Observatory, a learning center with exhibits and programs (772-0210). Sign out a free "Discovery Kit," a backpack with binoculars, sketching materials, guidebook and map.
- The Carousel. Mid-park at 64th Street, 879-0244, 369-1010.
- Carriage Rides. Located on 59th Street between Fifth and Sixth Avenues or at Tavern on the Green.
- The Charles A. Dana Discovery Center. At 110th Street between Fifth and Lenox Avenues, 860-1370. Nature classes, arts and crafts, family workshops and fishing (photo ID required for fishing).
- Conservatory Garden. At 105th Street and Fifth Avenue.
- Conservatory Water. Enter the park at 72nd Street and head north along Fifth Avenue.

- The Dairy. Mid-park at 65th Street, 794-6564. Displays, interactive computer programs and models provide visitors with information on the design, architecture and history of Central Park.
- Delacorte Clock. North of the Central Park Zoo at 65th Street.
- Hans Christian Andersen Statue. On the east side of the park at 72nd Street.
- Lasker Rink. Mid-park at 110th Street, 534-7639. Typically from November through March, the rink is open for outdoor private and group skating and ice hockey instruction. From July 4th to Labor Day, the rink is converted to a swimming pool.
- Loeb Boathouse. East Drive at 74th Street, 517-2233 for reservations for the restaurant. Rent boats with lifejackets; available mid-March through October. ID required.
- North Meadow Recreation Center. Mid-park at 97th Street, 348-4867. Youth center offering a variety of outdoor activities, including basketball and handball courts, and new indoor and outdoor climbing walls. Some activities are available on a drop-in basis; others require registration.
- Strawberry Fields. On the west side of Central Park at 72nd Street. John Lennon memorial.
- Trolley Tours of Central Park. Grand Army Plaza at Fifth Avenue and 60th Street, 360-2727 or 397-3809 for reservations.
- Wollman Rink. South of the 65th Street transverse in the center of the park, 396-1010. During the winter months, the rink is prepped for ice skating. In warmer weather, Wollman transforms into a rollerblading rink with a special area dedicated to a basketball challenge course

- Zoo/Central Park Wildlife Center/Tisch Children's Zoo. 64th Street near Fifth Avenue, 861-6030.

Some helpful hints

- When in Central Park, it is easy to forget you are in the center of one of the world's largest and busiest cities. Even though the park is well patrolled, use the same safety rules for your family as you would elsewhere in the city, such as staying away from isolated areas and being aware of your surroundings.
- Becoming geographically disoriented in the park is not an uncommon problem. Note that some lamp posts are marked with the cross street to help identify your location.

Playgrounds within Central Park:

EAST SIDE

- Billy Johnson Playground. Fifth Avenue between 67th and 68th Streets
- Fifth Avenue between 71st and 72nd Streets
- James Michael Levin Playground. Fifth Avenue between 75th and 76th Streets
- Three Bears Playground. Fifth Avenue between 79th and 80th Streets
- Ancient Playground. Fifth Avenue between 84th and 85th Streets
- Fifth Avenue between 95th and 96th Streets
- Bernard Playground. 108th and 109th Streets; enter on 110th Street and walk south
- 110th Street between Fifth and Lenox Avenues

WEST SIDE

- Heckscher Playground. Central Park South and 62nd Street; enter at Seventh Avenue and Central Park South and walk north
- Adventure Playground. Central Park West and 67th Street
- Diana Ross Playground. Central Park West and 81st Street
- Ross Pinetum. Central Park West and 84th Street; enter at 84th Street and walk east
- Belfer Playground. Central Park West between 84th and 85th Streets
- Spector Playground. Central Park West between 85th and 86th Streets
- Safari Playground. Central Park West between 90th and 91st Streets
- Wild West Playground. Central Park West between 93rd and 94th Streets
- Rudin Playground. Central Park West between 96th and 97th Streets
- Robert Bendheim Playground. Central Park West between 99th and 100th Streets
- Central Park West and 110th Street

Chelsea Piers Sports and Entertainment Complex Depends on ability/activity
Piers 59-62 at West 23rd Street and the Hudson River, 336-6666, www.chelseapiers.com
Batting cages, ice skating, rollerblading, golf, rock climbing, basketball, extreme skating/skateboarding/bmx biking and bowling available on a drop-in basis during scheduled times.

Circle Line 4+
Pier 83 at West 42nd Street, Pier 16 at the South Street Seaport, 563-3200, www.circleline.com
Three-hour cruise around the island of Manhattan leaving from Pier 83. Toddlers and very active children might find this too long an adventure. Bring lap activities to provide additional entertainment. The Pier 16 cruise is approximately one hour in length and tours lower Manhattan.

Claire's Storytelling Corner at Lord & Taylor up to age 6
Lord & Taylor, 424 Fifth Avenue at 39th Street, 7th floor, 382-7670
"Tell me a story" free storytelling and readings (often followed by activities) on Saturdays at 2 p.m.

Claremont Riding Academy 6+
175 West 89th Street between Columbus and Amsterdam Avenues, 724-5100
Private horseback riding instruction for all levels by appointment.

Coney Island
Surf Avenue, Brooklyn, 718 372-5159, www.coneyisland.com
Attracting locals and tourists alike for many decades, this famous waterside attraction includes Astroland, Coney Island USA and Deno's Wonder Wheel amusements parks, the renowned Cyclone Rollercoaster, tons of rides for adults and kids, side shows, freak shows, the New York Aquarium, Nathan's Famous Hot Dogs, a museum and a boardwalk.

The Craft Studio 3+
1657 Third Avenue between 92nd and 93rd Streets, 831-6626
Drop-in projects include painting plaster molds, flower pots and watering cans and decorating chocolate with edible paints.

Dieu Donne Papermill 5+
433 Broome Street between Crosby Street and Broadway, 226-0573, www.papermaking.org
Tour a genuine paper mill and see how paper is made. Papermaking workshops are also held.

Empire State Building Observatory All ages
350 Fifth Avenue between 33rd and 34th Streets, 736-3100, www.empirestatebuilding.com
Two observation decks offer great views of the city and surrounding areas. Don't miss the Guinness Exhibition of World Records. See also New York Skyride.

ESPN Zone 5+
1472 Broadway at Times Square, 921-3776, www.espn.go.com
Sports entertainment complex, including a restaurant, lots of televisions for watching the big games and high-tech interactive and sports simulation games.

Extra Vertical Climbing Center 5+
61 West 62nd Street in the Harmony Atrium, 586-5718
Climb the walls, literally.

Family Disco infants+
Jack Rose Ballroom, 771 Eighth Avenue at 47th Street, 586-7425
A dance party for the whole family on Sundays from 5–6:30 p.m. featuring a full bar for adults and 'wacky' snacks for kids. Here's your chance to "boogie with your baby" and learn the hula, hora and twist.

FDNY Fire Zone 5+
34 West 51st Street between Fifth and Sixth Avenues, 698-4520, www.fdnyfirezone.com
State-of-the-art fire safety learning center operated by the FDNY includes hands-on exhibits, a recreated firehouse and a fire scene. Takes about 30 minutes.

14th Street Y 3+
Sol Goldman YM-YWHA of the Educational Alliance, Inc.
344 East 14th Street at First Avenue, 780-0800, www.edalliance.org
Indoor playground available at scheduled weekly times.

French Institute/Alliance Française 5+
22 East 60th between Park and Madison Avenues, 355-6100, www.fiaf.org
Occasional dance, films and other events geared to young audiences.

Frozen Ropes 3+
207 West 74th Street between Broadway and Amsterdam Avenue, 362-0344, www.frozenropesnyc.com
This national network of baseball and softball training centers offers training, professional instruction and an assortment of batting cages for all skill levels on a drop-in basis. Reservations for batting cages recommended.

Fulton Fish Market Tour 10+
165 John Street near the South Street Seaport, 748-8590
The country's oldest wholesale fish market. Tours are offered through the South Street Seaport Museum and require a minimum of eight people or the tour is canceled. Reservations required; call for scheduled dates.

Galactic Circus 7+
1540 Broadway at 46th Street, 869-9397
Entertainment complex with games, motion ride simulators, live performers, prizes and a café.

Gracie Mansion 11+
East End Avenue at 88th Street, 570-4751, www.nyc.gov/html/om/html/gracie.html
Weekday tours of the official residence of the Mayor of New York. Reservations required.

Horse Drawn Carriage Rides All ages
A quintessential New York Experience. Carriages are available at 59th Street and Fifth Avenue, along Central Park South and at Tavern on the Green (inside Central Park at 67th Street and Central Park West). Fare is currently $34 for the first half-hour, $10 for each additional 15 minutes.

Ice Rink at Rockefeller Plaza 3+
49th and 50th Streets between Fifth and Sixth Avenues, 332-7654
Experience the magic of skating in one of the most recognized spots in the world. Skate rentals available. Call for public skating hours.

Institute of Culinary Education 6+
50 West 23rd Street between Fifth and Sixth Avenues, 847-0700, www.iceculinary.com
Single-session cooking classes include pizza-making, baking and others.

Kids on Wheels 5+
Joel Rappelfeld's Rollerblading, 744-4444
In-line skating instruction offered after school and on weekends.

Lazer Park 7+
163 West 46th Street between Broadway and Sixth Avenue, 398-3060, www.lazertag.com
Laser tag for the intrepid.

Leisure Time Bowling 4+
625 Eighth Avenue and 40th Street in the Port Authority Bus Terminal, 268-6909
Bumper bowling for beginners, regular bowling for older children and adults.

Liberty Helicopters Parental discretion
West 30th Street Heliport, 967-6464, www.libertyhelicopters.com
Aerial tours of the Hudson, lower Manhattan and up to Central Park.

Libraries All ages
The New York Public Library system (www.nypl.org) contains a wealth of literary works for even the youngest of readers. The library branches listed

below have children's areas and even entire children's floors. Programs vary but can include films, story hours, workshops, computer games and instruction. The Donnell Library on West 53rd Street has the honor of being the permanent residence of Winnie-the-Pooh and his friends. Call the branch you wish to visit for specific hours. A monthly calendar of city-wide activities and events can be obtained at any branch.

- New York Public Library Offices of Children's Services, 340-0904
- 58th Street Branch, 127 East 58th Street, 759-7358
- 67th Street Branch, 328 East 67th Street, 734-1717
- 96th Street Branch, 112 East 96th Street, 289-0908
- 115th Street Branch, 203 West 115th Street, 666-9393
- Chatham Square Branch, 33 East Broadway, 964-6598
- Columbia Branch, 514 West 113th Street, 864-2530
- Donnell Library Center, 20 West 53rd Street, 621-0615
- Early Childhood Resource and Information Center, 66 Leroy Street, 929-0815
- Epiphany Branch, 228 East 23rd Street, 679-2645
- Harlem Branch, 9 West 124th Street, 348-5620
- Jefferson Market Branch, 425 Sixth Avenue, 243-4334
- Kips Bay Branch, 446 Third Avenue, 683-2520
- Lincoln Center Branch, 127 Amsterdam Avenue, 870-1633
- Muhlenberg Branch, 209 West 23rd Street, 924-1585
- Ottendorfer Branch, 135 Second Avenue, 674-0947
- Riverside Branch, 127 Amsterdam Avenue, 870-1810
- St. Agnes Branch, 444 Amsterdam Avenue, 877-4380
- Tompkins Square Branch, 331 East 10th Street, 228-4747
- Webster Branch, 1465 York Avenue, 288-5049
- Yorkville Branch, 222 East 79th Street, 744-5824

Lincoln Center Tours 6+
Broadway and 64th Street, 546-2656, 875-5350 (tour desk information), www.lincolncenter.org
Behind-the-scenes look at New York City's famous cultural center. Rehearsals viewed weekdays. Meet at the Metropolitan Opera House on the Concourse level next to the gift shop. Call for weekly schedules.

Little Shop of Plaster and Pottery 4+
431 East 73rd Street, 717-6636, www.littleshopofplasterandpottery.com
Paint plaster molds of your choice. Also available: glass painting, T-shirt painting and sand art.

Madame Tussaud's All ages
234 West 42nd Street between Broadway and Eighth Avenue, 800 246-8872, www.nycwax.com
View replicas of more than 150 of your favorite celebrities, including Lady Diana, Elton John, Jacqueline Kennedy Onassis, George W. Bush and more, at this 85,000 square foot New York location of the world-famous wax museum.

Madison Square Garden Tour 9+
Seventh Avenue between 31st and 33rd Streets, 465-5800, www.thegarden.com
See what's behind the bleachers, visit a corporate box, check out the locker rooms and more. Tickets available at the box office.

My Favorite Place 6 months–4 years; age specific
265 West 87th Street between Broadway and West End Avenue, 362-5320
Indoor playroom and toy store offering toddler and after-school drop-in programs at scheduled times, including a "Toddler Sing-Along" each weekday morning.

NBC Studio Tour Children under 6 not permitted
GE Building, 30 Rockefeller Center between 49th and 50th Streets, 664-3700, www.nbc.com
See what happens on television from the other side of the screen. Tickets are sold on a first-come, first-served basis and can be purchased on the website. Reservations are recommended. Call 664-3056 for tickets to NBC shows taped in New York.

Nelson A. Rockefeller Park (formerly Hudson River Park) All Ages
Battery Park City, 267-9700
Enter at the end of Chambers or Vesey Streets or at the World Financial Center and walk north along the river. This site offers a fabulous playground with breathtaking views. Special events are organized for all ages, including recreational and arts programs, music and storytelling, after-school programs, drawing classes, fishing and walking tours. May through October.

New York Skyride 3+
350 Fifth Avenue in Empire State Building at 34th Street, 2nd floor, 800 975-9743, www.skyride.com
Big-screen flight simulator takes you for a ride over Manhattan.

New York Stock Exchange 8+
Interactive Education Center, 20 Broad Street between Wall Street and Exchange Place, 656-5168, www.nyse.com
Self-guided tours weekdays at no charge. See what makes the ticker tape tick.

New York Waterway Cruises 4+
Pier 78 at 38th Street and Twelfth Avenue, 800 533-3779, www.nywaterway.com
A number of cruise opportunities available for various lengths of time. Toddlers and very active children might find some excursions too long an adventure. Bring lap activities to provide additional entertainment.

Our Name is Mud 4+
59 Greenwich Avenue at Seventh Avenue, 647-7899
1566 Second Avenue between 81st Street and 82nd Streets, 570-6868
506 Amsterdam Avenue between 84th and 85th Streets, 579-5575
Glaze the clay piece of your choice on a drop-in basis.

Parades, street festivals and other happenings
The Mayor's Street Activity Office, 788-7439
Calendar of community events delivered by automated voice system.

Parks
www.nyc.gov (city agencies, Parks & Recreation); Special Events Hotline, 888 NY PARKS (888 697-2757) or 360-3456 or 800 201 PARK (800 201-7275)
The City Parks & Recreation Department operates 35 recreation centers and hundreds of parks; playgrounds; playing fields (including softball, cricket, football and soccer fields); basketball, tennis, volleyball and bocce courts; golf courses; ice skating rinks; roller hockey rinks; marinas; running tracks; skate parks (inline skating, roller hockey and skateboarding); and bike paths. Visit the website for locations and operating hours.

Permits are required for special events held in a city park if 20 or more people will be present (yes, this includes birthday parties and school or class picnics), for certain sporting events and for organized sports leagues. Fees for permits vary depending on the nature of the permit. To obtain a permit, visit www.nyc.gov (city agencies, Parks & Recreation) or call 408-0226 (Manhattan), 718 430-1847 (Bronx), 718 965-8912 (Brooklyn), 718 520-5941 (Queens) or 718 390-8023 (Staten Island).

The Parks & Recreation Department operates 10 Urban Park Ranger Nature Centers that offer walking tours, workshops, educational programs and recreation.

- Bronx. Pelham Bay Nature Center, 718 885-3467; Crotona Park, 718 378-2061; Orchard Beach Nature Center, 718 667-6042 or 718 967-3542; Van Cortlandt Nature Center, 718 548-0912
- Brooklyn. Salt Marsh Nature Center, 718 421-2021
- Manhattan. Inwood Hill Nature Center, 304-2365; Belvedere Castle Visitor Center (Central Park), 628-2345; Dana Discovery Center (Central Park), 860-1370
- Queens. Alley Pond Nature Center, 718 217-6034 or 718 846-2731; Forest Park Nature/Visitor Center, 718 846-2731

- Staten Island. Blue Heron Nature Center, 718 967-3542; High Rock Nature Center, 718 967-3542

The Parks & Recreation Department operates 20 Historic Houses (see www .nyc.gov, City Agencies, Parks & Recreation, or www.nycparks.completei net.net for details). Some are individually listed in this chapter. In addition:

- Bronx. Bartow-Pell Mansion Museum, Van Cortlandt House Museum.
- Brooklyn. Leffert Homestead Children's Historic House Museum, Old Stone House Historic Interpretive Center, Pieter Claesen Wyckoff House Museum.
- Queens. King Manor Museum, Kingsland Homestead.
- Staten Island. Conference House, Seguine Mansion.

Playgrounds

With more than 200 playgrounds in Manhattan alone, you are never too far from a "play break" as you wend your way through the city. The most popular playgrounds are found in Central Park, Riverside Park (from 72nd to 100th Streets, along the Hudson River) and along the East River. However, there are many playgrounds, small and large, tucked within most residential neighborhoods. For a complete list of playgrounds in all boroughs, visit www.nyc.gov, City Agencies, Parks & Recreation, or www.nycparks.completeinet.net.

Some favorites:

- Bryant Park, 42nd Street and Sixth Avenue, behind the Public Library
- Hudson River Playground, Chambers Street at Greenwich Street
- John Jay Playground, 76th Street and the FDR Drive
- Mercer Street Playground, Mercer Street between Bleecker and West 3rd Street
- Hippo Park, in Riverside Park at 91st Street
- Union Square Park, Union Square between 14th and 17th Streets
- For older kids interested in extreme skating, Owls Head Park in Bay Ridge, Brooklyn

Post Office Tour—The Morgan Mail Facility — 7+ only

341 Ninth Avenue between 29th and 30th Streets

Tours on weekdays of the Post Office's automated mail processing. Generally, a two-week advance reservation is required.

Public Spaces

These areas, which are open to the public, offer a nice place to stop and rest while walking around midtown Manhattan. All offer seating and some have food concessions at certain hours or seasonally.

- Citicorp Center, 53rd Street with entrances on Lexington and Third Avenues. Shopping arcade.
- Crystal Pavilion, 50th Street at Third Avenue. Atrium with waterfalls.
- IBM Plaza, 56th Street at Madison Avenue. Atrium.
- Olympic Tower, 51st Street at Fifth Avenue. Atrium with waterfall.
- Paley Park, 53rd Street from Fifth to Madison Avenues. Passageway with waterfall.
- Park Avenue Plaza, Park Avenue from 52nd to 53rd Streets. Passageway with waterfall and shopping arcade.
- Water Tunnel, from 48th to 49th Streets between Sixth and Seventh Avenues. Passageway with waterfall.

Radio City Music Hall Tours 10+
1260 Sixth Avenue between 50th and 51st Streets, 632-4041, www.radiocity.com
Backstage tours of this world-famous theater.

Rain or Shine 6 months–6 years
115 East 29th Street between Park and Lexington Avenues, 532-4420
Indoor play space that resembles a natural rain forest.

Riverdale Equestrian Center 5+
West 254th Street and Broadway in Van Cortlandt Park, Riverdale, Bronx, 718 548-4848
Private riding lessons by appointment, pony rides on weekends from 1 to 3 p.m.

Rockefeller Center Tour 6+ only
GE Building, 30 Rockefeller Center between 49th and 50th Streets, 664-3700, 664-3700, www.nbc.com
Tour NBC, Radio City, the skating rink, gardens and more in this Art Deco jewel in the heart of Manhattan.

Sports Depends on event

Arenas

- Madison Square Garden. Seventh Avenue between 31st and 33rd Streets, 465-6741, www.thegarden.com. The Garden hosts basketball (professional, college and even high school championships), hockey, tennis, wrestling; the circus; dog, cat and horse shows; concerts and more. The teams that call the Garden home are the Knicks, the Rangers and the Liberty.
- Meadowlands Sports Complex. East Rutherford, New Jersey, 201 935-3900, www.njsea.com. Consisting of the Continental Airlines Arena, Giants Stadium and the Meadowlands Race Track, this sports/entertainment complex is home to the Giants, Jets and Metrostars.

- Nassau Veterans Memorial Coliseum. Uniondale, Long Island, 516 794-9300, www.nassaucoliseum.com. Long Island's sports and entertainment complex is home to the Islanders, New York Saints La Crosse and New York Dragons football.
- Shea Stadium. Flushing, Queens, 718 507-8499, www.ballparks.com. Home to the Mets.
- USTA National Tennis Center, Flushing Meadows-Corona Park Queens, 718 760-6200, tickets 888 673-6844, www.usta.com, www.usopen.org. Home to the U.S. Tennis Open.
- Yankee Stadium. Bronx, 718 293-6000, www.ballparks.com. Home to the Yankees.

Teams

BASEBALL

- New York Mets. Shea Stadium, 718 507-8499, www.newyorkmets
- New York Yankees. Yankee Stadium, 718 293-6000 www.yankees.mlb.com
- Brooklyn Cyclones. Keyspan Park, Coney Island, www.brooklyncyclones.com, 718 449-8497
- Brooklyn Kings. www.brooklynkings.com
- Staten Island Yankees. Richmond Country Bank Ballpark, Staten Island, 718 720-9265, www.siyanks.com

BASKETBALL

- New York Knicks. Madison Square Garden, 465-5867, www.nba.com/knicks
- New York Liberty. Madison Square Garden, 564-9622, www.wnba.com/liberty

FOOTBALL

- New York Giants. Meadowlands, 201 460-4370, www.giants.com
- New York Jets. Meadowlands, 201 935-3900, www.newyorkjets.com

HOCKEY

- New York Islanders. Nassau Coliseum, www.newyorkislanders.com
- New York Rangers. Madison Square Garden, www.newyorkrangers.com

SOCCER

- New York Metro Stars. Meadowlands, 201 583-7000, www.metrostars.com
- New York Power. Mitchel Athletic Complex, Uniondale, Long Island, 866 769-7849 (tickets), www.nypower.com

Television show tapings

While most television shows are taped in Los Angeles, quite a few are taped in New York. Dramatic shows typically do not allow visitors on the set, but talk shows, sitcoms and game shows tape before a studio audience. Audiences Unlimited (818 753-3470, www.tvtickets.com) offers free tickets to tapings. Most are in LA, but occasionally New York tickets are available for specific shows. See also www.nycvisit.com (look at visitors, things to do) for a list of shows that tape in the city as well as shows that can be seen from outside the studio (such as *The Early Show* at Fifth Avenue and 59th Street, *Good Morning America* at 44th Street and Broadway, *The Today Show* at 30 Rockefeller Plaza, and *Total Request Live* at 1550 Broadway between 44th and 45th Streets). Visit www.abc.com, www.nbc.com (or call 664-3056), www.fox.com, www.thewb.com and www.upn.com to see if your favorite New York–based shows have live tapings or studio visits.

Tennis Courts

There are a number of courts located in and around the city where you can pay a court fee and play or even arrange a lesson. The following is an abbreviated listing. See also www.parksnyc.completeinet.net for a list of public courts.

- Columbus Tennis Club. 795 Columbus Avenue at 98th Street
- Crosstown Tennis. 31st Street between Fifth and Broadway
- HRC Tennis and Yacht. Piers 13 and 14 at the Seaport, 422-9300
- HRC Village Courts. 110 University Place between 12th and 13th Streets, 989-2300
- Manhattan Plaza Racquet Club. 450 West 43rd Street between Ninth and Tenth Avenues

- Midtown Tennis Club. 341 Eighth Avenue at 27th Street, 989-8572
- Roosevelt Island Racquet Club. 280 Main Street (next to the tram), 935-0258
- Stadium Racquet Club. 11 East 162nd Street (across from Yankee Stadium), 718 588-0077
- Sutton East Tennis Club. 488 East 60th Street, 751-3452
- USTA National Tennis Center. Corona Park, Flushing Meadows, Queens, 718 760-6200

Tin Pan Alley Studios 5–13

One East 28th Street between Fifth and Madison Avenues, 3rd floor

Make your own CD. Studio musicians accompany child's performance of a collection of songs or instrumental selections.

United Nations Buildings and Gardens Children under 5 not permitted on tours
First Avenue between 42nd and 48th Streets; visitors' entrance at 46th Street.
45-minute tours given daily.

Waldorf Astoria Tea 7–11
301 Park Avenue between 49th and 50th Streets, 355-3000, www.waldorfastoria.com
Introduce to your child to formal tea at the Waldorf on Saturdays from 2:30–4:30 p.m. Participants enjoy full tea service, learn about the history of tea and take home a goody bag and certificate of completion.

World Financial Center Depends on program
Battery Park City between Vesey and Liberty Streets, 646 772-6885, www.worldfinancialcenter.com
The Center's Winter Garden is a most amazing indoor public space that hosts shows, concerts, dance programs and other family activities.

Cultural Institutions, Galleries, Gardens, Museums and Zoos

Cultivating culture is serious fun in the Big Apple. The city's museums offer a variety of classes, workshops, lectures, seminars and other programs geared to inspire a child's natural creativity and curiosity. New York City's Wildlife Conservation Society, which has for over 100 years encouraged visitors to care about our natural resources and heritage, is also creator of one of the nation's largest urban wildlife parks. In addition, there are dozens of galleries and gardens to explore. Many of the locations listed below will be familiar to you. You may have even spent time wandering their corridors and paths as a child. You will likely be surprised, however, at the breadth of programming that is available for children and families at those same places today.

We also remind you that it is worth considering becoming a member of some of the institutions listed in this section. If you plan on visiting a place several times over the course of the year, you may well find that the cost of membership beats the price of admission for multiple visits. Additionally, membership typically comes with privileges such as priority registration for programs, discounts and admission to special members-only events.

You may notice that the entries in this section sometimes take you off the island of Manhattan. The ones we have included outside Manhattan are, in our view, big enough, special enough or unique enough that we felt they deserved mention.

Entries are listed in alphabetical order and include the name of the facility, address, phone number, a brief description and the ages best served. Please keep in mind that in this section the indication for "ages best served" will sometimes apply specifically to the family programming that is offered. Many organizations provide an incredible number of opportunities for children of all ages to explore what they have to offer in special programs geared to particular ages. We recommend calling for detailed information and, when appropriate, registering in advance.

Abigail Adams Smith Museum 7+
421 East 61st Street between First and York Avenues, 838-6878
Experience New York City as it once was in this restored 18th-century carriage house that was built for President John Adams' daughter and her husband, even though they never got to live there. Evening and weekend programs for families. Special annual events for children. The museum contains nine period rooms furnished with American antiques.

Abyssinian Baptist Church 8+
132 Odell Clark Place between Adam Clayton Powell Jr. and Malcolm X Boulevards, 862-7474, www.abyssinian.org
One of the oldest churches in Harlem.

Alice Austen House 7+, programs for 5+
2 Hylan Boulevard, Rosebank, Staten Island, 718 816-4506, www.aliceausten.8m.com
Alice Austen was famous for her contribution to early photography. This one-room farmhouse, originally built in 1690, was home to the Austen family.

Alley Pond Environmental Center 3+
228-06 Northern Boulevard, Douglaston, Queens, 718 229-4000, www.alleypond.com
A 700-acre park is the setting for this center's many learning opportunities. The indoor facility, wetlands and many exploration trails allow visitors to study environmental history and science. An extensive educational department offers weekend and summer programs and special clubs.

American Craft Museum 7+, programs for younger children
40 West 53rd Street between Fifth and Sixth Avenues, 956-3535, www.americancraftmuseum.org
This museum was the first dedicated to the work of fine American craft artists. Exhibitions include works from both established and emerging artists. The museum also holds workshops, demonstrations and lectures.

American Museum of the Moving Image 5+
36-01 35th Avenue at 36th Street, Astoria, Queens, 718 784-0077, www.ammi.org
Near the Kaufman Astoria Studios complex at 36th Street. This museum houses a wonderful collection of films and all kinds of artifacts from the industry. Hands-on exhibits allow first-hand testing of the principles and techniques used by filmmakers.

American Museum of Natural History All ages, programs age-specific
Central Park West between 77th and 81st Streets, 769-5100, 769-5200 for reservations and program information, www.amnh.org
One of the world's largest museums, this amazing institution houses an extensive range of exhibits that cover the history of human life and natural evolution, including over 40 million natural specimens. Favorites include Dinosaur Hall, the Hall of Minerals and Gems, the Hall of Biodiversity (a new area featuring a rain forest) and the North American Indian exhibit. There is a Discovery Room for children that requires tickets but is free of charge. The Natural Science Center is also open to children for exploration at specified times.

American Museum of Natural History Hayden Planetarium, Rose Center for Earth and Space All ages
81st Street between Central Park West and Columbus Avenue, 769-5100, www.amnh.org
Now housed in a sleek new glass box, the Rose Center for Earth and Space and the Planetarium provide a virtual journey through time–space and the mysteries of the universe.

American Numismatic Society 8+
Broadway at 155th Street in Audubon Terrace Museum Complex, 234-3130, www.amnumsoc.org
The exhibition galleries have extensive collections of coins, medals and paper money. An appointment can be scheduled for a tour with a curator.

Anne Frank Center, USA 10+
584 Broadway between Houston and Prince Streets, 431-7993, www.annefrank.com
An exhibit that explores the life of Anne Frank, her family and other Jewish families during WWII in Europe.

The Aquarium for Wildlife Conservation All ages, programs age-specific
West 8th Street and Surf Avenue, Coney Island, Brooklyn, 718 265-FISH(3474), 718 265-3448 for program information, www.nyaquarium.com
Observe an abundance of sea life. Daily performances. Programs for children and families throughout the year plus summer and holiday programs, including lectures, beach walks, and "get wet" workshops.

The Asia Society 10+
725 Park Avenue at 70th Street, 288-6400, 517-NEWS for events information, www.asiasociety.org
Permanent and changing exhibitions create an awareness and understanding of Asian cultures.

The Bard Graduate Center for Studies in the Decorative Arts 6+
18 West 86th Street between Central Park West and Columbus Avenue, 501-3000, www.bgc.bard.edu
Interactive programs including gallery tours, artisan demonstrations, theatrical role-playing, book readings and arts-and-crafts projects. Educational programs are keyed into current exhibits.

Bronx Museum of the Arts 5+
1040 Grand Concourse at 165th Street, Bronx, 718 681-6000, www.bronxview.com/museum/
Founded in 1971 to serve the culturally diverse population of the Bronx and the rest of New York, the museum focuses on modern and contemporary art. There are Sunday family programs.

The Bronx Zoo/Wildlife Conservation Park All ages, programs age-specific
Bronx River Parkway at Fordham Road, Bronx, 718 367-1010 general information, 718 220-6854 program information, www.bronxzoo.com, www.wcs.org
Natural habitats house hundreds of species at this world-class zoo. Rides, shows, feedings and a special Children's Zoo. Seasonal exhibits, programs, lectures and workshops.

Brooklyn Botanic Garden All ages, programs age-specific
1000 Washington Avenue, Brooklyn, 718 623-7200, 718 623-7220 for tour information, www.bbg.org
Explore 59 acres and over 12,000 kinds of plants, and participate in a variety of special programs. Tours are given on weekends.

Brooklyn Children's Museum 2–13
145 Brooklyn Avenue at St. Mark's Avenue, Brooklyn, 718 735-4432 4400, www.brooklynkids.org
The exhibitions and many hands-on activities here provide the materials for children to learn about the world and different cultures around them. Many different kinds of children's programs are offered.

The Brooklyn Historical Society 5+
128 Pierrepont Street at Clinton, Brooklyn Heights, Brooklyn, 718 624-0890, www.brooklynhistory.org
Exhibitions on Brooklyn history with permanent exhibits on the Brooklyn Bridge, Coney Island, the Dodgers, the Navy Yard and Brooklynites. Note: the Historical Society building is closed for renovation until early 2003, and the Society is temporarily located at 45 Main Street, Suite 617. Only the photo archives are available, by appointment.

The Brooklyn Museum of Art 4+, programs age-specific
200 Eastern Parkway, Brooklyn, 718 638-5000, www.brooklynart.org
Some of the museum's permanent exhibits include traditional art of Africa, the South Pacific and the Americas. Paintings, sculpture, costumes, decorative arts and period rooms are on display. The museum is also home to preeminent collections of Egyptian, Classical, Middle Eastern and Asian art. "Arty Facts" is a weekly series of workshops and gallery visits for families. The museum offers many other programs for all different ages and interests.

Cathedral Church of St. John the Divine 8+
Amsterdam Avenue at 112th Street, www.stjohndivine.org
Begun in 1892 and home to the Episcopal Church, this is one of the world's largest cathedrals.

Central Park Wildlife Center, Wildlife Gallery and The Tisch Children's Zoo All ages, programs age-specific
Fifth Avenue at 64th Street behind the Arsenal Building in Central Park, 861-6030, www.wcs.org
A collection of habitats within various climate zones. Shows, activities, workshops and special events. Adjacent to the Central Park Wildlife Center is the Children's Zoo, which is filled with opportunities to "walk with the animals."

Central Synagogue 6+
55th Street and Lexington Avenue, www.centralsynagogue.org
The oldest Jewish house of worship in the city in continuous use. Serving a Reform congregation, the magnificent Moorish-style Sanctuary Building is a National and New York City historic landmark.

Children's Galleries for Jewish Culture all ages
515 West 20th Street, 4E, 924-4500, www.jcllcm.com
The Jewish Children's Learning Lab seeks to "engage school age children and accompanying adults in the exploration of Jewish culture and heritage through interactive exhibitions for children and related educational programs."

The Children's Interactive Jewish Museum 4+
14th Street Y, Sol Goldman YM-YWHA of the Educational Alliance
344 East 14th Street at First Avenue, 780-0800 ext. 254,
www.edalliance.org
A museum set up for families to learn about Jewish feasts, fasts, celebrations and holidays in an interactive and educational way.

Children's Museum of the Arts 2–10
182 Lafayette Street between Broome and Grand Streets, 274-0986,
www.cmany.org
The museum offers many types of programs for children and families, including dance and theater workshops.

Children's Museum of Manhattan All ages
212 West 83rd Street between Amsterdam Avenue and Broadway,
721-1224, www.cmom.org
Wonderful, original, interactive exhibits provide a unique setting for children and adults to learn about art, science and the world around them. The museum offers classes, workshops and many programs for children.

China House Gallery/
China Institute in America 12+, programs for younger children
125 East 65th Street between Park and Lexington Avenues, 744-8181,
www.chinainstitute.org
The gallery hosts special exhibits of Chinese art and other cultural items and offers accompanying workshops, which can range from exploring Chinese languages to instruction in calligraphy.

City Hall/Governor's Room 9+
City Hall, 788-6865, www.nyc.gov
Get a hands-on lesson in local government via a self-guided tour of City Hall and the Governor's Room (available for parties of ten or fewer). Larger groups can tour the facility with a sergeant. Requires a two-week advance reservation.

The Cloisters 4+
Fort Tryon Park, upper Manhattan, 923-3700, www.metmuseum.org
The Cloisters, on a hilltop overlooking the Hudson River, is a branch of the Metropolitan Museum of Art and is devoted to the art and architecture of medieval Europe. Special workshops are offered for families, typically on Saturdays.

Cooper-Hewitt National Design Museum Depends upon exhibits
2 East 91st Street at Fifth Avenue, 849-8300, www.si.edu/ndm
The Smithsonian Institution's National Museum of Design offers changing exhibits focusing on various aspects of contemporary and historical design, including anything from buttons to jewelry to kitchen utensils.

Dahesh Museum 10+

580 Madison Avenue at 56th Street, 759-0606, www.dasheshmuseum.org

A small museum dedicated to exploring 19th-century European academic art.

DIA Center for the Arts 10+

548 West 22nd Street, 431-9232, www.diacenter.org

Large-scale installations of contemporary art, usually by a single artist.

The Drawing Center All ages

35 Wooster Street, 219-2166, www.drawingcenter.org

This institution, which focuses on the exhibition of historical and contemporary drawings, offers Saturday morning "Line Readings for Children" where authors/illustrators read from their works.

The Dyckman Farm House 7+

4881 Broadway at 204th Street, 304-9422, www.dyckman.org

The last remaining Dutch colonial farmhouse in Manhattan contains period artifacts depicting life in colonial New York. Demonstrations can be scheduled in advance.

Edgar Allan Poe Cottage 10+

2460 Grand Concourse and East Kingsbridge Road, Bronx, 718 881-8900

The 1812 cottage where Edgar Allan Poe settled in 1846 has been restored and is dedicated to one of America's greatest literary masters. Tours by appointment during the week.

Eldridge Street Project 5+

12 Eldridge Street near Canal and Allen Streets, 978-8800, www.eldridgestreet.org

Tours are available of this historic landmark synagogue. Programs offered include storytelling.

Ellis Island Immigration Museum All ages will enjoy the boat ride, otherwise 6+

Ellis Island, by way of the Statue of Liberty ferry, 363-3200, ferry schedule 269-5755, www.ellisisland.org

The Ellis Island immigration station, which operated from 1892 to 1954, has been restored as a museum. Among its many exhibits, the museum displays countless artifacts belonging to the individuals who passed through years ago. Explore the passenger record archive (culled from arriving ships' manifests) for information on the individuals who entered this country at Ellis Island.

El Museo del Barrio 5+

1230 Fifth Avenue at 104th Street, 831-7272, www.elmuseo.org

Through paintings, sculpture, graphics, photography, archaeology, films, music and theater, the museum highlights the cultural heritage of Puerto

Ricans and all Latin Americans living in the United States. Traditional folk art and contemporary urban art of the barrio are displayed. El Museo is one of the city's foremost Hispanic cultural institutes, offering concerts, workshops and other programs, some of which are appropriate for children.

Fashion Institute of Technology 8+
Seventh Avenue at 27th Street, 217-5800, www.fitncy.suny.edu
With a huge collection of costumes, textiles and clothing, this museum, dedicated to the social and cultural contexts of style and fashion, will delight fashion-conscious kids.

The Forbes Magazine Gallery 7+
60 Fifth Avenue between 12th and 13th Streets, 206-5548, www.forbes.com
The galleries display 300 pieces of Fabergé art, 12,000 toy soldiers, 500 toy boats, an assortment of historical documents and other memorabilia and paintings from the permanent collection.

Fraunces Tavern Museum 3+
54 Pearl Street, 425-1778, www.frauncestavernmuseum.org
Tucked away in the historical Fraunces Tavern, the museum has a permanent collection of artifacts, decorative arts, paintings and prints from 18th-century America. One weekend each month, the museum conducts programs for families and children.

The Frick Collection Children under 10 not admitted
One East 70th Street at Fifth Avenue, 288-0700, www.frick.org
Formerly a single-family residence, now a museum, this grand mansion houses an incredible collection of 18th- and 19th-century art, and transports visitors into the grandeur of turn-of-the-century high society.

Guggenheim Museum (Solomon R. Guggenheim Museum)
Activity guide for 7 and under, programs age-specific
1071 Fifth Avenue at 88th Street, 423-3500, www.guggenheim.org
A diverse collection of contemporary art that grew out of the private collection of millionaire Solomon Guggenheim. The building has an upward spiraling ramp around a large atrium—a manageable space that is kid friendly. The museum offers programs for children and conducts family workshops at scheduled times throughout the year. Note that advance registration for these workshops is generally required; call 423-3587. A family activity guide is available and relates to current exhibitions.

Hispanic Society of America 10+
613 West 155th Street at Broadway, at the Audubon Terrace, 926-2234, www.hispanicsociety.org
The diverse collection of work housed at this reference library and museum represents the arts, literature and culture of Spain, Portugal and Latin America.

Historic Richmond Town 6+
441 Clark Avenue, Staten Island, 718 351-1611, www.historicrichmondtown.org
This authentic village of historic buildings, including a museum, takes you back in time. There is a story time for young children.

International Center of Photography 11+
1133 Sixth Avenue at 43rd Street, 857-0000, www.icp.org
ICP is Manhattan's only museum dedicated solely to photography. Great photographic works are restored and on permanent display and in special exhibits. Educational opportunities, lectures, and other events take place year round.

Intrepid Sea, Air and Space Museum 4+
Intrepid Square, Pier 86, West 46th Street and Twelfth Avenue, 245-0072, www.intrepidmuseum.com
A decommissioned aircraft carrier houses a museum of naval history. In addition to the aircraft carrier, other vessels are available to tour, including a submarine. Talks and workshops are offered occasionally.

Islamic Cultural Center of New York 8+
1711 Third Avenue at 96th Street, 288-3215
A modern (completed in the 1990s) mosque built at an angle to face Mecca.

Jacques Marchais Museum of Tibetan Art 6+
338 Lighthouse Avenue, Staten Island, 718 987-3500, www.tibetanmuseum.com
Tibetan and Asian works of art are housed in a building designed by Jacques Marchais to look like a Buddhist mountain temple. Surrounded by gardens, this museum seeks to promote a better understanding of Tibetan culture, art, philosophy and history. Weekend workshops, family programs, concerts, dances, performances and storytelling are scheduled.

The Jewish Museum 4+
1109 Fifth Avenue at 92nd Street, 423-3200, 423-3337 for family program information, www.thejewishmuseum.org
This museum houses the largest collection of Judaica in America. Contemporary and folk art exhibits depict Jewish culture throughout history. It has Sunday drop-in programs for children, story time and gallery talks.

Judaica Museum of the Hebrew Home for the Aged at Riverdale 6+
5961 Palisade Avenue, Bronx, 718 581-1787, www.hebrewhome.org/museum
This educational center houses objects, paintings, and textiles from the Jewish religion and culture.

The Liberty Science Center 2+

251 Phillips Street, Liberty State Park, Jersey City, New Jersey, 201 200-1000, www.libertysciencecenter.org

This huge world-class science-oriented museum features an Omni Max Theater, interactive activities, demonstrations, hands-on exhibits, classes, workshops, special events and more. You can get there by car or by taking a ferry from the World Financial Center to the Colgate Center in Jersey City (call 800 53 FERRY) and then a short shuttle bus to the museum.

Little Red Lighthouse 5+

Fort Washington Park, 178th Street and the Hudson River

This lighthouse, officially known as Jeffrey's Hook Lighthouse, is the star of the 1942 classic children's book *The Little Red Lighthouse and the Great Gray Bridge* by Hildegarde H. Swift.

Lower East Side Tenement Museum 6+

90 Orchard Street at Broome Street, 431-0233, www.tenement.org

The museum draws the visitor to America's urban immigrant roots through tours of its 1863 tenement building, neighborhood walking tours, exhibits, performances and media presentation. The Confino family apartment is open on weekends for viewing and provides an interactive experience for families with children.

Metropolitan Museum of Art 6+, programs age-specific

1000 Fifth Avenue at 82nd Street, 535-7710, www.metmuseum.org

One of the premier museums in the United States. Permanent and special exhibits are devoted to representing 5,000 years of human expression in over 32 acres of exhibition space and through more than 3.5 million pieces of art from all over the world. Special museum guides are available for children, facilitating interaction between adults and children during the self-guided tour. There is so much to see, it's best to pick and choose a few areas. Favorites for kids include exhibits on ancient Egypt, Arms and Armor and ancient Greece and Rome. Programs for children, families and teens are run through the membership and education departments.

Morris-Jumel Mansion 5+

65 Jumel Terrace at 160th Street in Washington Heights, 923-8008, www.morrisjumel.org

This restored building was built in 1765 as a summer house and in 1776 established by George Washington as the headquarters for the Continental Army. The museum highlights New York history, culture and the arts, and has 12 period rooms. Summer and after-school programs are occasionally arranged. Annual Washington's Birthday Celebration.

Museum for African Art 5+
593 Broadway between Houston and Prince Streets, 966-1313, www.africanart.org
Celebrate African history and culture via concerts, exhibits, lectures, workshops, films, family and weekend programs that bring African art to life. Note: The museum has temporarily moved to 36-01 43rd Avenue in Long Island City, Queens (718 784-7700), while its new permanent home is being constructed at the northern end of Museum Mile in Manhattan.

Museum of American Financial History 10+
28 Broadway across from Bowling Green Park, 908-4519, www.financialhistory.org
This very small museum contains a "wealth" of information and is a neat place to visit in conjunction with a look around the Stock Exchange.

Museum of American Folk Art 5+
45 West 53rd Street between Fifth and Sixth Avenues, 265-1040
Eva and Morris Feld Gallery, 2 Lincoln Square on Columbus Avenue between 65th and 66th Streets, 595-9533
www.folkartmuseum.org
Changing exhibitions explore the work of three centuries of American folk artists and their culture. Sunday workshops for families are scheduled periodically, generally requiring reservations.

Museum of American Illustration Depends upon exhibit
128 East 63rd Street between Park and Lexington Avenues, 838-2560, www.societyillustrators.org
Changing exhibitions feature the work of illustrators from around the world.

Museum of Bronx History/Valentine–Varian House 10+
3266 Bainbridge Avenue at East 208th Street, Bronx, 718 881-8900, www.bronxhistoricalsociety.org
The Museum of Bronx History is contained within the Valentine–Varian House, which is a restored farmhouse built in 1758. The museum hosts special exhibitions on Bronx culture, history and well-known residents.

Museum of Chinese in the Americas 4+
70 Mulberry Street at Bayard, 2nd floor, 619-4785, www.moca-nyc.org
Housed in a century-old school building, the museum is dedicated to preserving the history and culture of Chinese immigrants and their descendents in the Western hemisphere. It features exhibits, children's book readings, walking tours of Chinatown. Specially scheduled family programs.

The Museum of the City of New York 4+
1220 Fifth Avenue at 103rd Street, 534-1672, www.mcny.org
The museum collects, preserves and features original artifacts, documents, prints, maps and other items relating to the history of Manhattan. Various programs for children and several annual family events.

Museum of Jewish Heritage—A Living Memorial to the Holocaust 7+
18 First Place, Battery Park City, 509-6130, www.mjhnyc.org
Dedicated to teaching all ages and backgrounds about 20th-century Jewish life. Exhibits include photographs, artifacts and narratives of life during the Holocaust.

The Museum of Modern Art 5+
11 West 53rd Street between Fifth and Sixth Avenues, 708-9400, www.moma.org
This pre-eminent museum houses one of the world's largest collections of 19th- and 20th-century painting, sculpture, photography and design. Workshops, lectures, films, performances and special events are offered for children and their families, including Saturday morning tours. "Art Safari," a guide created especially for children, is available for sale in the gift shop. MOMA is undergoing a major renovation and is temporarily located at 45-20 33rd Street at Queens Boulevard in Long Island City, Queens. The museum offers Queens Artlink: a free weekend bus shuttle service to MOMA, P.S. 1 Contemporary Art Center, The Noguchi Museum, Socrates Sculpture Park and the American Museum of the Moving Image.

The Museum of Television and Radio Depends upon exhibit
25 East 52nd Street between Fifth and Madison Avenues, 621-6600, www.mtr.org
The museum's collection of over 90,000 radio and television programs offers everything from news, public-affairs programming and documentaries to the performing arts, children's programming, sports, comedy shows and advertising. There are special events for children during the International Children's Festival, typically in the fall and spring.

National Academy of Design 5+
1083 Fifth Avenue at 89th Street, 369-4880, www.nationalacademy.org
Houses one of the largest collections of American art in the country in a former home of a philanthropist. Offers after-school programs, seminars, weekend and family programs, workshops, lectures, art classes and concerts. Family Fun Days on Saturday.

National Museum of the American Indian 5+
One Bowling Green across from Battery Park, 514-3700, 514-3888 for program information, www.nmai.si.edu
Past and present Native American cultures are celebrated. Cultures from the Arctic to the Antarctic are represented. One Saturday each month, the museum features a Traditional Native American Performance program.

New Museum of Contemporary Art 7+
583 Broadway between Prince and Houston Streets, 219-1222, www.newmuseum.org
Founded in 1977, the museum has changing exhibits of contemporary art and offers talks and workshops.

The New York Botanical Garden 5+, although at any age a stroll through the gardens can be enjoyable

200th Street and Southern Boulevard near the Bronx Zoo, 718 817-8700, www.nybg.org

Located on 250 acres in the Bronx, the New York Botanical Garden offers educational programs and seasonal displays to teach visitors about the plant world.

The New York City Fire Museum 2+, programs age-specific

278 Spring Street between Varick and Hudson Streets, 691-1303, www.nycfiremuseum.org

This renovated 1904 firehouse displays equipment used to battle fires throughout history. Programs for children and their families.

The New York City Police Museum 7+

100 Old Slip, 480-3100, www.nycpolicemuseum.org

This museum is located in the Police Academy Training School and offers the opportunity to view badges, counterfeit money, fingerprinting equipment, firearms and uniforms. Weekend family activities. Open weekdays by appointment only.

New York Hall of Science 3+

47-01 111th Street, Flushing Meadows, Queens, 718 699-0005, www.nyhallsci.org

Designed to improve the public understanding of science and technology through exhibits, programs and media and ranked as one of the 10 top science museums, the hall features the largest collection of interactive exhibits in New York City. A variety of programs for children (including sleepovers!) are offered. The Discover Room and Bubble Area are designed for preschoolers.

New York Historical Society 8+

2 West 77th Street at Central Park West, 873-3400, www.nyhistory.org

The permanent collection includes everything from American paintings to sleighs. Changing exhibits highlight the history of the city and state.

The New York Transit Museum 4+

Boerum Place and Schermerhorn Street, Brooklyn Heights, Brooklyn, 718 694-5100, www.mta.nyc.ny.us

The Transit Museum is located in a decommissioned 1930s subway station. Learn about the history of our rapid transit system. Weekend family workshops. Note: The museum is currently closed for renovation but is scheduled to reopen in 2003.

New York Unearthed 7+

17 State Street at Pearl Street, 748-8628.

This archeology museum features dioramas filled with actual artifacts excavated from beneath New York City and a functioning glass-enclosed laboratory where you can view conservators at work.

Newseum/NY 10+

580 Madison Avenue between 56th and 57th Streets, 317-7596, www.newseum.org

Newseum is a media educational and cultural institute aimed at improving public understanding of journalism and First Amendment issues. Good for budding reporters.

North Wind Undersea Institute 6+

610 City Island Avenue, Bronx, 718 885-0701

An environmental museum with many ongoing and hands-on exhibits of marine life, deep-sea diving equipment, scrimshaw and sunken treasures. Weekend tours given on the hour.

The Old Merchant's House 10+

29 East 4th Street between Lafayette Street and Broadway, 777-1089, www.merchantshouse.com

This restored Greek Revival row house, built in 1832, was once owned by the merchant Samuel Treadwell. It provides an example of living conditions in 19th-century New York.

The Paine Webber Art Gallery Depends upon exhibit

1285 Sixth Avenue between 51st and 52nd Streets, 713-2885, www.ubspainewebber.com

This gallery features changing art exhibits. Closed on weekends.

The Pierpont Morgan Library 4+

29 East 36th Street at Madison Avenue, 685-0610, www.morganlibrary.org

J.P. Morgan's vast collection of rare books, sculpture, paintings, manuscripts and musical scores is housed here. The library will be closed until 2006 for an expansion project.

Poets House 4–10

75 Spring Street, 2nd floor, 431-7920, www.poetshouse.org

This literary center and poetry archive, housing a library containing 40,000 volumes of poetry, features a whimsical Children's Room just right for settling in with a volume of verse. Open on Saturdays from 11 a.m. to 1 p.m. Children must be accompanied by an adult. Programs for kids are held throughout the year.

Queens Botanical Garden 4+
43-50 Main Street, Flushing, Queens, 718 886-3800, www.queensbotanical.org
Over 39 acres of gardens to explore, including a Victorian wedding garden. Workshops for families are conducted, including seed planting for children.

Queens County Farm Museum 3+
73-50 Little Neck Parkway, Floral Park, Queens, 718 347-FARM (3276), www.queensfarm.org
This unique museum is a historical, full-size, working farm. Special events for families are offered on weekends. Note that this is primarily an outdoor experience.

The Queens Museum of Art 4+
New York City Building, Flushing Meadows–Corona Park, Queens, 718 592-9700, www.queensmuse.org
The museum hosts fine-arts exhibitions and the "Panorama of New York," an exact scale model of the five boroughs that was designed originally for the 1964 World's Fair and is updated as needed. Weekend drop-in programs are held year round.

The Riverside Church 8+
Riverside Drive at 122nd Street, www.theriversidechurchny.org
Interdenominational Gothic church modeled after the 13th-century Gothic cathedral in Chartres, France, known for its 392-foot-high tower. The Labyrinth on the floor of the chancel is quite interesting for kids.

Rose Center for Earth and Space.
See American Museum of Natural History

St. Patrick's Cathedral 8+
Fifth Avenue at 50th Street, www.ny-archdiocese.org
Begun in 1858 and renovated as recently at 1989, this is the largest (seats 2,200) decorated, Gothic-style Catholic Cathedral in the United States.

Schomburg Center for Research in Black Culture 6+
515 Malcolm X Boulevard at 135th Street, 491-2200, www.nypl.org
Part of the New York Public Library, this widely used research facility preserves materials relating Africa and the African Diaspora. It presents changing exhibits on African American culture and various programs.

Skandinavia House 3–10
Heimbold Family Learning Center, 58 Park Avenue, 847-9740, www.skandinaviahouse.org
Skandinavia House offers regular programs for families and children including storytelling and informal playgroups where kids can read, play with toys and dress up in Skandinavian costumes.

Skyscraper Museum 10+
44 Wall Street, 968-1961, www.skyscraper.org
The museum is dedicated to the study of high-rise buildings. Note: The museum is closed until mid-2003, when it will open in its new permanent home in Battery Park City.

Sony Wonder Technology Lab 7+
550 Madison Avenue between 55th and 56th Streets in Sony Plaza, 833-8100, www.sonywondertechlab.com
A one-of-a-kind interactive science and technology center designed to showcase the latest in communication technology. After-school, weekend and family programs.

The South Street Seaport Museum 5+
207 Fulton Street and the 11-square block historic district including Fulton Street, South Street and 17 State Street, 748-8600, www.southstseaport.org
Exhibits explore the workings of the waterfront district from colonial times to the present. Family and children's programs as well as workshops are offered. "NY Unearthed," a satellite exhibit of the museum, is located at 17 State Street. Also visit the Whitman Gallery at 209 Water Street to see ship models on display.

The Spanish Institute 2+ (language classes)
684 Park Avenue between 69th and 70th Streets, 734-4177, www.spanishinstitute.org
The museum was founded to promote the understanding of Spanish culture and its influence on the Americas. It offers changing exhibits and language classes for children.

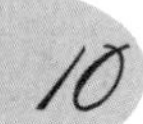

Staten Island Botanical Garden All ages
1000 Richmond Terrace, Snug Harbor Cultural Center, Staten Island, 718 273-8200, www.sibg.org
Explore 15 acres of wetlands and 13 acres of various gardens. Junior Green Team and family programming.

Staten Island Children's Museum 3–12
1000 Richmond Terrace, Staten Island, 718 273-2060, www.snug-harbor.org
The museum offers many opportunities for children to explore and learn by doing and an outdoor area for picnics. Weekend workshops and activities are offered for parents and children, including performances, storytelling, films, concerts and craft projects. No strollers allowed in the museum.

The Staten Island Institute of Arts & Sciences 7+
75 Stuyvesant Place, Staten Island, 718 727-1135, www.siiasmuseum.org
A two-block walk from the ferry terminus, this institute features changing and permanent exhibits as well as the Staten Island Ferry Collection, which explores the history of, and includes large-scale models of, the Ferry Line.

The Statue of Liberty National Museum All ages
Liberty Island, 363-3200, www.nps.gov/stli
Reached by boat from Battery Park North (for ferry information call 269-5755). View New York from the crown or visit the museum in the base, which features the history and development of the famous statue. Note: The statue itself is currently closed; only the grounds are open for visiting.

The Studio Art Museum in Harlem 5+
144 West 125th Street between Lenox and Seventh Avenues, 864-4500, www.studiomuseum.org
This museum showcases African American artists. Special exhibits feature a diversity of work produced by new and established talent. Classes, workshops, concerts and various programs are conducted on a regular and special-events basis.

Temple Emanu-El 8+
One East 65th Street at Fifth Avenue, 744-1400, www.emanuelnyc.org
Mingling Moorish and Romanesque architectural styles and completed in the late 1920s, this synagogue is home to the largest Reform congregation in the world. The Herbert and Eileen Bernard Museum houses an extraordinary collection of Judaica.

Theodore Roosevelt Birthplace, National Historic Site 8+
28 East 20th Street off Broadway, 260-1616, www.nps.gov/thrb
The boyhood home of Theodore Roosevelt features artifacts from Roosevelt's life and presidency.

Trinity Church Museum 10+
74 Trinity Place—Trinity Church at Broadway and Wall Street, 602-0872, www.trinitywallstreet.org
Exhibits highlight the church's history and the history of the city and nation throughout the Dutch, British and American eras.

The Ukrainian Museum 5+
203 Second Avenue between 12th and 13th Streets, 228-0110, www.ukrainian.org
Family workshops are typically conducted around major holidays such as Christmas and Easter.

Wave Hill 3+
675 West 252nd Street and Independence Avenue, Riverdale, Bronx, 718 549-3200, www.wavehill.org
Twenty-eight acres of public gardens feature an incredible number of plants from around the world. The Kerlin Learning Center offers workshops for visitors to gain a better understanding of the natural history of Wave Hill, the Bronx and the world we live in. Family art projects are offered on the weekends.

Whitney Museum of American Art 4+
945 Madison Avenue at 75th Street, 570-3676, www.whitney.org
Founded by Gertrude Vanderbilt Whitney, a sculptor herself, the Whitney is devoted to 20th-century art featured in permanent and changing exhibitions. The museum offers a Saturday gallery tour and conducts a Family Fun program once a month.

Yeshiva University Museum Depends upon exhibit
15 West 16th Street between Fifth and Sixth Avenues, 2294-8330, www.yu.edu/museum
Changing exhibitions highlight Jewish life, history and culture. Throughout the year, the museum offers special family workshops relating to Jewish holidays.

RESOURCES

www.centralpark.org
www.citysearch.com
www.culturefinder.com
www.digitalcity.com
www.dityguideny.com
www.museumstuff.com
www.newyorkled.com
www.nyc.com
www.nyc-arts.org
www.nycparks.org
www.nycvisit.com
www.nymuseums.com

Summer Camp

American Camping Association
www.acacamps.org

Association of Independent Camps
www.independentcamps.com

Camp Channel
www.campchannel.com

Camp Page
www.camppage.com

Camp Resource
www.campresource.com

KidsCamps.com
www.kidscamps.com

National Camp Association
www.summercamp.org

SummerCamps.com
www.summercamps.com

Thomson Peterson's
www.petersons.com

Chapter 11

The Ultimate Shopping Guide

Manhattan is a magnet for shoppers. From bargain to bespoke, you can find it, have it made or order it from here. Depending on whether you are a born consumer or hate to shop, the scope and variety of merchandise available in New York City is either a blessing or a curse. Wherever you fall on the buying spectrum, there is no question that if you want it, in all likelihood you can have it without ever leaving the borough.

Shopping for children in Manhattan is a unique experience. The vast selection of clothing, shoes, toys and other children's products and services can unnerve even the hardiest of shoppers. Our goal is to help you find your way to the products you want, both in terms of price and location of the shops convenient to you. In this book, you will find a list of stores specializing in children's clothing, shoes, books, toys and supplies as well as clothing and accessories for teens, tweens and expectant mothers.

Please note that we do not attempt to chronicle every shop that sells something for or related to children. In a city with an ever-changing landscape of hundreds of thousands of square feet of retail space, to do so would be virtually impossible. Therefore, we have not included every neighborhood candy store, pharmacy or stationery store that carries some children's items; adult clothing or gift stores that carry a few items of children's clothing, accessories or baby paraphernalia; bookstores that carry a small selection of children's books; furniture stores that carry a few pieces either designed or suitable for children's rooms; or sporting-goods stores that carry a few items for kids. Rather, we have focused on those businesses that are devoted primarily to children's goods or carry a significant or particularly unique inventory of products for children.

Each entry contains information about what is carried in the store, the general price range of merchandise and where exactly the store is located. At the end of the chapter, you will find the stores indexed by the type of goods sold and a neighborhood locator. Happy shopping!

The Shopping Landscape

There are basically three categories of stores in Manhattan: department stores, multi-unit stores and boutique/specialty stores. Department stores are large institutions that carry many types of goods for men, women, children and the home. Multi-unit stores are those that are individual locations of larger businesses, whether regional, national or even international in scope. Boutique or specialty stores are usually single-location businesses, although occasionally there may be an additional location in the city or in the tri-state area. Boutique and specialty stores, big or small, carry unique merchandise individually selected by the store's management.

▶ **Department Stores.** Several department stores in Manhattan carry children's merchandise. Department stores at the highest end of the spectrum, such as Bergdorf Goodman and Barney's, tend to carry exclusive, imported and expensive items for infants and young children as well as luxury accessories for the layette and nursery. Stores such as Bloomingdales, Saks Fifth Avenue, Macy's and Lord & Taylor have much more extensive children's departments, typically going up to pre-teen or teen sizes, stocking both premium or designer (i.e., more expensive) labels as well as more moderately priced labels and a respectable selection of accessories, stuffed animals and perhaps dolls. The discount department stores such as Kmart carry nationally known clothing labels as well as toys and baby supplies.

▶ **Multi-unit Stores.** Multi-unit stores range from the discount to luxury categories. Included within this group would be moderately priced stores you are likely to find in shopping malls, such as the Gap, Talbots Kids or Gymboree or national chains such as Toys R Us, as well as stores (in either the moderate or expensive price ranges) that have boutiques in various other cities in the U.S. or even around the world. For example, Manhattan is home to a number of higher-end European chains such as Jacadi, Catimini and Oilily. For us, these stores feel more like the boutique or specialty category by virtue of the unique merchandise they carry, but in fact they are not stand-alone stores. Also in this group are discount stores such as Daffy's.

▶ **Boutiques and Specialty Stores.** The plethora and variety of boutique and specialty shops are, to many, what New York shopping is all about. It is in these individually owned and operated stores that one can often find amazing merchandise. Some are big and well known while others are tiny retail spaces crammed full of goodies and good ideas. These stores can carry anything from antique toys to environmentally correct products and everything you could possibly need for your new baby or older child, from luxury layette to funky downtown clothes, from handmade playthings to science-fiction toys. Prices range from bargain to the stratosphere, depending on the nature of the merchandise carried. Some boutiques are known only to neighborhood cognoscenti while others are magnets for shoppers from all over. The boutiques and specialty stores of Manhattan truly offer something for everyone.

▶ **Malls.** New York is not really a mall town. However, there are a few containing stuff for kids and teens, for those who prefer a concentrated dose of shopping. The South Street Seaport Marketplace (732-7678), located in lower Manhattan, is an outdoor mall with a nautical theme. It includes a pedestrian mall at Fulton Street, the Fulton Market Building (the site of the original Fulton Fish Market) and the shops at Pier 17. Expect to find mall regulars such as the Gap, Ann Taylor, J. Crew, Victoria's Secret as well as a host of small and specialty stores and a food court. The Seaport tends to attract many tourists, especially on beautiful weekend afternoons.

The Manhattan Mall (465-0500), located in the garment district on Sixth Avenue and 33rd Street, is a glass-encased vertical mall featuring an atrium and food court and 55 stores, mostly in the moderately priced category. The Herald Center (634-3883), located at 1 Herald Square, just across from Macy's, also features lower-priced merchandise. Rockefeller Center, bordered by Fifth and Sixth Avenues and 48th and 51st Streets has a shopping plaza just off Fifth Avenue worthy of visiting as you stroll down Fifth Avenue and take in the sights of Rockefeller Center—Art Deco buildings, the skating rink and Radio City. Shops your older kids and teens may want to visit include Kenneth Cole, J. Crew, Banana Republic, Brookstone and the Sharper Image.

▶ **What you will find in this chapter.** We confess that putting together this listing of stores was not an entirely scientific process. Our list was culled from advertising sources, word of mouth and pounding the pavement. We have endeavored to be as current as possible, keeping in mind that small businesses tend not to advertise and do tend to open and close without much fanfare, all of which makes it difficult to be totally comprehensive.

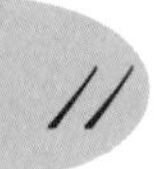

The goal is to provide you with a broad range of shopping options, both in terms of price, location and type of merchandise, to assist you in finding what you need when and where you need it. To be sure, there will be stores that we may have missed or that you think should have been included, but we think you will agree that this list, containing over 400 establishments, is by far the most comprehensive list of its type to date.

Please remember that we do not list every store that carries some children's items. We have focused on those businesses that either cater entirely to the younger set, carry a meaningful selection (in our subjective opinion!) of children's merchandise or offer merchandise so unique or special (even if only in a limited quantity) that we thought you would want to be aware of them. For teens, we have focused on stores that carry adult-sized clothing but whose merchandise is cool, trendy and youthful for maximum appeal to this savvy clientele.

▶ **How to use this directory.** All entries are listed in alphabetical order together with their addresses and cross streets and a brief description of what is carried in the store. The intention is to give you an objective listing of the merchandise carried and a general indication of the price point at which the majority of the goods in the store are sold. In compiling this information we developed a list of categories of children's merchandise, which we share with you.

Please note that these are the broadest descriptions of each category and not every store listed as carrying a certain type of merchandise will have each item we included in our definition. Additionally, even if a store does carry most of the items on our list for a particular category, quantities of particular items will vary among stores. The definitions are here mainly to serve as a very general guideline as to what you can expect, not an inventory of each individual store. Therefore, if you are shopping for a very specific item in a certain category, we urge you to call first and make sure that the store carries it.

- ACCESSORIES AND NOVELTIES—all types of trendy, popular, fun, cool, generally inexpensive personal accessories, small room accessories and little toys such as costume jewelry, mirrors, picture frames, inflatable and bean-bag pillows and furniture, lava lamps, charms, key chains, travel accessories, "bunk junk" for summer camp, purses, beads, pens, little desk toys and other items kids covet.
- ACTIVEWEAR—clothes and accessories for sports and dance, leotards, bathing suits, sports shorts, warm-ups and sweats.
- BABY GIFTS—special, usually expensive, gifts for new babies, including fine china and silver items such as frames, rattles, porringers, spoons, comb and brush sets, boxes and other engraved items.

- **BOOKS**—all types of books for children, hard and soft cover, board and/or fabric books for infants. Larger bookstores will also carry books for young readers (chapter books, series, classics, etc.).
- **CLOTHING AND ACCESSORIES**—all types of children's clothing, which generally also includes undergarments, pajamas, seasonal clothing (e.g., snowsuits and bathing suits) and outerwear. Stores that carry clothing also typically carry a variety of accessories such as hats, gloves, scarves, socks and tights, slippers, hair ornaments (bows, headbands), belts, ties, suspenders, bags (backpacks, children's purses) and sometimes water shoes (jellies, flip-flops). Stores that carry baby clothes often carry some stuffed animals and crib toys (and sometimes even a few baby books) to package with baby gifts. Most clothing stores carry clothing up to sizes 12–16 children's (fitting children between the ages of 10 and 12). Most stores organize merchandise by numerical sizes, while others categorize their merchandise by the age of the child it is meant to fit. For our purposes, if an entry does not contain a size or an age range, you can assume that the store carries items for infants up to 10- or 12-year-olds. When a particular store carries a more limited range of sizes (or only fits up to a certain age range), that information is specifically indicated.
- **COMICS/TRADING CARDS**—current, vintage and collectible comic books, sports cards and other types of trading cards and related merchandise, which usually consists of action figures, T-shirts and other collectible character representations and toys.

- **COSMETICS/BATH ACCESSORIES**—products for the bath including soaps, shampoos, bubble bath and bath oils, lotions; hair products; aromatherapy products; candles and potpourri and accessories such as sponges, washcloths, loofahs and bath toys. Cosmetics refer to products appropriate for teens or tweens such as lip gloss, glitter gel, cologne and accessories such as mirrors, cosmetic bags, hair brushes and so forth. Note that stores referenced may also carry full lines of adult makeup and products that may not be appropriate for young girls.
- **DECORATIVE ACCESSORIES**—accessories for the nursery or older child's room, such as toy boxes, grow sticks, hat/coat racks, easels, child-sized furniture (tables, chairs, miniature sofas), rocking toys, bulletin boards, decorative storage boxes and units, baskets, step stools, stor-

age cabinets, hampers, decorative pillows, picture frames, wall hangings and throws. Many of these items are hand wrought, hand-painted/decorated or personalized. Some stores will have a modest selection of lamps and perhaps even small area rugs. Decorative accessories for tweens and teens might include such things as inflatable furniture, kitschy lamps or desk accessories and storage units (CD holders, storage boxes, etc.).

- EQUIPMENT—merchandise for infants and toddlers (typically up to preschoolers) such as strollers, baby carriers, prams, car seats, playpens and portable cribs, swings, cloth diapers and burp cloths, crib sheets and accessories, toddler bedding, crib toys and mobiles, baby bathtubs, diaper bags, nursery monitors, gadgets, child-proofing and child-safety items, bottles, first cups, cutlery and dishes.
- FURNITURE—cribs, rockers, kid-sized tables and chairs, beds, changing tables, bureaus, armoires and upholstered furniture. Some stores carrying furniture may also include lamps and decorative accessories, window treatments and floor coverings (area rugs) for the nursery or child's room. Some stores may offer design services and customized furniture.
- GADGETS AND ELECTRONICS—CD players, boomboxes, video games (hardware and/or software), computers, computer software and accessories and all sorts of other cool (and, your children will insist, much needed) gadgets designed to make life easier (or more complicated, depending on your point of view) and more interesting.
- GAMES AND HOBBIES—model kits, merchandise specific to particular games such as chess or relating to collectibles or hobbies such as electric trains.

- LAYETTE—bedding for cribs, cradles and bassinettes, newborn clothing, hats, booties, receiving blankets, bibs, crib toys and stuffed animals, decorative pillows, quilts and blankets and accessories for the newborn. Bedding can consist of basic sheets and blankets or can include bumpers, bed skirts, wall hangings and coordinating window treatments.
- LINENS—a number of higher-end imported fine linen stores carry some bedding and bath accessories (towels, robes) for children.

- **MAGIC**—merchandise for the budding magician including tricks, gags and props. Magic stores often have personnel on-site to demonstrate tricks.
- **MATERNITY**—everything for the mother-to-be including clothing, undergarments, sleepwear, pantyhose, nursing paraphernalia and accessories. Many maternity shops also stock some items for the newborn and usually offer pregnancy and new baby books.
- **MUSEUM STORES**—stores operated by museums. These stores typically carry not only merchandise related to particular exhibits but items—toys, games, stuffed animals, souvenirs, books, videos, T-shirts, novelties—more generally related to the subject of the museum (art, history, animals, science, etc.) Museum gift shops range from modest little stores to full-blown emporia with extensive inventory, handcrafted items, furniture and decorative accessories and a wide range of unique merchandise.
- **OUTERWEAR**—coats, jackets and foul-weather gear. Some stores carry gear for particular activities such as skiing or camping.
- **SHOES**—casual shoes, dress shoes, sandals, sneakers and athletic shoes and water shoes.
- **SPORTING GOODS**—sports equipment, rackets, balls, skates, rollerblades, helmets, bats, gloves and gear for water sports. Sporting goods stores usually also carry athletic shoes and activewear.
- **STATIONERY**—writing papers and supplies, notebooks, desk accessories, photo albums, journals, gift wrapping supplies, writing implements and art supplies.

- **TEENS**—clothing and accessories for teens and, if you dare, tweens. The stores referenced in this category are not necessarily "teen" stores per se, but rather adult stores that because of their cool merchandise, trendy style, petite sizes and high concept presentation have become destinations for teens and teen wannabes. Clothing in the teen category is sized in adult sizes although some stores may have some junior sizes. Be aware that the stores that cater to teens are likely to have very adult prices!
- **THEME STORES**—stores with merchandise relating to particular brands or themes such as Disney, as well as stores devoted to particular sports or teams.

- TOYS—anything kids play with, including games, puzzles, dolls, stuffed animals, educational toys, building toys, arts and crafts supplies, models, cars and trucks, ride-on toys (which may include bicycles and tricycles), project kits, puppets, action figures, character figures (for example, Sesame Street, Pooh), classic toys, handmade toys, some sports toys, dress-up, crib and baby toys, etc. Some toy stores carry computer software, electronic toys, audio and/or video tapes and a few books.

▶ **Consumer information.** It is useful to be aware of your rights under local consumer law. You have the right: to know the price of any item, which must be clearly marked either on the item or on a display sign; to know the store's refund policy before you make your purchase (if there is no posted policy, you have the right to a full refund if you return the goods within 20 days of purchase); to obtain a receipt for all purchases over $20, which includes the price, description, tax, date, and name and address of the store; to know what you are purchasing (if the product is used or reconditioned, it must say so).

NYC Consumer Affairs urges consumers to beware of these practices at electronics stores: bait and switch—you are lured in with an advertisement for a low-priced item but told it is sold out when you arrive and you are offered something higher priced or of lower quality; Manufacturer's Suggested Retail Price—by law, the store must tell you this price; tourist traps—be wary of salespeople who ask you where you are from and how long you are staying as they may be setting you up for a scam on the theory that you will not be here long enough to complain or return the item. Be wary of buying expensive items from street vendors; note that their products are usually knock-offs (imitations) rather than the real thing.

If you have a consumer problem, call Consumer Affairs at 487-4444 or 718 286-2994 Monday through Friday from 9:30 a.m. to 4:30 p.m. or file a complaint on-line at www.nygov.com/consumers.

▶ **Sales tax.** There is a sales tax of 8.625% (4.25% for New York State, .25% for the Metropolitan Commuter Transportation District and 4.125% for New York City) on all purchases of clothing and shoes. If you ship your purchases out of state, meaning that you do not take possession of them in the store, you will have to pay shipping charges, but no New York sales tax will be charged on the items. You will, however, be charged the sales tax, if any, levied by the jurisdiction to which the item is being shipped.

▶ **A word about price.** Indicating the price range of merchandise carried in a store is extremely complicated. While it is easy to identify stores in the discount and luxury categories, the vast majority of stores sell somewhere in the middle or sell merchandise at multiple price points. To attempt to quantify price points specifically is an exercise in futility. As a result, we came up with a not-quite-perfect three-point system for looking at prices: $ for discount or value-priced goods, $$ for moderately priced goods and $$$ for expensive or luxury goods. It is best to think of these valuations as relative rather than as absolute—a way of distinguishing among choices when you are faced with a shopping expedition. For example, you may want to seek stores in the $ or $$ category for playclothes and the $$$ category for party clothes and baby gifts.

In addition, it is our experience that many of the stores in the $$ category stock inventory at the top and bottom of the range, or even into the next range. It is, for example, quite common to find a clothing store that carries great value leggings and T-shirts next to $200 hand-knit sweaters and $95 imported jeans. In such cases, we have indicated the store's price range as $$ to $$$. Also, even stores at the top of the $$$ category may have incredible blow-out sales for which you should be on the lookout.

Stores that sell items other than clothing, shoes or items for the home (decorative accessories and furniture) are extremely difficult, if not impossible, to differentiate in terms of price. For example, most toy stores carry an assortment of toys, small to large, inexpensive to expensive. Bookstores, too, may carry an array of inexpensive paperback books as well as full-price hardbound books. Stores that sell games, hobbies, comics, sports cards, and cosmetics/bath accessories will also have a range of merchandise at different price points. For that reason, in general we have noted price ranges only for stores purveying clothing, accessories, shoes and items for the home and not for stores selling toys, books, games/hobbies or theme stores unless the store is clearly in a particular price category.

In order to help you figure out where in the spectrum stores fall when no price range is indicated, here are some general rules.

- Boutique toy stores carrying unique, specialty, educational, imported and handmade toys will generally have a selection of merchandise more expensive than those carrying more commercial brands (such as Fisher Price) or national chains such as Toys R Us or Kmart.
- Books at the smaller specialty bookstores or neighborhood stores will likely not be discounted as they may be in the chain superstores.
- Stores carrying unique, exclusive lines of cosmetics, bath products, electronics, furniture or decorative accessories will be higher priced than chain stores or stores carrying widely available national brands.
- Wherever possible, we indicate in the store description the general nature of the merchandise, from which you can deduce whether it is of the pricier more exclusive variety or of a more commercial and mass merchandise nature.

Remember, prices are relative and identifying the prices of goods is a highly subjective process. A bargain to one family can be a luxury to another, while for other families price is not the top priority in making a purchase. The system we have used is neither foolproof nor perfect, but we hope it will help you identify, at least generally, the stores you want to start with when you need or want to shop.

Let's Go Shopping

ABC Carpet and Home **$$ to $$$**
888 Broadway at 19th Street, 473-3000, www.abchome.com
A huge, full-service home furnishings, carpet, fabric, furniture and decorative accessories emporium that carries beautiful linens and specialty and gift items (such as cashmere baby blankets). Design services available. Definitely worth a visit downtown.

Abercrombie & Fitch **$$ to $$$**
199 Water Street at Fulton Street, South Street Seaport, 809-9000
www.abercrombie.com
This popular brand delivers trendy casual clothes and accessories for kids ages 7 to 16 and adults. It is very popular among teens and tweens.

Abracadabra
19 West 21st Street between Fifth and Sixth Avenues, 627-5194
www.abracadabra-superstore.com
This magic superstore, complete with a stage and a café, also stocks costumes and novelties, theatrical makeup and props.

Adidas Originals **$$**
136 Wooster Street between Prince and Houston Streets, 777-2001
www.adidas.com
Sporty teens and tweens will love the Adidas footwear, clothing and accessories in this store that seeks to create a "fusion of sport authenticity and global street style."

Albee's **$$**
715 Amsterdam Avenue between 94th and 95th Streets, 662-8902/5740
www.albeebaby.com
This Upper West Side institution carries everything you need for the new baby and young child, including equipment, layette, furniture, toys, books and some clothing (basics only for ages 0–12 months).

Alex's MVP Cards
256 East 89th Street between Second and Third Avenues, 831-2273
This shop has a very good selection of vintage and new comics, sports cards and some non-sports toys.

Alphabets
47 Greenwich Avenue between Perry and Charles Streets, 229-2966
115 Avenue A between 7th and 8th Streets, 475-7250
2284 Broadway between 82nd and 83rd Streets, 579-5702
www.alphabetsnyc.com
Your kids will enjoy browsing among the unique retro toys, novelties, cards and reproductions of goodies from yesteryear.

Alphaville
226 West Houston Street between Sixth Avenue and Varick Street, 675-6850, www.alphaville.com
This store/gallery specializes in vintage toys, games and collectibles (think wind-up toys and ray guns) with an emphasis on toys made from the 1940s through 1960s, including a large collection of 3D toys and flickers (plastic images which change as you move them). Prices start at 95 cents. Alphaville also carries a small line of "retro contemporary" new toys inspired by their vintage predecessors.

Alskling **$$**
228 Columbus Avenue between 70th and 71st Streets, 787-7066
"Alskling," which means sweetheart in Swedish, carries a unique selection of Swedish designs for women and handknitted infant cardigans, dresses for girls 0–3 and some casual playclothes.

American Craft Museum Shop
40 West 53rd Street between Fifth and Sixth Avenues, 956-3535
www.americancraftmuseum.org
This well-stocked museum gift shop carries a large assortment of creative kits, small toys and some children's books.

American Museum of Natural History Store
Central Park West between 77th and 81st Streets, 769-5100
www.amnh.org
This 8,500-square-foot shop is a treasure trove of educational toys and books, many relating to current exhibits in the museum and planetarium, as well as souvenirs, stuffed animals and T-shirts.

America's Hobby Center
146 West 22nd Street between Sixth and Seventh Avenues, 675-8922
www.ahc1931.com
This is the place for "vehicular hobbies": model cars, trains, planes, boats and radio-controlled vehicles. For children ages 8+.

April Cornell **$$ to $$$**
487 Columbus Avenue between 83rd and 84th Streets, 799-4342
www.aprilcornell.com
This shop offers a large selection of quality classic clothing for girls ages 1–12 and women, including mother–daughter outfits.

Art & Tapisserie **$$ to $$$**
1242 Madison Avenue between 89th and 90th Streets, 722-3222
www.artandtapisserie.com
This neighborhood boutique stocks a unique selection of decorative accessories and some furniture (much of which can be personalized), toys and books.

Astor Place Hair Designers
2 Astor Place at Broadway, 475-9854
Downtown's own trendy, but basic, barbershop. Cash only.

Au Chat Botte **$$$**
1192 Madison Avenue between 87th and 88th Streets, 722-6474
This French shop is a great source for classic and elegant European layette, equipment, furniture and clothing for girls and boys up to size 2.

Avon Salon & Spa
725 Fifth Avenue at 57th Street, Trump Tower, 755-2866
This spa and salon featuring Avon products offers a full line of products (shampoo, soap and other items) for babies and children.

A/X Armani Exchange **$$ to $$$**
568 Broadway at Prince Street, 431-6000
645 Fifth Avenue at 51st Street, 980-3037
www.armaniexchange.com
Come here for Italian designer Giorgio Armani's less expensive casual clothes for men and women. Many of the items, often bearing the company logo, will appeal to your teens.

Baby Depot at Burlington Coat Factory **$**
707 Sixth Avenue at 23rd Street, 229-1300/2247
www.burlingtoncoatfactory.com
Discount department store for the whole family. The children's department carries clothing, equipment, layette and furniture for the nursery.

Ballantyne Cashmere **$$$**
965 Madison Avenue between 75th and 76th Streets, 988-5252
If you can get past the stacks of cashmere sweaters for men and women, you will find luxurious cashmere sweaters for infants 6 to 18 months and cashmere baby blankets.

The Balloon Man
209 West 80th Street between Broadway and Amsterdam Avenue, 874-4464, www.tshirtexpress.com, www.selectagram.com
On the West Side for 25 years, this shop creates party and event decorations, including helium balloons, and will customize T-shirts and hats for your special occasion or to commemorate your visit.

Bambini **$$$**
1367 Third Avenue at 78th Street, 717-6742, www.bambininyc.com
This lovely boutique has a unique selection of classic imported, mostly Italian, clothes (up to size 8–10 for girls and boys), layette and a good selection of unique imported shoes.

Bambi's Baby Center **$**
2150 Third Avenue at 117th Street, 828-8878
This is upper Manhattan's source for everything you need for the new baby and young child, including equipment, layette, furniture, toys, books and some clothing (basics only for ages 0–12 months).

Banana Republic **$$**
205 Bleecker Street at Sixth Avenue, 473-9570
528 Broadway at Spring Street, 334-3034

550 Broadway between Prince and Spring Streets, 925-0308
111 Eighth Avenue between 15th and 16th Streets, 645-1032
89 Fifth Avenue between 16th and 17th Streets, 366-4630
114 Fifth Avenue at 17th Street, 366-4691
107 East 42nd Street at Vanderbilt Avenue, Grand Central Terminal, 490-3127
130 Lexington Avenue at 59th Street, 751-5570
1110 Third Avenue at 65th Street, 288-4279
17 West 34th Street between Fifth and Sixth Avenues, 244-3060
626 Fifth Avenue at 50th Street, Rockefeller Center, 974-2350
1136 Madison Avenue between 84th and 85th Streets, 570-2465
1529 Third Avenue at 86th Street, 360-1296
215 Columbus Avenue at 70th Street, 873-9048
2360 Broadway at 86th Street, 787-2064
888 BRSTYLE (277-8953) for automated listing of stores
www.bananarepublic.com
This national chain, offering stylish, modern, basic clothing, accessories and shoes for men and women at reasonable prices, has a large selection appropriate for your teen.

Bank Street Bookstore
610 West 112th Street at Broadway, 678-1654, 877 676-7830
www.bankstreetbooks.com (links to Barnes & Noble College Bookstore)
The knowledgeable, helpful staff will guide you through this bookshop's extensive selection of children's books, educational toys, games and books on education, learning and parenting.

Barnes & Noble Superstores
4 Astor Place at Broadway, 420-1322
396 Sixth Avenue at 8th Street, 674-8780
33 East 17th Street at Union Square North, 253-0810
105 Fifth Avenue at 18th Street, 807-0099
675 Sixth Avenue at 22nd Street, 727-1227
385 Fifth Avenue at 36th Street, 779-7677
750 Third Avenue at 47th Street, 697-2251
160 East 54th Street at Third Avenue, Citicorp Building, 750-8033
600 Fifth Avenue at 48th Street, 765-0590
240 East 86th Street between Second and Third Avenues, 794-1962
1280 Lexington Avenue between 86th and 87th Streets, 423-9900
1972 Broadway at 66th Street, 595-6859
2289 Broadway between 82nd and 83rd Streets, 362-8835
www.bn.com
Books for all ages, many discounted. Some stores have specific B & N Jr. departments, music departments and cafés.

Barney's New York **$$$**
660 Madison Avenue between 60th and 61st Streets, 826-8900
236 West 18th Street between Seventh and Eighth Avenues, 593-7800 (Co-op)

116 Wooster Street between Prince and Spring Streets, 965-9964 (Co-op)
www.barneys.com
This high-end department store carries trendy maternity fashions as well as unique, stylish, mostly imported children's clothing (up to size 6), decorative accessories and some nursery furniture and linens. Barney's Co-op (within the main store and two downtown locations) has a great selection of trendy clothing and accessories for teens at less than stratospheric prices.

Bath & Bodyworks **$ to $$**
Pier 17, South Street Seaport, 349-1561
693 Broadway at West 4th Street, 979-2526
141 Fifth Avenue between 20th and 21st Streets, 387-9123
304 Park Avenue South at 23rd Street, 674-7385
441 Lexington Avenue at 44th Street, 687-1231
7 West 34th Street between Fifth and Sixth Avenues (in the Express Store), 629-6912
1240 Third Avenue at 72nd Street, 772-2589
www.intimatebrands.com
The Bath & Bodyworks chain carries a full line of moderately priced bath, body, hair- and skin-care products and accessories. Young girls will enjoy the line created especially for them, including body and hair glitter, lip gloss, fragrances and bath products (which make great inexpensive party favors or gifts).

Bath Island **$$**
469 Amsterdam Avenue between 82nd and 83rd Streets, 787-9415, 877 234-3657, www.bathisland.com
This fragrant oasis on the Upper West Side offers natural and biodegradable bath and aromatherapy products and accessories. Parents and kids will love their all-natural Bath Island Baby products.

A Bear's Place Inc. **$$ to $$$**
789 Lexington Avenue between 61st and 62nd Streets, 826-6465
This stocked-to-the-rafters boutique carries a varied selection of unique toys as well as decorative accessories and some children's furniture.

Bebe **$$**
100 Fifth Avenue at 15th Street, 675-2323
805 Third Avenue at 50th Street, 588-9060
1127 East 66th Street at Third Avenue, 935-2444
www.bebe.com
Very trendy high-fashion clothes and accessories for your teen. Although some of the clothing tends towards the skimpy (think bare midriffs, tight fitting and low cut) and is for a more mature clientele, the pants, suits and dresses are quite popular among the (ladies) size 0–4 set.

Bebe Thompson **$$ to $$$**
1216 Lexington Avenue between 82nd and 83rd Streets, 249-4740
This boutique carries a unique selection of clothing, contemporary to classic, much of it imported (European), accessories, layette, some toys and handmade items.

Bed Bath & Beyond **$ to $$**
620 Sixth Avenue between 18th and 19th Streets, 255-3550
410 East 61st Street between York and First Avenues, 215-4702
www.bedbathandbeyond
Discount department store for all things for the bed, bath and kitchen. For children, look for bedding, bath accessories (towels, robes, accessories for the sink and tub), toys, some books, dishes, storage units and closet organizers, decorative accessories and gadgets galore.

Bellini Juvenile Designer Furniture **$$ to $$$**
1305 Second Avenue between 68th and 69th Streets, 517-9233
www.bellini.com
A good selection of higher-end furniture, decorative accessories and bedding for the nursery and older children.

Benetton (United Colors of Benetton) **$$**
10 Fulton Street, South Street Seaport, 509-3999
749 Broadway at 8th Street, 533-0230
597 Fifth Avenue between 48th and 49th Streets, 593-0290
188 East 78th Street at Third Avenue, 327-1039
555 Broadway between Prince and Spring Streets, 941-8010
666 Third Avenue at 42nd Street, 818-0449
120 Seventh Avenue between 17th and 18th Streets, 646 638-1086
www.benetton.com
Contemporary, well-priced sportswear and casual clothing with the Italian Benetton label for teens, tweens and adults.

Bergdorf Goodman **$$$**
754 Fifth Avenue at 57th Street, 753-7300
This high-end department store now has an in-store Best & Co. department offering classic imported layette, furniture for the nursery, linens and clothing and accessories for children up to size 8.

Berkley Girl **$$$**
410 Columbus Avenue between 79th and 80th Streets, 877-470
This boutique for tween girls specializes in up-to-date, stylish clothing and accessories for girls sizes 7–16 as well as a good selection of special-occasion dresses (including Nicole Miller), separates and suits.

Betsey Johnson **$$**
138 Wooster Street at Houston and Prince Streets, 995-5048
1060 Madison Avenue between 80th and 81st Streets, 734-1257

248 Columbus Avenue between 71st and 72nd Streets, 362-3364
251 East 60th Street between Second and Third Avenues, 319-7699
www.betseyjohnson.com
Avant-garde designer Betsey Johnson, known for her "exuberant, embellished and over the top" fashion, offers very trendy and funky clothes for your teen (and you, if you dare!).

Betwixt **$$ to $$$**
245 West 10th Street between Hudson and Bleecker Streets, 243-8590
Especially for tween girls, this boutique features cool, stylish casual clothes (for example, Monkey Wear, Roxy, Juicy) for girls sizes 7–16 and junior sizes 0–13. They have a good selection of accessories as well as special-occasion dresses, sportswear for kids and juniors, party/dressy outfits, school clothes and accessories (bags, jewelry).

Big City Kite Company
1210 Lexington Avenue at 82nd Street, 472-2623, 888 476-5483
www.bigcitykites.com
This tiny store specializes in all types of kites and other airborne toys.

Big Fun Toys
636 Hudson Street at Horatio Street, 414-4138, www.bigfuntoys.com
This toy emporium, where you are urged to "shop yourself silly," is full of cool stuff for kids of all ages.

Blades Board & Skate **$$**
659 Broadway between 3rd and Bleecker Streets, 477-7350
Roller Rink at Chelsea Piers, at 23rd Street and the Hudson River, Pier 62, 336-6299
Sky Rink at Chelsea Piers, at 23rd Street and the Hudson River, Pier 61, 336-6199
160 East 86th Street between Lexington and Third Avenues, 996-1644

120 West 72nd Street between Columbus Avenue and Broadway, 787-3911
www.blades.com
These shops have the latest in ultra-cool skates (in-line, roller and ice), skateboards, snowboards and gear.

Bloomers **$$**
1042 Lexington Avenue between 74th and 75th Streets, 570-9529
This local shop, which has a great selection of women's nightgowns, pajamas and robes, also carries cute playwear for boys and girls up to size 6x and girls sleepwear up to size 14.

Bloomingdales **$$ to $$$**
1000 Third Avenue at 59th Street, 705-2000, www.bloomingdales.com
This full-service department store boasts a large (two floors) children's department that carries clothes, layette and trendy accessories, featuring

many popular brands and designer labels. Your teens and tweens will love the second floor, which is stocked with popular sportswear labels. Bloomies also features Belly Basics and Babystyle clothing for the fashionable expectant mom.

The Body Shop **$ to $$**
16 Fulton Street, South Street Seaport, 480-9876
747 Broadway at Astor Place, 979-2944
135 Fifth Avenue at 20th Street, 254-0145
479 Fifth Avenue between 40th and 41st Streets, 661-1992
509 Madison Avenue at 53rd Street, 829-8603
714 Lexington Avenue between 57th and 58th Streets, 755-7851
901 Sixth Avenue at 33rd Street, Manhattan Mall, 268-7424
1270 Sixth Avenue and 51st Street, Rockefeller Center, 397-3007
142 West 57th Street between Sixth and Seventh Avenues, 582-8494
2151 Broadway at 76th Street, 721-2947
1 East 125th Street at Fifth Avenue, 348-4900
1145 Madison Avenue between 85th and 86th Streets, 794-3046
www.thebodyshop.com
This international company with a conscience produces naturally inspired products from traditional recipes for the skin, hair and bath. The company creates "sustainable trade relationships with communities in need around the world," does not believe in animal testing and actively promotes protection of the environment and human rights internationally.

Bombalulu's **$$ to $$$**
101 West 10th Street at Sixth Avenue, 463-0897
244 West 72nd Street between Broadway and West End Avenue, 501-8248
www.bombalulus.com
This is a great shop to find unique contemporary clothing for girls and boys up to size 8, toys and wonderful handmade quilts.

Bonne Nuit **$$$**
30 Lincoln Plaza at 62nd Street and Broadway, 489-9730
Enjoy this charming boutique stocked with fine imported classic clothing for girls up to size 10 and boys up to size 6, as well as layette and some crib and baby toys.

Bonpoint **$$$**
811 Madison Avenue at 68th Street, 879-0900
1269 Madison Avenue at 91st Street, 722-7720
www.bonpoint.com
Your children will fit in on the Champs Élysées in the fine, elegant imported classic clothing, shoes and layette from this French company. The 68th Street store carries up to size 12 for girls, up to size 8 for boys. The 91st Street store carries up to size 16 for girls, up to size 12 for boys. It's just the place to splurge for that perfect party dress.

Bookberries
983 Lexington Avenue between 71st and 72nd Streets, 794-9400
Bookberries is a fine neighborhood bookstore with a good selection of children's books.

Books of Wonder
16 West 18th Street between Fifth and Sixth Avenues, 989-3270
www.booksofwonder.com
This downtown institution houses an extensive selection of children's books and related items, such as dolls and puzzles, and a knowledgeable staff.

Borders Books and Music
550 Second Avenue between 31st and 32nd Streets, 685-3938
461 Park Avenue at 57th Street, 980-6785
www.borders.com
Books and music for all ages, some of it discounted.

Brooklyn Museum of Art Shop
200 Eastern Parkway, Brooklyn Museum, Brooklyn, 718 638-5000
www.brooklynart.org
The Brooklyn Museum of Art carries a large selection of toys, art materials, activity kits, books and other cool stuff for kids.

Brooks Brothers **$$ to $$$**
346 Madison Avenue at 44th Street, 682-8800
666 Fifth Avenue at 53rd Street, 261-9440
LaGuardia Airport, US Air Terminal, 718 779-6300
www.brooksbrothers.com
This store, famous for its classic business attire and casual clothing for men (and classic fashions for women), also carries traditional clothing, including suits and formalwear, for boys sizes 6–20.

Brookstone **$$ to $$$**
16 West 50th Street at Rockefeller Center, 262-3237
20 West 57th Street between Fifth and Sixth Avenues, 245-1405
JFK Airport, domestic terminal, Concourse D, 718 553-6306
JFK Airport, international terminal, Concourse level, 718 244-0192
LaGuardia Airport, departure level, Concourse D, 718 505-2440
LaGuardia Airport, departure level, center section, 718 505-2415
www.brookstone.com
This national chain (found in many shopping malls) carries a variety of gadgets and electronics, many of which are intriguing to kids of all ages. Kids (and their weary parents!!!) are drawn like magnets to the massage chairs.

Bu and the Duck **$$ to $$$**
106 Franklin Street at Church Street, 431-9226, www.buandtheduck.com
Unique, funky, original casual clothing for infants and children up to age 8 and European shoes, including those made for the store in Italy, for children

up to age 6. This charming store also carries vintage furniture and decorative accessories and a selection of handmade Raggedy Ann/Andy dolls.

Bunnies Children's Department Store **$**
100 Delancey Street between Essex and Ludlow Streets, 529-7567
www.bunnies.com
Discount children's department store that carries clothing for girls up to size 14 and boys up to size 20, equipment, layette and furniture.

Burberry **$$$**
9 East 57th Street between Madison and Park Avenues, 371-5010
131 Spring Street between Wooster and Greene Streets, 925-9300
www.burberry.com
This venerable British label has transformed itself into a very hip shopping destination. For children, you can find outerwear and some clothing for ages 18 months to 7 years. The ubiquitous plaid scarves and accessories are popular among the prep-school set.

BuyBuy Baby **$**
270 Seventh Avenue between 25th and 26th Streets, 917 344-1555
www.buybuybaby.com
This discount store has everything for your baby including clothing up to size 4, equipment, furniture, layette, books and toys.

Cadeau **$$$**
254 Elizabeth Street between Prince and Houston Streets, 674-5747
www.cadeaumaternity.com
Created by two former Barney's executives, this new line of maternity wear is made in Italy and reflects the owners' philosophy that pregnant women need not sacrifice their style. The line includes both casual basics and dressy pieces in a range of stretch and luxury fabrics.

Calypso **$$$**
280 Mott Street at Houston Street, 965-0990
424 Broome Street at Lafayette Street, 274-0449
935 Madison Avenue at 74th Street, 535-4100
This unique store houses a collection of clothing that incredibly manages to blend French style with an island flair. Calypso is best known for its women's collection of brightly colored silk bustle skirts, sarongs, silk and cotton dresses, delicious sorbet-colored cashmeres and Navajo-inspired summer sandals. The Madison Avenue store carries miniature versions of its adult line for girls up to size 8 and Vilebrequin bathing suits and some other items for boys. Teens will love the selection at all stores but especially the Mott Street shop, which specializes in small sizes.

Calypso Enfants & Bébé **$$$**
426 Broome Street between Crosby and Lafayette Streets, 966-3234
This Calypso location is just for kids and carries clothes for girls and boys

up to size 10. You can find Calypso classics for kids (the tiny sarongs and bustle skirts are particularly adorable), imported clothing, layette and baby cashmere, handcrafted wooden toys, European toys and books and stuffed animals.

Canal Jean Co. **$**
504 Broadway between Spring and Broome Streets, 226-1130
www.canaljean.com
Dress the whole family from three levels of discount casual clothing (mostly Levis) for children and adults starting at size four months. The upper levels carry popular designer labels for your teen.

Capezio **$$**
1650 Broadway at 51st Street, 2nd floor, 245-2130
1776 Broadway at 57th Street, 586-5140
136 East 61st Street between Lexington and Park Avenues, 758-8833
1651 Third Avenue between 92nd and 93rd Streets, 3rd floor, 348-7210
www.capeziodance.com
Not just for ballerinas, Capezio is a great source for dance and activewear for dancers of all ages.

Cartier **$$$**
653 Fifth Avenue at 52nd Street, 753-0111, www.cartier.com
This renowned jeweler is the perfect gift source for luxurious traditional silver baby gifts such as rattles, combs, brushes, porringers, cutlery and picture frames.

Catimini **$$$**
1284 Madison Avenue between 91st and 92nd Streets, 987-0688
www.catimini.com
This charming boutique has a great selection of adorable and distinctive European (mostly casual) clothing and layette with the Catimini label, many items featuring characters and animals from French children's stories.

CBS Store
1697 Broadway at 53rd Street, 975-8600, www.cbs.com
Visit this store for memorabilia, novelties, collectibles and T-shirts relating to your favorite CBS shows and personalities.

Century 21 **$**
22 Cortlandt Street between Broadway and Church Streets, 227-9092
472 86th Street between Fourth and Fifth Avenues, Bay Ridge, Brooklyn, 718 748-3266
www.c21stores.com
Many seasoned shoppers consider this discount department store to be "New York's best kept secret." The children's department carries discounted major brands and designer-label clothing for kids up to 8 years old, shoes

and layette. There is also plenty for your tweens and teens. You need a bit of patience to work through the merchandise, and the inventory can be hit or miss, but you can luck out with incredible designer bargains.

Chameleon Comics
3 Maiden Lane between Nassau Street and Broadway, 587-3411
A great source for new comics, sports cards and all kinds of trading cards, sports memorabilia, T-shirts, model kits, figures and related toys.

Chelsea Kids Quarters **$$**
33 West 17th Street between Fifth and Sixth Avenues, 627-5524
www.chelseakidsquarters.com
If you are furnishing a child's room, you will appreciate the large selection of solid wood furniture, decorative accessories and some linens (no crib sizes) for older children's rooms. Some custom furniture and design services available.

Chess Forum
219 Thompson Street between 3rd and Bleecker Streets, 475-2369
www.chessforum.com
For the chess lover, this chess club, store and café provides an opportunity for play. The store carries chess boards, books and magazines as well as other board games. It is possible to arrange for private instruction.

Chess Shop
230 Thompson Street between 3rd and Bleecker Streets, 475-9580
www.chess-shop.com
This chess emporium carries more than 1,000 chess sets as well as other board games. You can play a game here or arrange for private instruction.

Children's General Store
91st Street between Second and Third Avenues, opening in 2003
Grand Central Terminal, 628-0004
This store features a good selection of unique and educational toys.

Children's Museum of Manhattan Store
212 West 83rd Street between Amsterdam Avenue and Broadway, 721-1223, www.cmom.org
Whether or not you visit this excellent, hands-on children's museum, the shop has a good selection of unique and educational toys and books, many tied in to current exhibitions.

Children's Place **$ to $$**
901 Sixth Avenue at 33rd Street, Manhattan Mall, 268-7696
22 West 34th Street between Fifth and Sixth Avenues, 904-1190
1460 Broadway at 41st Street, 398-4416
1164 Third Avenue at 68th Street, 717-7187
173 East 86th Street between Lexington and Third Avenues, 831-5100

2039 Broadway at 70th Street, 917 441-2374
2187 Broadway at 77th Street, 917 441-9807
36 Union Square East between 16th and 17th Streets, 529-2201
650 Sixth Avenue between 19th and 20th Streets, 917 305-1348
248 West 125th Street between Seventh and Eighth Avenues, 866-9616
877-PLACEUSA (752-33872) for other locations
www.childrensplace.com
This national chain features a good selection of reasonably priced basics for school and play as well as some trendier items.

Children's Resale **$**
303 East 81st Street between First and Second Avenues, 734-8897
This consignment shop sells a wide variety of "pre-owned" clothing, accessories, toys, books and shoes for children up to about eight years old.

Chimera **$$**
77 Mercer Street between Spring and Broome Streets, 334-4730
This cute shop stocks fun stuff for kids—everything from stuffed animals and hand puppets to umbrellas, animal-motif rainboots and slippers, hats, accessories and onesies for infants. A fun place for the kids to visit.

Chocks **$**
74 Orchard Street between Broome and Grand Streets, 473-1929
www.chockcatalog.com
In this shop, located on the famed Orchard Street in the heart of the Lower East Side, you will find discount layette, sleepwear, underwear and hosiery for children and adults as well as some wooden toys.

Christofle Pavilion **$$$**
680 Madison Avenue at 62nd Street, 308-9390
This purveyor of fine silver, crystal and china has a collection of beautiful silver baby gifts, including cutlery, cups, figurines, picture frames, trays and baby china.

City Store
1 Centre Street, North Plaza Municipal Building, 669-8246
1560 Broadway between 46th and 47th Streets (in the Times Square Visitors Center)
www.nyc.gov/citystore
Run by the city government, this store carries books (everything from official publications to coffee-table books) about or relating to the city as well as novelty and souvenir items.

C. J. Laing
30 East 74th Street between Park and Madison Avenues, 819-0248
www.cjlaing.com
This store, well known in Locust Valley, has landed in Manhattan and is

known for its trademark "delightfully unique collection" of whimsically embroidered classic clothing for children in sizes 2–14.

Claire's Accessories **$**
Pier 17, South Street Seaport, 566-0193
755 Broadway at 8th Street, 353-3980
720 Lexington Avenue at 57th Street, 644-8665
1385 Broadway between 37th and 38th Streets, 302-6616
This shop features trendy, very inexpensive accessories for girls, including jewelry (from earrings, bracelets, necklaces to belly chains), walls of hair accessories, some cosmetics (lip gloss, glitter gel and the like), novelty home accessories (picture frames, pillows, pillow covers), boas, cute p.j.s, sunglasses and more. Most items are under $10. Beware, some locations offer ear piercing!

Classic Toys
218 Sullivan Street between Bleecker and West 3rd Streets, 674-4434
www.classictoysnyc.com
This unique shop features classic toys for children and adults, including puppets, tin toys, lead soldiers, classic cars, small character figures and novelties, some books and magazines, die-cast toys, classic games and some vintage toys.

Club Monaco **$$**
121 Prince Street between Wooster and Greene Streets, 533-8930
520 Broadway at Spring Street, 941-1511
160 Fifth Avenue at 21st Street, 352-0936
Fifth Avenue and 57th Street, opening in 2003
1111 Third Avenue at 65th Street, 355-2949
2376 Broadway at 87th Street, 579-2587
www.clubmonaco.com
Your fashion-forward teens (boys and girls) will love the trendy, current, casual fashions available here at reasonable prices.

Clyde's
926 Madison Avenue at 74th Street, 744-5050
www.clydesonmadison.com
This tony pharmacy and department store offers high-end bath and skin-care products (for kids and adults), cosmetics and some toys (including a good selection of Steiff stuffed animals).

Collector's Universe
31 West 46th Street between Fifth and Sixth Avenues, 922-1110
www.cunyc.com
Visit this shop for a wide selection of sports cards (both vintage and new), comic books, action figures, all types of trading cards and collectible figures.

Compleat Strategist
11 East 33rd Street between Fifth and Madison Avenues, 685-3880
www.compleatstrategist.com
If your family loves board games, then do not miss this shop, which features games (including role-playing and strategy games) and toys for children ages 3+ and adults.

Contempo Casuals **$**
65 East 8th Street between Broadway and Mercer Street, 228-6188
www.wetseal.com
Teens flock to this shop for trendy, inexpensive, fun clothes, many of which come in junior sizes.

Conway Stores **$**
151 William Street at Fulton Street, 374-1072
45 Broad Street at Exchange Place, 943-8900
201 East 42nd Street at Third Avenue, 922-5030
11 West 34th Street between Fifth and Sixth Avenues, 967-1370 (no kids department)
225 West 34th Street between Seventh and Eighth Avenues, 967-7390
450 Seventh Avenue between 34th and 35th Streets, 967-1371
1333 Broadway at 35th Street, 967-3460
General Information, 967-5300
The children's department in this discount department store for all ages carries clothing and layette. Some stores may have a modest selection of toys.

Cooper-Hewitt National Design Museum Shop
2 East 91st Street at Fifth Avenue, 849-8355, www.si.edu/ndm
The gift shop carries some children's books and a modest selection of toys and puzzles.

Corner Bookstore
1313 Madison Avenue at 93rd Street, 831-3554
This friendly neighborhood bookstore with a knowledgeable and friendly staff has books for all ages.

Cosmic Comics
10 East 23rd Street between Park Avenue and Broadway, 460-5322
Come here for new and vintage comics as well as action figures, trading cards and models.

Cozy's Cuts for Kids
1125 Madison Avenue between 84th and 85th Streets, 744-1716
448 Amsterdam Avenue at 81st Street, 579-2600
www.cozyscutsforkids.com
Haircuts for children up to age 12 in a totally child-friendly and fun setting. The store also carries a good selection of hair accessories and is well stocked with unique toys. Appointments are recommended.

Cradle & All **$$ to $$$**
1384 Lexington Avenue between 91st and 92nd Streets, 996-9990
This Upper East Side shop offers beautiful things for the new baby and young child, including layette, some furniture, linens, decorative accessories for the nursery and bath and clothing for infants up to 6 months. Some items can be hand painted or personalized.

Crate & Barrel **$$**
650 Madison Avenue at 59th Street, 308-0011
611 Broadway at Houston Street, 780-0004
www.crateandbarrel.com
While this huge home-furnishings store does not cater particularly to kids, there are plenty of fabulous, well-priced items that are very kid friendly, including furniture that is perfect for your older child's room, linens, melamine and plastic dishes and glasses, colorful bath accessories and kid-friendly decorative accessories. During the holiday season, the store offers specific gift items for kids and some child-sized furniture, such as table and chair sets.

Crawford Doyle Booksellers
1082 Madison Avenue between 81st and 82nd Streets, 288-6300
A fine neighborhood bookstore with a selection of quality children's books.

Crembebe
68 Second Avenue between 3rd and 4th Streets, 979-6848
This tiny shop offers a good selection of mostly imported stylish casual clothing for boys and girls up to size 4T as well as some toys for young children.

Crush—Hip Stuff You'll Want **$$**
860 Lexington Avenue between 64th and 65th Streets, mezzanine level, 535-8142, www.crushstore.com
Your tween or teen will love all the goodies this store—formerly located in Brooklyn—has to offer. Not only is there cool vintage stuff, but there is plenty of Hello Kitty merchandise, bags of all sorts, novelties and Powerpuff Girl goodies.

Daffy's **$**
462 Broadway and Grand Street, 334-7444
111 Fifth Avenue at 18th Street, 529-4477
335 Madison Avenue at 44th Street, 557-4422
125 East 57th Street between Park and Lexington Avenues, 376-4477
1311 Broadway at 34th Street, 736-4477
www.daffys.com
The children's department of this discount department store carries major brand clothing, shoes, layette and some toys. The inventory changes frequently and the selection is hit or miss, but a patient shopper can find some great bargains.

Danskin **$$**
159 Columbus Avenue between 67th and 68th Streets, 724-2992
www.danskin.com
Not just for dancing, this store carries dance and activewear for leisure and for serious dancers.

Dave's Army & Navy Store **$**
581 Sixth Avenue between 16th and 17th Streets, 989-6444
This store offers a broad selection of play clothes and Levis for adults and children (starting at size 4).

David Z **$$**
655 Sixth Avenue at 21st Street, 807-8546
1384 Fifth Avenue between 35th and 36th Streets, 917 351-1484
821 Broadway at 12th Street, 253-5511
This shoe store for adults, featuring comfort shoes (for example, Birkenstock, Mephisto, Ecco, Dansko), also carries Timberland and some sneakers for children sizes 3 and up.

Details **$$**
347 Bleecker Street at West 10th Street, 414-0039
142 Eighth Avenue at 17th Street, 366-9498
188 Columbus Avenue between 68th and 69th Streets, 362-7344
This eclectic home-accessories shop carries a unique selection of items for the home and bath that would appeal to kids, including a good selection of bath products and accessories (from animal-shaped sponges to cute shower curtains), totes and messenger bags for your school-age kids, cards, candles and lots of other fun stuff.

Diesel **$$ to $$$**
StyleLab, 416 West Broadway between Prince and Spring Streets, 343-3863
1 Union Square West at 14th Street, 646 336-8552
770 Lexington Avenue at 60th Street, 308-0055
www.diesel.com

For a totally cool shopping experience, your older kids will love these funky, hip, casual clothes and accessories with the Diesel label (think club- and streetwear) for men and women. The Lexington Avenue store has a kid's department that carries clothing with the signature look for toddlers to size 16. Neither the brand-new Union Square store, which features the new sports (think skates and skateboards) line, nor the SoHo StyleLab, which features the higher priced, more cutting-edge merchandise, has a kids' section, but your teens will love them.

Dinosaur Hill **$$ to $$$**
306 East 9th Street between First and Second Avenues, 473-5850
www.dinosaurhill.com
This Village shop is a great source for quality educational toys (many hand-made or hand finished) and unique casual clothes in sizes 0–6, including

hand-knit sweaters and one-of-a-kind items, baby blankets, infant shoes, hats and other accessories.

Disney Store
711 Fifth Avenue at 55th Street, 702-0702
218 West 42nd Street between Seventh and Eighth Avenues, 302-0595
147 Columbus Avenue at 66th Street, 362-2386
www.disney.com
This national chain offers clothing, toys, books and gift and novelty items with Disney themes for the whole family.

DKNY **$$$**
655 Madison Avenue at 60th Street, 223-DKNY (3569)
420 West Broadway between Prince and Spring Streets, 646 613-1100
www.dkny.com
These stores carry the DKNY line for women, men and the home. Your teens (girls and boys) will covet these stylish, pricey clothes and accessories. DKNY for kids can be found at Bloomingdales and Macy's.

Dollhouse
400 Lafayette Street at East 4th Street, 539-1800
This downtown shop has a treasure trove of stylish, trendy casual clothing for tweens and teens featuring Italian and French labels as well as their own Dollhouse jeans. Skinny moms will have fun here, too.

Dylan's Candy Bar
1011 Third Avenue at 60th Street, 646 735-0078
This brand-new, two-level candy store opened by Dylan Lauren is a candy-lover's dream. You can satisfy your sweet tooth with everything from Pez to M&Ms and pick your own personal favorites from walls of candy choices. Custom orders available.

Earl Jeans **$$$**

160 Mercer Street between Prince and West Houston Streets, 226-8709
www.earljean.com
They are expensive, but teen girls can not seem to live without these low-rise tight jeans.

East Side Kids **$$ to $$$**
1298 Madison Avenue at 92nd Street, 360-5000
This Upper East Side institution stocks a full selection of children's shoes from classic to trendy as well as sneakers and dance shoes.

Eastern Mountain Sports **$$ to $$$**
591 Broadway between Prince and Houston Streets, 966-8730
20 West 61st Street between Columbus Avenue and Broadway, 397-4860
www.EMSonline.com
This outdoor specialist carries everything for the outdoors for all ages, including outerwear and camping supplies for children.

E.A.T. Gifts **$$ to $$$**
1062 Madison Avenue between 80th and 81st Streets, 861-2544
This pricey boutique features a unique, eclectic selection of toys, books, decorative accessories, some furniture, party goods, high-end novelties, seasonal items (rain boots, flip-flops), accessories (umbrellas, tote bags) and dishes. Your children can spend hours in here and it is hard to leave empty-handed.

E. Braun & Co., Inc. **$$$**
717 Madison Avenue between 63rd and 64th Streets, 838-0650
This venerable boutique offers imported luxury linens, including child-sized sheets, duvet covers, silk comforters and cashmere blankets.

Eclipse **$$**
400 Lafayette Street at 4th Street, 539-1800
Teens love the casual, funky clothing for teen girls, including tank and tube tops, jeans, sweaters, some dresses, jackets and accessories.

Economy Handicrafts **$**
50-21 69th Street off Queens Boulevard, Woodside, Queens, 800 216-1601
www.economyhandicrafts.com
If you love projects, do not miss this store, which stocks everything you could possibly need for arts-and-crafts projects, all at a discount. Mail/telephone ordering available.

Enchanted Forest
85 Mercer Street between Spring and Broome Streets, 925-6677
www.sohotoys.com
This charming shop carries unique nostalgic toys and books in an incredible setting.

Ethan Allen **$$**
192 Lexington Avenue at 32nd Street, 213-0600
1107 Third Avenue at 65th Street, 308-7703
103 West End Avenue at 64th Street, 201-9840
www.ethanallen.com
No longer just the home of reproduction colonial furniture, Ethan Allen has morphed into a very stylish and well-priced home furnishings store with lines for all tastes and budgets. These stores feature several well-priced lines just for kids, including beds, storage and media units, desks

and dressers. The stores offer design services and can even dress the bed and windows.

Exploration Station
1705 First Avenue between 88th and 89th Streets, 426-5424
www.explorationstation.net
This store offers a "full line of teacher supplies for the classroom and also carries fun and educational games and kits for the home and school." A great source for math tools, geography games, puppets, anatomy models, science kits, dinosaur digs and arts-and-crafts supplies.

Express **$ to $$**
Pier 17, South Street Seaport, 693-0096
130 Fifth Avenue at 18th Street, 633-9414
733 Third Avenue at 46th Street, 949-9784
477 Madison Avenue at 51st Street, 644-4453
722-728 Lexington Avenue at 58th Street, 421-7246
584 Broadway at Prince Street, 625-0313
901 Sixth Avenue at 33rd Street, Manhattan Mall, 971-3280
7 West 34th Street between Fifth and Sixth Avenues, 629-6838
321-327 Columbus Avenue at 75th Street, 580-5833
www.expressfashion.com
This national chain has a broad selection of trendy, casual, well-priced clothes based on the season's hottest fashions, along with accessories perfect for your teen.

FAO Schwarz **$$ to $$$**
767 Fifth Avenue at 58th Street, 644-9400, www.fao.com
This huge toy store (and popular tourist destination) houses an extensive selection of toys (from commercial brands to unique items), stuffed animals, dolls, art supplies, party goods, books, costumes, entire departments dedicated to Barbie, Madame Alexander dolls, Lego and Star Wars, video games and accessories, a new FAO Baby shop and some clothing, all in an amazing setting.

Farmers Daughter and Son **$$ to $$$**
1001 First Avenue at 55th Street, 421-0484
This neighborhood ladies' boutique carries onesies and sweaters, some hand knitted, for infants.

Filene's Basement **$ to $$**
620 Sixth Avenue at 18th Street, 620-3100
2222 Broadway at 79th Street, 873-8000
www.filenesbasement.com
This discount department store does not have a children's department, but your tween (if he or she fits into adult sizes) or teen can find well-priced clothing, accessories and shoes.

Fire Zone
34 West 51st Street, 50 Rockefeller Plaza, between Fifth and Sixth Avenues, 698-4520, www.fdnyfirezone.com
Operated by the FDNY's Fire Safety Education Fund, this location houses both a store that sells officially licensed and trademarked products of the Fire Department and terrific hands-on and multimedia presentations about fire safety (including a firehouse, fire scene and empowerment zone).

First & Second Cousin **$$**
142 Seventh Avenue South between 10th and Charles Streets, 929-8048
This shop offers mostly casual and some party clothes for boys and girls (including such labels as Flapdoodles and OshKosh) up to size 10 as well as toys.

Flora and Henri **$$$**
943 Madison Avenue between 74th and 75th Streets, www.florahenri.com
Scheduled to open in summer 2003, this children's clothier from Seattle specializes in pure and simple vintage-inspired natural fabric clothing in "classic styles with beautiful appointments and hand-stitched details."

Forbidden Planet
840 Broadway at 13th Street, 473-1576
This unusual store features a wide selection of science-fiction toys, action figures, video games, role-playing games, comic books, fantasy literature and some accessories and T-shirts. For ages 5+.

Fossil **$$**
530 Fifth Avenue between 44th and 45th Streets, 997-3978
103 Fifth Avenue at 17th Street, 243-7296
www.fossil.com
The source for very cool watches, sunglasses, messenger bags and other accessories with the Fossil label for your tweens and teens.

Freed of London **$$**
21-01 43rd Avenue, Long Island City, Queens, 718 729-7061
www.freedoflondon.com
This shop is the place to go for serious dancewear and supplies for dancers ages 2 to adult.

French Connection **$$**
435 West Broadway between Prince and Spring Streets, 219-1139
700 Broadway at 4th Street, 473-4486
1270 Sixth Avenue at 51st Street, 262-6623
304 Columbus Avenue between 74th and 75th Streets, 496-1470 (women's only)
www.frenchconnection.com
Teens are drawn to the current and trendy styles based on runway looks, which are found here at quite reasonable prices.

Fresh $$$
57 Spring Street between Lafayette and Mulberry Streets, 925-0099
1061 Madison Avenue between 80th and 81st Streets, 396-0344
388 Bleecker Street between Perry and 11th Streets, 917 408-1850
www.fresh.com
Your teenage girl will love the luxurious natural products for skin, hair and body and some products and accessories for the home (they also make great gifts). Fresh also carries a line of lovely all-natural children's bath products.

Frette $$$
799 Madison Avenue between 67th and 68th Streets, 988-5221
www.frette.com
Indulge in imported luxury linens from this Italian company. For kids, you will find fine crib bedding and blankets.

Funny Business Comics
660B Amsterdam Avenue between 92nd and 93rd Streets, 799-9477
This shop is packed full of collectible comics.

Galo Shoes $$$
895 Madison Avenue at 72nd Street (opening in 2003)
825 Lexington Avenue at 63rd Street, 832-3922
1296 Third Avenue between 74th and 75th Streets, 288-3448
www.galoshoes.com
This women's shoe boutique carries a good selection of fashionable, mostly European shoes for boys and girls from one year up.

Game Show
474 Sixth Avenue between 11th and 12th Streets, 633-6328
1240 Lexington Avenue between 83rd and 84th Streets, 472-8011
If your family enjoys games, then this store is a great source for all kinds of games for adults and children ages 4+.

Games Workshop
54 East 8th Street between Broadway and University Place, 982-6314
www.games-workshop.com
This downtown outpost of the Games Workshop organization is dedicated to serious role-playing and battle simulation games. For ages 8+.

Gap $$
113 Front Street, South Street Seaport, 374-1051 (adults, kids, baby)
1 Astor Place at Broadway, 253-0145 (women)
345 Sixth Avenue at 4th Street, 727-2210 (adults)
750 Broadway at 8th Street, 674-1877 (men)
122 Fifth Avenue between 17th and 18th Streets, 917 408-5580 (adults, kids, baby)
1466 Broadway at 42nd Street, 382-4500 (adults, kids, baby)
657-659 Third Avenue at 42nd Street, 697-3590 (adults, kids, baby)

757 Third Avenue at 47th Street, 223-5140 (adults, kids)
900 Third Avenue at 54th Street, 754-2290 (adults)
527 Madison Avenue at 54th Street, 688-1260 (adults)
734 Lexington Avenue between 58th and 59th Streets, 751-1543 (adults)
277 West 23rd Street at Eighth Avenue, 646 336-0802 (adults)
60 West 34th Street at Broadway, 760-1268 (adult, kids, baby)
1212 Sixth Avenue at 48th Street, 730-1087 (adult, kids, baby)
680 Fifth Avenue at 54th Street, 977-7023 (adult, kids, baby)
250 West 57th Street at Broadway, 315-2250 (adults, kids, baby)
1131-1149 Third Avenue at 66th Street, 472-4555 (adults, kids, baby)
1037 Lexington Avenue at 74th Street, 327-2614 (baby)
1066 Lexington Avenue at 75th Street, 879-9144 (adults, kids)
1511 Third Avenue at 85th Street, 794-5781 (adults)
1535 Third Avenue at 87th Street, 423-0033 (kids, baby)
1988 Broadway at 67th Street, 721-5304 (adults, kids, baby)
335 Columbus Avenue at 76th Street, 873-9270 (women)
341 Columbus Avenue at 76th Street, 875-9196 (baby)
2373 Broadway at 86th Street, 873-1244 (adults)
Visit www.gap.com or call 800 GAP-STYLE to locate the store nearest to you.

This phenomenon is the epitome of American casual, offering stylish, contemporary, reasonably-priced basics for babies to adults.

The Gazebo **$$$**
306 East 61st Street between First and Second Avenues, 6th floor, 832-7077, www.thegazebo.com

This charming home-accessories shop offers country-inspired bedding, handmade quilts, decorative accessories for the nursery and some lovely hand-knit sweaters and crib blankets.

G. C. William **$$$**
1137 Madison Avenue between 84th and 85th Streets, 396-3400

Personal service is emphasized at this very chic Upper East Side boutique, which carries a variety of fashion-savvy classic and contemporary clothing for children ages 6–16, junior sizes for girls and husky sizes for boys. While there is a terrific assortment of cutting-edge casual clothes and accessories of all kinds, this is also the place to buy elegant, fashionable dress clothes (including Armani Jr. and Burberry), such as boys' suits and tuxedos and chic dresses for girls. Petite moms who fit into the junior sizes will appreciate the selection of Juicy, Petit Bateau and other hip T-shirts. You can also find Roxy and Kenneth Cole shoes for girls and Kenneth Cole shoes for boys.

Geiger **$$$**
505 Park Avenue at 59th Street, 644-3435, www.geiger-fashion.com

This boutique is the US home of the original Austrian boiled wool jacket (with or without appliqués) for children ages 18 months to 8 as well as jackets and clothing for women.

Geppetto's Toybox
10 Christopher Street at Greenwich Avenue, 620-7511, www.nyctoys.com
This downtown toy store offers a great selection of higher-end quality and educational toys (some handmade) and books.

G-Factory **$$**
458 West Broadway between Houston and Prince Streets, 260-4570
www.casio.com
This store is the place to go for the latest and best selection of Casio G-Shock and Baby-G watches.

Girlprops.com **$**
153 Prince Street between West Broadway and Thompson Street, 505-7615
203 Spring Street between Sullivan Street and Sixth Avenue, 625-8323
33 8th Street between University Place and Broadway, 533-3240
www.girlprops.com
For girls 3 to 83, very cool, fun, trendy accessories including hair accessories, "house props" such as picture frames and pillows, jewelry, makeup, sunglasses, wigs and bags. The price is right, too: Girlprops' motto is "inexpensive. . .we never say cheap."

Good Byes Children's Resale Shop **$**
230 East 78th Street between Second and Third Avenues, 794-2301
This resale shop is packed with clothing (sizes 0–6), equipment, toys and books.

Gotham City Comics
800 Lexington Avenue between 61st and 62nd Streets, 2nd floor, 980-0009
This East Side shop has a large selection of new and collectible comics, sports and other trading cards, action figures and toys.

Gracious Home **$$$**
1217 Third Avenue between 70th and 71st Streets (hardware), 988-8990
1220 Third Avenue between 70th and 71st Streets (bed and bath), 517-6300
1992 Broadway at 67th Street, 231-7800
www.gracioushome.com
This housewares store carries everything from hardware, home appliances, gadgets, organizers and everything for the kitchen to home furnishings and now a high-end baby department, too. The baby department carries furniture for the nursery, layette, linens, decorative accessories as well as wall and window coverings. Custom design services available.

Granny Made **$$ to $$$**
381 Amsterdam Avenue between 78th and 79th Streets, 496-1222
www.granny-made.com
This charming shop, known for its excellent selection of hand-knit sweaters, has quality clothing (including handmade items) for adults and children up to size 8/10. For kids, there are casual clothes (including such labels as Heartstrings, Sweet Potatoes and My Boy Sam), layette, decorative accessories, soft sculpture wall hangings, decorative quilts and a particularly good selection of boy stuff.

Granny's Rentals
876-4310, 410-9464
If you are hosting out-of-town guests, you can rent baby furniture (cribs, changing tables, rocking chair for mom) and equipment (strollers, high chairs, etc.) as well as kid-size party supplies. A week's notice is usually sufficient, except around major holidays when advance reservations are crucial.

Great Feet **$$**
1241 Lexington Avenue at 84th Street, 249-0551, www.striderite.com
This popular children's shoe store has a full selection of shoes, from classic to trendy, and sneakers along with toys to play with while you wait. The salespeople are real pros.

The Green Onion **$$**
247 Smith Street between Sackett and Degraw Streets, Brooklyn, 718 246-2804
Proprietor Shelley Kruth has created a charming shop filled with cool, funky, fun, upscale stylish clothing and shoes for kids 0 to 7 (some items for girls up to size 10), featuring a terrific layette selection, hand-knit sweaters, unique shoes, educational toys, books and some decorative accessories.

Greenstone's **$$ to $$$**
442 Columbus Avenue between 81st and 82nd Streets, 580-4322
Greenstone's, too, 1184 Madison Avenue between 86th and 87th Streets, 427-1665
These boutiques offer fun, contemporary and unique clothing, including a large selection of hand-knit sweaters and very cute hats.

Gryphon Bookshop
2246 Broadway between 80th and 81st Streets, 362-0706
This neighborhood used-book store has a modest children's section.

Gucci **$$$**
685 Fifth Avenue at 54th Street, 826-2600
840 Madison Avenue between 69th and 70th Streets, 717-2619
www.gucci.com
This high-end Italian leather goods, accessories and clothing store for adults carries signature soft infant shoes for the well-heeled baby.

Guess? $$
23 Fulton Street at South Street Seaport, 385-0533
537 Broadway between Prince and Spring Streets, 226-9545
www.guess.com
Teens love these trendy casual clothes and accessories.

Guggenheim (Solomon R.) Museum
1071 Fifth Avenue at 89th Street, 423-3615, www.guggenheim.org/store
This fabulous museum gift shop has a good selection of educational toys and books and some decorative accessories.

Gymboree Store $$
1049 Third Avenue at 62nd Street, 688-4044
1332 Third Avenue between 76th and 77th Streets, 517-5548
1120 Madison Avenue between 83rd and 84th Streets, 717-6702
2015 Broadway at 69th Street, 595-7662
2271 Broadway between 81st and 82nd Streets, 595-9071
www.gymboree.com
This national chain offers colorful, reasonably priced basic clothing and some shoes up to age 7.

H & M $
558 Broadway between Prince and Spring Streets, 343-8313
640 Fifth Avenue at 51st Street, 489-0390
Herald Square at 34th Street and Sixth Avenue, 646 473-1165
www.hm.com
Sweden's answer to the Gap offers inexpensive, up-to-the-minute, stylish clothes and accessories for men, women and kids. Only the Herald Square store has a kids' department (sizes 0–14), but tweens and teens will love the clothes and accessories in all of the stores. Inventory is constantly changing in these huge stores, so do not pass up that item you fall in love with, because it may be gone by next week.

H2O+ $$
460 West Broadway between Houston and Prince Streets, 505-3223
650 Madison Avenue between 59th and 60th Streets, 750-8119
www.h20plus.com
Well-priced, water-based natural products for skin, hair and body, which your teens and tweens will love (and they make great gifts and party favors). H20+ also stocks some great bath products and accessories just for kids.

Halloween Adventure
104 Fourth Avenue between 11th and 12th Streets, 673-4546
www.halloweenadventure.com
Not for the timid, this unusual store stocks magic tricks, gag gifts, costumes, wigs, disguises, makeup, novelties and decorations. A magician is often on the premises to demonstrate the magic tricks.

Hammacher Schlemmer **$$ to $$$**
147 East 57th Street between Lexington and Third Avenues, 421-9000
www.hammacher.com
This lifestyle store, famous for its catalogue and "best of" products, carries items, tools, retro-inspired novelties, electronics and gadgets for the home, recreation and personal care, designed to make life easier, more fun or more interesting. Kids will definitely enjoy visiting the showroom and testing the merchandise.

Harry's Shoes **$$**
2299 Broadway at 83rd Street, 874-2035, www.harrys-shoes.com
This Upper West Side institution is a full-service shoe store for children and adults, featuring a large selection of comfort shoes (Birkenstock, Mephisto, Rockport, Dansko, Timberland and others). The children's department carries everything from basics to party shoes. The salespeople are real pros.

Henri Bendel **$$$**
712 Fifth Avenue at 56th Street, 247-1100, www.bendels.com
This tony, fashion-forward department store has a tiny children's boutique tucked away on the second floor (near the housewares) with a selection of charming items for children 0–2 such as high-end onesies, bathrobes, silver baby accessories and a few items of clothing.

Hermes **$$$**
691 Madison Avenue at 62nd Street, 751-3181, www.hermes.com
This famed shopping destination of very high end—and high priced—luxury leather goods, clothing and accessories offers a truly extravagant selection of luxe blankets, robes, towels, china and silver accessories for babies and toddlers.

HMV
234 West 42nd Street between Seventh and Eighth Avenues, 302-1451
565 Fifth Avenue at 46th Street, 681-6700

308 West 125th Street between Fredrick Douglas Boulevard and Eighth Avenue, 932-9619
www.hmv.com
This British import has a huge selection of music of all types as well as some videos and DVDs.

Hombons
1500 First Avenue between 78th and 79th Streets, 717-5300
This well-stocked neighborhood store has a good selection of toys (from Barbie and Playskool to games and more unique toys) and a large section of crafts and art supplies.

Hoofbeats **$$ to $$$**

232 East 78th Street between Second and Third Avenues, 517-2633

This little boutique specializes in gifts for new babies: stuffed animals, pillows, diaper bags, robes, tote bags, hooded towels and decorative nursery accessories, many of which can be personalized or monogrammed.

Hoyt & Bond **$$ to $$$**

246 Smith Street between Degraw and Douglas Streets, Brooklyn, 718 596-5089

This charming shop for women and children offers a varied line of mostly European clothing for children up to 8 years old, featuring such labels as Marimekko and Petit Bateau and kilts from Scotland and Johnson Woolen Mills (American-made logger jackets). You'll also find original designs by owner Elizabeth Beer, hand-knit sweaters and some books, toys and shoes (such as Sonnet shoes from England).

Hyde Park Stationers

1060 Madison Avenue between 80th and 81st Streets, 861-5710

This friendly neighborhood stationers offers a great selection of school supplies, some toys and books, cards, invitations and custom stationery.

Ibiza Boutique **$$ to $$$**

42 & 46 University Place between East 9th and East 10th Streets, 533-4614

This very cool Village shop features hip European and eclectic clothing, handmade and unique goods, toys and books and whimsical accessories.

Infinity **$$ to $$$**

1116 Madison Avenue at 83rd Street, 517-4232

This packed shop is literally stuffed with fashion-forward trendy clothing, small toys, accessories (to wear and for your daughter's room) and novelties for girls and women. There is a terrific selection of casual and dressy clothing for tweens and teens.

Integral Yoga Bookstore

227 West 13th Street between Seventh and Eighth Avenues, 929-0586

This store is a great source for books for the New Age parent and yoga accessories.

Iris Brown's Victorian Doll Shop

253 East 57th Street between Second and Third Avenues, 593-2882

This shop houses a treasure trove of vintage and collectible dolls and dollhouse accessories.

It's a Mod, Mod World **$$**

85 First Avenue between East 5th and East 6th Streets, 460-8004

Lovers of kitsch will have a field day in this cool downtown shop packed to the rafters with collectible tin toys, unique toys and games (think Magic

8 Balls), candles, cards, items with pop images, as well as a line of unique fabricated items such as clocks made out of detergent boxes and lamps made out of vintage toasters.

It's "A" Nother Hit
131 West 33rd Street between Sixth and Seventh Avenues, 564-4111
www.itsanotherhit.com
Your little sports fan will want to check out the new and vintage baseball and other sports and trading cards, memorabilia, comics, action figures and collectibles.

J & R Music World
15-33 Park Row between Beekman and Ann Streets (just south of City Hall), 238-9000, www.jandr.com
This huge electronics store offers a large selection of computers, electronics, music (equipment and CDs), video games and more.

J. Crew **$$**
203 Front Street, South Street Seaport, 385-3500
99 Prince Street between Mercer and Greene Streets, 966-2739
91 Fifth Avenue between 16th and 17th Streets, 255-4848
30 Rockefeller Plaza at 50th Street, 765-4412
www.jcrew.com
Known originally for its catalogue, this store offers up the quintessential American preppy look with a cool twist. Teens will love the selection of basics for school, play and dressing up.

Jacadi **$$$**
787 Madison Avenue between 66th and 67th Streets, 535-3200
1296 Madison Avenue at 92nd Street, 369-1616
1260 Third Avenue between 72nd and 73rd Streets, 717-9292
www.jacadiusa.com
This popular French boutique offers a high-quality line of fine imported classic clothing, shoes, equipment, layette, furniture for the nursery and linens.

Jane's Exchange **$**
207 Avenue A between East 12th and East 13th Streets, 674-6268
A great source for resale kids' clothing and accessories, books, some toys and tapes, as well as maternity clothing and nursery furniture.

Jan's Hobby Shop
1557 York Avenue between 82nd and 83rd Streets, 861-5075
This shop specializes in models—wood, metal and plastic—for all ages, including airplanes, cars, ships. An on-site restorer is available to restore and repair old models and toys.

Jay Kos **$$$**
986 Lexington Avenue between 71st and 72nd Streets, 327-2382
This purveyor of fine men's clothing has recently added a complete boys' department featuring private-label classic, stylish casual and formal attire for boys sizes 1–16.

Jewish Museum Store
1109 Fifth Avenue at 92nd Street, 423-3200, www.jewishmuseum.org
This museum store (one part within the museum and one part next door) has a wonderful selection of Judaica and educational toys and books.

Jim Hanley's Universe
4 West 33rd Street between Fifth Avenue and Broadway, 268-7088
www.jhuniverse.com
One of the largest comic book stores in the city, this store stocks vintage and new comics, trading cards (except sports cards), action figures, statues, novels, comic-related apparel and books and supplies for comic artists.

Jodi's Gymwear **$$**
244 East 84th Street between Second and Third Avenues, 772-7633
Housed within Jodi's Gym (a popular venue for children's classes), this shop carries dance, gymnastics, ice-skating wear and activewear for girls through young junior sizes.

Joyce Leslie **$**
20 University Place at 8th Street, 505-5419, www.joyceleslie.com
Your teenage girl will be able to find up-to-the-minute trendiness—clothing, accessories and shoes—all in junior sizes, without spending a fortune.

Judy's Fancies **$$$**
By appointment only, 689-8663
Judy Correa specializes in christening gowns and custom-made clothing for children of all ages. Special-occasion clothes are available for girls through size 8 and boys through size 6. Other clothing goes up to size 6 for girls and boys. Judy, who uses only natural fabrics and favors a Victorian-inspired look, will create her own designs or work with your ideas.

Julian & Sara **$$$**
103 Mercer Street between Prince and Spring Streets, 226-1989
This SoHo boutique features fine European clothing and accessories (such as Kenzo and Jean Bourget), baby cashmeres, shoes, mobiles, music boxes and some toys. The look ranges from classic to cool. The layette selection includes some handmade items.

Jumpin' Julia's **$$$**
240 Seventh Avenue between 4th and 5th Streets, Brooklyn, 718 965-3535
This boutique carries a good assortment of classic, fine European clothing and shoes for children up to size 8.

Juno **$$$**
550 Broadway between Prince and Spring Streets, 925-6415
www.junokids.com
This downtown shop features cool, hip fashionable shoes for the whole family.

Just for Tykes **$$$**
83 Mercer Street between Spring and Broome Streets, 274-9121
This upscale children's boutique located in the heart of SoHo is one-stop shopping for kids 0–4. In addition to a large selection of cool European and American clothing, you will find unique bedding (custom and pre-made), furniture, equipment, decorative accessories, toys and a new-mother section. The play area keeps the kids busy while you shop.

Kar'ikter **$$ to $$$**
19 Prince Street between Elizabeth and Mott Streets, 274-1966
www.karikter.com
This shop is chock full of decorative accessories, dishes, backpacks and other accessories and small toys inspired by popular European characters such as Tintin, the Little Prince, Babar and Noddy. You will also find a colorful selection of modern European home furnishings.

Kate Spade Store **$$$**
454 Broome Street at Mercer Street, 274-1991, www.katespade.com
These cool, clean-lined, pricey fabric handbags have become de rigueur for the well-dressed teen. Moms may prefer the luxury leather versions, although the large fabric totes have been known to make hip, elegant diaper bags.

Kate's Paperie
561 Broadway between Prince and Spring Streets, 941-9816
8 West 13th Street between Fifth and Sixth Avenues, 633-0570
1282 Third Avenue between 73rd and 74th Streets, 396-3670
www.katespaperie.com
This stationer offers a broad variety of items for the serious writer—paper (from handmade to computer friendly), pens, stationery, wrapping papers and writing and desk accessories. A children's section features some books, arts-and-crafts supplies and kids' stationery. The stores offer periodic events (such as papermaking and crafts activities) for children and adults.

KB Toys
1411 St. Nicholas Avenue at 181st Street, 928-4816
901 Sixth Avenue at 33rd Street, Manhattan Mall, 629-5386

2411 Broadway at 89th Street, 595-4389
www.kbtoys.com
Come here for a large selection of commercial toys and art supplies.

Kenneth Cole **$$**
597 Broadway between Houston and Prince Streets, 965-0283
95 Fifth Avenue at 17th Street, 675-2550
130 East 57th Street at Lexington Avenue, 688-1670 (Reaction)
107 East 42nd Street at Park Avenue, 949-8079
610 Fifth Avenue at 49th Street, 373-5800
353 Columbus Avenue between 76th and 77th Streets, 873-2061
www.kennethcole.com
This hip young label, popular among older teenagers, features shoes, bags and accessories, jackets and some clothing for men and women.

Kidding Around **$$**
60 West 15th Street between Fifth and Sixth Avenues, 645-6337
This shop offers a good selection of educational and unique toys, books and fun and unique clothing and accessories (up to size 8). A good source for handmade quilts and baby blankets.

Kids Cuts
201 East 31st Street between Second and Third Avenues, 684-5252
Haircuts for children in a totally child-friendly and fun setting. The store also carries a selection of hair accessories and unique toys. Haircuts available for adults too.

Kids Foot Locker **$$**
120 West 34th Street between Sixth and Seventh Avenues, 465-9041
1504 Second Avenue between 78th and 79th Streets, 396-4567
www.footlocker.com
This national chain offers a large selection of sneakers and activewear (warm-ups, windbreakers, T-shirts) for babies on up.

Kids Supply Co. **$$ to $$$**
1343 Madison Avenue at 94th Street, 426-1200, www.kidssupplyco.com
This well-stocked shop offers children's higher-end furniture, some decorative accessories and linens. Custom design services available.

Kidstown **$**
10 East 14th Street between Fifth Avenue and University Place, 243-1301
This store is literally piled high with value-priced clothing, layette, furniture, equipment and toys.

Kiehl's **$$**
109 Third Avenue between 13th and 14th Streets, 677-3171, www.kiehls.com
Kiehl's natural products for skin, hair and body have been around since 1851. The Village flagship store is worth a visit just to see the collection of memorabilia. In addition to all kinds of products for adults, there is a line of baby products (many swear by the diaper cream) and great products for "problem" skin. Kiehl's products are also available at Barney's, Bergdorf Goodman, Saks Fifth Avenue and Zitomer's.

Kirna Zabete **$$$**
96 Greene Street between Prince and Spring Streets, 941-9656
www.kirnazabete.com
This high-end, cutting-edge designer boutique for women has a unique, seasonal selection of tiny luxurious infant cashmere sweaters and accessories.

Kmart Stores **$**
770 Broadway at Astor Place, 673-1540
One Penn Plaza at 34th Street between Seventh and Eighth Avenues, 760-1188
www.bluelight.com
The New York branches of this famed discount department store have large children's departments that carry major brand-name clothing, shoes, equipment, toys and books.

La Layette et Plus **$$$**
170 East 61st Street between Lexington and Third Avenues, 688-7072
www.lalayette.com
This boutique offers a treasure trove of fine imported layette, custom linens, baby cashmeres, clothing (up to size 2), hand-knits, silver and customized porcelain gift items and handpainted and carved furniture.

Lacoste **$$$**
551 Madison Avenue between 54th and 55th Streets, 800-4-Lacoste (800 452-2678), www.lacoste.com
Best known for the classic piqué crocodile-emblemed tennis shirt, this once-again trendy boutique offers up candy-colored cotton sportswear for adults and kids sizes 2–16. The logoed tops are very popular among teens and tweens. A flagship store on Fifth Avenue at 49th Street is due to open in 2003.

Laura Ashley **$$ to $$$**
398 Columbus Avenue at 79th Street, 496-5110, www.laura-ashleyusa.com
Best known for home furnishings, this shop also sells traditional, classic clothes for girls sizes 2–9.

Laura Beth's Baby Collection **$$**
By appointment only, 717-2559
This former department-store buyer helps expectant moms design the perfect nursery by offering a collection of high-end designer linens and deco-

rative accessories at prices below retail. Custom orders can be accommodated.

Le Chateau **$$**
611 Broadway at Houston Street, 260-0882
704 Broadway at Washington Place, 674-5560
34 West 34th Street between Fifth and Sixth Avenues, 967-0024
www.le-chateau.com
This Canadian import, which caters to young adults, is known for well-priced trendy clothes, many of which are done in rayon. Great for teens.

Le Sportsac **$$**
176 Spring Street between Thompson Street and West Broadway, 625-2626
1065 Madison Avenue between 80th and 81st Streets, 988-6200
www.lesportsac.com
A terrific source for distinctive, reasonably priced nylon bags in all shapes, colors, prints and sizes. Young girls particularly love the tiny shoulder bags. Moms enjoy the light-weight travel and tote bags, which make convenient diaper bags.

Leeper Kids
79 Grand Central Terminal, Lexington Passage, 499-9111
Located in the heart of Grand Central Terminal, this small shop offers trendy, colorful and fun casual clothing and accessories for children up to age 10.

Lee's Art Shop **$$**
220 West 57th Street between Broadway and Seventh Avenue, 247-0110
This huge full-service art supply store has not only everything the serious artist needs in the way of supplies, but also materials suitable for arts-and-crafts projects, school projects and other kids' art activities (non-toxic paint, crayons, big brushes, modeling clay, and lots more).

Lenox Hill Bookstore
1018 Lexington Avenue between 72nd and 73rd Streets, 472-7170
www.lenoxhillbooks.com
This wonderful neighborhood bookstore has a fine selection of children's and parenting books

Leron **$$$**
750 Madison Avenue at 65th Street, 753-6700, www.leron.com
In this shop, known for fine luxury linens for the bed, bath and table and customized embroidery, you can also find beautiful quilts, sheets, towels, robes (for all ages) and embroidered pillows for your child.

Lester's **$$ to $$$**
1534 Second Avenue at 80th Street, 734-9292
This recently expanded Upper East Side boutique is popular for its selection of up-to-the-minute contemporary-to-classic clothing, accessories, shoes, and layette as well as some toys, novelties (pillows, "bunk junk" and other hot items) and books. The shoe salespeople are true pros at fitting kids. The lower level houses a full junior department.

Lilliput **$$ to $$$**
240 Lafayatte Street between Prince and Spring Streets, 965-9201
265 Lafayette Street between Prince and Spring Streets, 965-9567
www.lilliputsoho.com
These boutiques feature cool, chic, contemporary, mostly European clothes, shoes, layette and specialty toys. The 265 Lafayette Street store fits children up to eight years old, and the 240 Lafayette Street store fits from babies to teens. These shops offer a mix of high-fashion labels such as Diesel, Replay and Juicy and fine European brands such as I Golfini della Nonna.

Lincoln Center Performing Arts Gift Shop
136 West 65th Street, Lincoln Center, concourse level, 917 441-1195
www.lincolncenter.org
The Lincoln Center gift shop offers merchandise related to the performing arts for all ages.

Little Eric **$$ to $$$**
1331 Third Avenue between 76th and 77th Streets, 288-8987
1118 Madison Avenue between 83rd and 84th Streets, 717-1513
This boutique offers a huge selection of high-fashion and adorable shoes for the younger set.

Little Extras **$$ to $$$**
676 Amsterdam Avenue at 93rd Street, 721-6161

Come here for an assortment of unique decorative accessories, stuffed animals, backpacks, art supplies and furniture and toys, much of which can be personalized.

Little Folk Art **$$ to $$$**
159 Duane Street between Hudson Street and West Broadway, 267-1500
www.littlefolkart.cc
This California-based company offers original designs and hand-crafted furniture and decorative accessories for the nursery, older child's room and playroom. Design services are available.

Little Folks **$ to $$**
123 East 23rd Street between Park and Lexington Avenues, 982-9669
This discount children's department store has two floors of everything you need for your baby and young child, including clothing in sizes 0 to 6x (basics from major brands and some imported), furniture (featuring CNT

cribs from Italy), equipment and layette. For older kids, look for underwear, pajamas and outerwear up to size 14. Look for a large selection of infant toys and some toys for older kids.

Liz Lange **$$$**
958 Madison Avenue between 75th and 76th Streets, 879-2191
www.lizlange.com
Who said expectant mothers cannot have stylish, fabulous clothes? Not Liz Lange who serves up her very fashionable signature "must haves": slim pants, cashmere twin sets, skirts, bathing suits and evening clothes for chic moms-to-be.

Logos
1575 York Avenue between 83rd and 84th Streets, 517-7292
This neighborhood bookstore, which carries books for all ages and specializes in Christian literature, has a large children's section that stocks all kinds of books, including some Christian and Hebrew themed works.

Lord & Taylor **$$**
424 Fifth Avenue between 38th and 39th Streets, 391-3344
www.maycompany.com
The large children's department of this full-service department store carries clothing, layette, and some toys. This store, while not known for a super high-fashion look, has a very good selection of basics and designer labels.

Loro Piana **$$$**
821 Madison Avenue between 68th and 69th Streets, 980-7961
The New York outpost of this Italian luxury brand, known for its sumptuous cashmeres and casual clothing for adults, carries miniature versions of its signature quilted jackets and cashmere robes, sweaters, blankets and slippers for children up to sizes 4–6.

Lucky Brand Dungarees **$$**
38 Green Street at Grand Street, 625-0707
172 Fifth Avenue at 22nd Street, 917 606-1418 (no kids' department)
1151 Third Avenue at 67th Street 646 422-1192 (no kids' department)
216 Columbus Avenue at 70th Street, 579-1760
www.luckybrandjeans.com
This L.A.-based retailer specializes in casual clothes with a hip spin. In addition to great-fitting jeans and tops for adults, they have cute jeans, tops and more for children sizes 2–6. There are also some very stylish casual looks for tweens.

M & J Trimmings
1008 Sixth Avenue between 37th and 38th Streets, 391-9072
www.mjtrim.com
If your kids are into crafts, they will love perusing the trimmings (buttons, ribbons, tassels and more) and sewing supplies for all types of craft projects.

MacKenzie-Childs, Ltd. **$$$**
824 Madison Avenue at 69th Street, 570-6050, www.mackenzie-childs.com
This high-end home accessories emporium carries a selection of unique and whimsical multi-colored and multi-patterned goods (mostly handmade, handpainted or handfinished), some of which are appropriate for children's rooms, baby gifts or children.

Macy's Herald Square **$$**
151 West 34th Street at Herald Square, 695-4400
www.macys.com
The very large children's department of this landmark full-service department store carries a broad variety of both designer and more moderate clothing, shoes, layette and toys. You can also find a full-service maternity department and a large selection of fashions and accessories for teen and tweens.

Magic Windows **$$$**
1186 Madison Avenue at 87th Street, 289-0028
M. W. Teen, 1188 Madison Avenue at 88th Street, 289-0181 (girls only)
Classically styled imported layette and clothing and accessories for boys and girls. You can also find bassinettes, infant baskets and changing tables. M.W. Teen has a large selection of special-occasion dresses and casual wear for preteen and junior-size girls.

Malo **$$$**
125 Wooster Street between Prince and Spring Streets, 941-7444
814 Madison Avenue at 68th Street, 396-4721
www.malo.it
Wrap your newborn in luxurious Italian cashmere sweaters, hats, booties and blankets. A real treat is the cashmere-covered hot-water bottle.

Mandee **$$**
2550 Broadway between 95th and 96th Street, 666-1652
www.mandee.com

This shop, which offers junior-size clothing, is popular among teens because of its mission to "deliver fashion at a fabulous price." Look here for well-priced, popular brands of clothing and shoes.

Manhattan Comics and Cards
228 West 23rd Street between Seventh and Eighth Avenues, 243-9349
Come here for new and vintage comics, sports cards, trading cards and action figures.

Manhattan Dollhouse
236 Third Avenue between 19th and 20th Streets, 253-9549
www.manhattandollhouseshop.com
A great source for new and vintage dollhouses and dollhouse accessories. Repair service is available.

Manny's Music
156 West 48th Street between Sixth and Seventh Avenues, 819-0576
www.mannysmusic.com
For your budding rock and roller, you will find a selection of guitars, drums, amplifiers, keyboards and recording equipment.

Marsha D. D. **$$ to $$$**
1574 Third Avenue between 88th and 89th Streets, 831-2422
A must-visit for cool kids, this is the place for the hottest clothing, small toys, "bunk junk" for camp, novelties and costume jewelry for ages 7 through preteen, teen and some adult sizes for girls and sizes 8–20 for boys.

Mary Arnold Toys
1010 Lexington Avenue between 72nd and 73rd Streets, 744-8510
More than just a neighborhood toy store, this shop has an extensive selection of high-quality toys, dolls (Madame Alexander and Carroll), Steiff animals and books.

Mason's Tennis Mart **$$$**
56 East 53rd Street between Madison and Park Avenues, 755-5805
This tennis shop stocks a decent selection of racquets and gear for kids ages 5 and up.

Maternity Works **$**
16 West 57th Street between Fifth and Sixth Avenues, 3rd floor, 399-9840
www.maternitymall.com, www.babystuff.com
Find discounted Mimi, Motherhood and A Pea in the Pod maternity basics at this outlet-style maternity store.

Maxilla and Mandible
451 Columbus Avenue between 81st and 82nd Streets, 724-6173
www.maxillaandmandible.com
Your young scientist will love "the world's first and only steological store" stocked with bones and fossils and "world renowned natural history and science emporium museum quality specimens and reproductions."

Metropolitan Museum of Art Shop
113 Prince Street between Wooster and Greene Streets, 614-3000
151 West 34th Street at Herald Square (in Macy's), 268-7266
15 West 49th Street, Rockefeller Center, 332-1360
1000 Fifth Avenue between 80th and 84th Streets, 535-7710
The Cloisters at Ft. Tryon Park, 923-3700
LaGuardia Airport, Central Terminal WR1, 718 396-8594
www.metmuseum.org/store
This world-famous museum features a world-class gift shop with a terrific and bountiful selection of educational toys and books. The main store (located within the museum) stocks the most kids' stuff.

Mets Clubhouse Shop
143 East 54th Street between Lexington and Third Avenues, 888-7508
11 West 42nd Street between Fifth and Sixth Avenues, 768-9534
www.sportsavenue.com
What about those Mets? Get all your team paraphernalia and novelties in their official stores.

Michèle Saint-Laurent **$$$**
1028 Lexington Avenue between 73rd and 74th Streets, 452-4200
www.michelesaintlaurent.com
The elegant French maternity clothes in this shop will make you look and feel downright Parisienne. If you need something for a special occasion, custom designs are available.

Mimi Maternity **$$**
1021 Third Avenue between 60th and 61st Streets, 832-2667
1125 Madison Avenue at 84th Street, 737-3784
2005 Broadway between 68th and 69th Streets, 721-1999
www.maternitymall.com
This national chain offers great well-priced, fashionable basics for work and play as well as some high fashion labels.

Miss Pym **$$$**
By appointment only, 879-9530, www.misspym.com
Miss Pym is where to turn for custom-made, lovely special-occasion dresses for girls 0–12. Made of the finest materials, these dresses are elegant, sophisticated and lovely. Accessories, including crinolines, slips, purses, jackets, capes and hair ornaments, are also available.

Modell's **$$**
1293 Broadway between 33rd and 34th Streets, 244-4544
51 East 42nd Street at Vanderbilt Avenue, 661-4242

1535 Third Avenue between 86th and 87th Streets, 996-3800
300 West 125th Street between St. Nicholas and Eighth Avenues, 280-9100
www.modells.com
A great source for kid-sized (and grownup) sporting goods, gear and skates.

Mommy Chic **$$ to $$$**
235 Mulberry Street between Prince and Spring Streets, 646 613-1825
www.mommychic.com
Owner Angela Chew designs a line of chic maternity clothes, using mostly silk, cashmere and stretch fabrics with hand-done details (crochet and beading) from terrific basics to fabulous party clothes for the mother-to-be.

Mom's Night Out **$$ to $$$**
147 East 72nd Street between Lexington and Third Avenues, 744-6667
www.momsnightout.com
The expectant mom who needs an outfit for a special night out can rent one from this shop's own label maternity evening-wear and special-occasion clothing. If you prefer, you can have an outfit made for you to keep.

Morgane Le Fay **$$$**
67 Wooster Street between Broome and Spring Streets, 219-7672
746 Madison Avenue between 64th and 65th Streets, 879-9700
This boutique, known for its women's designs that combine romantic with interesting angles and shapes, also carries beautiful and unique party dresses for girls up to size 12.

Morris Bros. **$ to $$**
2322 Broadway at 84th Street, 724-9000
This New York institution has a very large selection of casual clothes for children and teens (which includes some adult sizes) and some layette. You can count on this store for a big selection of poplar brands (such as Quicksilver and And One for boys and Petit Bateau for girls) for your fashion-conscious kids. Morris Brothers also makes name labels (sew-in or iron-on) and is an official camp outfitter.

Moschino **$$$**
803 Madison Avenue between 67th and 68th Streets, 639-9600
Tucked within the Moschino store for adults are unique, very fashionable designer clothing and shoes for children ages 2 to 8.

Motherhood Maternity **$**
641 Sixth Avenue at 20th Street, 741-3488
901 Sixth Avenue at 33rd Street, Manhattan Mall, 868-9478
36 West 34th Street between Fifth and Sixth Avenues, 695-9106
16-18 West 57th Street between Fifth and Sixth Avenues, 399-9840
2384 Broadway at 86th Street, 917 441-4009
1449 Third Avenue at 82nd Street, 734-5984
www.motherhood.com
This is the place for excellent value in stylish maternity basics.

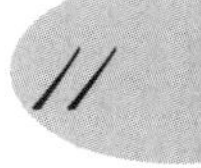

MTV Store
1515 Broadway at 44th Street, 846-5654, www.mtv.com
Visit this store for novelties, memorabilia and collectibles relating to your favorite MTV shows and personalities.

Museum of the City of New York Store
1220 Fifth Avenue at 103rd Street, 534-1672, www.mcny.org
This museum shop stocks a good selection of books and toys.

Museum of Modern Art Design Store
44 West 53rd Street between Fifth and Sixth Avenues, 767-1050 ext. 72
81 Spring Street between Crosby and Broadway, 646 613-1367
www.momastore.org
The Design Store offers a treasure trove of modern design for the home, art books and a good selection of educational books and toys for kids. While the Museum (located at 11 West 53rd Street) undergoes a major renovation, visit MOMA QNS in Long Island City, Queens.

Natalie and Friends **$$$**
205 East 60th Street between Second and Third Avenues, 759-9077
This boutique offers a great selection of fun, colorful, casual clothing, including plenty of hand-knits and accessories, for babies, girls up to size 16 and boys up to size 8 and features such labels as Lipstick, Submarine, Melina and Tina Neuman.

N.B.A. Store
666 Fifth Avenue at 52nd Street, 515-NBA1 (515-6221)
www.nba.com, www.wnba.com
If your kids love basketball, they will be in heaven in this megastore filled with NBA team paraphernalia and novelties. The store also hosts on-site special events.

NBC Experience Store
49th Street between Fifth and Sixth Avenues, in Rockefeller Plaza, 664-3700
www.nbcsuperstore.com
Visit this store for memorabilia, novelties, collectibles and T-shirts relating to your favorite NBC personalities and shows. Check the website for scheduled in-store celebrity events.

Neutral Ground
122 West 26th Street between Sixth and Seventh Avenues, 4th floor, 633-1288, www.neutralground.com

Games enthusiasts will love this shop filled with trading cards, role-playing games, sci-fi books and magazines, miniatures (and painting supplies), computer games and some board games. There is even a play area where the shop holds daily tournaments.

New York City Kids **$$**
495 Seventh Avenue between 36th and 37th Streets, 868-6925, www.nyck.net
This fashion-district store is a great source of contemporary, popular-label clothing and shoes with brands such as Guess, Calvin Klein, Nicole Miller, Kenneth Cole, Candies and Timberland. Dresses are available up to size 18, and boys suits are stocked for sizes 4–20. The store also carries christening gowns, Communion dresses and tuxedos for boys.

New York Doll Hospital
787 Lexington Avenue between 61st and 62nd Streets, 2nd floor, 838-7527
This shop is your source for antique dolls, stuffed animals and related collectibles. Repair services are available.

New York Exchange for Woman's Work **$ to $$$**
149 East 60th Street between Lexington and Third Avenues, 753-2330
www.nywomans-exchange.com
This not-for-profit store sells wonderful handmade items, including children's clothing, toys, blankets, quilts and dolls.

New York Firefighter's Friend **$$**
263 Lafayette Street between Prince and Spring Streets, 226-3142
www.nyfirestore.com
Your little firefighter will love this store filled with firefighter-motif clothing, toys and official-looking boots. For children and adults.

New York Public Library Shop
455 Fifth Avenue at 40th Street, 340-0849
476 Fifth Avenue at 42nd Street, 930-0641
www.thelibraryshop.com
A visit to the main branch of the New York Public Library, and photo op with the lions, warrants a visit to this well-stocked shop. The children's section contains books as well as some toys, decorative accessories and novelties. The 40th Street shop has a larger selection of children's books.

New York Transit Museum Gift Shop
Boerum Place and Schermerhorn Street, Brooklyn, 718 243-3060 (closed while under renovation)
Grand Central Terminal, 42nd Street, Main Concourse, 878-0106
Times Square Visitors Center, Broadway between 46th and 47th Streets
www.mta.info
Remember your commuter experiences with a treasure trove of New York transit system souvenirs, toys, novelties and other goodies.

Niketown **$$**
6 East 57th Street between Fifth and Madison Avenues, 891-6453
www.nike.com
Shopping here is a real experience. Totally devoted to athletes and those who just want the look, this store sells all types of Nike activewear, accessories and athletic shoes for children and adults.

Nine West **$$**
577 Broadway between Houston and Prince Streets, 941-1597
115 Fifth Avenue at 19th Street, 777-1752
341 Madison Avenue at 44th Street, 370-9107
757 Third Avenue between 47th and 48th Streets, 371-4597

675 Fifth Avenue at 53rd Street, 319-6893
750 Lexington Avenue between 59th and 60th Streets, 486-8094
901 Sixth Avenue at 33rd Street, Manhattan Mall, 564-0063
1230 Sixth Avenue at Rockefeller Center, 397-0710
1195 Third Avenue between 69th and 70th Streets, 472-8750
184 East 86th Street between Lexington and Third Avenues, 987-9004
2305 Broadway between 83rd and 84th Streets, 799-7610
425 Lexington Avenue between 43rd and 44th Streets, 949-0037
179 Broadway between John Street and Maiden Lane, 346-0903
2 Broadway at Bowling Green, 968-1521
www.ninewest.com
Your teen (and your wallet) will love the well-priced trendy shoes and accessories inspired by designer looks from this chain.

Nursery Lines **$$$**
1034 Lexington Avenue at 74th Street, 396-4445
This exclusive boutique carries fine imported classic clothing (up to size 4), linens and unique handpainted furniture. Custom linens and design services available.

Oilily **$$$**
820 Madison Avenue between 68th and 69th Streets, 628-0100
www.oililyusa.com
This Dutch label is known for its whimsical collection of signature multicolor and multi-patterned clothing for women and children up to age 12 as well as distinctive accessories and crib bedding.

Old Navy Clothing **$**
610 Sixth Avenue at 18th Street, 645-0663
150 West 34th Street at Broadway, 594-0049
300 West 125th Street at Eighth Avenue, 531-1544
511 Broadway at Spring Street, 226-0865
www.oldnavy.com

This relative of the Gap offers the same casual look at meaningfully lower prices. At these prices, it is easy to indulge your child's fashion whims for cool, trendy clothes and accessories.

Olive & Bette's **$$$**
1070 Madison Avenue between 80th and 81st Streets, 717-9655
252 Columbus Avenue between 71st and 72nd Streets, 579-2178
www.oliveandbettes.com
Teens, and petite moms, frequent this shop for trendy casual clothes and great jeans from such labels as Michael Stars, Bulldog, Theory and Diesel.

Original Levi's Store $$
3 East 57th Street between Fifth and Madison Avenues, 838-2188
750 Lexington Avenue at 59th Street, 826-5957
www.levi.com
This is the spot for all types of Levis jeans and other clothing. The mezzanine floor of the flagship 57th Street store is devoted to kids up to size 16. The Lexington Avenue store does not stock kids' sizes, but has plenty for teens. Both stores feature "create your own" departments (custom-fit jeans) for adults.

Origins $$
402 West Broadway at Spring Street, 219-9764
175 Fifth Avenue at 22nd Street, 677-9100
75 Grand Central Terminal, Lexington Avenue, 808-4141
44 West 50th Street, Rockefeller Center, 698-2323
2327 Broadway between 84th and 85th Streets, 769-0970
www.origins.com
Origins features natural products for skin, hair and body as well as bath accessories. There is an entire line just for babies, and your teens and tweens will love the delicious-smelling bath products and aromatherapy gum balls.

OshKosh B'Gosh $$
586 Fifth Avenue between 47th and 48th Streets, 827-0098
www.oshkoshbgosh.com
Famous for its overalls, this label offers an entire line of children's basics and casual clothes (up to size 16) and several styles of shoes (up to age 5).

Paper House $
1020 Third Avenue between 60th and 61st Streets, 223-3774
180 East 86th Street between Lexington and Third Avenues, 410-7950
269 Amsterdam Avenue between 72nd and 73rd Streets, 724-8085
This shop is stocked with party supplies, seasonal decorations, wrapping papers and party paraphernalia.

Papoose $$$
311 East 81st Street between First and Second Avenues, 639-9577
This lovely shop carries fine European, classically-inspired-yet-modern clothing and accessories for children 0–8.

Paragon Athletic Goods $$
867 Broadway at 18th Street, 255-8036, www.paragonsports.com
Since 1908, this huge emporium has been selling sporting goods and outdoor/camping supplies for all ages, including a large selection of sporting goods and activewear for children.

Party City **$**
38 West 14th Street between Fifth and Sixth Avenues, 271-7310
www.partycity.com
You can find everything you need for a great party at Party City, including paper goods featuring your child's favorite characters.

Patagonia **$$ to $$$**
101 Wooster Street between Prince and Spring Streets, 343-1776
426 Columbus Avenue between 80th and 81st Streets, 917 441-0011
www.patagonia.com
This high-end outdoor specialist for adults also carries a great line of high-performance and good-looking outerwear for children.

Paul and Shark **$$$**
772 Madison Avenue between 66th and 67th Streets, 452-9868
www.paulshark.it
This is Italian preppy at its most high tech. With a nautical spin (think yachting), this venerable Italian label offers high performance outerwear (in advanced high-tech fabrics) and very stylish casual clothing for men, women and boys (sizes 4–8).

Paul Mole
1031 Lexington Avenue at 74th Street, 2nd floor, 535-8461
For 80 years, barbers at this barbershop have cut and styled the hair of Upper East Side adults and children.

Payless Shoe Source **$**
34 East 14th Street at Union Square, 924-1492
1 Herald Square at 34th Street and Sixth Avenue, 947-0306
484 Eighth Avenue at 34th Street, 594-5715
590 Fifth Avenue between 47th and 48th Streets, 398-3823
250 West 57th Street at Broadway, 586-8625
www.paylessshoesource.com
As the name suggests, this is your source for very inexpensive contemporary shoes for the entire family.

A Pea in the Pod **$$ to $$$**
151 West 34th Street (in Macy's)
860 Madison Avenue at 70th Street, 988-8039
www.apeainthepod.com, www.maternitymall.com
This national chain carries a broad selection of well-priced, modern, chic maternity clothes and accessories.

Peanut Butter & Jane **$$ to $$$**
617 Hudson Street between Jane and West 12th Streets, 620-7952
This Village shop offers a terrific selection of mostly imported fun, upbeat and cool clothing (up to size 14/16 for girls and up to size 10 for boys), shoes and toys.

Pearl Paint $
308 Canal Street between Church Street and Broadway, 431-7932
www.pearlpaint.com
If you love arts and crafts, you will be in heaven in five floors of discounted art and craft supplies (for the serious artist as well as for the dabbler). Pearl also has a home-decorating center.

Pearl River Mart $
277 Canal Street at Broadway, 431-4770
200 Grand Street at Mulberry Street, 966-1010
www.pearlriver.com
Both Chinatown residents and fashionistas patronize this Chinese department store, which features a wonderful assortment of Chinese products, including silk pajamas, hats, purses, slippers, birdcages, novelties, housewares and games. The prices are great, too.

Peck & Goodie $$
917 Eighth Avenue between 54th and 55th Streets, 246-6123
In business for more than 50 years, this shop specializes in skates (in-line and ice), skateboards and accessories

Penny Whistle Toys
1283 Madison Avenue between 91st and 92nd Streets, 369-3868
448 Columbus Avenue between 81st and 82nd Streets, 873-9090
These cozy shops offer a selection of unique toys, art supplies and some books for younger children.

Peter Elliot $$$
1071 Madison Avenue at 81st Street, 570-1551
This women's boutique specializing in luxurious, casual clothing offers its signature cashmere sweaters and quilted and toggle jackets for children sizes 2 and up.

Peter Elliot, Jr. $$$
1067 Madison Avenue between 81st and 82nd Streets, 570-5747
This shop, complete with an on-site personal shopper and tailor and a play area for children, offers high-end (including special label cashmeres), mostly imported clothing and accessories for children sizes 2–12 as well as layette and infant clothing, gifts and novelties.

Petit Bateau $$ to $$$
1100 Madison Avenue at 82nd Street, 988-8884, www.petitbateau.com
This popular French brand has been making fine cotton garments since 1893 and now has a flagship store with a huge selection of adorable clothes for preemies and newborns and children up to size 18 (the larger sizes fit most moms). The T-shirts, which are available in a variety of styles and colors, are extremely popular with tweens, teens and adult women.

Pierre Deux **$$$**
625 Madison Avenue at 59th Street, 521-8012
www.pierredeux.com
You will feel transported to Provence in this home accessories and furniture shop featuring items made with traditional Provençal fabrics, pottery and pewter accessories and an especially popular quilted fabric diaper bag.

Plain Jane **$$ to $$$**
525 Amsterdam Avenue between 85th and 86th Streets, 595-6916
www.plainjanekids.com
This Upper West Side boutique offers unique vintage and retro-styled decorative accessories, furniture, bedding and layette for your child's room.

Planet Kids **$$**
247 East 86th Street between Second and Third Avenues, 426-2040
2688 Broadway between 102nd and 103rd Streets, 864-8705
www.planetkidsny.com
Planet Kids stocks everything you need for the new baby and young child, including equipment, furniture, layette, toys and books. The 86th Street store offers some clothing (up to size 4T); the Broadway store offers clothing up to teen sizes.

Pokemon Center
10 Rockefeller Plaza at 48th Street, 307-0900, www.pokemoncenter.com
Your Pokemon-loving child will adore this multimedia store dedicated to everything Pokemon, including the latest toys, cards and video games, with plenty of hands-on Pokemon.

Polo/Ralph Lauren **$$$**
867 Madison Avenue at 72nd Street, 606-2100
872 Madison Avenue at 71st Street, 606-2100 (Ralph Laruen Kids)
www.polo.com

Ralph Lauren creates his classically styled clothing for girls up to age 4, boys up to age 14, including cashmere sweaters, casual and dressy clothes and lots of logoed "polo" shirts. You will also find a good selection of suits and blazers for boys. Teens may want to shop in the adult department for expensive preppy looks or the Polo Sport store directly across the street for pricey activewear. The shop at 872 Madison brings the classic look to babies and children from newborns to age 4.

Pop Shop **$$**
292 Lafayette Street between Houston and Prince Streets, 219-2784
www.haring.com/popshop
This not-for-profit store for adults and children carries all things Keith Haring, including clothing and toys.

Sam Flax **$$$**
12 West 20th Street between Fifth and Sixth Avenues, 620-3038
425 Park Avenue at 55th Street, 935-5353
www.samflax.com
This very upscale and serious stationery and office- and art-supply store offers a number of items for your budding artist as well as lots of great notebooks, presentation books, folders and photo albums. Some of the more avant-garde office furniture and furnishings would work well in an older child's room.

San Francisco **$$**
975 Lexington Avenue between 70th and 71st Streets, 472-8740
This shop, which sells adult clothing, also offers nostalgic classic clothing and some toys for girls and boys to size 6x.

Sanrio
233 West 42nd Street between Seventh and Eighth Avenues, 840-6011
www.sanrio.com
This store is dedicated entirely to Hello Kitty and all her friends—Chococat, Pocchaco, Badtz-Maru and others. You can get everything from school supplies to room accessories to hats, bags and T-shirts. Fun for the boys, too.

Sansha **$$**
1717 Broadway, between 54th and 55th Street, 2nd floor, 246-6212,
www.sansha.com
This is the spot for serious dancewear and supplies for dancers of all ages.

Schneider's Juvenile Furniture **$$**
20 Avenue A at East 2nd Street, 228-3540
This is your source for everything for the new baby and young child, including equipment, layette, furniture and toys as well as furniture for your older child's room.

The Scholastic Store
557 Broadway between Prince and Spring Streets, 343-6166
www.scholastic.com/sohostore
Your family can spend hours exploring 5,500 square feet of Scholastic products with displays featuring characters (Clifford, Harry Potter, Magic School Bus and others) and hands-on activities.

Schweitzer Linen **$$$**
1053 Lexington Avenue between 74th and 75th Streets, 570-0236
1132 Madison Avenue at 84th Street, 249-8361
457 Columbus Avenue between 80th and 81st Streets, 799-9629
www.schweitzer-linen.com
For more than 35 years, this family-owned and -run company has provided New Yorkers with high quality, luxury linens, including classic items for the nursery and children's rooms.

Scoop **$$$**
532 Broadway between Prince and Spring Streets, 925-2886
1273-1277 Third Avenue between 73rd and 74th Streets, 535-5577
873 Washington Street at 14th Street, 929-1244
www.scoopnyc.com
This hip women's store features very expensive high-fashion clothing and accessories. Because the shop carries a lot of very tiny sizes, it is very popular among older teen girls. In addition to items by cutting-edge designers, the shop features T-shirts from popular labels such as Juicy. Scoop also carries a line of Petit Bateau items for infants.

Screaming Mimi's **$$**
382 Lafayette Street between Great Jones and 4th Streets, 677-6464
Teens adore the huge selection of vintage clothing, shoes (vintage, but never worn) and accessories (some vintage, some new) at this popular downtown boutique.

Sephora **$$**
555 Broadway between Prince and Spring Streets, 625-1309
119 Fifth Avenue at 19th Street, 674-3570
130 West 34th Street between Broadway and Seventh Avenue, 629-9135
1500 Broadway between 43rd and 44th Streets, 944-6789
Columbus Circle location opening in 2003
1129 Third Avenue at 67th Street, 452-3336
2103 Broadway at 73rd Street, 362-1500
www.sephora.com
This high concept cosmetics emporium, stocked with top brands of makeup, fragrances and bath products as well as an extensive collection of excellent private-label products, is the perfect destination for teenage girls (and their moms) who love to play with makeup. Preteens can have fun searching for the perfect lip gloss.

Shakespeare & Co. Booksellers
1 Whitehall Street between Bridge and Stone Streets, 742-7025
716 Broadway between Astor Place and 4th Street, 529-1330
939 Lexington Avenue between 68th and 69th Streets, 570-0201
137 East 23rd Street at Lexington Avenue, 505-2021
www.shakeandco.com
This New York institution, known for its knowledgeable staff, stocks a comprehensive selection of books for all ages.

Shanghai Tang **$$$**
714 Madison Avenue between 63rd and 64th Streets, 888-0111
www.shanghaitang.com
This department store imported from Hong Kong carries a unique selection of upscale clothing, accessories and housewares, as well as lovely and original children's clothing for boys and girls in sizes 2–12. The sweaters and Chinese jackets and pajamas are especially cool.

This Upper West Side source for comfort shoes (such as Birkenstock, Mephisto, Ecco) has finally opened an outpost for kids. The store features Stride Rite, New Balance, Keds, Timberland and more.

T. J. Maxx **$**
620 Sixth Avenue between 18th and 19th Streets, 229-0875
www.tjmaxx.com
As one of the largest off-price retailers in the country, T. J. Maxx is a great place to shop for brand-name and designer fashions for the entire family (from newborns through adults) and home accessories, as well as some toys and books.

Tod's **$$$**
650 Madison Avenue between 59th and 60th Streets, 644-5945
www.tods.com
Adults have become addicted to these high-quality, high-style casual driving moccasins, loafers and other shoes. Your well-heeled child can be shod just like mom and dad. The children's line is available in European sizes 23–35.

Tower Records
692 Broadway at 4th Street, 505-1500
383 Lafayette Street at 4th Street, 505-1166
721-725 Fifth Avenue at 56th Street (Trump Tower lower level), 838-8110
1961 Broadway at 66th Street, 799-2500
www.towerrecords.com
This chain, which pioneered the music superstore, offers up a terrific selection of music and other entertainment media for all ages and tastes.

Toys R Us **$$**
24-32 Union Square East at 15th Street, 674-8697
44th Street at Times Square, 800-869-7787
www.toysrus.com
It is hard to drag your children out of this store, which stocks an enormous selection of name-brand toys in every category you can imagine as well as strollers, car seats, bicycles and equipment of every type. The flagship store in Times Square, complete with Ferris wheel, is a total shopping experience.

Toys Tokyo
121 Second Avenue, between Seventh Street and St. Mark's Place, 2nd floor, 673-5424
This East Village shop specializes in vintage and collectible Japanese toys from the 1940s through the 1990s but also stocks Star Wars stuff, wind-ups and current favorites.

Train World
751 McDonald Avenue between Cortelyou Road and Ditmus Avenue, Brooklyn, 718 436-7072, www.trainworld.com
Your little engineer will have a field day in this large store full of electric trains and train stuff.

Trash and Vaudeville
4 St. Marks Place between Second and Third Avenues, 982-3590
Strictly for teens, this store has a treasure trove of funky, trendy clothing, shoes and accessories that live up to the promise of the shop's name.

Triple Five Soul
290 Lafayette Street between Houston and Prince Streets, 431-2404
www.triplefivesoul.com
Teen boys (but not necessarily their parents) love the hip-hop streetwear and accessories from this SoHo shop.

Trouvaille Française
By appointment only, 737-6015
If you are looking for that special christening gown, visit Muriel Clark for a unique, finely preserved, mostly English vintage Victorian-style selection, ranging in price from $125 to $500. You can also find antique table and bed linens here.

Tutti Bambini
1490 First Avenue between 77th and 78th Streets, 472-4238
This boutique is stocked with a great selection of contemporary and stylish clothing (a mix of European and American labels) and accessories for girls up to size 12, boys up to size 8/10.

United Colors of Benetton, see Benetton

United Nations Gift Center
United Nations, 46th Street at First Avenue, 963-7700
Complete a visit to the U.N. with a stop at the gift shop for such souvenirs as international dolls and flags and books.

Urban Outfitters
374 Sixth Avenue between Waverly and Washington Places, 677-9350
628 Broadway between Bleecker and Houston Streets, 475-0009
162 Second Avenue at 11th Street, 375-1277
2081 Broadway at 72nd Street, 579-3912
526 Sixth Avenue at 14th Street, 646 638-1646
www.urbanoutfitters.com
Teens love the hip, trendy, casual clothes for men and women and decorative accessories for their rooms.

Utrecht
111 Fourth Avenue between 11th and 12th Streets, 777-5353
www.utrechtart.com
Since 1966, Utrecht has been supplying quality, well-priced canvas, paints, papers, graphic arts and framing materials and other art supplies to New Yorkers. It's the perfect place to stock up for arts-and-crafts projects.

Veronique
1321 Madison Avenue at 93rd Street, 831-7800
www.veroniquematernity.com
This Carnegie Hill boutique offers an exclusive line of chic maternity clothing and accessories imported from Paris and Milan.

Versace
647 Fifth Avenue between 51st and 52nd Streets, 317-0224, www.versace.com
The fourth floor of the Versace store is home to the Italian label's stylish collection for children ages 2 to 12. The kids' clothes are mostly casual, and there are usually some shoes as well.

Vilebrequin
436 West Broadway at Prince Street, 431-0673
1070 Madison Avenue at 81st Street, 650-0353
www.vilebrequin.com
Men and boys (sizes 2–12) hit the beach via San Tropez with these festive, bright-colored and printed bathing suits from France.

Village Chess Shop
230 Thompson Street at West 3rd Street, 475-9580, www.chess-shop.com
Since 1972, this shop, located in the heart of Greenwich Village, not only specializes in chess sets from around the world, but also offers a friendly environment in which to play chess. Chess instruction is available by appointment.

Village Comics
214 Sullivan Street between Bleecker and West 3rd Streets, 777-2770
www.villagecomics.com
This large store has a huge selection of comics (new and vintage), collectibles, model kits, figures and trading cards for kids of all ages.

Village Kidz
3 Charles Street between Seventh and Greenwich Avenues, 807-8542
This Greenwich Village boutique offers a great selection of contemporary, casual and stylish clothing, shoes, layette and specialty toys.

Violet
203 East 75th Street between Second and Third Avenues, 879-3605
Violets are "Blue" at this uptown outpost of the East Village's custom-designed Blue label party dresses. This location offers chic, stylish ready-to-wear party dresses for pre-teens, teens and women.

Virgin Megastore
52 East 14th Street at Union Square, 598-4666
1540 Broadway between 45th and 46th Streets, 921-1020
www.virginmega.com
This British import offers a huge selection of music, DVDs, videos and other entertainment media for all ages and all tastes.

Warehouse of London
581 Broadway between Prince and Houston Streets, 941-0910
150 Fifth Avenue between 19th and 20th Streets, 243-7333
Teens will love the stylish, trendy, well-priced clothing from these downtown stores.

Wee Bee Kids
285 Broadway at Chambers Streets, 766-2147
93 Nassau Street at Fulton Street, 766-1494
A downtown source for everything for the new baby and young child, including equipment, layette, furniture and clothing for girls up to size 16 and boys up to size 20.

West Side Kids
498 Amsterdam Avenue at 84th Street, 496-7282
Not just a neighborhood toy store, this shop carries an excellent selection of unique and educational toys and books.

Wet Seal
670 Broadway at Bond Street, 253-2470
65 East 8th Street at Broadway, 228-6188
901 Sixth Avenue at 33rd Street, Manhattan Mall, 216-0622
www.wetseal.com
This national chain offers fashionable, trendy and hip brand-name and private-label well-priced clothes and accessories for fashion-conscious teen girls.

Whitney Museum of American Art Store
Madison Avenue at 75th Street, 570-3614, www.whitney.org
This museum shop has a children's section with a good selection of unique toys and books and some decorative accessories.

The Wicker Garden **$$$**
1327 Madison Avenue between 93rd and 94th Streets, 410-7001
This Upper East Side institution is the place to go for classic nursery furniture, decorative accessories and fine, imported, lovely layette and infant

clothing up to size 18 months. You can also choose from a selection of beautiful party dresses for girls up to size 2.

The Wiz
726 Broadway between Astor and Waverly Places, 677-4111
17 Union Square West at 15th Street, 741-9500
555 Fifth Avenue at 46th Street, 557-7770
212 East 57th Street between Second and Third Avenues, 754-1600
871-873 Sixth Avenue at 31st Street, 594-2300
1534-1536 Third Avenue between 86th and 87th Streets, 876-4400
2577 Broadway at 97th Street, 663-8000
www.thewiz.com
New Yorkers know that "nobody beats the Wiz." The sales staff can be somewhat aggressive, but The Wiz is still a good source for electronics for the family.

Yankees Clubhouse
393 Fifth Avenue between 36th and 37th Streets, 685-4693
110 East 59th Street between Park and Lexington Avenues, 758-7844
245 West 42nd Street between Seventh and Eighth Avenues, 768-9555
8 Fulton Street, South Street Seaport, 514-7182
www.sportsavenue.com
Do not worry if you cannot get to a game, because you can get team paraphernalia, souvenirs and novelties at the official Yankees store.

York Barber Shop
981 Lexington Avenue between 70th and 71st Streets, 988-6136
This local barbershop, in business for over 75 years, is a great place to take your child for a haircut.

Zany Brainy
112 East 86th Street between Park and Lexington Avenues, 427-6611
2407 Broadway between 88th and 89th Streets, 917 441-2066
www.zanybrainy.com
Offering "extraordinary toys for extraordinary kids," this chain stocks an extensive selection of high-quality, safe, non-violent, gender-neutral educational toys, craft kits and art supplies at value pricing.

Z'Baby Company **$$ to $$$**
996 Lexington Avenue at 72nd Street, 472-2229
100 West 72nd Street between Columbus Avenue and Broadway, 579-2229
www.zbabycompany.com
This lovely boutique carries a fantastic selection of charming, chic, mostly European clothing (including labels such as Sonia Rykiel and Kenzo), accessories and some shoes for boys and girls up to age 10.

Z Girl **$$$**

976 Lexington Avenue between 71st and 72nd Streets, 879-4990

This cool boutique carries hip, trendy clothes and some accessories for pre-teens and teens (cool moms can shop here too) in sizes 10 (girls) through adult sizes.

Zitomer and Zittles **$$ to $$$**

969 Madison Avenue between 75th and 76th Streets, 737-4480

www.zitomer.com

The emphasis is on service at this unique pharmacy and department store. The first floor has a large selection of high-end (including Kiehl's) skincare, bath products (including products especially for children and babies) and cosmetics. The second floor has a large selection of layette and fabulous children's and pre-teen clothing, from basics to imported to designer and from classic to trendy as well as some decorative accessories. The Zittles toy store on the third floor is an Upper East Side favorite and carries both commercial and unique and educational toys and books.

GENERAL RESOURCES

www.allny.com
www.citidex.com
www.cityguideny.com
www.citysearch.com
www.digitalcity.com
www.go-newyorkcity.com
www.metronewyork.com
www.nyc.com
www.nyctourism.com
www.nycvisit.com
www.nytoday.com
www.urbanbaby.com

SHOPPING INDEX

Neighborhood Locator

bkln	Brooklyn
es	East Side, East 23rd Street through and including East 60th Street
jfk	John F. Kennedy Airport
lga	LaGuardia Airport
lm	Lower Manhattan, below 23rd Street
qns	Queens
ues	Upper East Side, East 61st Street up to 110th Street
um	Upper Manhattan, 110th Street and above
uws	Upper West Side, West 61st Street up to 110th Street
ws	West Side, West 23rd Street through and including West 60th Street

Accessories and Novelties
Alphabets **lm, uws**
Alphaville **lm**
Chimera **lm**
Claire's Accessories **es, lm, ws**
Details **lm, uws**
Dylan's Candy Bar **es**
E.A.T. Gifts **ues**
Fossil lm, **ws**
G.C. William **ues**
Girlprops.com **lm**
Halloween Adventure **lm**
Ibiza Boutique **lm**
Infinity **ues**
It's a Mod, Mod World **lm**
Kar'ikter **lm**
Kate Spade Store **lm**
Kids Cuts **es**
Le Sportsac **lm, ues**
Lester's **ues**
Little Extras **uws**
Marsha D.D. **ues**
Pearl River Mart **lm**
Peter Elliot, Jr. **ues**
Pop Shop **lm**
P.S. I Love You **ues**
Reminiscence **ws**
Sanrio **ws**
Screaming Mimi's **lm**
Shoofly **lm, uws**
Tah Poozie **lm**
Tender Buttons **ues**

Activewear, Dancewear, Outerwear, Sporting Goods and Swimwear
Blades Board & Skate **lm, ues, uws, ws**
Capezio **es, ues, ws**
Danskin **uws**
Diesel **lm**
Eastern Mountain Sports **lm, uws**
Freed of London **qns**
Jodi's Gymwear **ues**
Kids Foot Locker **ues, ws**
Mason's Tennis Mart **es**
Modell's **es, ues, um, ws**
Niketown **es**
Paragon Athletic Goods **lm**
Patagonia **lm, uws**
Peck & Goodie **ws**
Princeton Ski Shop **lm**
Sansha, **ws**
Speedo Authentic Fitness **es, uws, ws**
Sports Authority **es, lm, ws**
Vilebrequin **lm, ues**

Art Supplies and Crafts
American Craft Museum Shop **ws**
Ben's For Kids **ues**
Brooklyn Museum of Art Shop **bkln**
Economy Handicrafts **qns**
Exploration Station **ues**
FAO Schwarz **es**
Hombons **ues**
Kate's Paperie **lm, ues**
KB Toys **um, uws**
Lee's Art Shop **ws**
Little Extras **uws**
M & J Trimmings **ws**
Pearl Paint **lm**
Penny Whistle Toys **ues, uws**
Sam Flax **es, lm**
Staples **es, lm, ues, uws, ws**
Stationery & Toy World **uws**
Tender Buttons **ues**
Utrecht **lm**
Zany Brainy **ues, uws**

Baby Gifts
ABC Carpet and Home **lm**
Cartier **es**
Christofle Pavillion **ues**
Gucci **es**
Henri Bendel **ws**
Hermes **ues**
Hoofbeats **ues**
Kirna Zabete **lm**
La Layette et Plus **ues**
MacKenzie-Childs, Ltd. **ues**
Peter Elliot, Jr. **ues**
Takashimaya **es**
Tiffany & Co. **es**
Trouvaille Française

Bookstores
Bank Street Bookstore **um**
Barnes & Noble Superstores **es, lm, ues, uws, ws**
Bookberries **ues**
Books of Wonder **lm**
Borders Books and Music **es**
City Store **lm, ws**
Corner Bookstore **ues**
Crawford Doyle Booksellers **ues**
Gryphon Bookshop **uws**

Integral Yoga Bookstore **lm**
Lenox Hill Bookstore **ues**
Logos **ues**
New York Public Library Shop **es, ws**
Rand-McNally Map Store **es**
Rizzoli Bookstores **ws**
Ruby's Book Sale **lm**
St. Marks Bookshop **lm**
Shakespeare & Co. Booksellers **es, lm, ues**
Strand Book Store **lm**
Teacher's College Bookstore **um**
The Scholastic Store **lm**

Clothing and Accessories
Abercrombie & Fitch **lm**
Albee's **uws**
Alskling **uws**
April Cornell **uws**
Au Chat Botte **ues**
Baby Depot at Burlington Coat Factory **ws**
Ballantyne Cashmere **ues**
Bambi's Baby Center **um**
Bambini **ues**
Barney's New York **lm, ues**
Bebe Thompson **ues**
Bergdorf Goodman **ws**
Berkley Girl **uws**
Betwixt **lm**
Bloomers **ues**
Bloomingdales **es**
Bombalulu's **lm, uws**
Bonne Nuit **uws**
Bonpoint **ues**
Brooks Brothers **es, lga, ws**
Bu and the Duck **lm**
Bunnies Children's Department Store **lm**
Burberry **es, lm**
BuyBuy Baby **ws**
Calypso Enfants & Bébé **lm**
Calypso **lm, ues**
Canal Jean Co. **lm**
Catimini **ues**
Century 21 **bkln, lm**
Children's Place **lm, ues, um, uws, ws**
Chimera **lm**
Chocks **lm**
C.J. Laing **ues**
Conway Stores **es, lm, ws**
Cradle & All **ues**

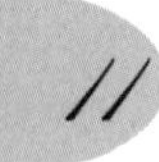

Crembebe **lm**
Daffy's **es, lm, ws**
Dave's Army & Navy Store **lm**
Diesel **es**
Dinosaur Hill **lm**
Farmers Daughter and Son **es**
First & Second Cousin **lm**
Flora and Henri **ues**
G.C. William **ues**
Gap **es, lm, ues, uws, ws**
Geiger **es**
Granny Made **uws**
The Green Onion **bkln**
Greenstone's **uws**
Greenstone's, too **ues**
Gymboree Store **ues, uws**
H & M **lm, ws**
Henri Bendel **ws**
Hermes **ues**
Hoyt & Bond **bkln**
Ibiza Boutique **lm**
Infinity **ues**
Jacadi **ues**
Jay Kos **ues**
Judy's Fancies
Julian & Sara **lm**
Jumpin' Julia's **bkln**
Just for Tykes **lm**
Kidding Around **lm**
Kidstown **lm**
Kirna Zabete **lm**
Kmart Stores **lm, ws**
La Layette et Plus **ues**
Lacoste **es**
Laura Ashley **uws**
Leeper Kids **es**
Lester's **ues**
Lilliput **lm**
Little Folks **lm**
Lord & Taylor **ws**
Loro Piana **ues**
Lucky Brand Dungarees **lm, uws**
Macy's Herald Square **ws**
Magic Windows **ues**
Malo **lm, ues**
Marsha D.D. **ues**
Miss Pym
Morgane Le Fay **lm, ues**
Morris Bros. **uws**
Moschino **ues**
Natalie and Friends **es**
New York City Kids **ws**

New York Exchange for Woman's Work **es**
Nursery Lines **ues**
Oilily **ues**
Old Navy Clothing **lm, um, ws**
Original Levi's Store **es**
Osh Kosh B'Gosh **ws**
Papoose **ues**
Paul and Shark **ues**
Peanut Butter & Jane **lm**
Pearl River Mart **lm**
Peter Elliot **ues**
Peter Elliot, Jr. **ues**
Petit Bateau **ues**
Planet Kids **ues, uws**
Polo/Ralph Lauren **ues**
Pop Shop **lm**
Prince & Princess **ues**
Rain or Shine General Store **es**
Ralph Lauren (see Polo) **ues**
Reminiscence **ws**
Replay **lm**
Robin's Nest **ues**
Saks Fifth Avenue **es**
San Francisco **ues**
Scoop **lm, ues**
Shanghai Tang **ues**
Small Change **ues**
Sotto Baby **lm**
Space Kiddets **lm**
Spring Flowers **ues**
The Stork Club **lm**
Syms **es, lm**
T.J. Maxx **lm**
Takashimaya **es**
Talbots Kids & Babies **ues**
Terra Verde **lm**
Tigers, Tutu's & Toes **lm**
Trouvaille Française
Tutti Bambini **ues**
Versace **es**
Village Kidz **lm**
Wee Bee Kids **lm**
The Wicker Garden **ues**
Z'Baby Company **ues, uws**
Z Girl **ues**
Zitomer and Zittles **ues**

Comics/trading cards
Alex's MVP Cards **ues**
Chameleon Comics **lm**
Collector's Universe **ws**
Cosmic Comics **es**
Forbidden Planet **lm**
Funny Business Comics **uws**
Gotham City Comics **ues**
It's "A" Nother Hit **ws**
Jim Hanley's Universe **ws**
Manhattan Comics and Cards **lm**
Neutral Ground **ws**
Pokemon Center **ws**
St. Mark's Comics **lm**
Village Comics **lm**

Cosmetics/bath accessories
Avon Salon & Spa **es**
Bath & Bodyworks **es, lm, ues, ws**
Bath Island **uws**
Bed Bath & Beyond **lm, ues**
The Body Shop **es, lm, um, ues, uws, ws**
Clyde's **ues**
Details **lm, uws**
Fresh **lm, ues**
H2O+ **es, lm**
Kiehl's **lm**
Origins **es, lm, uws, ws**
Sephora **lm, ues, uws, ws**
Shu Uemura **lm**
Zitomer **ues**

Dollhouses and Dollhouse Accessories
FAO Schwarz **es**
Iris Brown's Victorian Doll Shop **es**
Manhattan Dollhouse **lm**
New York Doll Hospital **ues**
Tiny Doll House **ues**

Equipment
Albee's **uws**
Au Chat Botte **ues**
Baby Depot at Burlington Coat Factory **ws**
Bambi's Baby Center **um**
Bunnies Children's Department Store **lm**
BuyBuy Baby **ws**
Granny's Rentals
Jacadi **ues**
Just for Tykes **lm**
Kidstown **lm**
Kmart Stores **lm, ws**
Little Folks **lm**
Planet Kids **ues, uws**
Schneider's Juvenile Furniture **lm**

Toys R Us **lm, ws**
Wee Bee Kids **lm**

Furniture and/or Decorative Accessories
ABC Carpet and Home **lm**
Albee's **uws**
Art & Tapisserie **ues**
Au Chat Botte **ues**
Baby Depot at Burlington Coat Factory **ws**
Bambi's Baby Center **um**
Barney's New York **ues**
A Bear's Place Inc. **ues**
Bed Bath & Beyond **lm, ues**
Bellini Juvenile Designer Furniture **ues**
Bergdorf Goodman **ws**
Bombalulu's lm, **uws**
Bu and the Duck **lm**
Bunnies Children's Department Store **lm**
BuyBuy Baby **ws**
Chelsea Kids Quarters **lm**
Cradle & All **ues**
Crate & Barrel **es, lm**
Details lm, **uws**
E.A.T. Gifts **ues**
Ethan Allen **es, ues, uws**
The Gazebo **ues**
Girlprops.com **lm**
Gracious Home **ues, uws**
Granny Made **uws**
Granny's Rentals
The Green Onion **bkln**
Guggenheim (Solomon R.) Museum **ues**
Jacadi **ues**
Just for Tykes **lm**
Kar'ikter **lm**

Kids Supply Co. **ues**
Kidstown **lm**
La Layette et Plus **ues**
Laura Beth's Baby Collection
Little Extras **uws**
Little Folk Art **lm**
Little Folks **lm**
MacKenzie-Childs, Ltd. **ues**
Magic Windows **ues**
Nursery Lines **ues**
Pierre Deux **es**
Plain Jane **uws**
Planet Kids **ues, uws**
Promises Fulfilled **ues**
Rain or Shine General Store **es**
Schneider's Juvenile Furniture **lm**
Space Kiddets **lm**
T.J. Maxx **lm**
Terra Verde **lm**
The Terrence Conran Shop **es**
Wee Bee Kids **lm**
The Wicker Garden **ues**

Gadgets and Electronics
Brookstone **jfk, lga, ws**
Hammacher Schlemmer **es**
J & R Music World **lm**
Radio Shack **es, lm, ues, uws, ws**
The Sharper Image **lm, ues, ws**
Staples **es, lm, ues, uws, ws**
The Wiz **es, lm ues, uws, ws**

Games and Hobbies
America's Hobby Center **lm**
Chess Forum **lm**
Chess Shop **lm**
Compleat Strategist **es**
Exploration Station **ues**
FAO Schwarz **es**
Game Show **lm, ues**
Games Workshop **lm**
Jan's Hobby Shop **ues**
Maxilla and Mandible **uws**
Neutral Ground **ws**
Red Caboose **ws**
Star Magic **lm, ues**
Stuyvesant Trains & Hobbies **lm**
Train World **bkln**
Village Chess Shop **lm**

Haircuts
Astor Place Hair Designers **lm**
Cozy's Cuts for Kids **ues, uws**
Kids Cuts **es**
Paul Mole **ues**
SuperCuts
York Barber Shop **ues**

Layette
Albee's **uws**
Au Chat Botte **ues**
Baby Depot at Burlington Coat Factory **ws**
Bambini **ues**
Bambi's Baby Center **um**
Bebe Thompson **ues**
Bergdorf Goodman **ws**
Bloomingdales **es**
Bonne Nuit **uws**
Bonpoint **ues**

Bunnies Children's Department Store **lm**
BuyBuy Baby **ws**
Calypso Enfants & Bébé **lm**
Catimini **ues**
Century 21 **bkln, lm**
Chocks **lm**
Conway Stores **es, lm, ws**
Cradle & All **ues**
Daffy's es, lm, **ws**
Dinosaur Hill **lm**
Flora and Henri **ues**
Gracious Home **ues, uws**
Granny Made **uws**
The Green Onion **bkln**
Hoofbeats **ues**
Jacadi **ues**
Julian & Sara **lm**
Kidstown **lm**
La Layette et Plus **ues**
Lester's **ues**
Lilliput **lm**
Little Folks **lm**
Lord & Taylor **ws**
Macy's Herald Square **ws**
Magic Windows **ues**
Morris Bros. **uws**
Peter Elliot, Jr. **ues**
Petit Bateau **ues**
Plain Jane **uws**
Planet Kids **ues, uws**
Prince & Princess **ues**
Robin's Nest **ues**
Saks Fifth Avenue **es**
Schneider's Juvenile Furniture **lm**
Space Kiddets **lm**
Spring Flowers **ues**
The Stork Club **lm**
Syms **es, lm**
Takashimaya **es**
Terra Verde **lm**
Toys R Us **lm, ws**
Village Kidz **lm**
Wee Bee Kids **lm**
The Wicker Garden **ues**
Zitomer and Zittles **ues**

Linens
ABC Carpet and Home **lm**
Barney's New York **ues**
Bed Bath & Beyond **lm, ues**
Bellini Juvenile Designer Furniture **ues**
Bergdorf Goodman **ws**
Chelsea Kids Quarters **lm**
E. Braun & Co., Inc. **ues**
Frette **ues**
Gracious Home **ues, uws**
Jacadi **ues**
Just for Tykes **lm**
Kids Supply Co. **ues**
La Layette et Plus **ues**
Laura Beth's Baby Collection
Leron **ues**
Nursery Lines **ues**
Plain Jane **uws**
Porthault Linens **ues**
Pratesi **ues**
Rain or Shine General Store **es**
Schweitzer Linen **ues, uws**
Trouvaille Française

Magic
Abracadabra **lm**
Halloween Adventure **lm**
Tannen's Magic Company **ws**

Maternity
Barney's New York **ues**
Bloomingdales **es**
Cadeau **lm**
Just for Tykes **lm**
Liz Lange **ues**
Macy's Herald Square **ws**
Maternity Works **ws**
Michèle Saint-Laurent **ues**
Mimi Maternity **es, ues, uws**
Mommy Chic **lm**
Mom's Night Out **ues**
Motherhood Maternity **lm, ues, uws, ws**
A Pea in the Pod **ues, ws**
Pumpkin Maternity **lm**
Veronique **ues**

Museum Stores
American Craft Museum Shop **ws**
American Museum of Natural History Store **uws**
Brooklyn Museum of Art Shop **bkln**
Children's Museum of Manhattan Store **uws**
Cooper-Hewitt National Design Museum Shop **ues**
Guggenheim (Solomon R.) Museum **ues**
Jewish Museum Store **ues**
Lincoln Center Performing Arts Gift Shop **uws**

Metropolitan Museum of Art Shop **lga, lm, ues, um, ws**
Museum of Modern Art Design Store **lm, ws**
Museum of the City of New York Store **ues**
New York Public Library Shop **es, ws**
New York Transit Museum Gift Shop **bkln, es**
United Nations Gift Center **es**
Whitney Museum of American Art Store **ues**

Music
Borders Books and Music **es**
HMV **es, um, ws**
J & R Music World **lm**
Lincoln Center Performing Arts Gift Shop **uws**
Manny's Music **ws**
Tower Records **es, lm, uws**
Virgin Megastore **lm, ws**

Party Goods
The Balloon Man **uws**
Dylan's Candy Bar **es**
E.A.T. Gifts **ues**
FAO Schwarz **es**
Paper House **es, ues, uws**
Party City **lm**
Stationery & Toy World **uws**

Resale
Children's Resale **ues**
Good Byes Children's Resale Shop **ues**
Jane's Exchange **lm**

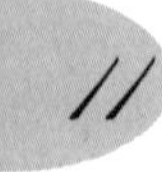

Shoes
Bambini **ues**
Bombalulu's **lm, uws**
Bonpoint **ues**
Bu and the Duck **lm**
Calypso **lm, ues**
Century 21 **bkln, lm**
Daffy's **es, lm, ws**
David Z **lm, ws**
East Side Kids **ues**
G.C. William **ues**
Galo Shoes **ues**
Great Feet **ues**
The Green Onion **bkln**
Gucci **es**
Harry's Shoes **uws**
Hoyt & Bond **bkln**
Jacadi **ues**
Jumpin' Julia's **bkln**
Juno **lm**
Kids Foot Locker **ues, ws**
Kmart Stores **lm, ws**
Lester's **ues**
Lilliput **lm**
Little Eric **ues**
Macy's Herald Square **ws**
Moschino **ues**
New York City Kids **ws**
Niketown **es**
Nine West **es, lm, ues, uws, ws**
Osh Kosh B'Gosh **ws**
Payless Shoe Source **lm, ws**
Peanut Butter & Jane **lm**
Prada **es, ues, ws**
Replay **lm**
Shoofly **lm, uws**
Skechers **lm, uws, ws**
Space Kiddets **lm**
Spring Flowers **ues**
Steve Madden **lm, ues, uws, ws**
Syms **es, lm**
Tigers, Tutu's & Toes **lm**
Timberland **ues**
Tip Top Kids Shoes **uws**
Tod's **es**
Versace **es**
Village Kidz **lm**
Z'Baby Company **ues, uws**

Stationery
Hyde Park Stationers **ues**
Kate's Paperie **lm, ues**
Sam Flax **es, lm**
Staples **es, lm, ues, uws, ws**

Teens
Abercrombie & Fitch **lm**
Adidas Originals **lm**
A/X Armani Exchange **es, lm**
Banana Republic **es, lm, ues, uws, ws**
Barney's New York **lm, ues**
Bath & Bodyworks **es, lm ues, ws**
Bath Island **uws**
Bebe **es, lm, ues**
Benetton **es, lm, ues**
Betsey Johnson **es, lm, ues, uws**
Bloomingdales **es**

The Body Shop **es, lm, ues, um, uws, ws**
Burberry **es, lm**
Calypso **lm, ues**
Canal Jean Co. **lm**
Century 21 **bkln, lm**
Club Monaco **es, lm, ues, uws**
Clyde's **ues**
Contempo Casuals **lm**
Crush—Hip Stuff You'll Want **ues**
Diesel **es, lm**
DKNY **es, lm**
Dollhouse **lm**
Earl Jeans **lm**
Eclipse **lm**
Express **es, lm, uws, ws**
Filene's Basement **lm, uws**
Fossil **lm, ws**
French Connection **lm, uws, ws**
Fresh **lm, ues**
G.C. William **ues**
Gap **es, lm, ues, uws, ws**
Guess? **lm**
H & M **lm, ws**
H2O+ **es, lm**
Infinity **ues**
J. Crew **lm, ws**
Joyce Leslie **lm**
Kate Spade Store **lm**
Kenneth Cole **es, lm, uws, ws**
Kiehl's **lm**
Lacoste **es**
Le Chateau **lm, ws**
Lester's **ues**
Lilliput **lm**
Lucky Brand Dungarees **lm, ues, uws**
Macy's Herald Square **ws**
Magic Windows (M.W. Teen) **ues**
Mandee **uws**
Marsha D.D. **ues**
Morris Bros. **uws**
Nine West **es, lm, ues, uws, ws**
Olive & Bette's **ues, uws**
Original Levi's Store **es**
Origins **es, lm, uws, ws**
Petit Bateau **ues**
Planet Kids **uws**
Polo/Ralph Lauren **ues**
Reminiscence **ws**
Ricky's **es, lm, ues, uws, ws**
Saks Fifth Avenue **es**
Scoop **lm, ues**
Screaming Mimi's **lm**
Sephora **lm, ues, uws, ws**
Shu Uemura **lm**
Sisley **lm, uws**
Skechers **lm, uws, ws**
Space Kiddets **lm**
Steve Madden **lm, ues, uws, ws**
Strawberry **es, lm, ws**
Stussy **lm**
T.J. Maxx **lm**
Trash and Vaudeville **lm**
Triple Five Soul **lm**
Urban Outfitters **lm, uws**
Violet **ues**
Warehouse of London **lm**
Wet Seal **lm, ws**
Z Girl **ues**

Theme Stores
CBS Store **ws**
City Store **lm, ws**
Disney Store **es, uws, ws**
Fire Zone **ws**
MetsClubhouse Shop **es, ws**
MTV Store **ws**
N.B.A. Store **ws**
NBC Experience Store **ws**
New York Firefighter's Friend **lm**
Sanrio **ws**
Yankees Clubhouse Shop **es, lm, ws**

Toys and/or Books
Albee's **uws**
Alex's MVP Cards **ues**
Alphabets **lm, uws**
Alphaville **lm**
American Craft Museum Shop **ws**
American Museum of Natural History Store **uws**
Art & Tapisserie **ues**
Bambi's Baby Center **um**
Bank Street Bookstore **um**
A Bear's Place Inc. **ues**
Bebe Thompson **ues**
Bed Bath & Beyond **lm, ues**
Big City Kite Company **ues**
Big Fun Toys **lm**
Bombalulu's **lm, uws**
Bonne Nuit **uws**
Books of Wonder **lm**
Brooklyn Museum of Art Shop **bkln**
BuyBuy Baby **ws**
Calypso Enfants & Bébé **lm**

Children's General Store **es, ues**
Children's Museum of Manhattan Store **uws**
Chimera **lm**
Classic Toys **lm**
Clyde's **ues**
Cooper-Hewitt National Design Museum Shop **ues**
Cozy's Cuts for Kids **ues, uws**
Crembebe **lm**
Daffy's **es, lm, ws**
Dinosaur Hill **lm**
E.A.T. Gifts **ues**
Enchanted Forest **lm**
FAO Schwarz **es**
First & Second Cousin **lm**
Forbidden Planet **lm**
Geppetto's Toybox **lm**
The Green Onion **bkln**
Guggenheim (Solomon R.) Museum **ues**
Homboms **ues**
Hoyt & Bond **bkln**
Hyde Park Stationers **ues**
Ibiza Boutique **lm**
It's a Mod, Mod World **lm**
Jewish Museum Store **ues**
Julian & Sara **lm**
Just for Tykes **lm**
KB Toys **um, uws**
Kidding Around **lm**
Kids Cuts **es**
Kidstown **lm**
Kmart Stores **lm, ws**
Lilliput **lm**
Little Extras **uws**
Little Folks **lm**
Lord & Taylor **ws**
Macy's Herald Square **ws**
Mary Arnold Toys **ues**
Metropolitan Museum of Art Shop **lga, lm, ues, um, ws**
Museum of Modern Art Design Store **lm, ws**
Museum of the City of New York Store **ues**

New York Exchange for Woman's Work **es**
New York Public Library Shop **es, ws**
New York Transit Museum Gift Shop **bkln, es**
Peanut Butter & Jane **lm**
Penny Whistle Toys **ues, uws**
Planet Kids **ues, uws**
Pokemon Center **ws**
Pop Shop **lm**
Promises Fulfilled **ues**
Rain or Shine General Store **es**
Reminiscence **ws**
San Francisco **ues**
Schneider's Juvenile Furniture **lm**
Sotto Baby **lm**
Space Kiddets **lm**
Star Magic **lm, ues**
Stationery & Toy World **uws**
Syms **es, lm**
T.J. Maxx **lm**
Terra Verde **lm**
The Terrence Conran Shop **es**
Toys R Us **lm, ws**
Toys Tokyo **lm**
Village Kidz **lm**
West Side Kids **uws**
Whitney Museum of American Art Store **ues**
Zany Brainy **ues, uws**
Zitomer and Zittles **ues**

Vintage

Crush—Hip Stuff You'll Want **ues**
Reminiscence **ws**
Screaming Mimi's **lm**
Space Kiddets **lm**
Trouvaille Française

Watches

Fossil **lm, ws**
G-Factory **lm**
Swatch **es, lm, uws**

Chapter 12

The Playdating Game

City kids do not typically run out of the house after school to play with the other kids on the block. While some kids are lucky enough to have playrooms in their building or a playground on their block, most city children see their friends during scheduled playdates. Even for the most socially adept adult, the world of playdating, and its attendant etiquette, is elusive at best. There are no official rules, nor is there a resource to which we can direct you for the up-to-the-minute protocol. Instead, we conducted a highly unscientific poll of Manhattan parents about playdate "issues" and present to you these thoughts.

Little Kids

There is no right or wrong way to organize playdates. The only rule of thumb is that the mission of the playdate is to set the scene for

the children to enjoy the experience of playing together and having a good time. The best advice we can give, therefore, is to be sensitive to the children's needs and feelings. Be prepared to supervise and intervene as necessary, but most of all, enjoy the opportunity to watch them at play. It will not be long before you are banished from their kingdom, at least for part of the day.

Be sensitive to the fact that in some households the parent may not make playdate arrangements.

▶ **Making a date.** Be sensitive to the fact that in some households the parent may not make playdate arrangements. When setting up a first playdate, ask with whom you or your babysitter should make plans to ensure that the plans you make end up on the family calendar and conflicting plans do not end up disrupting your schedule. Confirm playdates the evening before. Make sure that times and meeting locations, if outside the home, are clear.

▶ **Drop-off playdates.** Usually sometime around kindergarten, drop-off playdates (in which children go on playdates without their parent or caregiver) become the norm. It is important to discuss with the other parent (or caregiver) what the plans are, who will be supervising the children and what the pickup arrangements will be. If the playdate is to be at your house, let the other parent know your plans for the playdate, including what snacks or meals you will give the children, the activities you expect to do and whether you will be taking the children anywhere. Ask the other parent if the child has any special restrictions (no video games, TV, candy).

If the playdate is at the other child's house, confirm who will be picking up the children from school and how they will get to the next place, where they will be going and so forth. This way, for example, if you are not comfortable with the babysitter taking the children on the subway to a park in another part of town, you can do something about it. You should also let the other parent know about anything your child is not allowed to do (for example, go to the corner store without an adult) or to have (such as soda or candy) or any allergies your child may have.

Do not assume that all parents share your views, so if there is anything specific you want to discuss or there is something you think the other person may appreciate knowing when the playdate is at your house (for example that you will be going out and leaving the children with your sitter), do it before the playdate. Finally, if you are running late to pick up your child from someone else's house, call.

▶ **Remember to keep your child in mind when making plans.** A plan or activity that sounds fantastic to you may be awful for your child. For example, if you are invited along with another family for a day at their club and then to dinner, make sure your child will make it the full eight hours; otherwise, what sounds like a wonderful plan can turn into a horror show.

▶ **The blind playdate.** It is not uncommon to meet a person through a friend or discover that a colleague has a child of around the same age as yours. Making a date to all do something together seems a natural thing, as everyone will have someone to "play" with during your date. This logic, however, does not always apply. As you remember back to days of blind dating, you might approach these kinds of situations with some careful planning. With babies, this matchmaking usually works well, but for older kids it is the luck of the draw, so when scheduling your first date you might keep it short and sweet to avoid an awkward situation.

▶ **The playdate disaster.** There are playdates that seem to get off to a bad start or that dissolve into chaos and the kids begin to hit the wall, both figuratively and literally. Do not be afraid to call it quits before the time is up. If the child is not yet due to be picked up from your house, separate the children or introduce a neutral activity such as a video until things calm down. If the other parents were not there to witness the event, call and let them know what happened so they hear about the disaster from you first. It is much easier to reschedule a playdate that is not working out than to live through the event and potentially have two children who do not want to play together again.

▶ **Sharing.** Despite the fact that most parents battle to get their children to share or to let a playmate go first or take a turn on the computer, there are generous kids out there who like to give away their toys, clothing or whatever else is readily available. Though generosity is to be encouraged, you cannot allow your child to take home someone else's things or give away yours. Make sure to check with the parent or make arrangements to return the items after they have been "borrowed."

At the opposite end of the spectrum, if your child has trouble sharing, consider letting him or her put away special toys before the playdate with the understanding that items not put away must be shared.

▶ **Cleanup.** Nobody likes it but it is something we all need to help out with. Make sure that you let your children know you expect them to help, and if they are too young to take on the entire task themselves, show them how it is done.

▶ **Each family has different house rules.** Your child should be aware of that fact and be prepared to follow them. When a child comes to your house for the first time, let him or her know in advance any particular rules you may have, for example, no playing in the living room or no food in the bedroom. For small infractions simply let the child know that in your house the particular behavior is not permitted, and gently let him or her know you would appreciate it if next time he or she tries to remember. Remind your child that rules at someone else's house may be different from your rules and that he or she is expected to follow them. If, however, you find that a playdate in someone else's house leaves you or your child less than comfortable, try to schedule future dates at your house and avoid judgmental comments like, "I really don't think the kids should be playing Playstation all afternoon."

▶ **Nobody likes to get sick.** If your child has been under the weather, let the parent of the child he or she plans on visiting know. A choice in this situation is nothing less than a goodwill gesture and in some cases can make you a friend for life.

▶ **Shorter is better.** Children love to play, but a playdate that goes on too long leaves everyone unhappy. Whenever possible, err on the side of scheduling the playdate for too little rather than too much time. If the playdate is destined to be long (for example, a sleepover), try to have some backup activities to keep the children happy or be prepared to hang out with them for a while until they settle back into a better rhythm.

▶ **The terrible triad.** Threesomes are often difficult to handle, for adults as well as children. Too often, there is one child who feels left out and the playdate dissolves into a mess. If you have the choice, two or four children playing together works better than three. If there is no way around a triad, set some ground rules with the children at the beginning of the playdate so that everyone leaves with their feelings intact, and be prepared to be a referee.

▶ **Playdating lite.** As much as our kids may love playdates and as much as their having playdates gives us a break from having to be the sole source of a child's entertainment, it is truly not necessary to book a date for your child every day of the week. Children benefit from down time and sometimes need a break from the constant activity of a full schedule of school, classes or other programs, lessons, sports and playdates. It is also important for our children to learn to occupy and entertain themselves and play with their toys and games without the pressure of sharing and compromising.

Middle Schoolers

Once children reach the middle school years (grades five through eight), the world of playdates changes dramatically. First of all, the word "playdate" disappears from their vocabularies and is replaced by such notions as "having plans" or "hanging out" with friends. Second, these plans and hanging-out opportunities are no longer made by parents contacting each other and reviewing the calendars but rather are made by the children themselves. Third, the plans are often intended to include groups of kids getting together rather than structured one or two hour one-on-one dates. Fourth, the plans often involve the kids doing several different things and moving from place to place. Fifth, and perhaps most upsetting to parents, is that other than providing transportation, snacks and perhaps some spending money, parents are absolutely not included in the activities and are often specifically requested to be neither seen nor heard.

The middle school years, particularly from sixth grade on, are very complicated for parents and children alike. These tweens and young adolescents are anxious to get a taste of independence and seek to spend enormous amounts of unsupervised time with groups of friends. As parents, we know that they lack the skills, maturity and judgment to make all of their decisions for themselves and that it is inappropriate for them to be constantly cruising the city streets unattended. However, we also understand that in order for them to develop their street skills and sharpen their judgment, it is important for them to experience some modicum of independence. Finding a balance between unsupervised and supervised activities that is acceptable to children and adults is a challenge for all families, but one which is important for us all to deal with in a thoughtful, calm and deliberate way.

Finding a balance between unsupervised and supervised activities that is acceptable to children and adults is a challenge for all families, but one which is important for us all to deal with in a thoughtful, calm and deliberate way.

▶ **Making plans.** Perhaps the hardest thing for an adolescent to do is to make plans in advance. Adolescents relish living in the moment and the mere idea of committing to something other than spontaneously seems boring and old-fashioned. Additionally, in the quest to stay cool, kids are often reluctant to commit to an advance plan just in case something better comes along.

However, the lack of advance planning makes it difficult for families to make arrangements for picking up, dropping off or otherwise scheduling appointments for or supervising or transporting not only the adolescent, but other members of the household. While most parents will, whenever possible, make every reasonable effort to accommodate their children's social lives, it is also important for kids to understand that they operate within a family unit and their plans cannot always take precedence over the needs of other family members.

To deal with the battle between the kids and adults on the need for advance planning, some families set up basic parameters and contingency plans. For example, the child may be allowed to make spontaneous plans only on the weekend or on Friday afternoons, but not on other school days when there is homework or chores to be done. Or, the rule may be that the child can call a parent with a spur-of-the-moment idea, but if the parent cannot be reached to give permission, the child must stay with the original plans for that day. For instance, if the child regularly comes home on the school bus but wants to go to a friend's house instead, if the child cannot reach the parent for permission to go, she would have to forgo going home with her friend and come home on the school bus as originally planned.

► **Logistics.** Adolescents are notorious for making grandiose plans that totally disregard the logistics of executing those plans and for planning events and activities that do not actually materialize. When presented with a plan that seems to deny all logic, many of us automatically react by saying no to the idea. This immediate reaction usually results in a big fight between parent and child, often raising such familiar protests as "I'm never allowed to do anything," "everyone else can go," "you're not fair," "you don't trust me" and a litany of other complaints and grievances.

To avoid going down this path, a sage mother of several grown children advises that in many situations, the best strategy is to defer reacting and to say neither yes nor no when the plan is first raised, but to calmly wait it out ("hmmm," "let's see," or "let's wait until the details are worked out" are good delay tactics), because more often than not, the plan will fall apart before you are put to the test. Another method is to agree to the idea in principle, subject to determining that the details and specifics are realistic and appropriate (such as, "yes you can go to the party provided that the host's parents will be home"). And, should the plan actually

materialize, you have time to work out the logistics with your child as a condition to giving your permission for him or her to participate.

▶ **House rules.** As your child enters the teen years, he or she will likely have increasing freedom to go out without an adult, stay at home alone and spend time with groups of friends. For those times when your child has friends over (both in groups or one-on-one), it is extremely important to be very clear with your child about your house rules, particularly if the planned activities include boys and girls or use of the computer, the kids will be going out from or returning to your house as part of another plan, or the kids will be home without an adult present (even if only for a short time). Some things to consider in developing your house rules.

- Internet use. Be clear about time limits on computer use; what sites or chat rooms can or cannot be visited; your instant messaging rules; whether or not you will put parental controls on your computer; whether your child is allowed to create (and if so, what may be contained in) a "personal profile" that is posted on the Internet; and your rules on giving out personal information on the Internet.
- Phone calls. Be clear about time limits for calls and the times during which the phone can or cannot be used (during meals, after homework is done, before or after a certain hour); who can or cannot be called; and the rules concerning making long-distance calls. Since for some odd reason adolescents with cell phones consider their cell phones to be separate and distinct from the home land line and therefore potentially not subject to the house phone rules, be clear as to the rules for using cell phones (for calls or text messaging) in the house outside of regular "phone hours."
- Ordering things. Discuss whether and from which local establishments (restaurants, grocery store, pharmacy, video store) the kids are permitted to order (particularly if there is no adult home when the items will be delivered), whether the kids are permitted to order movies from pay-per-view services and, if so, any restrictions on what may be ordered.

- Going out. Be clear about when (daylight only? not before or past a certain time?), where and under what circumstances (getting permission first, particular agreed upon rules) children can go out on their own from your house. Make sure other kids have permission from their parents, too.
- Off-limits areas (or open-door-only areas) in the house (bedrooms, basement, terrace, building common areas) and off-limits activities (such as cooking, using the computer, video games or particular appliances or equipment, such as gym equipment, elaborate stereo or other media systems). Be clear about who can be where with whom, when and under what circumstances. This is particularly important in situations when boys and girls are in the house together (even if you are home!).
- Moving from place to place and checking in. Work out basic rules for calling in to parents (at particular intervals, upon arrival, before leaving, if plans change).
- Transportation. Be specific about what forms of transportation the child may use (walking, bus, subway, taxi, car service) and under what circumstances (time of day, with others, alone, only certain routes) the various means of transportation may be used.
- How many guests. Since adolescents prefer to travel in packs, it is important to be clear how many children are permitted in your home and whether and under what circumstances you permit co-ed groups at your home, both when there is an adult in the house and when there is not an adult in the house.
- Boys and girls. If boys and girls are in the house together, be specific about what activities are permitted and what activities are not permitted.

- Smoking, sex, alcohol, drugs and other substances. It cannot be emphasized enough that it is crucial to be very clear and specific with your child about your views, expectations and rules—both in your home and outside your home—for smoking; the use of drugs, alcohol and other substances; and sexual contact (from kissing to intercourse). Do not assume that your child "just knows" how you feel about these important issues, even if you have had general discussions about them in the past. Adolescents have short attention spans and even shorter memories, so regularly take the time to discuss and engage your child in conversation about the effects and consequences of substance use and sexual contact both in your own home and out in the world at large.

- Other families' rules. Since families all have different rules for their children, be clear about what your child may or may not do at others' homes when the other family has rules different from yours. For example, if the other child is allowed to go to the local pizza place without an adult but your child does not have permission to do that, make sure your child understands that he or she is subject to your rules, not those of the other parent.

► **Contact the other parents.** If your child has plans to attend a party or other gathering at someone's home or to participate in an event to be organized or supervised by other parents (such as attending a show, concert, sporting event, movie; visiting a theme park, sports facility; going to a restaurant or other establishment), no matter how much your child complains and tells you that you are treating him or her like a baby, be strong and make that phone call to the other parents to confirm details of the plans. If the plans are to be at the other child's home, confirm who (parent, older sibling, housekeeper or babysitter) will be home and whether someone will be home during the entire event, what activities are scheduled, whether the children are allowed to leave on their own and, if so, where they are allowed to go. If the plans involve an event outside of the home, confirm who will be supervising and how transportation and other logistics are being handled. If you are not satisfied that the party or event will be properly supervised, stand your ground and have your child decline the invitation.

Conversely, when you are on the receiving end of a call from another parent, do not be offended about getting such a phone call or feel that the other parent does not trust you with his or her child. Rather, welcome the call as an opportunity to have clear and open communication with the other parent and, if you do not already know that person, as an opportunity to become acquainted.

► **An escape hatch.** Unanticipated situations may arise where your child finds him- or herself in an uncomfortable situation that he or she would like to get out of. Since adolescents are extremely sensitive to how their behavior appears to their peers, they may be reluctant to stand up in front of their friends and announce that they want to go home. To avoid having your child feel stuck in a place he or she does not want to be and give your child an easy way to get extricated from a bad situation, many parents and children agree in advance to a "signal" that tells the parent "come and get me" without tipping off the other kids. For example, the child may call a parent and use an agreed-upon particular phrase or expression that provides a "reason" for the call and sounds innocuous to the child's friends but says it all to you (such as "I forgot my keys" or "I left my computer on"). Also, you can arrange to have your child call you at a specific time, at which point you can ask the questions and all your child has to do is respond. This allows your child not to have to initiate the call asking to be picked up.

► **The impossible years.** There is no doubt that living with your adolescent can try your patience and fortitude in every imaginable way. However, as parents, it is our job to do our best to help launch our children into adulthood. To that end, while we constantly remind them and ourselves that we are the adults and they are still children, we must also allow them the room and opportunity to grow up. And in that struggle to balance keeping them safe and letting them grow, it is important to take the time to enjoy these amazing, challenging, emerging, smart and wonderful people.

Chapter 13

About Birthdays

Making a birthday party for a child is like putting an exclamation point after the words "I love you." It is an opportunity to let your child know what a very important person he or she is. Birthdays are special events no matter how big or small, simple or elaborate the party may be. It is a time designated to celebrate the birthday child. It is no wonder children love birthdays. It is great to feel special, and if cake and presents are involved, all the better. Even a rough childhood can be sprinkled with happy birthday memories.

In the proverbial olden days, birthday parties used to follow a fairly predictable formula. Parties were typically held in the home of the birthday child. The guests arrived, party games were played, cake and ice cream were served, gifts were opened, loot bags were given out and good-byes were said. Parties rarely lasted more than an hour and a half. It was easy to stick to the golden birthday rule: keep it small, short, simple and moving.

Much has changed since the days when we had our own birthday parties. Parties have become bigger, grander and more sophisticated.

Not only are there facilities solely dedicated to housing children's parties, but almost all children's activity establishments will organize or accommodate a birthday party. Manhattan birthday parties have become big business, and with that has come an increase in both the expectations and requirements of children and parents for ever better birthdays.

Unfortunately, it is not always easy to avoid the temptation to keep pace with the level and type of birthday parties to which your child may have been exposed. On the other hand, it is more important for the birthday party you plan for your child to reflect your own family values than those of other families. It is up to you to set the tone and make the birthday special in the most appropriate way for your family.

The demands of busy schedules can make it hard to plan and organize birthday parties. There are many books on planning parties and there are even party planners for the younger set. Parties can be organized at any number of out-of-home locations, many of which will even supply you with invitations and order the cake.

What is the best party in town? Who is the hottest entertainer? The answers to questions like these depend on the age of your child, what time of year the party will take place and your own personal preferences. We will direct you to some wonderful resources for making your child's birthday special as well as give you some tips on getting it together. Whether you arrange it yourself or have someone else do it for you, getting it right starts with understanding what your child has in mind, exercising your own good judgment and planning with care.

It's My Party

▶ **Whose party is it?** Let your child and his or her interests provide the initial direction for the party. Planning a party can be a wonderful shared experience, and your child may enjoy planning it as much as attending the party. Consider the interests, ages and abilities of the guests as well as the personality and sociability of the birthday child. Be realistic about what the birthday child and the children attending can do. No one will have any fun if the activity is frustrating or not age appropriate or if the entertainment is incomprehensible or frightening to the audience. If your child has chosen a party that you know will not work for the age group, gently guide your child in another direction.

Do remember that a first birthday is really for the parents. Second birthdays create a great deal of excitement but are rarely remembered by the child. By the age of three, a child can anticipate and enjoy a birthday party, which can be the source of conversation for weeks. With each year thereafter, children take great pleasure in planning and hosting birthday parties, and become, as they mature and with your guidance, good hosts and hostesses.

▶ **Picking the date and time of the party should be made with the child in mind.** Too often, this detail of the party is determined by the schedules of busy entertainers and the availability of party spaces. It is important, however, to choose the timing of the party carefully. For younger children, many of whom nap, the time of day can be critical. A tired child, regardless of age, may rally for a party initially but is likely to fall apart long before the birthday candles are lit. Timing is also relevant for older children who have busy after-school schedules and homework.

There is no perfect time to have a party, but here are some things to think about when you make your plans:

- Many children leave the city on weekends.
- Parties on school nights that go into the evening may interfere with homework or after-school commitments.
- If your party will be occurring during mealtime hours, be prepared to serve the children a meal or you may end up with a group of hungry, cranky children. On the other hand, if you do not want to serve a meal, schedule the party for a reasonable time after the meal hour and before the next one.

- If your guests will have to travel across town, consider potential travel problems. There is nothing like trying to get to Rockefeller Center for a skating party on December 20 at 4:00 p.m.

Are Manhattan parents sabotaging their children's birthdays by going overboard on the guests? Sometimes. Smart mothers and fathers do their best to keep the numbers down, and when they cannot, to select an activity that engages the crowd and to enlist a lot of helpers.

Here are some thoughts on developing your guest list and determining how many people are appropriate for the party you have in mind:

◩ **The nature of the activity can limit or expand the guest list.** Some activities lend themselves to large groups (e.g., sports parties) while others work best for small gatherings (e.g., crafts parties). Once you get to the age of drop-off parties, large numbers of children become hard to manage and monitor, particularly if the party is in a place that is open to the public or does not have a separate party room. If you are taking responsibility for a lot of kids, make sure you can maintain security and have enough other adults around to keep track of everyone. If the group is very large, plan an activity, such as a gym party, that will engage children of different skill levels and attention spans and have backup for kids who do not want to participate.

◩ **Offer your child options.** Older children can be given the choice of different types of parties that would accommodate different numbers of children. For example, the child can choose among a gym party for a lot of children, a museum party for 12, five kids to a sporting event or three for a sleepover. A young birthday boy we know happily reduced the number of guests he wanted to invite when he was reminded that he would have to send a handwritten thank-you note for each gift he received.

◩ **Set a reasonable budget.** Parties in Manhattan are not cheap. When you add up the cost of everything from invitations to party favors, you can easily run up a birthday bill beyond your wildest dreams. Making your child feel special on his or her birthday does not require you to give him or her the moon and take out a second mortgage on your co-op.

◩ **Be aware of school birthday party policies.** Many schools have a specific policy regarding birthday invitations, the goal of which is to promote a sense of community and minimize the quotient of hurt feelings. If your school has a policy, by all means honor it. If it does not, you may want to consider following a typical policy, which is to either invite the whole class, keep the party single sex or invite less than half of the class. This type of policy prevents one or two children in a class from being left out. However you handle your invitations, be sensitive to the fact that children do discuss birthday parties in school and are very well aware of who has been or has not been invited.

◩ **Be prepared to deal with the siblings of your guests.** Many parents find themselves with more guests than they bargained for when their guests show up at the party with siblings. It is often difficult for some of your guests, whose parents work or who may not have a babysitter to watch a sibling during the party, to avoid bringing older or younger brothers or sisters. Depending on when and where the party is, this may or may not be a problem. Keep in mind that some facilities do charge for siblings, adding to the cost of the party.

Sometimes you can avoid the situation by timing the party to when siblings will be in school or by specifying that the party is a drop-off one. You may want to clarify with those parents who you think may have an issue whether they intend to bring siblings or to let them know that bringing siblings may not be feasible. In the latter case, you may want to arrange transportation to and from the party for the child to make it easier for the family. However you deal with the issue, know that you may potentially have additional guests of assorted ages, so have a plan, communicate with the parents of guests with siblings and bring an extra favor or two just in case.

◩ **Be alert to the composition of the group.** Many times we find ourselves in awkward party situations. Some examples: your daughter is having an all-girl ballet party but you feel funny not inviting the sons of your two close friends; everyone at your son's party is from his school except one friend from camp with whom he likes to play occasionally; or your daughter is having the whole class and some friends from last year's class, but wants to omit a friend from last year with whose parents you have become friendly. There are endless permutations of complicated situations, and, unfortunately, there are no official rules.

What to do? First and foremost, it is your child's birthday and, within the bounds of good manners, his or her wishes should prevail. Sometimes, however, birthday desires have to bend so as not to hurt the feelings of schoolmates or otherwise good friends. Your decision may depend in part on the personality of the child in question and the nature of the relationship you have with the family. In some cases it is best to err on the side of inclusiveness rather than exclusiveness and use the experience to talk to your child about empathy and kindness. If you do invite someone who will not know anyone at the party, be sure to introduce the child to the others and make sure that he or she is included in activities.

In other cases it may make sense not to invite a particular child or children. If you choose not to invite a child because, for instance, she would be the only girl at an all-boy hockey party, you can arrange for your child to have a separate birthday celebration, perhaps lunch or a special playdate, to mark the occasion. Whatever you choose, if your child is old enough to understand the issue, discuss the decision and its ramifications with your child. It may offer a useful opportunity to talk about your family values.

► **Répondez, s'il vous plaît.** Invitations should include instructions for the RSVP, including a date by which you want a response. Responses will allow you to get enough of whatever you will need for the party. Also, many party places require a head count in advance of the party so that they have enough staff on hand to run the party.

When parents call you about the party, it is a good time to inquire about any issues such as food allergies, special situations (such as how to handle a child with a fear of animals at a zoo party) and whether they intend, or are invited, to bring siblings. You may want to assist in organizing transportation, particularly if it is a drop-off party or at a distant location. You may be asked to give gift suggestions so be prepared and be careful not to give the same idea

out too many times. Most important, if you have not heard from a guest, call. Invitations have been known to be lost in the mail or thrown away by mistake.

▶ **Snacks, meals and birthday treats.** If you plan to serve a meal, keep it small and simple, because most kids simply do not eat much at a party. If you expect parents to stick around during the party, have some grown-up refreshments on hand. As for cakes, some of the best looking ones do not cut it when it comes to taste, at least as rated by kids. Simple is better, with lots of icing. Keep in mind, too, that those festive birthday candles can be dangerous when too close to loose hair or clothing.

If you plan to serve a meal, keep it small and simple, because most kids simply do not eat much at a party.

Food allergies have become more and more common among children. For some children, even the most traditional birthday treats can be forbidden. It certainly is not necessary to create a menu to address every guest's sensitivities, but it is a good idea to eliminate some of the most common problem foods like nuts, which also happen to be a choking hazard. If you are aware of the allergies of a particular child, be sure to contact the parents about what you are serving. You can either have special food on hand that the child can eat or ask the parents to send specially prepared safe food for the child, which you will serve when the children are eating.

▶ **Birthday presents.** It used to be customary to open gifts at the party. Most parties today do not include gift opening as an activity. Some disadvantages to opening presents during the party: perceived and actual differing gift values that create a sense of competition among the guests; receipt of duplicate gifts; uncensored remarks among the children; comments from the birthday child that may hurt the gift giver's feelings.

If you decide that these issues can be managed and want to make opening presents part of the event, set some ground rules ahead of time to ensure that all moves smoothly. Such rules might include asking your child to say something nice about, and say thank you for, each gift; letting the children know that only positive comments are appropriate; and announcing whether the children can play with the gifts once they are opened. Whenever you open the presents, remember to make a list of who gave each gift for the thank-you notes.

▶ **A word on thanks.** No matter how old your child may be, thank-you notes will require some effort on your part. You will either have to write them yourself or nag your older child to get them done. The trick is to make them as painless as possible while still making them meaningful. If your child is too young to write the note, he or she can decorate your note or a printed form note (with crayons, markers, stamps or stickers), write his or her name or put stamps on the envelope. If you use a computer, your child can participate in designing the note by choosing clip art or typing with your assistance. Older children can create their own notes on the computer or hand write a simple thank you.

▶ **Preserving your memories.** It seems like a silly thing to have to remind parents, but people do forget. Sometimes, even when parents remember the camera, they run out of film or battery power at the crucial moment. Whether you take pictures or video yourself, delegate the job to a friend or hire a professional, be clear about the images you want (e.g., candids or staged shots). If you want to hire a professional photographer or video service, check the parents' papers and with friends for referrals. Do not hesitate to ask for references and make sure that the assignment does not turn into a major movie production. The only lights you want shining on your child's face are those of the candles.

If you want to remember the way things looked before the festivities began, make sure to tell the photographer. It can be fun to photograph or video the different stages of the party. Planning, selecting items, set up, the party and the aftermath can all be documented and enjoyed at a later date. When developing your pictures, consider ordering an additional set so you can send pictures of your guests along with your thank you.

▶ **Bring a party to school.** Many schools allow parents to bring cupcakes or other special treats to school for a class party. If this is permitted at your child's school, be sure that you do whatever the children have come to expect from a school party. Contact the teacher to determine what to provide and how the party will be run. Some teachers allow parents to attend while others do not. If parents are not invited to join and you send in a camera, most teachers will be happy to take some pictures for you. Never assume anything, and ask your child for details about customary practice. One parent we know was put to shame by her daughter for not providing a cupcake for the nursery school director. The teachers had never mentioned this custom, but her daughter was clear about the routine.

▶ **A basic birthday checklist.** Most of the birthday books and articles on birthday party planning list many suggestions for creating a successful party that you should certainly peruse. Some basics to put on your birthday checklist:

- Invitations. Mail invitations rather than distributing them in class. This ensures that the invitations will make it home and can prevent hurt feelings among children who are not being invited. Allow approximately three weeks advance notice for a party, because city kids tend to have very full social calendars. Include details about the party on the invitation such as: attire (sneakers, dress for a mess, outdoor gear); directions (cross streets are helpful); whether a meal will be served; whether the party is a drop-off; details about the party (skating, crafts, rock climbing). A tip for busy parents: address the invitations and thank-you cards at the same time to speed up the thank-you process.
- Decorations and supplies. If not being provided by the party place, you will need paper goods (cups, plates, utensils, napkins, tablecloths) and other decorations (balloons, streamers, banner, etc.). Rubber balloons can be dangerous for young children, so use with caution. Piñatas can provide both decoration and an activity. You can use decorations to carry out your theme. Homemade decorations can be fun to make and build excitement for the birthday child. Remember to bring your camera, video, flash, batteries, film, candles and matches, a knife to cut the cake and large bags to bring home the gifts.

- Music. You can play music while the children eat or for dancing as an activity. Select the music carefully. Sometimes even young children like popular music more than a Barney sing-along. You can also use music to reflect your theme.
- Games and activities. Have enough supplies on hand so that all children get a turn, and have a plan for how and when activities will be done. It is always a nice touch to make certain that everyone goes home a winner by having a participation prize.
- Favors. Be sure that the favor is age appropriate and does not pose any hazards. If the favors are not identical, they should have the same perceived value. Activities that become a favor (for example, T-shirt painting) are always popular. It is often worth the extra time to put names on favors, or the bags they are in, to avoid fighting among the children. If you have a theme, you can buy, make or package favors in keeping with the theme.

► **Planning is the key to success.** It is really true. One of the reasons that birthday party places seem to execute flawless parties is because they have a formula that works for them. The party flows from start to finish and the children are kept moving throughout. You do not need to be a party professional to achieve the same results. A good plan does not have to be perfect or action packed. The bottom line is to keep the kids busy and engaged. In your planning, have ideas on what to do with children who arrive early or late; how much time to dedicate to the show, to various activities and to refreshments; how and when to distribute favors; and which games or activities you will propose if there is a lull or while you wait for the children to be picked up.

► **There are many ways to make children feel special on their birthdays, and a party is just one of them.** Each family has its own routines and traditions. The party does not have to be the only way to recognize the birthday child. You can make the day special in many ways. You can start the day off right with a birthday breakfast, complete with decorations. You can create birthday privileges such as deciding what is for dinner. You can review the videos or

photos from prior birthdays, take an annual birthday portrait, display a birthday banner, or create a birthday scrapbook that is added to each year. However you choose to honor family birthdays, you will have a chance to create happy memories for your children.

▶ **Spreading birthday cheer.** For many parents, the Manhattan birthday party scene seems at times to go too far. The celebration of a child's birth among good friends somehow gets lost when parties become extravaganzas, costs get out of hand and the goal of the party turns into how much loot the birthday child can bring home. There is an alternative that, for families so inclined, creates an opportunity for parents to encourage their children to use the occasion of a birthday for helping others.

Families can, in connection with a birthday party or other celebration, donate money, in any amount, by either reducing the cost of the party or making a separate contribution, to the Children for Children Foundation. The Foundation will in turn use the donated funds to make donations to New York City public schools. Participating children receive materials from the Foundation to include in their party invitations and a Certificate of Appreciation. For more information, you can contact Children For Children Foundation at 985 Fifth Avenue, New York, NY 10021, 759-1462, www.childrenforchildren.org.

▶ **Too much birthday.** Birthdays can be great, but sometimes too much of a good thing all at once is no fun at all. As parents, we want so much to show our children how much they are loved. In Manhattan, with the world at our fingertips, it is often tempting to take an idea one step further and perhaps one step too far. Just because we can have a tea party at the Plaza does not mean it is appropriate for a second birthday. When we try too hard to make a party more unique, more novel, we are in danger of creating an atmosphere where the event is more important than the child. So relax, take a step back from the birthday mania, and have a party that makes sense to you and the birthday boy or girl.

Thirteen

Thirteen can be a very lucky number. When a Jewish child turns thirteen, he or she becomes an adult member of the Jewish community, responsible for observing the commandments (the rules of Jewish life) and moral and ethical obligations of the faith. This milestone is marked by the child participating in leading a religious service and being called to the Torah (a scroll containing the five Books of Moses). This ritual is called becoming a Bar Mitzvah (son of the commandments) for boys or a Bat (or Bas) Mitzvah (daughter of the commandments) for girls. While not all Jewish children observe this tradition and families who worship according to the tenets of the various Jewish philosophical movements (such as the Orthodox, Conservative and Reform movements) observe this tradition somewhat differently, those who do observe generally celebrate this momentous occasion with a party.

Whether or not you are Jewish, if your seventh grader attends school in Manhattan or participates in extracurricular activities (sports, dance, summer programs) with other seventh graders from around the city, he or she is likely to be invited to one or more Bar or Bat Mitzvah celebrations during the school year. These parties can range from modest family celebrations at the child's home to tony Saturday night black-tie parties for 300 and, like everything else in New York, will reflect the differing values and priorities of families.

▶ **Be my guest.** A typical celebration of becoming a Bar or Bat Mitzvah usually commences with a service at the family's synagogue, at which time the child helps to lead the service with the Rabbi. The service can take place during the regular Saturday morning Sabbath service, on Saturday afternoon, on Saturday at sundown (the end of the Sabbath) or on Sunday.

At the service, the child usually reads (or chants) from the Torah and other texts (in Hebrew or English), conducts various prayers and may deliver a speech of his or her own. Sometimes other family members are called up to read certain prayers with the child. A service can last anywhere from 45 minutes (a private service in a more Reform setting) to more than three hours (in a Conservative or Orthodox setting). In Orthodox congregations, the men and women do not sit together. In many synagogues, boys and men are expected to cover their heads with *kipot* or *yarmulkes,* which are usually provided by the synagogue or the family. In some congregations, girls and women are expected to cover their heads with small veils (held on the hair with a bobby pin) provided by the synagogue.

The party following the service can take many forms. At some synagogues, the service is immediately followed by a reception at the synagogue where guests and other congregants are offered a light refreshment (Kiddush). Thereafter, families celebrate in many different ways. Some families have a party directly following the service (a luncheon or dinner, depending on the time of the service) while other families have a service during the day on Saturday and a separate party on Saturday night. Still others have two parties, either on the same day or on different days: one for the adults and a separate one for the kids. In many situations the hosts will provide transportation for the children from the service to the party. Most parties will include music and dancing as well as organized entertainment for the children.

▶ **Etiquette basics.** Some considerations:

- The service. Despite the emphasis on the party, the most important part of becoming a Bar or Bat Mitzvah is the service. As a result, the service, even if it is separate from the party, is really the main event. In respect for the traditions and meaning of the day and in support of the child who has worked hard to prepare for the day, it is respectful for your child to attend and sit quietly throughout the service (even if it is long or boring). If your child cannot attend the service due to some conflict, but will attend the party, it is appropriate to so inform the hosts. It is not necessary for parents to attend the service if they are not invited to the party.

- Attire. Children should dress appropriately for the service: jackets and ties for the boys (with shoes, not sneakers!); modest, age-appropriate skirts or dresses for the girls (if a girl wants to wear dress pants or a pants suit to the service, she should check with the host to see if that is appropriate attire for the particular synagogue). If a girl is wearing a strapless dress to a party that directly follows the service, she should wear a cover-up of some sort over her dress during the service. Attire for the party is generally indicated on the invitation, but if not, it is best to check with the host as to proper dress.

- RSVP. Most families send formal invitations to these carefully planned events. Children (with your help, if necessary) should formally reply to the invitation well in advance of the event. Most invitations include a response card (many with a "reply by" date), which should be promptly completed and sent by the child. This is an excellent way to introduce the art of correspondence to children used to writing in jargon on the Internet! If your child has accepted an invitation and subsequently determines that he or she cannot attend, it is appropriate to call the hosts (since in many cases seating plans and other arrangements and expenditures have been made to include your child) and express regrets. A previously accepted invitation should not be abandoned for a later invitation to a more "desirable" party. If your child has to cancel at the last minute (due, for example, to illness), it is polite to call the next morning to apologize for missing the party.
- Gifts. Always a touchy subject in New York, there is no clear answer as to the right gift. That being said, while it is appropriate to give a gift to the Bar or Bat Mitzvah, there is no need to go overboard and send a gift that is beyond your budget or good sense. Particularly if your child will be attending many such parties, reasonable gifts should be the order of the day. Many parents give gift certificates or cash gifts (in the form of a check) while others prefer to purchase something specific. Some families give monetary gifts for amounts in multiples of $18 (36, 54, 72 and so on), since 18 is considered a life-affirming number. At some schools, parents informally join together for group gifts, give gift certificates to the same establishment so the child can combine them to make a larger purchase or agree to a basic amount that they will give to the various celebrants.

► **Hostess (or host) with the most-est.** If you are planning to celebrate your child becoming a Bar or Bat Mitzvah, there are many things to consider as you organize your event.

- When. The date for your event will be governed by the date you arrange with your synagogue for your child's service. Depending on your synagogue, you will generally be able to schedule your date when your child is in fourth, fifth or sixth grade. Since many schools will have more than one child celebrating becoming a Bar or Bat Mitzvah during the seventh-grade year, we highly recommend that families communicate with each other and set up a calendar of dates for the children's parties (in some schools, this is an annual process, usually handled by a parent volunteer). This is very important because without a calendar, date conflicts are almost guaranteed to occur (especially if there will be many parties in the grade), and conflicts can lead to unfortunate crises. The most upsetting conflict is when two events are scheduled for the same day. In such a case the children of the grade are put in the position of deciding which party to attend. The likely result is that most kids will go to one party, leaving the other child with very few or no guests and lasting wounds. Such conflicts are easily avoided (or at least reduced) by parents' communicating and planning ahead.

- What. Early in the process, it is important to decide what type of event you want to have: daytime, evening, formal, casual, kids and adults together, kids and adults separately, an extravaganza, a modest event. Your planning will be guided by your preferences, priorities, budget, the desires of your child, your anticipated guest list (how many and where they are traveling from) and your family traditions and expectations. There is no right or wrong way to plan your event. What matters is creating an event that is realistic for your budget, honors the experience in an authentic way that is relevant to your child, reflects your values, allows you to celebrate with the people whom you care about and is meaningful for your family.

- Where. To a great extent, the "where" is a function of the "what." A Sunday afternoon event for 50 requires a very different venue from that of a black-tie party for 200 on Saturday night. As you consider the various alternatives, it is useful to consider the accessibility of the venue to your guests. For example, if you are planning an evening event in Tribeca that will go until midnight and most of the children coming to the party live on the Upper East Side, consider how children will get home from the party. As you will experience when your own child is a guest, setting out to a distant neighborhood in the wee hours is not always a welcome activity. This does not mean that you should not have your event in the desired location, just that you might want to consider providing a bus for the children who need transportation to another location. Many parents solve this by setting an early pick up time (usually around 10:00 p.m.) or arranging buses to convenient pick-up points, thereby reducing inconvenience to the parents of their child's guests.

- How. Planning a celebration can feel overwhelming for already busy parents. For many, the answer is to hire a professional party planner who can oversee all the details. For those who would rather do it themselves, the key is to be extremely organized and diligent. With sufficient lead time and a great checklist, it is possible to create a memorable and beautiful event.
- Checklist. Planning a big party is an exercise in managing a giant list of details, from the sublime to the ridiculous. Even the simplest party requires advance planning. Certain very basic items need to be booked or ordered in advance of the party (many will require advance deposits): date for the service; venue; party planner if you plan to use one; caterer; florist; photographer and/or videographer; entertainment, including band or disc jockey and possibly other entertainment for the kids (dancers, motivators, emcee, games or activities); party favors (for children and, if desired, for adults); accommodations and travel arrangements for out-of-town guests. You will also need to develop your guest list, select and order invitations (it is useful to order coordinating thank-you notes at the same time) and work out dates for sending invitations and dates by which guests must reply.
- Who. The composition of the guest list can become a huge issue in planning your event. Because thirteen-year-olds are acutely aware of the perceived pecking order of popularity in their grade, friendships are in a constant state of flux, and there is a high quotient of drama in the daily lives of these adolescents, who gets added on or left off each classmate's guest list is much debated among the kids and is extremely sensitive. In some schools with smaller grades, it may be feasible and customary to invite the entire grade to the party. In most

schools, however, where there are a fairly large number of students in the grade, inviting everyone may not be realistic. In such cases, the composition of the guest list becomes an exercise in the very grownup process of balancing desires (to invite only favorite friends) with obligations (to invite some guests your child may not prefer to include who, for various reasons, should be invited). While there is no magic formula for getting it right, it is often appropriate to err on the side of inclusion rather than exclusion. In any case, it is important to work through with your child the ramifications of his or her choices.

- Why. As you go through the process of planning your event, it is always worth taking a moment to remember what all of this is for. The goal of the day is to celebrate your child's becoming an adult in the eyes of the faith and your joy in being able to bring friends and family together to honor this age-old tradition. As you become enmeshed in the details of event management, remind yourself to take the time to honor your child and yourself as you mark this milestone in the life cycle of your family.

RESOURCES

Children For Children Foundation, 985 Fifth Avenue, New York, NY 10021, 759-1462, www.childrenforchildren.org.

Parents League of New York, Inc. (open only during the school year), 115 East 82nd Street, New York, NY 10028, 737-7385, www.parentsleague.org. Produces *The Parents League Guide to New York and Calendar* and has on-site birthday files (available to members only).

Periodicals

Big Apple Parent. 889-6400, www.parentsknow.com. Monthly. Free. Widely distributed throughout the city. Produces an annual birthday party guide and *Parents' Source Book.* Subscriptions available.

Family Entertainment Guide. 787-3789, www.familybuzzguide.com. Five issues per year (seasonal plus holiday). Free. Available at schools, libraries and family facilities. Produces an annual *Kids Birthday Party Directory* in the spring.

It is helpful to try to put together a picture of the child's behavior, including cognitive and motor skill abilities and social skills, noting when milestones were achieved and when difficulties appeared. A detailed profile can greatly assist a professional in determining what diagnostic tools are appropriate, at what point intervention would be beneficial and what the potential ramifications of postponing intervention might be.

Take your observations and any other relevant information to an individual you feel confident can help direct your inquiry. Such individuals might include your pediatrician or another health care provider; teacher or school administrator; school psychologist; or session leader from a parenting class. If you start with your pediatrician, even if the problem is not medical in nature, your pediatrician can refer you to specialists in different fields or to a developmental pediatrician, who has additional training in developmental issues. If your pediatrician is not in tune with issues that are not purely medical in nature or you feel that he or she is not giving your concerns sufficient attention, you may need to seek guidance elsewhere.

> ***As best as you can, respect your child's privacy and make sure that the individuals with whom you discuss his or her situation treat the information as privileged.***

Depending on the type of problem that is suspected, you may need to consult one or several types of professionals to conduct evaluations or for opinions on diagnosis and treatment. It is fair to say that in general, if the source of the problem is not immediately evident, it is useful to rule out medical conditions such as vision, hearing, allergy and other physical and neurological problems before focusing on nonmedical conditions. You must also consider environmental factors such as family stress or school pressure, both of which can have a dramatic impact on performance, behavior and health. As you begin to explore what might be at the root of a problem, remember that some diagnoses are more elusive than others and require more patience to be properly identified.

Depending on the age of your child, he or she may be very sensitive to your discussing details of his or her life with your friends or professionals. As best as you can, respect your child's privacy and make sure that the individuals with whom you discuss his or her situation treat the information as privileged. It is a good idea to discuss the issue with your child in an age-appropriate way, perhaps with the advice of the professional you are consulting, emphasizing that you love him or her no matter what. Each family will cope with the situation its own way. Some families are more open and others are more private. Finding the right balance between publicly and privately acknowledging your child's situation is up to the individuals involved.

Getting professional help

▶ **Finding a professional.** Having decided to seek the services of a professional, you must find your way to a practitioner in the appropriate field. While this may sound obvious, many problems are multidimensional and your first step may involve exploring the possibilities. Do you need to consult with a psychiatrist or psychologist, a psychopharmacologist, a learning specialist, an occupational therapist, a speech therapist or some combination of specialists? Depending on your child's diagnosis and how you arrived at that diagnosis, he or she may need various types of intervention, either contemporaneously or over time, to tackle the situation.

New York City is filled with specialists of every ilk and school of thought. One of the most anxiety-producing tasks for parents is to find the right type of intervention and the right person (or people) to work with their child. Your first line of attack is to talk about your situation both with professionals whose opinion you value and perhaps with other parents facing a similar issue. Your pediatrician, mental health professionals, therapists, physicians and, if your child is in school, professionals at your child's school can frequently provide important information and referrals and, in some cases, help you put together a team.

There are many wonderful parent support groups for specific conditions that can offer both excellent and current information about treatment and referrals as well as emotional support for you. Additionally, numerous local and national organizations and foundations address various problems and illnesses and offer information, access to research findings and lists of practitioners to contact. The Internet is a tremendous resource for sharing information and helping parents sort out complex problems and competing treatment plans; though be aware that not every site you visit on the Internet will provide accurate or current information. The list at the end of this chapter can help you get started.

Parents of school-age children are often unclear as to whether to involve the school in their inquiry. The answer to this question is "it depends." In both private and public schools, school psychologists, administrators and teachers often have good insights and resources to offer and can arrange for evaluations and services to be delivered to your child at school or can refer you to a network of specialists with whom they have worked in the past. If your child is in school and you want your child to receive the evaluations and services the public school districts have the legal obligation to provide at no cost to you (as detailed below), you will need to involve the school.

Your decision will depend on your confidence in the school to be of help to your family and protective of your child. While the school does not need to know everything about your child and family, do remember that, depending on the nature, severity and extent of the problem, it is quite possible that the school is already aware that there is a problem.

▸ Interviewing and selecting professionals to work with your child. Once you have gotten names of specific practitioners, whether in one field of practice or in several, the process of choosing the right person, or people, begins. The individual you consult for an evaluation may or may not be the person who conducts the intervention. The person you choose to work with your child will do so over a period of time on what may be very emotionally charged issues. To get the most from the work done together, the intervention requires a positive and (ultimately) trusting relationship between professional and client. This is true for all types of

intervention—psychotherapy, speech therapy, work with learning specialists and even physical therapy.

It is important to keep in mind that the most esteemed authority in a particular field may not necessarily be the right person to work with your child. No matter how fabulous the professional's credentials, if he or she does not establish a good rapport with your child, the value of the therapy may be meaningfully diluted.

When considering therapists and other practitioners, it is worth thinking about the proximity of their offices to your home or your child's school. Particularly if your child will be working with more than one specialist, it is important to look at the kind of schedule you will be creating for your child. You do not want your child's whole life to be about intervention. Children need down time, the opportunity to pursue personal interests, the chance to build friendships and participate in extracurricular activities and time to do homework. Fitting everything into the week can be difficult, and so the logistics of getting to an office is a relevant concern. In some cases, a practitioner who can work with your child in your own home may be a good alternative.

You will probably have several people you want to talk to before settling on a person to work with your child. Before making an appointment to meet with any practitioner, you will want to make sure that he or she has available appointment hours at appropriate times to work with your child, and you will certainly want to discuss rates. If the person will not actually be able to work with your child, you may still want a consultation in order to get a professional opinion about the case. You may be able to do some initial screening on the telephone, but, in general, you should be prepared to have an in-person meeting—for which you will probably be charged—to discuss the details about your child with any professional whom you are seriously considering retaining.

It is important for parents to meet the professional before bringing in their child.

It is important for parents to meet the professional before bringing in their child. This meeting gives you an opportunity to tell your story, get an initial read on a possible course of action or explanation of alternatives, ask questions about the nature of the work to be done with the child and give the professional a case history without the child being present. You can also use the time to ask questions about the professional's training, credentials and approach.

Because selecting a professional to work with your child is such an important decision and likely to be complicated, you should feel free to ask whatever questions you require to get you comfortable with the person to whose care you may be entrusting your child. Intervention works best when the parents and child feel comfortable, confident and clear about the process and goals of the intervention.

Michelle Ascher Dunn, C.S.W., a Manhattan psychoanalyst and child therapist, suggests that you inquire into the professional's training, school of thought (if any in particular) behind the therapeutic approach, technique and philosophy. She advises discussing how he or she plans to deal with parents. Does the therapist meet with parents together with the child, separately from the child or not at all? How will progress be evaluated and communicated to parents? Does the therapist work only with children or does he or she treat adults? What type of general time frame should parents expect for the intervention? Dunn stresses that not only must the child trust the professional, but the parents must as well. Parents need to feel secure that the information they provide will be private and confidential and that they are free to discuss anything relevant without fear of being criticized or feeling threatened.

Once you have decided to have your child work with a particular person, he or she will probably want to take an extensive case history from you and, if appropriate, other relevant adults. Depending on the situation and type of intervention, this may be accomplished at the initial meeting or in one or more subsequent meetings. In some situations, it is sometimes possible for the therapist to guide the parents in conducting the intervention without ever working directly with the child. In such cases, the therapist will meet with the parents at scheduled intervals to review progress and adjust the strategy.

When a child works directly with a professional (either for an evaluation or for ongoing intervention), it becomes necessary to make introductions. While you will probably want to discuss with the professional how he or she should be introduced to your child,

Michelle Ascher Dunn offers these basic guidelines: In general, children under the age of four do not need much advance preparation. Simply telling them that they are going to play with a new adult may suffice. Children between the ages of four and six will probably need more of an explanation. In this age group, you may want to tell the child that he or she is going to meet a person who can help with his or her feelings or a specific issue (e.g., speech, coordination, reading).

A child between the ages of six and eight can handle more specific information and can be told that he or she is meeting an expert who can help solve a problem. A child between the ages of eight and 12 is more likely to be aware that he or she has an issue that needs to be addressed and about which his or her parents are concerned. A child of this age may be either relieved to see a specialist who can help or reluctant or embarrassed to go. The child may need to be told more definitively that meeting with a specialist is necessary.

If your child will be working with more than one professional, you may want to give some thought as to how to coordinate their efforts. Some therapists have a developed network of practitioners with whom your child can work, which will facilitate communication. If the people with whom your child will be working do not have any relationship, it can sometimes be very difficult to get them to talk to each other about your child's case. This leaves you, as the parent, in the middle, communicating with each specialist and trying to put the information together yourself. In this situation, you may want to propose having them meet, at your expense, for a conference or conference call (at various intervals or on an as-needed basis) in which you can participate.

Addressing a child's disabilities or facing a mental health issue requires your energy, commitment and financial resources. Certain types of therapy will be covered in whole or in part by health insurance; others will not. While it is optimal to create a multidisciplinary team for complex issues, if for financial or other reasons you must limit the intervention, you should prioritize the remediation tools with the help of a qualified professional.

A final important point on working with specialists. It is crucial to assess your child's progress several times a year to determine if the intervention is, in fact, producing maximum remediation and help for your child. If at all possible, your child's abilities should be quantitatively measured against age-appropriate norms. It is not always easy to tell if the program is working, but you should be able to determine if some progress, however subtle, is being made over a reasonable time period.

If the intervention is not producing results, be prepared to modify the intervention and, where necessary, change practitioners or reconfigure the remediation team or types of intervention being provided. It is not only reasonable to arrange for periodic reevaluation but vital to getting the most effective help for your child.

Your Child's Legal Rights

While there are a number of federal laws adddressing disabilities, there are two particularly important federal statutes that create legal rights for children with various disabilities: Section 504 of the Rehabilitation Act and the Individuals with Disabilities Education Act (IDEA).

Section 504 requires that schools that receive federal funds provide a free public education to each qualified handicapped person in the school's jurisdiction and not discriminate against students with disabilities. Schools are required to notify the public of a general right to nondiscrimination in an effort to identify children with disabilities in the district and specifically notify children known to be disabled about the responsibilities of the school district to: provide evaluation, educational and related services free of charge; put disabled children in the least restrictive environment possible; and provide the most appropriate education possible together with the services necessary to do so. To be eligible for Section 504 services, a student must have a mental or physical impairment that substantially limits one or more major life activities, as defined by the statute.

IDEA requires that a "free appropriate public education" be available to children with disabilities between the ages of 3 and 21 and that early intervention services be provided free of charge to infants and toddlers with qualifying disabilities. The statute also requires a general notice of rights to parents as well as specific notices if the school intends to take some action with respect to a child. The rights afforded by IDEA include rights to: free, full and independent evaluation (and subsequent periodic re-evaluations) of the child's needs; explanation and justification for any proposed action to be taken and options rejected by the school; the development of an Individualized Education Program (IEP) for a disabled student; services to support the IEP; and have the child mainstreamed (placed in the least restrictive environment) to the extent possible.

IDEA also addresses the timing and nature of notices to parents with respect to certain actions being taken (or not taken) by the school relating to their child, parental consent, confidentiality of information in the child's records and the right of parents to mediation or an impartial due process hearing to challenge the services to be provided to or withheld from a child. To be eligible for IDEA services, the child must fall into one of the statutory eligibility categories, each of which has its own diagnostic criteria.

In compliance with these and other federal laws, New York State has developed law and policy implemented through various agencies and the public school system to provide the services necessary to infants, toddlers and school-aged children with special needs. The law is extensive and complicated, but for parents of children who may qualify for services, it is important to become acquainted with your rights in greater detail. The resources listed at the end of this chapter can help you work your way through the system as it applies in New York City.

Special Programs For Children from Birth to Five

New York State has established 15 Early Childhood Direction Centers (ECDC) throughout the state. ECDCs are funded by the State Education Department and administered by the State Office of Vocational and Educational Services for Individuals with Disabilities (VESID). The ECDC in Manhattan is sponsored by New York-Presbyterian Hospital. The family of any child who has a suspected or diagnosed physical, mental, and/or emotional disability can receive, at no cost, confidential information and referrals with respect to diagnostic and evaluation services; medical, educational and social services; support group services; counseling; and entitlements. The ECDC can refer infants and toddlers to the Early Intervention Program and children between the ages of three and five to the Committee on Preschool Special Education (CPSE) of the school district in which the child resides.

▶ **Early Intervention Program.** The Early Intervention Program is a statewide program administered by the New York State Department of Health. Children under the age of three who have developmental or physical delays or mental conditions likely to cause a developmental delay, including cognitive, physical, visual, hearing, communication, social/emotional or adaptive impairment, are eligible for the Early Intervention Program. Children who are referred to the program (by doctors, childcare agencies, social service workers or other agencies) are entitled to a comprehensive developmental evaluation, which is provided free of charge.

If the evaluation demonstrates that the child is eligible for free services, an Individual Family Service Plan is created to address the child's specific needs. The program can provide, at no cost to the family and depending on the child's needs, services such as additional evaluation and diagnostic testing, coordination of services, support groups, home visits, assistive technology, various types of therapy (such as occupational, speech or physical therapy) and social services.

▶ **CPSE.** Children between the ages of three and five are eligible for evaluation by the CPSE in the school district in which they reside (or, if they are attending a public preschool, in the district in which that school is located). Referral for an evaluation can be made by a teacher or other professional in the child's preschool, doctors, judicial officers, social service workers or other agencies, an ECDC or, if the child participated in the Early Intervention Program, a

professional involved with that program. The local CPSE will arrange for an evaluation at no cost to the family, and, if a qualifying disability is found, the child will be recommended for preschool special education services to be delivered pursuant to an Individualized Education Program, free of charge.

▶ **Services.** The Early Intervention Program evaluations or CPSE-directed evaluations, as well as the services themselves (if the child is determined to be entitled to services), are provided by the Department of Education or private practitioners who are under contract with, or otherwise approved by, the state. It is often comforting to parents to know that the same individual authorized by a publicly supported program to service specific disabilities or limitations might have been the same individual they could have found after networking on their own.

If it is determined that your child is not entitled to services, you will be notified of that fact and also of the procedures you may pursue to challenge the determination, including mediation or an impartial hearing.

Special Needs at School

If your child is attending ongoing school, the evaluation, diagnostic and intervention process may very well involve the school, at least to some degree if not exclusively. Parents are often reluctant to bring their concerns to the school or advise the school of an ongoing intervention because of the fear that their child will be stigmatized and that confidentiality will not be maintained. Consider, however, that school is where a child will spend the bulk of the day and that support and cooperation from the school can really help. It is to everyone's advantage when parents and schools can work in partnership.

There are two ways that issues are addressed once a child is in school. Parents either bring their concerns to the attention of the teacher (or other school official such as the psychologist, learning specialist or principal) or the school approaches the parents with their observations and discusses how the situation should be pursued. If the problem was brought to your attention by school personnel or if it was otherwise evident in school, then the school already is aware of the issue and can probably assist you.

If your child is truly symptom free at school, your decision to advise the school is a function of your confidence in the school. If your child is working with a professional to address the problem, you should discuss with that person whether and when to raise it with the school and how much information is appropriate to give to the school under the circumstances. If you feel that the school cannot be made a partner in the evaluation and intervention process and cooperate in providing the necessary support, then you should consider if your child is in the right school.

▶ **Nonpublic schools.** Private schools (unless they are the recipients of federal funding) do not have the legal obligation to provide the types of services or facilities for special needs students that are provided as of right in the public school system. Nonpublic preschools and ongoing schools may or may not have, or may not have the inclination to allocate resources to, special education programs or to address the issues of particular students. Some schools are simply ill-equipped to be of much assistance when a child is experiencing difficulty. Each school will have its own level of dedication and expertise with respect to meeting the specific needs of each student, procedures for identifying issues and determining and executing the appropriate intervention.

Many of the private schools are very supportive and will work with a child on-site as well as with outside support services to ensure that a child is receiving optimal intervention. There are also some schools that have developed extensive programs for intervention and remediation. There is, however, no standard protocol. It is very much up to each school to determine what it can and will do.

For parents in the throes of dealing with a child's issues, this time can be one of great confusion and anxiety. Parents of private school students who may be accustomed to an intimate, nurturing and personalized support network at school may be disappointed and feel abandoned when their child's issues become involved to

a degree that the school is not prepared to support. Your child needs you to become his or her advocate and make sure that everything that can be done is being done. If that does not prove to be the case or if your child is suffering because he or she is struggling socially or in the classroom, be prepared to move on to a better environment.

At the same time, you must also realize that every individual and every resource has its limitations, and it is up to *you*, not the school, to seek out professionals to help you make decisions and implement interventions that are beyond what the school can offer. If you are not happy with what the school can provide, do not waste time being offended or dissatisfied. Consult with an outside professional and keep searching until you find the assistance and services you need. Remember, this is about getting your child appropriate help, and it is you who must protect and advocate for your child.

One last point for parents of private school students. By law, and depending on the nature of your child's issues, your child may be eligible for an evaluation and various forms of intervention at no cost and expense to you through your school district, even though your child does not attend public school. Consult your local school district office for information as to eligibility and available services. See Chapter 8 for information on school districts.

▶ **Public schools.** The Department of Education has established guidelines in compliance with applicable law (such as IDEA) to govern evaluation, diagnosis and intervention management for students with various disabilities. Each local school district has a Committee on Special Education (CSE) and a School Based Support Team (also known as a Subcommittee on Special Education), which coordinate and conduct evaluations and recommend programs, services and placements for students living or attending school in the district.

Three useful publications that outline the system guidelines and parents' and children's rights are the State Education Department booklet, *Special Education in New York State for Children Ages 3–21: A Parent's Guide*, available at www.vesid.nysed.gov; and two publications of the New York City Department of Education, *Getting*

Started, Special Education as Part of a Unified Service Delivery System (Continuum of Services) and *Special Education Services as Part of a Unified Service Delivery System (The Continuum of Services for Students with Disabilities),* both of which are available at www.nyc.gov (see Department of Education, Students with Special Needs).

Special education basics. New York City's model for the delivery of special education services, the New Continuum of Services for Students with Disabilities, which was developed in 2000, is intended to provide a "unified, whole school approach" to the delivery of special education services. The cornerstone of the policy is to make it possible for students with disabilities to be "held to similar standards as, and be educated with, their non-disabled peers to the maximum extent appropriate" in the least restrictive environment and, to the extent possible, be educated in their home school zone or neighborhood school.

In order to implement this philosophy, the Continuum consists of an array of possible alternatives to accommodate students with special needs, including general education classes that offer various services in the classroom for eligible students, special education teacher support services (to be provided both in the regular classroom and in separate classrooms), special classrooms that contain a regular teacher and a special education teacher (so-called Collaborative Team Teaching), special class services (both part-time and full-time) within a regular district school, full-time specialized schools (including so-called District 75 schools), state supported/operated and state approved nonpublic schools and home and hospital instruction.

The intention is that a student not be removed from the regular general education classroom unless or until either his or her needs cannot be met in the general education classroom (even with the use of supplementary aids or services) or the disabled student requires so much of the teacher's time or attention, or is so disruptive, that other students are adversely impacted.

Informal actions to make extra help available. Throughout the city, many dedicated educators are doing their utmost in the face of

budget constraints and the growing number of students needing intervention to make services available to children in whatever way they can. As a result, there are many innovative programs taking place in the public schools.

All city public schools are required to have a Pupil Personnel Team to discuss children at risk and possible intervention techniques. This committee comprises the principal (or a designee) and any of the following: guidance counselors, teachers, members of the School Based Support Team, psychologists, social workers, and educational evaluators and other relevant school personnel. The committee is supposed to use a multidisciplinary approach to evaluate each student who is having difficulty in school and recommend a plan of intervention using various school resources to assist the student. Note: Review by a Pupil Personnel Team is not a prerequisite to a full, formal CSE evaluation.

City public schools also each have Special Education Teacher Support Services through which students can receive direct or indirect services in the classroom from special education teachers. This program benefits children eligible to receive in-class assistance as well as those requiring just a little extra help.

Children identified by the School Based Support Team and the CSE as requiring Special Education Teacher Support Services can receive these services either in a separate location outside of the classroom (formerly called the Resource Room) or within the classroom itself. Outside-the-classroom help is in the form of so-called *pull out services* for a scheduled period of time each week. Within-the-classroom help is in the form of so-called *push in services* and includes such help as the use of specialized instructional methods or materials designed for the particular student and modification of the curriculum. This type of service can be provided either by the special education teacher alone or by the regular teacher with the guidance of the special education teacher. If this type of temporary intervention is not doing the job, the child will be referred for the full formal evaluation.

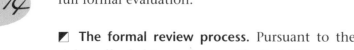

◩ **The formal review process.** Pursuant to the federal statutory rights afforded to students with disabilities as implemented under New York law, schools must follow certain formal procedures in identifying, evaluating and arranging for and delivering services to qualifying students. According to the State and City Education Departments, the formal evaluation process in New York City public schools generally operates as follows (except in particular or extrordinary situations, where certain specific regulations may apply):

- In order to receive special education services for the first time, a child must be referred to the CSE to be evaluated. The referral can be made by a teacher or other school professional, a parent or other interested professional (doctor, judicial officer, social worker, etc.). In most cases, the parents will meet with various school personnel to discuss the situation and decide on a course of action. If warranted, a written request to the CSE for an evaluation will be made. Parents may initiate a request directly to the district CSE for evaluation. Referral of the child for evaluation and diagnostic testing cannot proceed without the written consent of the parents.
- A battery of psychoeducational testing is conducted, and a social history of the child is outlined by the social worker in conjunction with the parents. All areas relating to the disabilities suspected must be explored. By law, this evaluation is conducted at the school's expense. A standard private evaluation can cost $1,000 and upward, although the cost can be much more or less depending on the nature of the suspected disability and the depth of testing. Parents have the right to provide the CSE with outside evaluations conducted at the parents' expense, although the CSE is not bound by the findings of such private evaluations.
- Once the evaluation is completed (whether done at the school or district office or by private testers at the school's expense), a recommendation is made by the IEP team, based on the diagnosis resulting from evaluation, to the school district's CSE. If you disagree with the findings of the CSE, you can request an independent evaluation. The CSE can either pay for the independent evaluation or request an impartial hearing to approve the CSE findings. If the CSE determines that your child is not eligible for services, you may request mediation or an impartial hearing to review the decision.

- Based on the diagnosis of the disabilities and determination of eligibility for services, an IEP is established, which outlines the services to be provided. The IEP must include a detailed description of the child's current level of educational performance, goals and the anticipated time frame for achievement; services to be delivered (for example, counseling, speech, occupational or physical therapy); the degree to which the child will participate in the general curriculum and whether the child will be removed (part- or full-time) from the general education classroom; for how long it is anticipated that services will be necessary; and the child's class placement.
- By law, students must be placed in the least restrictive environment. Parents have the right to participate in formulating the goals and the structuring of the IEP and must consent to its implementation. The IEP must be reviewed annually and modified to incorporate updated goals and strategies. It is required that the child be retested periodically. In certain situations, retesting of the child can be done on request if it is determined to be necessary or at specified intervals. At the very least, retesting must be done triennially.
- Throughout the process, there are specific notices to be sent to parents and opportunities for parents to participate in the process, including the right to protest the action taken (or not taken) and to call for mediation or a due process hearing.

▶ The special education experience is a positive one for most. If you trust in the professionals guiding you through the identification, evaluation and diagnostic process, and those individuals are worthy of that trust, the result will be genuine help for your child. Owing in part to the legislation passed in recent years, labels cannot be given to children at the whim of a teacher or principal. Documentation must validate any label applied to a child's disability. Your consent must be obtained for an evaluation, an IEP and the annual review.

On the other hand, you need to be aware that the public schools are faced with the obligation to provide services to a growing population in the face of budget cuts and increased class size. Does this mean your child is not getting quality intervention? Not necessarily, but it is reason enough to stay on top of your child's progress to be sure optimal intervention is being made available.

Parents must realize as well that there is a difference between not getting what your child is entitled to and not having your expectations met. Most disabilities are not cured. Rather, the child is taught strategies to compensate for, and when possible to overcome, obstacles. It is important to understand as well the distinction between what remediation is available for the identified disability and what the school is required by law to provide. The fact that a particular remediation or therapy exists does not mean that your school has the expertise, equipment or resources to provide that exact strategy or treatment. Recognizing this distinction will enable you to determine if you have grounds to challenge any decisions by the school system. If the therapy you seek is beyond what the school must give your child, you may want to consider supplementing the school-provided remediation with private therapy.

To be your child's advocate and a part of the educational team, you need to maintain a dialogue with those handling your child's education and intervention. Communicating with service providers is key to your child's success. As a parent, you are free to bring private consultants (learning specialists, psychologists or even a lawyer) to your meetings with public school officials. If your concerns or requests have not been addressed to your satisfaction, do not be intimidated by the system. Follow up at the school, and if that does not produce results, move up the hierarchy until you have the answers you need. It is not always easy to challenge the system, but the potential rewards for your child assuredly outweigh the burdens of "fighting City Hall."

RESOURCES

General Resources

American Association for Home-Based Early Interventionists
Utah State University
6500 Old Main Hill, Logan, UT 84322
800 396-6144, www.aahbei.org

American Self-Help Clearinghouse
Saint Clare's Health Services
25 Pocono Road, Denville, NJ 07834
973 326-6789, www.selfhelpgroups.org
Information on self-help groups. Publishes the *Self-Help Sourcebook,* which is available online at www.mentalhelp.net/selfhelp.

Child Study Center
New York University Medical Center
550 First Avenue, New York, NY 10016
263-6622, www.aboutourkids.org
Clinical care, research, educational outreach and advanced training for professionals; programs for AD/HD, developmental delays, behavioral difficulties, learning disabilities; gifted programs; and the research unit for Pediatric Psychopharmacology and clinical trials.

Easter Seal Society of New York
845 Central Avenue, Albany, NY 12206
518 438-8785, 800 727-8785
300 Park Avenue, New York, NY 10022
572-6227
www.ny.easter-seals.org

Federation for Children with Special Needs
1135 Tremont Street, Suite 420, Boston, MA 02120
617 236-7210, www.fcsn.org
Information and referral services.

Girls and Boys Town National Hotline
800 448-3000, www.girlsandboystown.org/hotline/index.asp
Referral and support for a variety of behavioral and learning issues.

Independent Parent Advocacy Network
277 Alexander Street, Suite 500, Rochester, NY 14607
www.advocacycenter.com

Internet Resources for Special Children (IRSC)
www.irsc.org

Jewish Board of Family and Children's Services, Inc.
120 West 57th Street, New York, NY 10019
888 JBFCS-NY (888 523-2769), 582-9100, www.jbfcs.org
Community-based residential and day treatment programs and referrals.

Manhattan Parent Resource Center
666 Broadway, 2nd floor, New York, NY 10005
614-6316, 529-7253, www.mhaofnyc.org/4parentfam.html
Information, referrals, support groups, telephone help line and other services. Designed and run by parents.

March of Dimes
Resource Center
888 663-4637, www.marchofdimes.com

National Easter Seal Society
230 West Monroe Street, Suite 1800, Chicago, IL 60606
312 726-6200, 800 221-6827, www.easter-seals.org

National Information Center for Children and Youth with Disabilities (NICHCY)
P.O. Box 1492, Washington, DC 20013
800 695-0285, www.nichcy.org
Information clearinghouse. Also provides list of state resources for all states.

National Organization for Rare Disorders (NORD)
55 Kenosia Avenue, P.O. Box 1968, Danbury, CT 06813
800 999-NORD (800 999-6673), 203-744-0100, www.rarediseases.org

New York City Self-Help Center
850 Seventh Avenue, Suite 1201, New York, NY 10019
586-5770 ext. 207
Information and referral to support and self-help groups.

New York Foundling Hospital
Pediatric Center
590 Avenue of the Americas, New York, NY 10011
633-9300, www.nyfoundling.org
Therapeutic inpatient rehabilitative facility for children 0 to 5 years old, emergency diagnostic reception centers and community-based prevention programs. Services geared toward families in crisis.

Parent to Parent of New York State
500 Balltown Road, Schenectady, NY 12304
800 305-8817, 518-381-4350
New York City office
75 Morton Street, Room 4C23, New York, NY 10014
741-5545
www.parenttoparentnys.org
Information and referrals by parents.

Parents Helping Parents
3041 Olcott Street, Santa Clara, CA 95054
408 727-5775, www.php.com

Resources for Children with Special Needs
116 East 16th Street, 5th floor, New York, NY 10003
677-4650, www.resourcesnyc.org
Publishes two invaluable books for families with children with special needs: *The Comprehensive Directory, Programs and Services for Children and Youth with Disabilties and Special Needs and Their Families in the Metro New York Area*, which contains more than 1,000 pages of listings for programs and services (childcare, respite, evaluation and diagnostic, legal and advocacy, family support, medical and health, vocational training), and *After School and More: After School, Weekend and Holiday Programs for Children and Youth with Disabilities and Special Needs in the Metro New York Area.*

Toys R Us Toy Guide for Differently Abled Kids
Catalogue free at Toys R Us stores.

Zero to Three
National Center for Infants, Toddlers and Families
2000 M Street, NW, Suite 200, Washington, DC 20036
202 638-1144, www.zerotothree.org

Governmental Resources

Early Childhood Direction Center (ECDC)
New York-Presbyterian Hospital
435 East 70th Street, Suite 2A, New York, NY 10021
746-6175
www.vesid.nysed.gov/lsn.ecdclocations.htm
www.nyp.org/socialwork/cp_early_child.html
Free confidential information and referral for services for young children (five-years-old or under) with diagnosed or suspected special needs. Funded in part by the New York State Department of Education and sponsored by New York-Presbyterian Hospital.

Health Resources and Services Administration
U.S. Department of Health and Human Services
Parklawn Building, 5600 Fishers Lane, Rockville, MD 20857
888 ASK-HRSA (888 275-4772), www.ask.hrsa.gov

Mayor's Office for People with Disabilities
100 Gold Street, 2nd floor, New York, NY 10038
788-2830, www.nyc.gov/html/mopd/home.html

National Institute for Child Health and Human Development
National Institutes of Health
9000 Rockville Pike, Rockville, MD 20852
302 496-4000, www.nih.gov

New York City Department of Education
School Programs and Support Services
Special Education Initiatives
52 Chambers Street, Room 220, New York, NY 10007
374-6085, 374-2363 Division of Student Services
www.nyc.gov (see Department of Education) or www.nycenet.edu
Publishes *Getting Started, Special Education as Part of a Unified Service Delivery System (Continuum of Services)* and *Special Education Services as Part of a Unified Service Delivery System (The Continuum of Services for Students with Disabilities).*

New York City Department of Health and Mental Hygiene
93 Worth Street, New York, NY 10013
219-5400
219-5580 Early Intervention Program
800 577-BABY (800 577-2229) TOT Line
219-5212 Mental Retardation and Disabilities Services Office
800 LIFENET (800 543-3638) Help line
www.nyc.gov/html/doh/html/bureau/earlyint.html
Information and referral services.

New York City Department of Health and Mental Hygiene
Physically Handicapped Children's Program (PHCP)
161 William Street, 6th floor, P.O. Box 34, New York, NY 10038
676-2950, www.nyc.gov/html/doh/html/phc/phcintro.html
Provides services for chronically ill and disabled children.

New York State Commission for the Blind and Visually Handicapped
Office of Children and Family Services
52 Washington Street, Rensselaer, NY 12144
518 473-1675
New York City office
20 Exchange Place, 2nd floor, New York, NY 10005
825-5710
www.ocfs.state.ny.us/main/cbvh

New York State Commission on Quality of Care for the Mentally Disabled
401 State Street, Schenectady, NY 12305
800 624-4143, www.cqc.state.ny.us
Protection and advocacy agency for mentally and physically disabled.

New York State Department of Education
Office for Special Education Services
Vocational and Educational Services for Individuals with Disabilties
One Commerce Plaza, 16th floor, Albany, NY 12234
518 486-7462
518 473-6108 Preschool Unit (ages 3 to 5)
518 486-7584 Special Education Unit (ages 5 to 21)
718 722-4544 New York City office
www.nysed.gov, www.vesid.nysed.gov
Publishes *Special Education in New York State for Children Ages 3–21: A Parent's Guide.*

New York State Department of Education
Vocational and Educational Services for Individuals with Disabilities
Early Childhood Direction Centers
One Commerce Plaza, Room 1624, Albany, NY 12234
518 486-7462, www.vesid.nysed.gov

New York State Department of Health
Bureau of Child and Adolescent Health
Corning Tower, Room 208, Empire State Plaza, Albany, NY 12237
518 474-2084, www.health.state.ny.us
Publishes *New York State Directory of Self-Help/Mutual Support for Children with Special Health Needs and Their Families*, which lists self-help clearinghouses and national organizations and support networks for more than 50 conditions and illnesses.

New York State Department of Health
Early Intervention Program
Bureau of Child and Adolescent Health
Corning Tower, Room 208, Empire State Plaza, Albany, NY 12237
518 473-7016
219-5580 Central New York City office
487-3920 Manhattan Borough office
800 522-5006 Growing Up Healthy Hotline
800 698-4543 Child Health Plus (insurance program)
www.health.state.ny.us/nysdoh/eip/index.htm
Telephone Growing Up Healthy Hotline to access services and information regarding physically handicapped children's programs and Early Intervention Programs.

New York State Developmental Disabilities Planning Council
155 Washington Avenue, 2nd floor, Albany, NY 12210
518 486-7505, www.ddpc.state.ny.us

New York State Office of the Advocate for Persons with Disabilities
Technology Related Assistance for Individuals with Disabilities (TRAID) Project
1 Empire State Plaza, Suite 1001, Albany, NY 12223
518 474-2825 or 800 522-4369 (SATIRN IV Database of services)
www.advoc4disabled.state.ny.us
Helps individuals access assistive technology services and devices. Links with SATIRN IV (resource directory of assistive technology devices), HyperAble Data (directory of devices) and TRAID-IN Equipment Exchange Program.

New York State Office of Mental Health
44 Holland Avenue, Albany, NY 12229
518 473-6902, 800 597-8481, www.omh.state.ny.us
State mental-health representative for children and youth.

New York State Office of Mental Retardation and Developmental Disabilities
44 Holland Avenue, Albany, NY 12229
518 473-9689
518 473-1890 Bureau of Consumer and Family Supports
518 474-5647 "Care at Home" Program
New York City regional office
75 Morton Street, New York, NY 10014
229-3231
229-3216 Metro New York Developmental Disabilities Services Office
www.omr.state.ny.us

New York State Office of Vocational and Educational Services for Individuals with Disabilities
6 Tower Place, 1st floor, Executive Park, Albany, NY 12203
800 272-5448, 518 473-8097
518 474-5652 Resource on Deafness
www.vesid.nysed.gov

Learning and Educational Issues

Advocates for Children of New York
151 West 30th Street, 5th floor, New York, NY 10001
947-9779, www.advocatesforchildren.org

Council for Exceptional Children
Division for Learning Disabilities
1110 North Glebe Road, Suite 300, Arlington, VA 22201
703 620-3660, www.cec.sped.org

Council of Parent Attorneys and Advocates
1321 Pennsylvania Avenue, SE, Washington, DC 20003
202 544-2210, www.copaa.com

Dial-a-Teacher (tutors)
United Federation of Teachers and Department of Education
777-3380, www.uft.org

Educational Resources Information Center (ERIC) Clearinghouse on Disabilities and Gifted Education
1110 North Glebe Road, Arlington, VA 22201
800 328-0272, www.ericec.org

Learning Disabilities Association of America
4156 Library Road, Pittsburgh, PA 15234
412 341-1515, www.ldaamerica.org

The Learning Disabilities Association of New York City
27 West 20th Street, Suite 303, New York, NY 10011
645-6730, www.learningdisabilitynyc.org

Learning Disabilities OnLine
www.ldonline.org

National Association for the Education of African American Children with Learning Disabilities
P.O. Box 09521, Columbus, OH 43209
614 237-6021, www.aacld.org

National Association of Private Schools for Exceptional Children
1522 K Street, NW, Suite 1032, Washington, DC 20005
202 408-3338, www.napsec.com

National Center for Learning Disabilities
381 Park Ave South, New York, NY 10016
545-7510, 888 575-7373, www.ncld.org

National Parent Network on Disabilities
1200 G Street, Suite 800, Washington, DC 20005
202 432-8686

New York Branch of the International Dyslexia Society
71 West 23rd Street, Suite 1527, New York, NY 10010
691-1930, www.interdys.org

Parents League of New York, Inc.
115 East 82nd Street, New York, NY 10028
737-7385, www.parentsleague.org

ReadingRockets.org
www.readingrockets.org

Schwab Learning
1650 South Amphlett Blvd., Suite 300, San Mateo, CA 94402
650 655-2410, www.schwablearning.org
Support for learning differences.

What Schools Forget to Tell Parents About Their Rights by Reed Martin, JD. This book describes students' rights to special services under Federal law and can be purchased from Reed Martin, P.O. Box 4003, Morgantown, WV 26504, 304 598-3406, www.reedmartin.com

Mental Health

Ackerman Institute for the Family
149 East 78th Street, New York, NY 10021
879-4900, www.ackerman.org

American Psychiatric Association
1000 Wilson Boulevard, Suite 1825, Arlington, VA 22209
888 35-PSYCH (888 357-7924)
New York County District Branch
150 East 58th Street, 31st floor, New York, NY 10022
421-4732/33/34, www.psych.org

American Psychological Association
750 First Street, NE
Washington, DC 20002
202 336-5500, 800 374-2721, www.apa.org

Child Intervention Research Center
Division of Columbia University, College of Physicians and Surgeons
New York State Psychiatric Institute
722 West 168th Street, New York, NY
543-5314, www.nyspi.cpmc.columbia.edu
Specialists in anxiety and depression.

Department of Child Psychiatry at Columbia University
New York State Psychiatric Institute
722 West 168th Street, New York, NY 10032
543-5948, www.nyspi.cpmc.columbia.edu

Federation of Families for Children's Mental Health
1101 King Street, Alexandria, VA 22314
703 684-7710, www.ffcmh.org

Institute for Contemporary Psychotherapy
1841 Broadway, 4th floor, New York, NY 10023
333-3444, www.icpnyc.org

LifeNet
800 LIFENET (800 543-3638), www.800lifenet.com
Information and referral network for emotional and substance abuse problems. LifeNet is a service of the Mental Health Association of New York City, Inc., in collaboration with New York City Department of Mental Health, Mental Retardation and Alcoholism Services.

Mental Health Association of New York City
666 Broadway, 2nd floor, New York, NY 10012
254-0333, www.mhaofnyc.org
Advocacy, information and education, direct services and referrals.

Mental Health Association of New York State
194 Washington Avenue, Suite 415, Albany, NY 12210
518 434-0439, www.mhanys.org

National Alliance for the Mentally Ill (NAMI)
Colonial Place Three
2107 Wilson Boulevard, Suite 300, Arlington, VA 22201
703 524-7600
800-950-NAMI (800 950-6264) NAMI HelpLine
www.nami.org
Information, list of family support groups, education, support, advocacy, support for research.

National Alliance for the Mentally Ill New York City Metro
(NAMI-NYC Metro)
432 Park Avenue South, Suite 710, New York, NY 10016
684-3365
684-3264 HelpLine
684-4237 EventsLine
www.nami-nyc-metro.org

National Alliance for the Mentally Ill of New York State (NAMI-NYS)
260 Washington Avenue, Albany, NY 12210
518 462-2000, www.naminys.org

National Mental Health Association
800 969-6642, www.nmha.org

New York Psychoanalytic Institute and Society
247 East 82nd Street, New York, NY 10028
879-6900, www.psychoanalysis.org

Post Graduate Center for Mental Health
Child, Adolescent and Family Services
138 East 26th Street, New York, NY 10010
576-4190, www.pcmh-institute.org

Saint Vincent Catholic Medical Centers
St. Vincent's Hospital Manhattan
Child and Adolescent Psychiatry Service
144 West 12th Street, 4th floor, New York, NY 10011
604-8211, www.svcmc.org

Specific Conditions and Disabilities

ADD Resource Center
215 West 75th Street, New York, NY 10023
724-9699

American Lung Association of the City of New York
Family Asthma Days
432 Park Avenue South, 8th floor, New York, NY 10016
889-3370, www.lungusa.org/newyork

American Speech-Language-Hearing Association
10801 Rockville Pike, Rockville, MD 20852
800 638-8255, www.asha.org

Asperger Syndrome Coalition of the United States
2020 Pennsylvania Avenue, NE, Box 771, Washington, DC 20006
www.asperger.org

Association for the Help of Retarded Children
200 Park Ave South, New York, NY 10003
780-2500, www.ahrcnyc.org

Autism Society of America
7910 Woodmont Avenue, Suite 300, Bethesda, MD 20814
301 657-0881
800 3-AUTISM (800 328-8476)
www.autism-society.org

Brain Injury Association of New York State
10 Colvin Avenue, Albany, NY 12206
518 459-7911, 800 228-8201, www.bianys.org

Children and Adults with Attention-Deficit/Hyperactivity Disorders (CHADD)
8181 Professional Place, Suite 201, Landover, MD 20785
800 233-4050, 301 306-7070, www.chadd.org

Children's Advocacy Center of Manhattan
333 East 70th Street, New York, NY 10021
517-3012, www.childhelpusa.org/manhattan
Intervention and treatment program for child victims of sexual and physical abuse.

Developmental Delay Resources
4401 East West Highway, Suite 207, Bethesda, MD 20814
301 652-2263, www.devdelay.org

Downtown Brooklyn Speech-Language-Hearing Clinic at Long Island University
175 Willoughby Street, Brooklyn, NY 11201
718 488-3480
www.brooklyn.liunet.edu/cwis/bklyn/depts/commsci/html/audiology_clinic.html
Speech-language-voice, swallowing and hearing services.

Epilepsy Foundation of New York City
305 Seventh Avenue, Suite 1202, New York, NY 10001
633-2930, www.efnyc.org

Food Allergy & Anaphylaxis Network
10400 Eaton Place, Suite 107, Fairfax, VA 22030
800 929-4040, 703 691-2713, www.foodallergy.org

Gay Men's Health Crisis (GMHC)
The Tisch Building, 119 West 24th Street, New York, NY 10011
807-6655 Hotline
800 AIDS-NYC (800 243-7692)
367-1267 Child Life Program for children and families dealing with AIDS
www.gmhc.org

Genetics Services Program
New York State Department of Health
Wadsworth Center Labs and Research
P.O. Box 509, Empire State Plaza, Room E299, Albany, NY 12201
518 474-7148, www.wadsworth.org

Goodson Parker Wellness Center
30 East 76th Street, 4th floor, New York, NY 10021
717-5273, www.goodsonparker.com
Provides therapeutic yoga for kids with special needs.

Jewish Board of Family and Children's Services
120 West 57th Street, New York, NY 10019
582-9100, www.jbfcs.org
A voluntary mental health and social service agency.

Lyme Disease (LDF)
One Financial Plaza, Hartford, CT 06103
800 866-LYME (800 866-5963) Lyme Disease Hotline
860 525-2000
www.lyme.org

National Attention Deficit Disorder Association (ADDA)
1788 Second Street, Suite 200, Highland Park, IL 60035
847 432-ADDA (847 432-2332), www.add.org

National Cancer Institute
6116 Executive Boulevard, MSC8322, Suite 3036A, Bethesda, MD 20892
800 4CANCER (800 422-6237) Cancer Information Service
www.nci.nih.gov

National Coalition for Auditory Processing Disorders
4304 Ivey Glen Road, Orlando, FL 32826
www.ncapd.org

National Heart, Lung and Blood Institute
Information Center
P.O. Box 30105, Bethesda, MD 20824
301 592-8573, www.nhlbi.nih.gov

New York State Speech-Language-Hearing Association
2 Northway Lane, Latham, NY 12110
518 786-0947, www.nysslha.org

Next Generation Yoga
200 West 72nd Street, Suite 58, New York, NY 10023
595-9306, www.nextgenerationyoga.com
Special needs yoga.

NYSARC, Inc. (New York State Association for Retarded Children)
393 Delaware Avenue, Delmar, NY 12054
518 439-8311, www.nysarc.org

NYU Medical Center
Neurology ADHD Program
550 First Avenue, New York, NY 10016
263-3580, www.nyuchildrens.org

Speech and Hearing Center of the Dyson College of Arts and Sciences
Pace University
41 Park Row, 5th floor, Room 511, New York, NY 10038
346-1644
Professional services for articulation, stuttering and delayed language development.

Stuttering Foundation of America
3100 Walnut Grove Road, Suite 603, P.O. Box 11749, Memphis, TN 38111
800 992-9392, 800 967-7700, www.stutteringhelp.org

United Cerebral Palsy Associations (National)
1660 L Street, NW, Suite 700, Washington, DC 20036
800 872-5827, www.ucpa.org

United Cerebral Palsy Associations of New York State
330 West 34th Street, New York, NY 10001
947-5770, www.cerebralpalsynys.org

Substance Abuse

American Council for Drug Education
www.acde.ocg

Center for Substance Abuse Prevention
www.samhsa.gov

DrugHelp
www.drughelp.org

National Clearinghouse of Alcohol and Drug Information
www.health.org

National Inhalant Prevention Coalition
www.inhalants.org

Parents. The antidrug
www.theantidrug.com

Partnership for a Drug Free America
www.drugfreeamerica.org

Talking with Kids about Tough Issues
www.talkingwithkids.org

Useful Phone Numbers and Websites

Baby Supplies

BabyLab's Baby Basics, 718 257-3000
Home delivery service for infant products and low birth weight and special care infants

General Information

(Note: Many of the websites for tourists include useful information on entertainment, dining and activities for children and families.)

www.allny.com
www.centralpark.org
www.citidex.com
www.cityguideny.com
www.citysearch.com
www.cuisinenet.com
www.culturefinder.com
www.dailycandy.com
www.digitalcity.com
www.fieldtrip.com/ny/index
www.findnyc.com
www.go-newyorkcity.com
www.kerrymenu.com
www.metronewyork.com
www.museumstuff.com
www.newyorkled.com

www.nyc.com

www.nyc-arts.org

www.nyckidsarts.org

www.nycparks.org

www.nyctourism.com

www.nyctourist.com

www.nycvisit.com

www.nymuseums.com

www.nytimes.com

www.nytoday.com

www.theinsider.com

www.timeoutny.com

www.urbanbaby.com

www.zagat.com

Government Resources

Emergency (police, fire, ambulance), 911

Citizen Service Center–New York City Government, 311 (can connect or direct call to all city government offices)

New York City official website, www.nyc.gov

New York State official website, www.state.ny.us

NYPD Switchboard, 646 610-5000

Office of the Manhattan Borough President, 669-8300, www.cvfieldsmbp.org

Terrorism Hotline, 888 NYC SAFE (692-7233)

U.S. government official web portal, www.firstgov.gov

U.S. government publications, 888 8 PUEBLO (888 878-3256), www.pueblo.gsa.gov

Health/Medical

Cancer, www.findcure.com

Children's Hospital Los Angeles, www.juniormed.com

Licenders, www.licenders.com, 888 LICENDERS, (542-3633)

Medline, www.nlm.nih.gov

Mental health, Psych Central, www.coil.com

Nemours Foundation, www.kidshealth.org

Oncology, OncoLink, www.oncolink.com

www.canceradvisors.com

www.cancerdecisions.com

www.webmd.com

D

N

O

P

U

Diane Chernoff-Rosen, mother of two, is a graduate of Cornell University, Georgetown University Law Center and New York University Stern School of Business and has practiced law in New York City. She is the author of *Grownup's Guide® Visiting New York City with Kids*, written with Lisa Levinson. In addition to raising her children, she is the principal of Grownup's Guide® Publishing LLC and is actively involved in volunteer activities. She has lived in Manhattan for 23 years.